981

HEATH CHEMISTRY
CANADIAN EDITION
LABORATORY EXPERIMENTS

Michael A. DiSpezio

Science Teacher and Chairman
Science Department
Cape Cod Academy
Osterville, MA

Ted Hall

Chemistry Teacher
Wayland High School
Wayland, MA

Duncan Morrison

Chemistry Teacher
David Thompson Secondary School
Vancouver, B.C.

Clifford L. Schrader

Chemistry Teacher
Dover High School
Dover, OH

Darrel Scodellaro

Chemistry Teacher and
Science Department Head
Seaquam Secondary School
Delta, B.C.

Jay A. Young, Ph.D.

Chemical Safety and Health Consultant
Silver Spring, MD

D.C. HEATH CANADA LTD.

THE HEATH CHEMISTRY PROGRAM: Canadian Edition

Heath Chemistry, Pupil's Edition

Heath Chemistry, Teacher's Annotated Edition

Heath Chemistry Laboratory Experiments, Pupil's Edition

Heath Chemistry Laboratory Experiments, Teacher's Edition

Heath Chemistry Teacher's Resource Binder (Includes Canadian Supplement)

The components below are available in their original American editions.

Heath Chemistry Chapter Worksheets

Heath Chemistry Tests, Spirit Duplicating Masters

Heath Chemistry Computer Test Bank

Heath Chemistry Computer Test Bank, Teacher's Guide

Heath Chemistry Courseware

Heath Chemistry Lab Assistant

Executive Editor: Ellen M. Lappa
Project Editor: Toby Klang
Editorial Development: John M. Bowmar, Mary M. Scofield
Design, Illustration, and Production: Navta Associates, Inc., Michelle Miodonski
Cover Design: Angela Sciaraffa
Cover Photograph: Courtesy of Richard Megna/Fundamental Photos
Canadianization: Olga Domján, Francine Geraci
Canadian Reviews: Bob Johnston, Margaret Redway and Wayne Rowley

Canadian Cataloguing in Publication Data

Main entry under title:

Heath chemistry laboratory experiments

Canadian ed.
ISBN 0-669-95291-5

1. Chemistry — Experiments.   2. Chemistry —
Laboratory manuals.   I. Dispezio, Michael A.

QD43.H42 1987   540'.76   C87-094509-2

Published simultaneously in the United States of America
Printed in Canada
International Standard Book Number: 0-669-95291-5

2   3   4   5   6   7   8   9   0

CONTENTS

Chapter 21 ELECTROCHEMISTRY

Chapter 22 ANALYTICAL PROBLEM SOLVING

Chapter 23 ORGANIC CHEMISTRY

Chapter 24 BIOCHEMISTRY

Safety Recommendations for the Laboratory

GENERAL SAFETY PRECAUTIONS

1. Unauthorized experiments are prohibited. Do only those experiments assigned by your teacher.
2. Never work alone in a science laboratory or storage area, and never work without the teacher's supervision.
3. Never eat, drink, smoke, or chew gum in a science laboratory or storage area. Do not store food or beverages in the laboratory environment.
4. Wear protective eye goggles and aprons at all times in the laboratory.
5. Restrain loose clothing (e.g., sleeves, full-cut shirts or blouses, neckties, etc.), long hair, and dangling jewelry.
6. Footwear should cover feet completely; no open-toe shoes.
7. Do not touch chemicals with your hands unless directed to do so. Wash your hands thoroughly before and after work in a science laboratory, and after spill cleanups.
8. Do not hold your face directly over an open container of chemicals. When observing the odor of a substance, fan a small amount of the vapor toward you by sweeping your hand over the top of the container.
9. Never reach over an exposed flame.
10. Use tongs, test-tube holders, or pot holders to handle hot laboratory equipment. Allow ample time for glassware to cool before handling. (Remember, hot glass looks like cool glass.)
11. When using electrical equipment, use only equipment that is in good working order. Never touch electrical equipment with wet hands or place equipment in areas that may be wet.
12. Never use broken or chipped glassware. Be sure all glassware is clean before you use it.
13. Never place flammable materials near an open flame.
14. When heating something in an open container such as a test tube, always point the open end of the container away from yourself and others.
15. Never pipette by mouth.
16. Keep chemicals, bottles, beaker, flasks, etc., away from the edges of the lab bench.
17. Become familiar with the safety precautions for each chemical to be used in an experiment.
18. Know the location of all safety equipment in the laboratory including fire extinguishers, fire blankets, sand, safety showers, an eyewash fountain, and a first-aid kit.

ACCIDENTS

1. Report any accident or injury, no matter how minor, to your teacher.
2. If a chemical spills on your skin or clothing, wash it off immediately with plenty of cool water and notify your teacher.
3. If a chemical gets into your eyes or on your face, wash immediately in the eyewash fountain with plenty of water. Notify your teacher. Follow your teacher's instructions for washing your eyes.
4. Clean up all spills immediately. Do not pick up broken glassware with your bare hands. Use a dustpan and a brush.
5. If a thermometer breaks, do not touch the mercury. Call your teacher immediately.
6. Smother small fires with a towel. Use a blanket or the safety shower to extinguish clothing fires.

SAFE CONDUCT AND PROCEDURES

1. Approach laboratory work with maturity. Never run, push, or engage in horseplay or practical jokes of any kind in the laboratory.
2. Always prepare for an experiment by reading the directions in the manual before you come to the laboratory. Follow the directions carefully and intelligently, noting all precautions.
3. Never leave heat sources unattended (e.g., gas burners, hot plates, heating mantles, sand baths, etc.). Turn off equipment when not in use.
4. Always use heat-resistant (Pyrex®) glassware for heating.
5. Use materials only from containers that are properly labeled. Read labels carefully before using chemicals.
6. Never return unused chemicals to the stock bottles. Do not put any object into a reagent bottle, except the dropper with which it may be equipped.
7. Follow the directions from your teacher for the disposal of all chemicals.
8. When diluting acid with water, *always add the acid to the water*.
9. Store all equipment and chemicals in appropriate storage areas.
10. Do not use the sink to discard matches, filter paper, or other solid or slightly soluble materials.
11. Use a lubricant to insert glass tubing or thermometers into rubber stoppers. Do not force glassware into stoppers.
12. Keep your apparatus and desk area clean. Store items not in use such as books, purses, etc., out of the way in designated storage areas.

Reading Reagent Labels

Before working with any chemical, you should familiarize yourself with any hazards associated with its use. The Canadian Hazardous Products Act requires chemical manufacturers to include the following on their product labels:
— a symbol and a word indicating the degree of hazard;
— a symbol and a statement indicating the nature of the primary hazard.
The latter symbol is superimposed on the appropriate degree of hazard symbol:

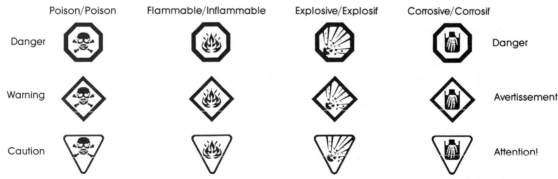

Symbols registered under the Trademarks Act, June 10, 1970, *Trademark Journal*, Vol. 17, No. 815

In addition, labels must provide:

— a statement of the nature of any secondary hazard(s);
— a statement of precaution;
— the words "First Aid Treatment," followed by the
   i) source of the hazard,
   ii) first aid antidote, and
   iii) directions for safe use and storage.

Most chemical products used in Canadian schools are manufactured and labeled in the United States. Though labeling systems vary, most contain the following common features:

(A) Name of Reagent

(B) Safety Equipment to wear when handling reagent

(C) Hazard Category/Rating
1. Flammability hazards
2. Reactivity hazards — Explosives, Oxidizers, Water and/or Air Reactive
3. Health hazards — Poisons, Carcinogens, Life, Radioactive
4. Contact hazards — Corrosives, Life

```
   0        1        2        3        4

  None            Moderate           Extreme
```

(D) Color Coding for Storage (color not shown)
1. R/Red — Flammability hazard
2. Y/Yellow — Reactivity hazard
3. B/Blue — Health hazard
4. W/White — Contact hazard
5. G/Gray — General storage
6. Exception — When this symbol appears, reagent is incompatible with other reagents of same color bar.

(E) Cautionary Instructions

(F) First Aid Instructions

(G) Physical Data for the Reagent

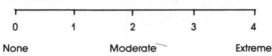

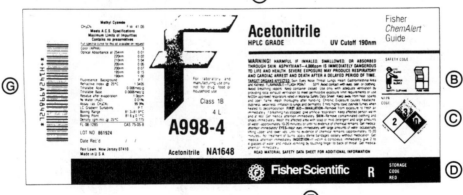

Label: Courtesy Fisher Scientific

For additional information, contact:

Publications Services Branch
British Columbia Ministry of Education
878 Viewfield Road
Victoria, B.C. V9A 4V1

— The B.C. Ministry is currently publishing a *Science Safety Manual* to familiarize educators fully with all aspects of safety in science education.

Canadian Government Publishing Centre
Supply and Services Canada
Ottawa, Ontario, K1A 0S9
(819) 997-2560

— Copies of the Hazardous Products Act are available for sale upon request.

COMMON LABORATORY EQUIPMENT

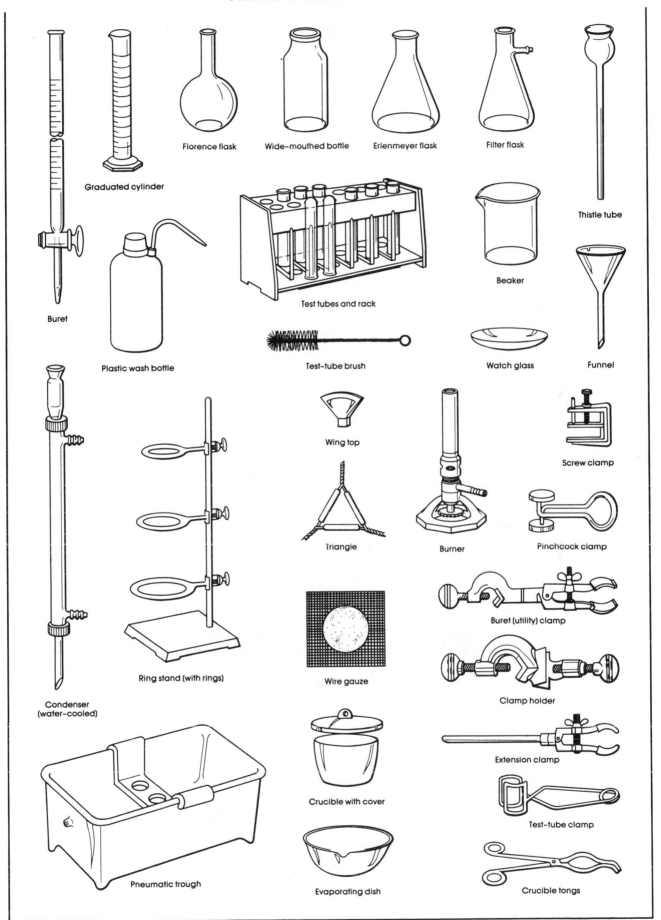

Graduated cylinder

Florence flask

Wide-mouthed bottle

Erlenmeyer flask

Filter flask

Thistle tube

Buret

Plastic wash bottle

Test tubes and rack

Beaker

Test-tube brush

Watch glass

Funnel

Condenser (water-cooled)

Ring stand (with rings)

Wing top

Triangle

Burner

Screw clamp

Pinchcock clamp

Buret (utility) clamp

Wire gauze

Clamp holder

Extension clamp

Crucible with cover

Test-tube clamp

Pneumatic trough

Evaporating dish

Crucible tongs

Working in the Chemistry Laboratory

One of the important components of your chemistry course is the laboratory experience. Perhaps you have done experiments in other science courses, so you are somewhat familiar with some of the lab equipment. The chemistry laboratory is unique, however. There is a great deal to be learned about the equipment and safety procedures in a chemistry lab.

A number of important procedures need to be mastered in order for you to be successful in the later experiments of this course. You need to know how to use a lab burner (Part I); how to filter liquids (Part III); how to manipulate glass tubing (Part II); how to handle solid chemicals and solutions (Parts III, IV, and V); and how to heat materials safely in the chemistry laboratory (Parts II and III). In addition, it is important that you learn to measure using graduated cylinders, thermometers, and balances.

In this introductory experiment, you will have a chance to learn about all of these lab techniques while doing an experiment involving an important chemical reaction (Parts IV and V). Limewater is a solution of calcium hydroxide, $Ca(OH)_2$, dissolved in water. Limewater is used as a test for carbon dioxide, an important product of animal respiration. When carbon dioxide is bubbled through some limewater, a cloudy appearance is noted. This is called a *precipitate*.

OBJECTIVES

1. to learn the following lab techniques:

    a. using a lab burner
    b. using a funnel and filter paper
    c. bending and fire-polishing glass tubing
    d. handling solid chemicals and solutions
    e. measuring mass with a balance
    f. measuring temperature with a thermometer
    g. measuring volume with a graduated cylinder

2. to correctly set up the equipment in order to perform an experiment

3. to observe the reaction between limewater and carbon dioxide

4. to test the gaseous products of two chemical reactions for the presence of carbon dioxide

MATERIALS

Apparatus

lab burner
centigram balance
flame spreader
funnel
filter paper
stirring rod
glass tubing (6 mm)
2 Erlenmeyer flasks
    (125 mL)
one-hole rubber
    stopper, to fit
    Erlenmeyer flask

two-hole rubber
    stopper, to fit
    Erlenmeyer flask
rubber or plastic
    tubing
ring stand and ring
wire gauze
thermometer
2 beakers (250 mL)
spark lighter or
    matches
file for glass tubing

graduated cylinder
    (100 mL)
metric ruler
marking pen
lab apron
safety goggles
plastic gloves
funnel holder
folded cloths or towels
face shield

Reagents

1M HCl (hydrochloric   glycerin
acid)   sodium carbonate
magnesium ribbon   calcium hydroxide

PROCEDURE

Part I   Using a Lab Burner

1. Most lab burners are constructed in a similar fashion. There is an inlet for the gas, an adjustment for the amount of gas, and an adjustment for the amount of air. (See Figure 1A-1.) A proper mix of air and gas will yield a faint blue flame for maximum heat and minimum soot.

Figure 1A-1 *Two common laboratory burners: (a) the Bunsen burner, (b) the Tirrill burner.*

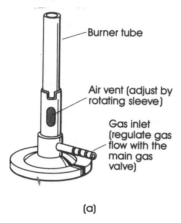

Burner tube

Air vent (adjust by rotating sleeve)

Gas inlet (regulate gas flow with the main gas valve)

(a)

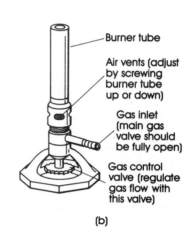

Burner tube

Air vents (adjust by screwing burner tube up or down)

Gas inlet (main gas valve should be fully open)

Gas control valve (regulate gas flow with this valve)

(b)

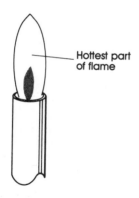

Hottest part of flame

Figure 1A-2 *The hottest part of the flame produced by a laboratory burner is just above the tip of the inner (blue) cone.*

2. Put on your safety goggles. Examine your burner before you try to light it. Identify the gas adjustment and air adjustment on your burner. To start the flame, turn the air adjustment to allow as little air as possible. Use a match (or a spark lighter) to light the burner by turning on the gas and holding the lighted match above the barrel of the burner.

3. Adjust the flame to a blue color without a roaring sound by changing the amount of air and the amount of gas. Note, for future reference, where the flame is hottest (Figure 1A-2).

4. Turn off the burner and go on to the next part of the experiment.

Part II   Working with Glass

1. Obtain a piece of glass tubing that is 50 cm long. Using a metric ruler and a marking pen, mark the tubing for cutting into two 20 cm pieces and one 10 cm piece.

CAUTION: To avoid cuts, wear gloves when you break glass tubing.

2. Place the tubing on a firm surface as shown in Figure 1A-3. Using a single firm stroke of a triangular file, make a deep scratch at the point where you want to cut the glass tubing. Wearing gloves, hold the tubing with both thumbs behind the scratch. (The scratch should be pointing away from you.) Push firmly with your thumbs and the tubing should break cleanly.

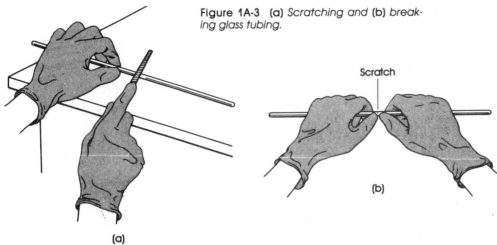

Figure 1A-3 (a) *Scratching and* (b) *breaking glass tubing.*

Scratch

(b)

(a)

3. Continue at each of the marks on your tubing.

4. In order to smooth the ends of the glass tubing, a technique called fire-polishing is used. Light the burner again and place the end of one piece of tubing into the flame. Rotate the tubing so that the heating is even. You will quickly notice that the end of the tubing is becoming smooth. Do not leave the glass in the flame for too long or the end of the tube will close. Continue the fire polishing with each piece of tubing.

5. Turn off the burner and place the flame spreader on the top of the burner, as in Figure 1A-4a. This will allow you to bend the glass tubing more easily.

6. Hold one of the 20 cm pieces of the tubing in both hands and place the centre of the tubing in the flame while rotating the tubing, as in Figure 1A-4b. Continue rotating until you feel the tubing getting soft. At this point, remove the tubing from the flame and bend it at a 90 degree bend in one smooth motion. Repeat with the other 20 cm piece.

7. Allow the bends to cool. Then place one or two drops of glycerin into the holes of a two-hole rubber stopper. The glycerin acts as a lubricant for the glass tubing. Protecting both hands with folded cloths, put one of the right-angle bends into one of the holes, extending the tubing as far as possible into the stopper. It is very important that care be taken to *gently* push the tubing into the rubber stopper. In the other hole, place the 10 cm piece so that it is just below the stopper. (See Figure 1A-5.) Save the second 20 cm bend for Part V.

CAUTION: Be careful with hot glass tubing. Place the hot pieces on a piece of wire gauze or other fireproof material and be careful to wait for each piece to cool down.

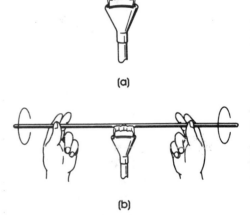

(a)

(b)

Figure 1A-4 (a) *Properly adjusted flame with a flame spreader on the burner.* (b) *How to heat glass tubing before bending it.*

Figure 1A-5 *Two-hole stopper with glass tubing, inserted in a flask for use in Parts IV and V.*

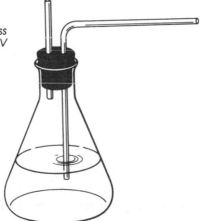

CAUTION: Protect your hands with cloth pads when inserting glass tubing into a stopper. Use glycerin as a lubricant. Protect your hands whenever you are adjusting or removing the tubing.

Part III   Preparing a Limewater Solution

1. In order to make the limewater solution, you must be able to use the lab balance. Two common balances are shown in Figure 1A-6.

Figure 1A-6   *Triple-beam centigram balance (left) and combination vernier-scale beam balance (right).*

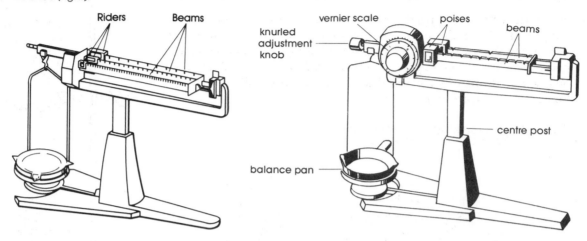

2. The balance must be zeroed before it is used to find masses. Place the balance on a level table and find the zero-adjusting screw. Adjust the balance to the zero point. Probably the balance that you are using has three beams on it, or a double beam with an adjustable, spring-loaded dial. In order to properly record the mass, you must add up the masses indicated by the riders on the beams.

3. When you find the mass of solid chemicals, it is important that you do not put the chemical directly on the pan or platform of the balance. Place a clean, dry 250 mL beaker on the pan of the balance and find the mass of the beaker. Record it in your notebook.

4. Now, get approximately 3 g of calcium hydroxide from your instructor and find the mass of the beaker plus the calcium hydroxide. Record it in your notebook.

5. Using the graduated cylinder, place 175 mL of distilled water into the 250 mL beaker. It is important that you know how to read a graduated cylinder. Graduated cylinders are designed to read correctly only if the bottom of the meniscus is the point where the volume is recorded. A *meniscus* is the slight curve that appears because the water is slightly higher on the surface of the glass and therefore lower in the middle of the cylinder. See Figure 1A-7 for the correct reading of the graduated cylinder.

CAUTION: Calcium hydroxide and limewater are both irritating to skin and eyes. Wear safety goggles, lab apron, and gloves. Do not touch the chemical; use a scoop or spatula for the calcium hydroxide. If you get any on your skin or in your eyes, wash it off immediately with plenty of water.

Figure 1A-7   *When you read a graduated cylinder, your eyes should be at the same level as the top of the liquid, and the scale reading should correspond to the bottom of the meniscus. In this example, the correct reading is 18.0 mL.*

6. Using a stirring rod, begin stirring the solution.

7. Calcium hydroxide is difficult to dissolve. Heating the solution will speed up the dissolving process. Set up the ring stand and ring with the wire gauze as shown in Figure 1A-8. Heat the solution gently, stirring constantly. Heat for approximately 5 min-10 min. Even after 10 min, you will probably find that some of the solid has not dissolved. Put the beaker down to cool and allow the solid to settle while you set up a funnel and filter paper to obtain a clear solution of limewater.

8. Set up the filtration apparatus shown in Figure 1A-10. Filter paper is supplied in the shape of a circle. You need to fold it two times, then open up the paper so that it forms a cone. (See Figure 1A-9a.) Before you pour the solution into the funnel, you should moisten the filter paper with a few drops of water, so that the filter paper will stick to the funnel, as in Figure 1A-9b.

Figure 1A-8 *Setup for heating the limewater solution.*

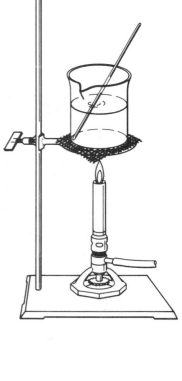

Figure 1A-9 (a) *Folding filter paper.* (b) *Fitting a moistened filter paper cone to a funnel.*

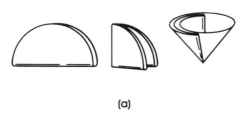

(a)

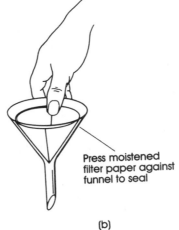

Press moistened filter paper against funnel to seal

(b)

9. Pour the solution into the funnel as shown in Figure 1A-10 and allow it to filter into the beaker below. You will need the clear limewater for Parts IV and V.

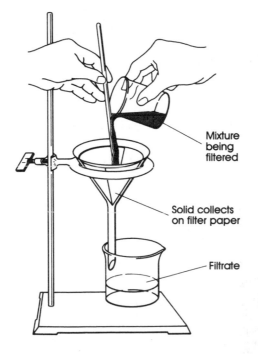

Mixture being filtered

Solid collects on filter paper

Filtrate

Figure 1A-10 *When filtering, use a glass stirring rod to control the flow of the solution into the funnel. If the stem of the funnel touches the side of the beaker, the liquid flows more smoothly into the beaker.*

Part IV Testing for Carbon Dioxide

1. Place just enough of the clear limewater into the flask so that the glass tubing is just below the liquid when the stopper that contains the glass tubing is inserted in the flask. Put the stopper on the flask tightly.

2. Gently blow into the right-angle bend. You will exhale carbon dioxide (among other gases). Continue to exhale until you observe a change. Write down your observations in your notebook.

Part V Testing Gases with Limewater

CAUTION: Protect your hands with cloth pads when inserting glass tubing into a stopper.

1. Place the second 90 degree bend into the one-hole stopper, using the glycerin as a lubricant. Again, be very careful to *gently* push the tubing into the rubber stopper. If you encounter any resistance, put more glycerin on the glass tubing. Attach a short piece of rubber or plastic tubing to the ends of both of the 90 degree bends and set up the flasks as shown in Figure 1A-11.

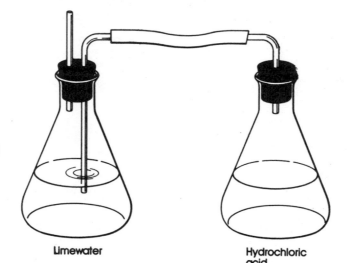

Figure 1A-11
Setup for testing gases with limewater.

Limewater   Hydrochloric acid

2. Rinse out the flask that you used for the limewater and fill it with fresh, clear limewater to the same level.

3. In the other flask, place 35 mL of $1M$ hydrochloric acid.

CAUTION: Hydrochloric acid is corrosive to skin, eyes, and clothing. When handling 1M hydrochloric acid, wear safety goggles, lab apron, gloves, and use a full face shield. Wash off spills and splashes with plenty of water. Call your teacher.

4. With a thermometer, measure the temperature of the acid and record it in your notebook in your copy of Table 1. Be sure to rinse the end of the thermometer after removing it from the acid.

5. Obtain a piece of magnesium ribbon from your instructor. Carefully drop the magnesium into the acid and quickly place the stopper on the top of the flask. Record your observations in Table 1.

6. As soon as the reaction stops, remove the stopper and measure the temperature of the acid. Record it in Table 1.

7. Rinse out all of the glassware and repeat Steps 2, 3, and 4. Then obtain approximately 2 g of sodium carbonate. Carefully pour the sodium carbonate into the flask and quickly put the stopper on the flask. Record your observations in Table 1.

8. As soon as the reaction stops, remove the stopper and measure the temperature of the acid. Record it in Table 1.

9. Rinse out all of the glassware and put away all of the equipment.

10. Before you leave the laboratory, wash your hands thoroughly with soap and water, using a fingernail brush to clean under your fingernails.

CAUTION: Always protect your hands with cloth pads when removing glass tubing from a stopper.

REAGENT DISPOSAL

If any unused limewater is left over, return it to the appropriate container, following your teacher's instructions. Rinse all solutions down the sink with copious amounts of water. Place all solids in the designated waste containers.

POST LAB DISCUSSION

Both reactions that you observed in Part V involved the formation of a gas. You observed in Part IV that carbon dioxide causes limewater to turn cloudy. This should help you in determining if carbon dioxide is formed in either of the last two reactions.

Reactions that give off heat are called *exothermic*, while reactions that absorb heat are *endothermic*.

The precipitate that forms when carbon dioxide reacts with limewater is calcium carbonate. Calcium carbonate is insoluble in water.

DATA AND OBSERVATIONS

Part III   Preparing a Limewater Solution

Mass of beaker

Mass of beaker + calcium hydroxide

Mass of calcium hydroxide alone

Part V   Testing Gases with Limewater

Table 1

	HYDROCHLORIC ACID/ MAGNESIUM REACTION	HYDROCHLORIC ACID/SODIUM CARBONATE REACTION
Temperature before		
Temperature after		
What happens in the reaction?		
What happens to the limewater?		

QUESTIONS

1. In Part V, was carbon dioxide produced in either of the reactions? How do you know?

2. Were the reactions exothermic or endothermic?

3. Why is it necessary to filter the limewater before using it in Parts IV and V?

4. Why is it necessary to use a beaker or the equivalent when finding the mass of solids?

FOLLOW-UP QUESTIONS

1. If you were to find the mass of the hydrochloric acid and the mass of the magnesium strip before the reaction, how would that mass compare with the mass of material that remained in the flask after the reaction was complete? If you could contain the gas that was produced, how would the "before" and "after" masses compare?

2. A number of SI units were used in this experiment. Review the Procedure and make a list of all of the units that you used in the measurements.

3. Matter in three different phases was observed in this experiment. Give examples from the experiment that are:
   a. solids
   b. liquids
   c. gases

CONCLUSION

State the results of Objective 4.

Making Observations

Observations are an important component of the *scientific method*, a means whereby scientists solve problems. The scientific method is cyclical in nature. First, a scientist makes observations and analyzes them in a search for patterns or relationships. Having discovered a relationship, the scientist checks it by making predictions of outcomes of further tests. In doing these further tests, the scientist naturally makes more observations, and so on.

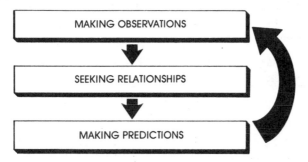

Figure 1B-1   *Primary activities of the scientific method.*

In chemistry, you will constantly be checking for changes when you do experiments. Sometimes you will observe that no change occurs. This type of observation is just as important as one in which a change does occur.

"Observing" is often associated only with "seeing"—that is, "using your eyes". However, in science, "observing" implies using any or all of the senses of sight, touch, smell, hearing, and taste. Obviously, in a chemistry lab no unauthorized observations, particularly those involving touch, smell, or taste, should be conducted. Since the unaided senses are limited, scientists rely on special laboratory equipment such as thermometers and balances to extend their senses. Scientific equipment is used extensively in homes to monitor and control temperatures in ovens, refrigerators, and rooms, as well as in industries such as chemical processing and services such as health care.

Observations are classed as one of two types: qualitative and quantitative. Qualitative observations tend to be rather general and use words, not numbers, to describe an object or event. An example of a qualitative observation would be, "A car drove quickly down the street." Quantitative observations are more specific and usually describe something in terms of numbers. The observation above is quantitative when expressed as, "A car drove down the street at 50 km/h." Because quantitative observations are more specific than qualitative ones, they are generally more useful in science.

In this experiment, you will practise making both qualitative and quantitative observations while doing two acitvities: combining two different metals with water (Part 1), and placing aluminum foil in copper(II) chloride solution (Part 2).

OBJECTIVES

1. to make observations while watching materials interact and undergo change

2. to record and classify these observations as qualitative or quantitative

MATERIALS

Apparatus

3 beakers (250 mL)
2 test tubes
  (16 mm × 150 mm)
thermometer
centigram balance
metric ruler
tweezers
safety goggles
lab apron

Reagents

mossy zinc
calcium metal
phenolphthalein
aluminum foil
1M copper(II) chloride
  solution

PROCEDURE

Part I Combining Two Different Metals With Water

1. Put on a lab apron and safety goggles.

2. Obtain two 250 mL beakers and fill each of them with about 150 mL of tap water. Label one beaker A and the other B.

3. Next fill two 150 mm test tubes with tap water. Fill them to the brim so that no air remains in them.

4. With your thumb covering the open end, invert each test tube *one at a time*. Place one in beaker A and one in beaker B. Leave each test tube filled with water upside down in the beaker, as in Figure 1B-2.

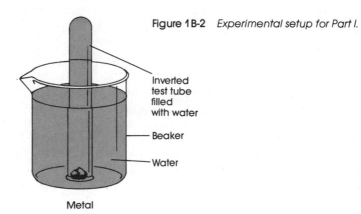

Figure 1B-2 *Experimental setup for Part I.*

Inverted
test tube
filled
with water

Beaker

Water

Metal

5. Place a piece of mossy zinc in beaker A and immediately shift the test tube over to cover the metal. Hold the test tube in place and record your observations in your copy of Table 1 in your notebook.

6. Add 2 drops of phenolphthalein to beaker A, and record your observations in Table 1.

7. Repeat Steps 5 and 6, this time adding a chunk of calcium metal to beaker B. Do not touch the calcium; use tweezers to pick it up. Record your observations in Table 2.

8. Repeat any steps of your choice in order to quantify your observations. Use any lab equipment that has been made available to you, as well as your imagination! Before going ahead, however, check your procedure with your teacher.

9. Refer to the section on reagent disposal which follows, and clean up your apparatus.

Part II   Aluminum Foil in Copper(II) Chloride Solution

1. Place 100 mL of copper(II) chloride solution in a clean 250 mL beaker, and record the temperature of the solution.

2. Cut a square of aluminum foil (approximately 15 cm × 15 cm) and roll it into a tube. To form the tube, you can roll the foil on a pencil.

3. Place the tube of aluminum foil in the beaker containing copper(II) chloride solution and immediately start recording your observations in your copy of Table 3.

CAUTION: Copper (II) chloride is poisonous. Do not get any in your mouth; wash away any spills or splashes with plenty of water.

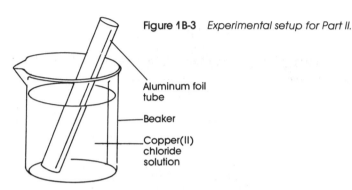

Figure 1B-3   *Experimental setup for Part II.*

Aluminum foil tube

Beaker

Copper(II) chloride solution

4. When no further changes appear, note down the temperature of the remaining solution in Table 3.

5. Refer to the section on reagent disposal, and clean up your apparatus.

6. Before you leave the laboratory, wash your hands thoroughly with soap and water; use a fingernail brush to clean under your nails.

REAGENT DISPOSAL

After Part I, pour all liquids down the sink. Place the remaining zinc and the remaining calcium into the designated containers. After Part II, place all liquids and the remaining solids in the designated container(s).

POST LAB DISCUSSION

Because of the nature of this experiment, you might well have expected a variety of observations. Did you use all your senses? Where possible, you should have tried to obtain some quantitative observations to extend your qualitative observations.

An interesting activity at this point would be to compare your observations with those of another lab group.

DATA AND OBSERVATIONS

Part I   Combining Two Different Metals With Water

Table 1   Zinc Metal in Water

QUALITATIVE OBSERVATIONS	CORRESPONDING QUANTITATIVE OBSERVATIONS (IF ANY)

Table 2   Calcium Metal in Water

QUALITATIVE OBSERVATIONS	CORRESPONDING QUANTITATIVE OBSERVATIONS (IF ANY)

Part II   Aluminum Foil in Copper(II) Chloride Solution

Table 3

QUALITATIVE OBSERVATIONS	CORRESPONDING QUANTITATIVE OBSERVATIONS (IF ANY)

QUESTIONS

1. In which of the tests did you observe a color change?

2. a. In which of the tests did you observe the formation of a gas?
   b. Which observations allowed you to conclude that a gas was produced?

3. In which test(s) did you observe no changes taking place?

FOLLOW-UP QUESTIONS

1. Suppose you wanted to collect and measure the volume of a gas produced in a chemical reaction. How would you do this?

2. Find out what phenolphthalein is, and what it is commonly used for.

CONCLUSION

Report a significant qualitative and quantitative observation for each test you did.

Analysis of Experimental Results

The results of many experiments are more significant than the results of a single experiment. A professional chemist repeats a given experiment many times until consistent results are obtained. These results are usually not all the same, so a method for comparing the results and selecting the best result is necessary. Only when several chemists, working independently, have obtained the same value for the result of an experiment is that value generally considered reliable. Then it is known as the "accepted value."

You usually do not have enough time to do a given experiment several times, but you can compare your data to those of others in the class. In this experiment you will determine a unitary rate: the mass, in grams, of one millilitre of water. The mass of a unit volume of a substance is called its *density*.

Density is an *intensive property* of matter, since it does not depend on the amount of material measured. A cupful of water has the same density as a teaspoonful. Properties such as mass and volume are known as *extensive properties*, because they depend on the amount of material measured.

OBJECTIVES

1. to use a graduated cylinder to measure volume and a balance to measure mass

2. to analyze experimental data and suggest causes for possible deviations from accepted values

3. to evaluate the suggested causes for results that deviate from accepted values

MATERIALS

Apparatus	Reagent
centigram balance	tap water
graduated cylinder	
beaker (150 mL)	
safety goggles	
lab apron	

PROCEDURE

1. Put on your lab apron and safety goggles.

2. Use the centigram balance to determine the mass of a clean, dry, empty 150 mL beaker. Record the mass in your notebook.

3. Measure the assigned volume of water in a graduated cylinder and record the volume in your notebook.

4. Pour the water into the 150 mL beaker.

5. Use the centigram balance to determine the mass of the beaker and water. Record the mass in your notebook.

6. Your teacher will have placed a copy of Table 1 on the chalkboard. Once you have obtained all the necessary data, place them in the table on the board. When all members of class have completed the table, copy it into your notebook.

POST LAB DISCUSSION

The accepted value for the mass of one millilitre of water is one gram. In other words, the density of water is 1 g/mL. It is more informative to compare the accepted value to the experimental values obtained by all class members than to any one result. If the class results are different from the accepted value, analysis of your experimental procedure may help you to decide why.

DATA AND OBSERVATIONS

Mass of 150 mL beaker

Volume of water

Mass of 150 mL beaker and water

Mass of water in 150 mL beaker

Table 1   Class Results

STUDENT	MASS OF WATER (g)	VOLUME OF WATER (mL)	DENSITY OF WATER (g/mL)

CALCULATIONS

1. Use the class results to calculate the mass of one millilitre of water for each experiment and record those masses in your copy of Table 1 (under "Density of Water").

FOLLOW-UP QUESTIONS

1. The mass of one millilitre of water is a unitary rate. What is the name given to this unitary rate?

2. What is the accepted value for the mass of one millilitre of water?

3. If your experiment gave a different value for the mass of one millilitre of water, analyze the experiment to determine three possible causes.

4. Make a list of the possible causes suggested by the other students.

5. Evaluate each suggested cause and indicate which are most likely to be true.

6. Select one cause that you think is the most probable cause and explain your selection.

7. Design an experiment to evaluate the cause you selected.

CONCLUSION

State the results of Objective 2.

Cooling and Heating Curves of a Pure Substance

Every pure substance has a characteristic temperature at which it melts. This property of individual melting points can be used by chemists to identify substances. Likewise, when a liquid pure substance cools, it freezes at a characteristic temperature. Freezing points can therefore be used to differentiate between methanol and water; methanol freezes at −94°C, whereas water freezes at 0°C.

In this experiment, the pure substance to be studied is paradichlorobenzene, one type of moth repellant. You will first heat solid paradichlorobenzene until it melts and forms a liquid, then investigate the cooling of this liquid paradichlorobenzene (Part I). In Part II you will reheat this substance to study the melting process. During the cooling and heating processes, temperature data will be recorded at regular intervals.

OBJECTIVES

1. to investigate the cooling process for liquid paradichlorobenzene

2. to investigate the heating process for solid paradichlorobenzene

3. to determine and compare the melting and freezing temperatures of paradichlorobenzene

MATERIALS

Apparatus
ring stand and ring support
buret clamp
lab burner
wire gauze with ceramic centre
test tube (18 mm × 150 mm)
beaker (400 mL)
2 thermometers
lab apron
safety goggles

Reagents
paradichlorobenzene

PROCEDURE

Part I The Cooling Process

1. Put on your lab apron and safety goggles.

2. With your partner, decide in advance the role each of you will perform in Part I. As you carry out the cooling process, one partner will act as observer, while the other will act as recorder. Later, in Part II, you can exchange roles. The recorder will be taking readings every 30 s for about 10 min, so one of you will need to prepare a data table in advance. Consult Table 1, which appears later in this experiment, for a model.

3. Obtain a stoppered test tube containing solid paradichlorobenzene from your instructor. Remove the stopper and save it for the end of the experiment.

CAUTION: Paradichlorobenzene is poisonous and flammable. In high concentrations its vapors can irritate the eyes.

4. Put 300 mL of cold tap water in a 400 mL beaker and place the beaker on the wire gauze on the stand. DO NOT place the test tube in the water bath yet.

5. Change the solid paradichlorobenzene into the liquid state by slowly heating the test tube over a burner flame while holding the test tube with a buret clamp. Move the test tube back and forth slowly in the flame to avoid overheating, as shown in Figure 2A-1. Do not heat it at the bottom only.

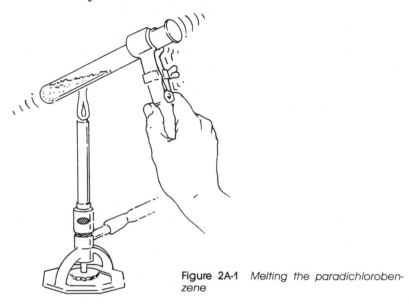

Figure 2A-1 *Melting the paradichlorobenzene*

6. Place a thermometer in the test tube and continue the heating process until you obtain a liquid temperature between 70°C and 75°C.

7. Clamp the test tube containing both the liquid and the thermometer onto the ring stand so that the test tube is suspended above the beaker.

8. Record the temperature readings of the liquid paradichlorobenzene, then lower the test tube so that the water level in the bath is higher than the level of the paradichlorobenzene (Figure 2A-2). Temperature readings should be taken every 30 s, until a temperature near 40°C is reached. Record the times when solidification begins and ends, as well as any other observations. (The thermometer will become embedded in the solid.)

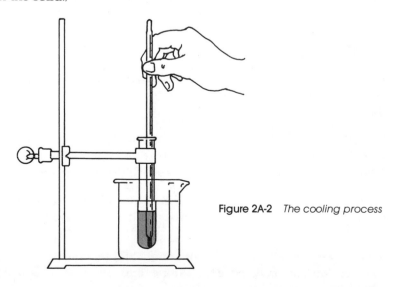

Figure 2A-2 *The cooling process*

Part II The Heating Process

1. Part II, like Part I, requires teamwork. You and your lab partner can exchange observing and recording duties at this point if you wish. Table 1 will be used for recording data from this part of the experiment as well.

2. The test tube from Part I now contains a thermometer embedded in solid paradichlorobenzene. Raise the test tube out of the water bath and swing it away from the beaker. See Figure 2A-3.

3. Use a lab burner to heat the water bath to approximately 75°C. Use your second thermometer to monitor this temperature.

4. Turn off the burner, but keep it in position in case you need to reheat the water bath later.

5. Initiate the heating process. Record the temperature of the solid paradichlorobenzene, then position the test tube in the hot water bath. Once again, make sure that the water level is higher than the level of the paradichlorobenzene.

6. Record the temperature of the paradichlorobenzene every 30 s until a temperature near 60°C is attained. As the paradichlorobenzene melts, stir it gently to mix the solid and liquid. Record when melting begins and ends, as well as any other observations. During the heating process, the temperature of the water bath should be monitored with the second thermometer to make certain that the water temperature remains above 60°C. (You may find it necessary to reheat the water bath with the burner.)

7. When a temperature at or near 60°C has been attained, remove the thermometer from the liquid paradichlorobenzene and immediately wipe it with a paper towel.

8. Raise the test tube out of the hot water bath to allow the paradichlorobenzene to resolidify. When the test tube has cooled, reseal it with the stopper and return it to your instructor.

9. After the heating apparatus has cooled, disassemble it and return all components to their proper location.

10. Before you leave the laboratory, wash your hands thoroughly with soap and water, using a fingernail brush to clean under your nails.

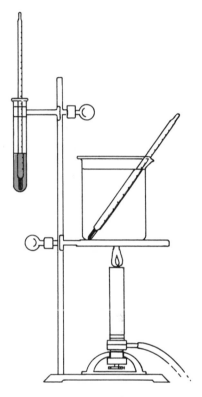

Figure 2A-3   *The heating process*

REAGENT DISPOSAL

The solidified paradichlorobenzene is to be kept in the test tube and sealed with a rubber stopper for future use.

POST LAB DISCUSSION

The data you have collected can now be analyzed with a graph which will represent the cooling and heating curves of paradichlorobenzene.

DATA AND OBSERVATIONS

Table 1   Cooling and Heating of Paradichlorobenzene

TIME (min)	COOLING PROCESS			HEATING PROCESS		
	TEMPERATURE (°C)	OBSERVATIONS		TEMPERATURE (°C)	OBSERVATIONS	
0						
0.5						
1.0						
1.5						
2.0						
2.5						
. .						

ANALYSIS OF DATA (GRAPHING)

Part I   The Cooling Process

1. Using the data you obtained during the cooling process, construct a graph of temperature versus time. Use small circles for these data points, and sketch a smooth curve.

2. Indicate on the graph where solidification began and ended.

Part II   The Heating Process

1. On the same graph as the cooling curve, plot temperature versus time for the heating process. Use small squares to distinguish these data points, and sketch a smooth curve.

2. Indicate on the graph where melting began and ended.

QUESTIONS

1. What property of paradichlorobenzene may convince you that it is an ingredient in mothballs?

2. From your cooling curve, determine the freezing point of paradichlorobenzene.

3. From your heating curve, determine the melting point of paradichlorobenzene.

4. Compare your melting and freezing points with those of two other lab groups, and explain any similarities or differences.

5. What can you conclude about the melting points and freezing points of a pure substance?

FOLLOW-UP QUESTIONS

1. How would you explain the plateaus in your heating and cooling curves?

2. Suppose that more paradichlorobenzene had been used in Part I. What would be the appearance of the new cooling curve?

CONCLUSION

State the results of Objective 3.

Chemical and Physical Change

There are two types of change that are of particular interest to chemists: chemical change and physical change. A *chemical change* is one in which new substances are formed. A common example of a chemical change is the combustion of paraffin wax in a candle. The new substances formed as a result of this chemical change are carbon dioxide and water.

In a *physical change*, no new substance is formed. Sometimes physical changes are confused with chemical changes when heat and bubbles are involved. For example, when a liquid is heated to boiling, a physical (not a chemical) change occurs, since no new substance is formed. The liquid merely changes to a vapor with the same chemical composition. In the distillation of crude oil, the various components are separated by a series of physical changes. These components, which include gasoline, kerosene, and motor oils, have characteristic boiling points. Therefore, the individual components can be vaporized at a variety of temperatures and separated from the liquid mixture.

In this experiment, various chemical changes will be observed. Chemical changes are characterized by changes in such observable properties as color, odor, solubility, and phase, among others. Learning to recognize chemical and physical changes is important in explaining the behavior of matter.

OBJECTIVES

1. to observe some changes in the laboratory

2. to infer whether each is a chemical or a physical change

3. to record some recognizable characteristics of chemical changes

MATERIALS

Apparatus

4 small test tubes
(10 mm × 75 mm)
test-tube rack
4 medicine droppers
glass square
safety goggles
lab apron

Reagents

set of 4 unknown solutions

PROCEDURE

1. Put on your safety goggles and lab apron.

2. Label four test tubes *A, B, C, D*. Obtain one third of a test tube of each of the unknown solutions.

3. Place a clean medicine dropper in each test tube. Set the test tubes in the test-tube rack on the lab bench.

4. Obtain a clean glass square. On a piece of white paper the size of the glass square, draw a grid like the one that appears at the top of the next page, on which to conduct tests. Place the grid directly beneath the glass square.

CAUTION: Remember A, B, C, and D are unknowns; whether they are hazardous or not, it is always a good practice to minimize your contact with unknown chemicals. Some of these chemicals are corrosive to skin, eyes, or clothing. Wear safety goggles and gloves when handling the chemicals. Wash spills and splashes off with plenty of water. Call your teacher.

	A	B	C	D
A	▓		▓	▓
B		▓		▓
C			▓	▓
D				▓

5. On each cell of the grid, combine the solutions as shown. Place just one drop of each on the glass square. There are only six different combinations.

6. Draw up a data table like the one below. Make brief comments on any changes you observe. If no change occurs, record this as well.

7. Clean up, following the instructions for reagent disposal.

8. Before you leave the laboratory, wash your hands thoroughly with soap and water, using a fingernail brush to clean under your fingernails.

REAGENT DISPOSAL

All solutions can be rinsed down the sink with copious amounts of water.

POST LAB DISCUSSION

As a review, note how the results of this experiment can be related to the discussion of physical and chemical changes in the introduction. If you observed in any instance that no change took place, you were probably overlooking the fact that mixing occurred, so the concentrations of the solutions changed. In such instances, a physical·change has occurred.

DATA AND OBSERVATIONS

Table 1

UNKNOWN	A	B	C	D
A				
B				
C				
D				

QUESTIONS

1. State whether a physical or a chemical change occurred for each combination of solutions.

FOLLOW-UP QUESTIONS

1. Describe (a) two chemical changes and (b) two physical changes that you might observe occurring in your everyday life.

CONCLUSION

State the results of Objective 3.

Recognizing Elements, Compounds, and Mixtures

In simple terms, chemistry can be defined as the study of the composition and interaction of matter. Matter is anything that has mass and occupies space. The universe is made up of many types of matter—water, rock, plants, air, people, to name just a few. It is quite easy to think of examples of matter, but it is more important to be able to organize them into groups. In order to better understand matter, chemists have developed a classification scheme for it. See Figure 2C-1.

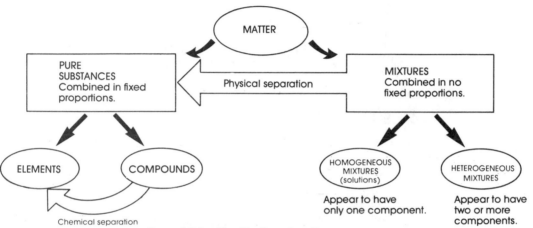

Figure 2C-1   Classification of matter

Among the many people who can appreciate the importance of classifying matter are workers in the mining industry. For example, the process for the production of the element copper often begins with the mining of a heterogeneous mixture called "copper ore". See Figure 2C-2.

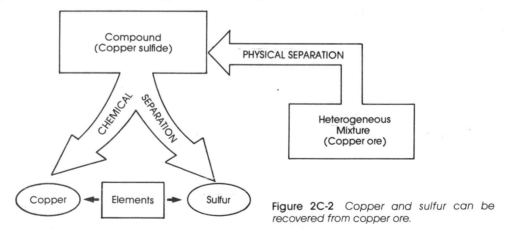

Figure 2C-2 Copper and sulfur can be recovered from copper ore.

In this experiment, you will act like a chemist by classifying matter. You will be given a number of unknown samples which you will test in various ways. You must decide whether a given sample is an element, a compound, or a mixture. As you know, mixtures consist of two or more substances physically combined in any proportion. Therefore, you will find that mixtures can be separated by physical means such as picking apart the components, selective dissolving, filtration, or evaporation. Compounds, on the other hand, can only be separated into elements by chemical means that are beyond the scope of this experiment.

OBJECTIVES

1. to use simple laboratory procedures to test a set of unknown samples of matter

2. to classify unknown samples of matter as elements, compounds, or mixtures

MATERIALS

Apparatus

tripod magnifier
stereomicroscope
  (if available)
tweezers
plastic spoon
3 test tubes
  (13 mm × 100 mm)
test tube rack
lab burner

evaporating dish
crucible tongs
ring stand and
  ring support
filter paper and funnel
250 ml beaker
lab apron
safety goggles

Reagents

set of 5 unknown
  samples

PROCEDURE

1. Put on your safety goggles and apron.

2. Obtain a sample of each unknown from your instructor. Take care to number your samples according to your instructor's numbering system. If the unknown is solid, place about one half spoonful on a piece of paper. Fill a test tube half full with any liquid sample.

3. Use a data table similar to Table 1 to help organize your observations in your notebook.

4. Observe the unknowns carefully and record their properties.

5. Of the three solid unknowns, one is an element, one is a compound, and one is a mixture. Devise a method to separate the solid mixture, then try it.

6. Of the two liquid unknowns, one is a compound and one is a mixture. Devise a means (other than tasting) of classifying them, and try it.

7. Clean up according to the reagent disposal instructions.

8. Before leaving the laboratory, wash your hands thoroughly with soap and water; use a fingernail brush to clean under your nails.

CAUTION: You must not taste any unknowns, as some are poisonous.

REAGENT DISPOSAL

Any remaining liquids can be rinsed down the sink with copious amounts of water. Any solid waste should go into the designated container.

POST LAB DISCUSSION

Distinguishing between a mixture and a pure substance is fairly straightforward. If the unknown can be separated by physical means such as those available in this experiment, then it is a mixture. However, if the unknown is a pure substance, further tests may be required to determine whether it is an element or a compound.

DATA AND OBSERVATIONS

Table 1

UNKNOWN	PROPERTIES OBSERVED	POSSIBILITIES		
		ELEMENT	COMPOUND	MIXTURE
1				
2				
3	(Leave several spaces			
4	between each unknown.)			
5				

QUESTIONS

1. Classify each of the solid unknowns as an element, compound, or mixture, and explain your decisions. If you are uncertain about any of the unknowns, explain why.

2. Which of the liquids was the compound, and which was the mixture? How did you determine this?

FOLLOW-UP QUESTIONS

1. In some countries, desalination plants are used to separate salt from sea water. Consult a reference book and describe the process used in these plants. (Use the terms elements, compounds, and mixtures where appropriate in your description.)

2. In this experiment, one of the solids you tested was a compound, and one was an element. What further tests would you perform to tell them apart?

CONCLUSION

State the results of Objective 2.

Separation of a Mixture by Paper Chromatography

Chromatography is one technique used by chemists to separate mixtures of chemical compounds in order to identify or isolate their components. In chromatography, mixtures are separated according to the different solubilities of the components in liquids, or their adsorptions on solids.

Chromatography has many applications, including the detection and measurement of pesticides in foods, and drugs in urine specimens. It is also used extensively in biological research to separate alcohols, amino acids, and sugars; in plants, for example. In addition, the pharmaceutical industry relies on chromatography for the production of high-purity chemicals.

There are a variety of chromatographic techniques, but all share two features: a moving carrier phase, and a stationary phase. In the stationary phase of paper chromatography, the sample to be analyzed is spotted onto a piece of filter paper. The sample is carried along this stationary phase by a solvent which acts as the moving carrier. The components of the sample are carried different distances along the paper, depending on their individual solubilities. (See Figure 2D-1.) After a length of time, therefore, the original spot is spread out into a series of bands. These bands are then analyzed, to determine their identities.

Figure 2D-1 *A typical paper chromatogram.*

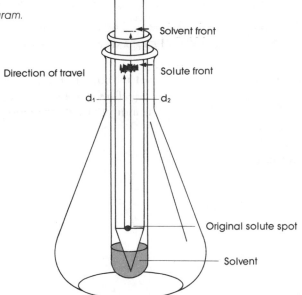

In paper chromatography, one method of identifying these separated components of a mixture is to calculate the R_f value of each. ("R_f" stands for "ratio of fronts".) An R_f value is simply the ratio of the distance travelled by the solute to the distance travelled by the solvent:

$$R_f = \frac{d_1}{d_2}$$

where d_1 = distance travelled by solute
d_2 = distance travelled by solvent

The R_f value of a substance is a characteristic of that substance for a specific solvent. A substance having a high solubility in the moving phase will be carried further and consequently will have a high R_f value. By definition, R_f values vary from 0 to 1.

In this experiment, you will become acquainted with paper chromatography. In Part I you will assemble a paper chromatography apparatus. In Part II you will examine chromatographic results for a variety of food colorings. Then in Part III you will separate two mixtures of these colorings, and study the significance of the R_f values. Unfortunately, many chromatography tests on substances present two problems for the school chemistry lab:

1. The solvents required are often classified as hazardous and are therefore not recommended for school use.
2. In many cases, the time required for the separation of mixture is too long for a typical laboratory period.

For these reasons, this experiment is restricted to the analysis of food colorings, which are readily soluble in water.

OBJECTIVES

1. to assemble and operate a paper chromatography apparatus

2. to study the meaning and significance of R_f values

3. to test various food colorings and to calculate their R_f values

4. to compare measured R_f values with standard R_f values

5. to separate mixtures of food colorings into their components

6. to identify the components of mixtures by means of their R_f values

MATERIALS

Apparatus

per class:
  5 glass stirring rods
  several pairs of scissors
per lab station:
  3 large test tubes
    (25 mm × 200 mm)
  3 Erlenmeyer flasks (250 mL)
  metric ruler
  pencil
  chromatography paper strips
    (2.5 cm wide × 66 cm long)

Reagents

set of food colorings
  (yellow, green, blue, red)
unknown mixture of food colorings

PROCEDURE

Part I   Setting Up

1. Obtain three large test tubes and three Erlenmeyer flasks. (The sizes of these pieces of apparatus are important to the rest of the procedure.) Place a test tube in each of the flasks, and label the test tubes *A*, *B*, and *C*.

2. Obtain a 66 cm length of chromatography paper and cut it into three strips of 22 cm each. Using a pencil, lightly draw a line across each strip 4.0 cm from one end. (See Figure 2D-2). Use a pair of scissors to trim this end of the strip into a point, as shown in the drawing.

Figure 2D-2

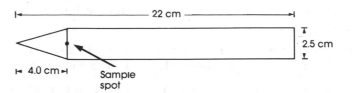

3. Place some water (the solvent for this experiment) in each test tube so that it is 2.0 cm deep.

Part II   R$_f$ Values of Individual Food Colorings

1. You will be assigned one food coloring to test: red, yellow, or blue. Take one strip of chromatography paper over to the station of food colorings. Using a glass stirring rod, spot the strip with the color assigned to you. (Refer again to Figure 2D-2.) Be careful not to make too large a sample spot; it should not exceed 0.5 cm in diameter. (The smaller the spot, the better.) Write the color at the top of the strip.

2. Insert the strip in test tube A. Be very careful not to push the strip down too far; its tip should just touch the bottom of the test tube, and the water should cover about half of its point. (See Figure 2D-3.) Do not allow the flat surface of the strip to rest against the walls of the test tube. (Achieving this should not be difficult, since the width of the paper and the inside diameter of the test tube are almost the same.)

Figure 2D-3 *The final arrangement of the apparatus.*

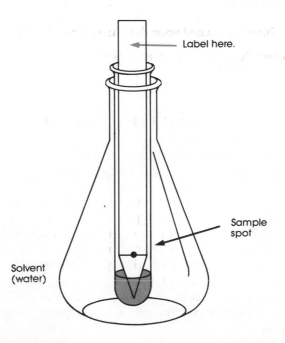

3. Observe what happens to your sample spot as the water moves slowly up the paper as a result of capillary action.

4. Continue to make observations for the next 10 min. Try to identify two fronts as they move up the paper. One is the solute front (the food coloring) and should be easy to identify in this experiment. The other is the solvent front (water) and can only be seen upon close examination.

5. See whether or not your sample separates into component colors. Copy Table 1 into your notebook, and record your results.

6. Since the movement of fronts is a rather slow process, you could start Part III of the experiment at this point. However, once you have begun Part III, you should return to Part I and complete it.

7. After about 20 min have elapsed, when you are satisfied that no further separation of color will occur, remove the strip from the test tube. *Immediately* draw a pencil line across the top edge of the solvent front, before it evaporates!

8. Referring to Figure 2D-4, measure d_2 and d_1 on your strip as precisely as possible. Record these values in Table 1. Calculate the R_f value for your sample, and record it as well.

9. Your instructor will have a data table similar to Table 2 on the chalkboard for the class results. Place your own results on this table, and copy it into your notebook when it is complete.

10. Clean up, following the instructions for reagent disposal.

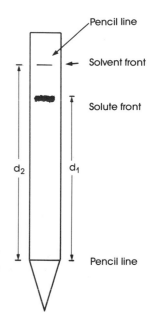

Figure 2D-4 *Making measurements on the chromatography paper.*

Part III   Separation of Mixtures into Their Components

1. Take your second strip of chromatography paper and spot it with a sample of green food coloring. Spot the third strip with a sample of the unknown mixture of food colorings. Remember to label both strips at the top.

2. Insert the strips in test tubes B and C, and follow the same procedures as in Part II, Steps 2 to 7.

3. When you have finished, record your data in a copy of Table 3.

4. Clean up, following the reagent disposal instructions.

REAGENT DISPOSAL

The chromatography paper can be placed in the designated container, or saved and placed in your lab report.

POST LAB DISCUSSION

The separation of a mixture of food colorings is a good introduction to paper chromatography, because the components can be seen clearly spread out on the strip. Each component color has a characteristic R_f value that can be compared to a table of standard R_f values. The list of values provided in Table 4 is a partial list and may not correspond to your R_f values if the dyes used by the manufacturers of the food colorings are not identical. Therefore, the measured R_f averages (Table 2) will be more reliable than those in Table 4 when you are identifying the component colors of your mixtures.

DATA AND OBSERVATIONS

Part II   R$_f$ Values of Individual Food Colorings

Table 1   Results for Lab Station

Color tested
Distance solute travelled (d_1)
Distance solvent travelled (d_2)
Ratio of fronts (R_f)

COMPLETE IN YOUR NOTEBOOK

Table 2   Class Results

LAB STATION	COLORS TESTED		
	RED R_f	YELLOW R_f	BLUE R_f
1			
2			
3			
. . .			
Average R_f Values			

COMPLETE IN YOUR NOTEBOOK

Part III   Separation of Mixtures into Their Components

Table 3 R_f Comparisons for Component Colors

	COMPONENT COLORS	d_1 (cm) d_2 (cm)	CALCULATED R_f	COMPONENT R_f (FROM TABLE 2)
Green Coloring				
Unknown Mixture				

COMPLETE IN YOUR NOTEBOOK

Table 4   Some of the Dyes Approved for Food Colorings

DYE	RED #2	RED #3	RED #4	YELLOW #5	YELLOW #6	BLUE #1	BLUE #2
R_f	0.81	0.41	0.62	0.95	0.77	1.0	0.79

QUESTIONS

1. a. Which of the colors you tested in Part II of the experiment appeared to contain one or more of the approved dyes listed in Table 4?
   b. Which, if any, of the colors you tested did not correspond to any of the approved dyes?

2. From your results in Part III, what are the components of the green food coloring? Support your answer both qualitatively and quantitatively.

3. What can you conclude about the identity of the components in the unknown mixture? What qualitative and quantitative evidence supports your answer?

4. What might happen if ink, rather than pencil, were used to mark the sample line on the chromatography paper?

5. Why should green food coloring be classified as a mixture, whereas yellow, blue, or red should not?

FOLLOW-UP QUESTIONS

Figure 2D-5

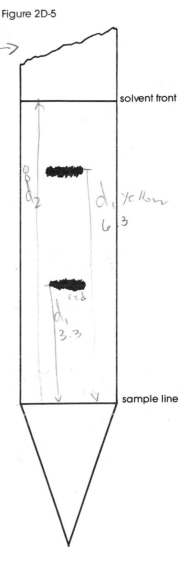

1. Identify the dyes that appear on the chromatogram in Figure 2D-5. (Consult Table 4 for R_f values.) The original sample was orange food coloring.

2. A pharmaceutical chemist runs a chromatography test on a substance and identifies two of its components by comparing their R_f values against certain standards. If the two components have R_f values of 1.0 and 0.41, and the solvent front has travelled 12.0 cm from the sample's origin, what is the separation distance on the chromatogram?

3. A chemist performs an R_f calculation, obtains a value of 1.2, and decides that the answer is unacceptable. Why?

CONCLUSION

State the results of Objective 6.

Law of Definite Composition

Elements are a kind of matter that cannot be decomposed. Compounds are combinations of elements. However, not all combinations of elements are compounds. The combination must be a chemical combination. For example, the combination of nitrogen gas and oxygen gas in air is a mixture. The gases are physically combined and therefore can be mixed in an infinite variety of proportions. Compounds, on the other hand, are special combinations of elements.

The way in which compounds are formed has been shown to obey certain laws. One of these laws is the Law of Conservation of Mass, which you have previously studied. Another law obeyed by chemical reactions is the Law of Definite Composition (also called the Law of Definite Proportions). The Law of Definite Composition states that the elements that form a compound always combine in the same proportion by mass. The compound water, H_2O, always is a chemical combination of hydrogen and oxygen in a 1:8 ratio by mass. If a mixture of hydrogen and oxygen in some other ratio, say 1:2, were reacted, there would be water formed, but there would also be some unreacted hydrogen, because water always forms in the 1:8 ratio by mass.

In this experiment, you will examine the reaction between magnesium metal, Mg, and the oxygen in the air, O_2. The magnesium will be heated strongly in a crucible for several minutes. The mass of magnesium will be compared with the mass of the material produced.

Magnesium reactions are interesting. Because of the intensity of reaction, a magnesium fire is extremely difficult to put out. It will continue to burn even in the carbon dioxide gas from a CO_2 fire extinguisher! "Incendiary bombs" designed to burn through a building from top to bottom contain magnesium metal.

OBJECTIVES

1. to observe the reaction between magnesium and oxygen
2. to calculate the ratio of mass of product to mass of magnesium
3. to verify the Law of Definite Composition
4. to make careful mass measurements that are adequate for appropriate results

MATERIALS

Apparatus

crucible and lid
crucible tongs
medicine dropper
centigram balance
pipestem triangle
ring stand and ring
burner and lighter

wire gauze with
  ceramic centre
sandpaper or
  emery cloth
safety goggles
lab apron

Reagents

magnesium ribbon
distilled water

PROCEDURE

1. Put on your apron and goggles. Hot crucibles and magnesium can cause burns, so use with caution. Handle hot crucibles with tongs and place the hot crucible on the wire gauze to cool.

2. Obtain a piece of magnesium from your instructor. If the surface of the magnesium is not shiny, use a piece of sandpaper or emery cloth to shine the surface.

3. Obtain a clean and completely dry crucible and cover. Find the mass of the crucible and cover and record it in your copy of Table 1 in your notebook.

4. Roll the magnesium into a loose coil and place it in the crucible. Find the mass of the crucible, cover, and magnesium, and record it in Table 1.

5. Set up the ring stand, ring, burner, and pipestem triangle as shown in Figure 2E-1. Place the crucible on the pipestem triangle. Begin heating the crucible gradually with the *lid completely on*. Heat slowly by moving the flame around underneath the crucible. Remove the heat temporarily if a large amount of smoke comes out of the crucible.

6. After about four minutes of direct heating with no smoke, remove the lid slightly. Heat the crucible to *redness* for four minutes. Finally, remove the lid completely and heat strongly for four more minutes.

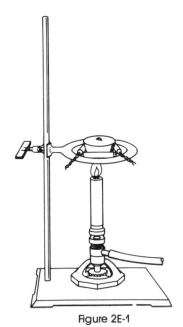

Figure 2E-1

7. Turn off the burner and put the lid back on the crucible. Allow the crucible and cover to cool to a temperature low enough so that you can touch the crucible. Find the mass of the crucible, contents, and cover. Add ten drops of distilled water. Smelling cautiously, note any odor. Put the crucible back on the ring-stand setup and heat again for four minutes with the *lid on*. Allow to cool again.

8. Find the mass of the crucible, cover, and product. Record it in Table 1.

9. If enough time remains, reheat the crucible for four minutes, allow it to cool, and again find the mass. If this mass differs by more than 0.03 g from the mass you found in Step 8, repeat this procedure until the masses are within the 0.03 g range.

10. If enough time remains, repeat the whole procedure for a second trial.

11. Clean and put away all of the materials.

12. Wash your hands thoroughly with soap and water, using a fingernail brush to clean under your fingernails.

REAGENT DISPOSAL

Place all wastes in the designated waste containers.

POST LAB DISCUSSION

The magnesium metal is an element that combines with another element, oxygen gas, to form the compound magnesium oxide. The ratio of the mass of magnesium oxide to the mass of magnesium should be constant for all of your trials, regardless of the mass of magnesium that you started with.

The strong heating ensured that all of the magnesium reacted with the oxygen in the air to form magnesium oxide. Since some magnesium nitride (magnesium + nitrogen) could have formed, the addition of water and subsequent heating were done to remove that product from the crucible.

In order to calculate the ratio, you must first find the masses of magnesium oxide alone and of magnesium alone by subtracting the mass of the crucible from the masses that you recorded. The ratio is then calculated by:

RATIO = MASS OF MAGNESIUM OXIDE/MASS OF MAGNESIUM.

DATA AND OBSERVATIONS

Table 1

	TRIAL ONE	TRIAL TWO
Mass of crucible and cover		
Mass of crucible, cover, and magnesium		
Mass of crucible, cover, and product (before adding water)		
Mass of crucible, cover, and product (second time)		

CALCULATIONS

1. For each of the trials, calculate:

   a. mass of magnesium alone
   b. mass of magnesium oxide alone
   c. ratio of mass of magnesium oxide to mass of magnesium

2. The accepted ratio for the mass of magnesium oxide to the mass of magnesium is 1.65. Calculate the percent of error for each of your trials by using the formula:

$$\text{Percent error} = \frac{(\text{Accepted Value} - \text{Experimental Value})}{\text{Accepted Value}} \times 100\%$$

FOLLOW-UP QUESTIONS

1. Use your textbook to determine the formula for the magnesium oxide that is formed in this experiment.

2. Use the accepted ratio to find the mass of magnesium that would be needed to combine with 16.0 g of oxygen.

3. What mass of magnesium oxide would be formed in item 2?

4. Suppose you tried to combine 42.0 g of magnesium with 45.0 g of oxygen. How much magnesium oxide would be formed? Would there be any magnesium or oxygen left over? If so, which element and how much?

CONCLUSION

State the results of Objective 2. Compare your ratio to the accepted value.

Investigating Conservation of Matter and Uncertainty of Measurements

Two of the fundamental questions in chemistry are:
1. What is the identity of the matter I have?
2. How much matter do I have?

Exact measurement is very important in the chemical industry. The exact reproduction of a paint color, for example, demands that the proportions of pigments added be measured most accurately. In fact, chemistry became a science only after experimenters believed that conservation of matter offered them a starting point from which they could interpret their results.

In the next experiment you will learn to determine the identity of matter. For this experiment, you will assume that matter in the bottle labeled potassium sulfate is K_2SO_4. In most experiments, chemists assume that the identity of the substance in the bottle is the same as that given on the label. Before the bottle was labeled, the manufacturer did experiments to determine the identity of the substance. If unexpected results are obtained, the chemist will check the labels and contents of the reagent bottles.

Some of the most significant experiments in chemistry are quantitative which means they include measurements of how much matter is present or is changed. Since no measurement is exact, all measurements include some uncertainty. The exact value for a measurement can be assumed to lie within a range expressed by the best estimate for the measurement and the estimated uncertainty. If a measurement is expressed as 20 cm ± 2 cm, for example, the exact answer probably lies within the range of 18 cm to 22 cm.

In Part I of this experiment, you will learn the limitations of measurements and the skills involved in determining the mass of a substance and the volume of a liquid. In Part II, you will learn to make careful measurements and try to avoid losing any matter during a physical change. In addition, you will develop skills involved in stirring, dissolving, and filtering.

OBJECTIVES

1. to learn to handle chemicals and equipment safely

2. to use a centigram balance to determine mass

3. to use a graduated cylinder to measure volume

4. to dissolve and filter a solution

5. to learn to estimate the uncertainty in calculated masses

MATERIALS

Apparatus

centigram balance	stirring rod	safety goggles
2 beakers	filter paper	lab apron
(150 mL or 250 mL)	graduated cylinder	spatula
funnel	hot plate	plastic gloves
funnel holder	(for the class)	fume hood

Reagents

solid potassium
    sulfate, K_2SO_4
distilled water

PROCEDURE

You will measure the mass of a beaker three times on three different balances. Your lab partner will also make three measurements. You will then have a total of six measurements that you can use to select a best estimate and an estimated uncertainty.

Part I   Uncertainty of Measurements (Day 1)

1. Put on your lab apron and safety goggles.

2. Label a clean, dry 150 mL or 250 mL beaker with your name and the letter *A*.

3. Find the mass of beaker *A* on a centigram balance to the nearest 0.01 g. Record the mass and balance number in your notebook.

4. Determine the mass of beaker *A* on two additional centigram balances and record the data in your copy of Table 1 in your notebook.

5. Label a second clean, dry 150 or 250 mL beaker with your name or locker number and the letter *B*.

6. Find the mass of beaker *B* on three different centigram balances as you did beaker *A* and record the data in your copy of Table 1.

7. Use the following procedure to add between 5 g and 7 g of K_2SO_4 to beaker *A*: a) balance beaker *A*, move the gram mass up 5 g, and add K_2SO_4 until the beam goes up. The beaker will then contain at least 5 g of K_2SO_4. b) Measure the mass of the beaker on three different centigram balances, and record it in Table 1. (By using this procedure instead of measuring the K_2SO_4 separately, you are less likely to contaminate the supply bottle of K_2SO_4.)

8. Determine the mass of a piece of filter paper on three different centigram balances and record the data in Table 1.

9. Using a graduated cylinder, add 37 mL $\pm$ 1 mL of distilled water to beaker *A*. Stir for three minutes.

10. Filter the liquid in beaker *A* into beaker *B*. Leave any undissolved potassium sulfate in beaker *A*.

11. After filtering, fold the filter paper flat and put it into beaker *A*. Put beaker *A* in your locker.

12. Put beaker *B* on the hot plate in the fume hood and evaporate the liquids.

Part II   Conservation of Matter (Day 2)

1. Measure the mass of beaker *A* and contents on three different centigram balances and record the data in your copy of Table 2.

2. Measure the mass of beaker *B* and contents on three different centigram balances and record the data in Table 2.

3. Rinse the potassium sulfate into a container provided by your teacher.

4. Before you leave the laboratory, wash your hands thoroughly with soap and water; use a fingernail brush to clean under your fingernails.

REAGENT DISPOSAL

All solutions can be rinsed down the sink with copious amounts of water.

POST LAB DISCUSSION

You may have found several different masses for beaker *A*. The beaker does not have several different masses. If it is invariant, it has one exact mass that we cannot find. Even if a balance could be made that would measure the exact mass of a beaker (it cannot be done!) and print out the answer on a slip of paper, it would take forever to print the infinite number of decimal places required to express an exact mass. In the meantime the beaker might change slightly in mass, so this answer would still not be exactly right.

Since you cannot find the exact mass (or any measurement exactly), it is necessary to find the best measurement possible for the given conditions and available instruments. This measurement is called the *best estimate*. Find a best estimate for the masses of beaker *A*, beaker *B*, beaker *A* and potassium sulfate, and the filter paper.

The best estimate that you have found may be different from the exact mass. You cannot ever find the exact mass, but you need to be able to express the uncertainty in your best estimate in such a way that the exact mass is probably included within the range expressed by the best estimate and the uncertainty. You can always make sure the exact answer is included in the range by making the range of the mass go from zero to infinity. However, this makes the measurement meaningless. If you make the range too small, the exact value may not be included within the range, and the measurement would not be valid. This sort of conflict is common in science. You should attempt to make the range as small as possible, but large enough to be reasonably sure the exact answer is within the range.

You may notice that, under certain circumstances, you can never be completely sure your best estimate is valid without making the range so large that the answer is meaningless. This is an inevitable consequence of the nature of science. Science is a statistical process in which the probability of a measurement or an experimental result being true increases as the number of experiments increases. You use estimates of probability in your everyday experience when you cross the street, drive a car, drink a glass of milk, or predict the outcome of a coin flip or a game.

Scientists and mathematicians have developed elaborate processes for analyzing data statistically to estimate probabilities. You do not need to know these statistical procedures at this time. You can develop a useful method that makes sense to you if you keep the previous discussion in mind.

You will also need to develop a method for estimating the uncertainty in an answer calculated from measurements.

DATA AND OBSERVATIONS

Part I   Uncertainty of Measurements (Day 1)

Table 1

	MASS	BALANCE NO.	MASS	BALANCE NO.	MASS	BALANCE NO.	BEST ESTIMATE
Beaker A							
Beaker A + K$_2$SO$_4$							
Beaker B							
Filter paper							

Part II   Conservation of Matter (Day 2)

Table 2

	MASS	BALANCE NO.	MASS	BALANCE NO.	MASS	BALANCE NO.	BEST ESTIMATE
Beaker A, dry K$_2$SO$_4$, + filter paper							
Beaker B + dry K$_2$SO$_4$							

QUESTIONS AND CALCULATIONS

1. Calculate the mass of potassium sulfate in beaker A at the beginning of the experiment. Estimate the uncertainty in the mass of K$_2$SO$_4$. Label your calculation.

2. Calculate the mass of potassium sulfate in beaker A at the end of the experiment (after filtering and drying). Estimate the uncertainty in the mass of K$_2$SO$_4$. Label your calculation.

3. Calculate the mass of K$_2$SO$_4$ in beaker B at the end of the experiment (after filtering and drying). Estimate the uncertainty in the mass of K$_2$SO$_4$. Label your calculation.

4. Calculate the total amount of K$_2$SO$_4$ remaining at the end of the experiment. Estimate the uncertainty in the mass of the K$_2$SO$_4$. Label your calculation.

5. Compare the mass of the K$_2$SO$_4$ at the beginning and end of the experiment.

6. Analyze your experimental results. If the results are different from those expected, explain why.

FOLLOW-UP QUESTIONS

1. Why is it important to use distilled water in this experiment?

2. If tap water were used in this experiment, how would the experimental results be affected?

3. How much K$_2$SO$_4$ dissolved in your experiment?

4. How much K$_2$SO$_4$ did not dissolve in your experiment?

5. Why didn't all of the K$_2$SO$_4$ dissolve in your experiment?

CONCLUSION

How does the amount of matter change during a physical change?

The Thickness of a Thin Aluminum Sheet

In science, we make use of large and small numbers much of the time. In addition, we must often make use of one set of measurements and known properties (such as density) to indirectly measure other quantities. One example of this type of "measurement" will be found in this experiment. The laboratory tools normally available would not be suitable for the direct measurement of the thickness of a piece of aluminum foil.

The formulas that will enable you to find the thickness of the foil are familiar to you. The *volume* of a regular object is found by using the formula $V = L \times W \times H$, where L = length, W = width, and H = height. Imagine that the regular object is a rectangular-shaped piece of foil. Then the formula might be revised to $V = L \times W \times T$, where T = thickness of the foil. Going one step further, the area of the foil can be expressed as $A = L \times W$, so the original formula for volume can be restated as $V = A \times T$. Since this experiment involves finding the thickness, it would be better to rearrange the formula once again. Dividing both sides of the equation by A, we get the new equation: $T = V/A$.

The next problem will be to find the volume and area of a piece of aluminum foil. Remember that *density* is a property that is expressed as $D = m/V$. The density of aluminum is known, and the mass of a piece of aluminum foil can be measured with a balance. The volume of the aluminum can then be calculated by using the rearranged equation: $V = m/D$.

Even thinner than aluminum foil is the hard layer of aluminum oxide that forms on the surface of aluminum exposed to the air. This tenacious coating prevents further corrosion and can be given a constant thickness and a variety of bright colors in a commercial plating process known as *anodizing*.

OBJECTIVES

1. to correctly apply the principles of significant figures in calculating the thickness of aluminum foil

2. to correctly use exponential notation in expressing the results of the thickness calculation

MATERIALS

several rectangular pieces of aluminum foil
centimetre ruler
centigram balance

PROCEDURE

1. Cut four rectangular pieces of aluminum foil. Be sure that the dimensions are at least 10 cm on each side. If samples of more than one type of foil (heavy duty and regular) are available, get two pieces of each type.

2. Using a centimetre ruler, carefully measure the length and width of each piece of foil. Record the measurements in Table 1. How precise can your measurements be? Think carefully before you record your results.

3. Using a balance, find the mass of each piece of aluminum foil. Record the masses in Table 1. Again, be careful to be as precise as possible. Ask your instructor if you are unsure of the precision to which your balance can be read.

REAGENT DISPOSAL

Place the used aluminum foil in the wastepaper basket.

POST LAB DISCUSSION

Accuracy is the closeness of an experimental value to an accepted value. For example, if you were measuring the length of a 100 m track, the accepted value would be 100 m. If your measurement was close to 100.0 m, then your measurement would be considered to be accurate. Precision is the closeness of your repeated measurements to each other. Using the same example, if you measured the track three times and each time found the length to be 98.6 m, your measurements would be precise, but not accurate.

In this experiment, the accepted values for the thickness might be available on the aluminum foil packages, or your instructor might have determined what (s)he believes are the accepted values. The closeness to these accepted values will determine the accuracy of your measurements. If you do two or three trials with the same type of aluminum foil, you can determine the precision of your measurements.

Exponential notation is used in the calculations because of the magnitude of the thickness measurements. Whenever very large or very small numbers are encountered in scientific work, it is best to express those numbers in exponential notation.

DATA AND OBSERVATIONS

Table 1

SHEET NO.	TYPE	LENGTH (cm)	WIDTH (cm)	MASS (g)
1				
2				
3				
4				

QUESTIONS AND CALCULATIONS

1. For each of the pieces of aluminum foil, you will need to calculate the following:

   a. Area (A)

   b. Volume (V)

   c. Thickness (T)

   Refer to the beginning of this experiment for the formulas to be used. The density of aluminum is 2.70 g/cm³. Show all of your work and results. Your answers should have the correct number of significant figures and be expressed in exponential notation, where appropriate.

2. Compare your answers with those of other students or, if available, look at the box from the aluminum foil. How do your answers compare? Can you determine how accurate your measurements are? (Why or why not?)

3. How precise are your answers? Recall the definition of precision.

4. If you had used a crude balance that allowed only one significant figure, how would this have affected your results for a. area; b. volume; c. thickness?

FOLLOW-UP QUESTIONS

1. Could this method be used to determine the thickness of an oil spill? What information would be needed? Yes, the information needed would be the volume of oil spilled and the area of the oil spill.

2. A very thin layer of gold plating was placed on a metal tray that measured 25.22 cm by 13.22 cm. The gold plating increased the mass of the plate by 0.0512 g. Calculate the thickness of the plating. The density of gold is 19.32 g/cm³.
2.65×10^{-3} cm³ / 333.4 cm².

3. By mistake, one litre (1000 cm³) of oil was dumped into a swimming pool that measures 25.0 m by 30.0 m. The density of the oil was 0.750 g/cm³. How thick was the resulting oil slick? Be careful with significant figures and exponential notation. 1.33×10^{-8} cm.

4. How might this method of finding thickness be used in finding the size of molecules?

CONCLUSION

State the results of Objectives 1 and 2.

How Big is a Molecule?

Our bodies contain numerous large complex molecules consisting of atoms of carbon, hydrogen, oxygen, and nitrogen. One term "molecule" comes from the Latin word *moles*, meaning "a mass." The word was coined by the Italian physicist Avogadro (1776–1856) in 1811.

Atoms and molecules are the smallest pieces of elements and compounds that exist. They are much too small to observe with the unaided eye. Scientists have been able to observe some molecules with the electron microscope, but an electron microscope is very expensive and certainly not a piece of equipment that you would expect to find in a high school chemistry lab. It is relatively easy for us to speak about the size of objects that we can see. The width of the fingernail on your smallest finger is approximately one centimetre. The diameter of a needle is about one millimetre. When we begin to talk about the sizes of atoms and molecules, we need to use numbers that are in exponential notation to indicate just how small an atom or a molecule is.

In the last experiment, you used an indirect method to find the thickness of a piece of aluminum foil. Recall that you found the area of the foil by multiplying the length by the width. You found the volume of the foil by dividing the mass of the foil by the density of aluminum. Then you found the thickness by dividing the volume by the area. In this experiment, you will use the same technique to find the approximate thickness of a molecule. By making some assumptions about the material we are using, we can go one step further and calculate the approximate mass of a molecule.

Oleic acid is made primarily of hydrogen and carbon. It is not soluble in water, and has the property of spreading out to a very thin layer when placed on the surface of water. A single drop of pure oleic acid will spread out into a thin layer at least as large in area as a swimming pool. In fact, scientists believe oleic acid will spread out to a thickness of one molecule.

Oleic acid will float on the surface of water because the density of oleic acid is less than that of water. Its density is 0.895 g/cm³. In this experiment, you will use an approximate density of 1 g/cm³ for your calculations involving the density of oleic acid.

There are several assumptions that you will make when you do the calculations for this experiment:

1. Oleic acid molecules will spread out to a thickness of one molecule.

2. Oleic acid molecules, when spread out, will stand up like a column.

3. Oleic acid molecules are ten times as tall as they are wide. The base of the molecule is a square.

4. The density of oleic acid is approximately 1 g/cm³.

OBJECTIVES

1. to experimentally determine the approximate size of an oleic acid molecule

2. to use the size calculation to determine the approximate mass of an oleic acid molecule

3. to determine the number of molecules of oleic acid in a single drop of oleic acid solution

4. to use exponential notation in expressing the values calculated in this experiment

MATERIALS

Apparatus

large tray (at least 40 cm wide)
graph paper with 1 cm squares

overhead transparencies
overhead transparency pens
medicine dropper
graduated cylinder (10 mL)

beaker (600 mL)
safety goggles
lab apron

Reagents

oleic acid solution (0.50% dissolved in methanol)
lycopodium powder (or zinc stearate powder)

strips of newspaper approx. 5 cm wide and longer than the tray

PROCEDURE

1. Put on your lab apron and safety goggles.

2. Obtain a medicine dropper and use it and a graduated cylinder to determine how many drops will make up 1 cm³ of water. Repeat two more times. Record in your copy of Table 1 in your notebook.

3. Bring a tray to your lab table. Fill a 600 mL beaker with water and put the water into the tray. If you need more water, get the water in the beaker and pour it into the tray.

4. Allow the water to settle down so that you have a calm surface of water before going on to the next step. Pass a strip of newspaper over the surface to remove any unwanted dust.

5. Sprinkle a very fine layer of lycopodium powder on the entire surface of the water. If the powder is moving around, you have not let the surface of the water become calm enough. Wait until all is calm.

6. Put one drop of the oleic acid solution on the water in the middle of the tray. The powder should move away, leaving an area that is clearly defined. Place an overhead transparency above the thin layer of oleic acid and accurately trace the shape of the oleic acid layer.

7. Using graph paper with 1 cm squares, determine the area of the thin layer of oleic acid. Large areas can be squared off and measured, while the edges of the layer can be estimated. The area of one square on the graph paper is equal to 1 cm².

8. If you have enough time, repeat Steps 3-7. Be sure that you have removed all of the powder from the tray before starting over.

9. When cleaning up, REMEMBER NOT TO CARRY A TRAY FILLED WITH WATER ACROSS THE ROOM. Instead, remove the water at your lab table.

10. Before you leave the laboratory, wash your hands thoroughly with soap and water; use a fingernail brush to clean under your fingernails.

CAUTION: Do not try to fill the tray with water and then carry it across the lab. You could spill the water and make the floor dangerously slippery.

CAUTION: Lycopodium powder (or zinc stearate powder) can be harmful to your lungs if you inhale the dust. Sprinkle the dust carefully to avoid inhaling.

CAUTION: Before using the oleic acid solution, be sure that all flames are extinguished in the lab. The solution of oleic acid contains methanol, which is toxic and extremely flammable.

REAGENT DISPOSAL

The oleic acid dissolved in CH_3OH should be poured into the designated waste container. The water with oleic acid film can likewise be rinsed down the sink with plenty of water. Place any solids in the designated waste container.

POST LAB DISCUSSION

In the calculations for this experiment, you will be asked to progress from the number of drops in 1 cm³ to the size of a molecule. A few hints will make the calculations more understandable:

1. In calculating the volume of one drop, remember that the units that you have recorded are in drops/cm³. In order to find the volume of one drop, the units will need to be cm³/drop.

2. Since the oleic acid that is used in this experiment is very dilute, the actual volume of pure oleic acid in one drop will be very small. Remember that the solution is 0.50% oleic acid.

3. Once you know the volume of pure oleic acid, you can figure out the thickness as you did in the previous experiment when you found the thickness of aluminum foil.

DATA AND OBSERVATIONS

Table 1

	TRIAL 1	TRIAL 2	TRIAL 3
Number of drops in 1 cm³			
Area of oleic acid layer in cm²			

COMPLETE IN YOUR NOTEBOOK

QUESTIONS AND CALCULATIONS

1. Calculate the average number of drops from your medicine dropper that add up to a volume of 1 cm³.

2. Calculate the volume of one drop of liquid. Express your answer in exponential notation.

3. Calculate the volume of pure oleic acid in one drop of 0.50% oleic acid solution. Express in exponential notation.

4. Calculate the thickness of one molecule of oleic acid by dividing the volume calculated in item 3 by the area of the oleic acid layer that you determined in Step 7 of the Procedure. Express your answer in exponential notation.

5. Calculate the volume of one molecule, assuming that the length and width are each one tenth of the thickness. Express in exponential notation.

6. Calculate the mass of one molecule of oleic acid by multiplying the volume by the density.

7. How many significant figures do you have in all of your calculations?

8. Compare your answers with others in your class. How close are the values? Remember that you can only depend on one significant figure in all of the calculations.

FOLLOW-UP QUESTIONS

1. Do you think an atom will be bigger or smaller than the value that you calculated for the size of an oleic acid molecule? Explain.

2. Approximately how many molecules of oleic acid were in the drop of oleic acid solution? Remember that you know the volume of one molecule and you know the total volume of pure oleic acid that you used.

3. Using the values that you obtained for thickness, what area (in cm²) would be covered if 10 cm³ of pure oleic acid spread over a large body of water? What is the area in km²?

CONCLUSION

State the results of Objective 3.

Graphing as a Means of Seeking Relationships

You will recall from Experiment 1B that the scientific method involves a cyclical process of making observations, seeking relationships, and making predictions. A scientist who looks for a relationship between two variables is often hoping to discover a *mathematical* relationship.

Just as people rely on language for communicating, scientists rely heavily on mathematics to better understand scientific concepts and communicate their ideas. While conducting an experiment, a scientist will typically produce a set of data as a part of the observations made, then will attempt to make sense of the data.

In this experiment, you will attempt to find a relationship between the mass and the volume of three liquids: water, methanol, and a salt solution. You will collect data on mass and volume, then analyze the data by constructing and interpreting the graphs.

OBJECTIVES

1. to make measurements of mass and volume for three different liquids

2. to analyze the data by means of graphing techniques

3. to determine a mathematical relationship between mass and volume for each liquid

MATERIALS

Apparatus

per class:
   several burets
   lab aprons
   safety goggles
per lab group:
   centigram balance
   250 mL Erlenmeyer flask

Reagents

water
methanol
salt (sodium chloride)
   solution

PROCEDURE

In order to make better use of lab time, you will be sharing your data with the other members of the class. You will therefore be depending on each other for good results. You will produce two data tables: one that consists of only your own lab station's data, and one that includes the data from the entire class. Your teacher will assign you a volume of liquid that you are to measure. Use this same volume for all three solutions.

1. Put on your lab apron and safety goggles.

2. Determine and record the mass of a clean, dry 250 mL Erlenmeyer flask. Since different flasks, although they appear to be identical, can have different masses, it is important that you use this same flask throughout this experiment.

3. Go to one of the burets that contains water, methanol, or salt solution (the order of the liquids is not important) and dispense your assigned volume into your Erlenmeyer flask as accurately as possible. If you do not obtain precisely your assigned volume, do not be concerned. What is important is that you accurately record in Table 1 the volume you do obtain.

CAUTION: Methanol is highly flammable and toxic. Extinguish all flames in the area. Do not get methanol in your mouth, do not swallow any.

4. Measure the total mass of the liquid and the flask. Subtract the previous mass of the flask in order to determine the mass of the liquid. Record this figure in Table 1.

5. Now repeat Procedure Steps 2 and 3 for the other two liquids. Do not empty the flask each time you add a different liquid—just keep determining the mass of each volume by subtracting the previous balance reading.

6. A data table similar to Table 2 will be on the chalkboard. Record your results from Table 1 in the table on the board.

7. When all lab stations have recorded their data on the board, copy the completed Table 2 in your notebook.

8. Before you leave the laboratory, wash your hands thoroughly with soap and water; use a fingernail brush to clean under your fingernails.

REAGENT DISPOSAL

Pour any leftover methanol into the designated waste container. Sodium chloride solution can be rinsed down the drain with plenty of water.

POST LAB DISCUSSION

A mathematical relationship can be expressed in the form of an equation. Graphs are extremely useful tools for scientists, since certain characteristic shapes of lines on graphs can lead to mathematical equations. For instance, any straight-line graph can be represented by a mathematical equation of the form $y = mx + b$. You may recall from mathematics courses that this equation is sometimes called the *slope-intercept form.*

A brief mathematics review might be helpful here.

the x variable

$$y = mx + b$$

the y intercept

the slope of the line

the y variable

How is this equation related to the lab you just did? First, the y and x variables are defined by the terms "mass" and "volume" respectively. Second, the y intercept will be zero because mass = 0 when volume = 0. Finally, the slope, m, must be calculated along with its appropriate units:

$$m = \frac{\Delta y}{\Delta x}$$

When reporting your mathematical relationship, you must ensure that it is meaningful. In other words, your final equation in the slope-intercept form would include the terms "mass" and "volume" rather than "y" and "x".

DATA AND OBSERVATIONS

Table 1 For Lab Station _____

WATER		ALCOHOL		SALT SOLUTION	
VOLUME (mL)	MASS (g)	VOLUME (mL)	MASS (g)	VOLUME (mL)	MASS (g)

Table 2 Class Results

LAB STATION	WATER		ALCOHOL		SALT SOLUTION	
	VOLUME (mL)	MASS (g)	VOLUME (mL)	MASS (g)	VOLUME (mL)	MASS (g)
1						
2						
3						
4						
5						
6						
7						
8						
9						
10						
11						
12						

COMPLETE IN YOUR NOTEBOOK   COMPLETE IN YOUR NOTEBOOK

ANALYSIS OF DATA (GRAPHING)

1. Whenever a graph is constructed, the first question that arises is, "Which variable goes on the *y*-axis and which goes on the *x*-axis?" The answer is that the dependent variable goes on the *y*-axis and the independent variable goes on the *x*-axis. The *independent* variable is the one over which you have control; it is the variable that you decided to measure. (Did you decide to obtain a certain volume or a certain mass of each liquid?)

2. Following the rules of good graphing, plot a graph showing mass vs. volume for each liquid. You should plot the results for all liquids on the same graph, but be careful to differentiate the results. For example, use circles for the data points of water, squares for those of methanol, and triangles for those of the salt solution.

3. If the lines on your graph illustrate straight-line relationships, determine the mathematical relationship between mass and volume for each liquid.

QUESTIONS AND CALCULATIONS

1. Use your graph to predict the mass of 6.5 mL of methanol.

2. Use your mathematical relationship to calculate the mass of 6.5 mL of methanol.

3. Compare your answers to Questions 1 and 2, and explain why they might not be identical.

FOLLOW-UP QUESTIONS

1. Suppose you have a large supply of sponge balls with weights in the centre, so that when the balls are piled on each other the bottom balls are flattened. Sketch a graph that generally describes mass vs. volume for these sponge balls.

2. Would weighted sponge balls represent a good model for liquid molecules such as water or methanol? Use the shapes of your graphs to support your answer.

CONCLUSION

State the results of Objective 3.

Investigating the Density of Four Liquids

In Experiment 2C, you learned to determine how much matter you have by making measurements. You found that it is not possible to make exact measurements. You learned how to find a best estimate and to estimate the uncertainty in measurements and in answers calculated from measurements. In this experiment, you will use those skills and extend the ideas to other measurements. In addition, you will learn to use an intensive property to answer the question: "What is the identity of this matter I have?" The intensive property is density, which you used in Experiment 1C. Density is discussed in Section 3-17 of the textbook.

Differences in the densities of liquids are important in many industrial processes such as the production of iron. The less dense molten impurities or "slag" float on the surface of the molten iron. This difference in density means the two substances can be tapped from different parts of the furnace, thus effecting a separation.

The purpose of this experiment is to determine whether the four liquids labeled *A*, *B*, *C*, and *D* in this experiment are the same by measuring densities of the liquids. If the densities are approximately the same, it is necessary to determine whether or not the densities are the same within the range of experimental uncertainty.

You know how to estimate the uncertainty in mass by making a series of measurements. In this experiment you will learn to estimate the uncertainty in measuring volume when using a graduated cylinder. You should read the volume and estimate the uncertainty. Have your lab partner do the same independently. Then compare your answers to determine whether they are the same within experimental uncertainty.

OBJECTIVES

1. to measure the mass and volume of each of four liquids and to estimate the uncertainty of each measurement

2. to calculate the density and the uncertainty in the density for each liquid

3. to compare the densities of the liquids to determine whether the densities are the same or different within experimental uncertainty

4. to use an intensive property to determine the identity of matter

MATERIALS

Apparatus

centigram balance   plastic gloves
graduated cylinder   lab apron
safety goggles   face shield

Reagents

liquids *A*, *B*, *C*, and *D*

PROCEDURE

1. Put on your lab apron and safety goggles.

2. Clean and dry the graduated cylinder.

3. Determine the mass of the graduated cylinder on two different balances. If you have a lab partner, have your lab partner determine the mass of the graduated cylinder on two different balances. Record your data in your copy of Table 1 in your notebook.

4. Add liquid A to the graduated cylinder.

5. Determine the mass of the graduated cylinder and liquid A on two different balances. Have your lab partner do the same and record your data in Table 1.

6. Read the volume of liquid A in the graduated cylinder and estimate the uncertainty. Have your lab partner read the volume of liquid A and estimate the uncertainty. If your volume reading is not the same as your lab partner's reading within experimental uncertainty, analyze both the readings and the uncertainties. Discuss possible parallax error and the proper way to read the meniscus. Record your data in Table 1.

7. Carefully pour liquid A back into the bottle marked A.

8. Repeat Steps 2-7 with liquids B, C, and D, recording your data in Tables 2, 3, and 4, respectively.

9. Before you leave the laboratory, wash your hands thoroughly with soap and water; use a fingernail brush to clean under your fingernails.

REAGENT DISPOSAL

Rinse all solutions down the sink with copious amounts of water.

POST LAB DISCUSSION

To determine whether liquids A, B, C, and D are the same or different you must investigate the characteristic properties of the liquids. In this experiment, density was used for two reasons: so that you could determine whether the densities found are the same within experimental uncertainty, and to help you understand how to compare densities and the uncertainties. If another liquid labeled G has a density of 1.35 g/mL ± 0.03 g/mL and liquid H has a density of 1.41 g/mL ± 0.04 g/mL, both apparently have the same density within experimental uncertainty. Your conclusion should be that liquids G and H could be the same.

Liquid J has a density of 1.25 g/mL ± 0.04 g/mL and liquid K has a density of 1.08 g/mL ± 0.05 g/mL. These densities cannot be the same within experimental uncertainty, and you can conclude that liquids J and K are not the same.

DATA AND OBSERVATIONS

It would be useful to have these data tables ready in your notebook before you come to the laboratory.

Table 1 (Liquid *A*)

	YOUR READINGS		PARTNER'S READINGS	
	1	2	1	2
Mass of graduated cylinder				
Mass of graduated cylinder and liquid *A*				
Volume of liquid *A*	±		±	
Best estimate and uncertainty for the mass of the graduated cylinder		±		
Best estimate and uncertainty for the mass of the graduated cylinder and liquid *A*		±		
Best estimate and uncertainty for the volume of liquid *A*		±		
Best estimate and uncertainty for the mass of liquid *A*		±		
Density of liquid *A*				
Minimum density of liquid *A*				
Maximum density of liquid *A*				
Best estimate and uncertainty of the density of liquid *A*		±		

Table 2 (Liquid *B*)

	YOUR READINGS		PARTNER'S READINGS	
	1	2	1	2
Mass of graduated cylinder				
Mass of graduated cylinder and liquid *B*				
Volume of liquid *B*	±		±	
Best estimate and uncertainty for the mass of the graduated cylinder		±		
Best estimate and uncertainty for the mass of the graduated cylinder and liquid *B*		±		
Best estimate and uncertainty for the volume of liquid *B*		±		
Best estimate and uncertainty for the mass of liquid *B*		±		
Density of liquid *B*				
Minimum density of liquid *B*				
Maximum density of liquid *B*				
Best estimate and uncertainty of the density of liquid *B*		±		

COMPLETE IN YOUR NOTEBOOK

Table 3 (Liquid *C*)

	YOUR READINGS		PARTNER'S READINGS	
	1	2	1	2
Mass of graduated cylinder				
Mass of graduated cylinder and liquid *C*				
Volume of liquid *C*	±		±	
Best estimate and uncertainty for the mass of the graduated cylinder		±		
Best estimate and uncertainty for the mass of the graduated cylinder and liquid *C*		±		
Best estimate and uncertainty for the volume of liquid *C*		±		
Best estimate and uncertainty for the mass of liquid *C*		±		
Density of liquid *C*				
Minimum density of liquid *C*				
Maximum density of liquid *C*				
Best estimate and uncertainty of the density of liquid *C*		±		

COMPLETE IN YOUR NOTEBOOK

Table 4 (Liquid *D*)

	YOUR READINGS		PARTNER'S READINGS	
	1	2	1	2
Mass of graduated cylinder				
Mass of graduated cylinder and liquid *D*				
Volume of liquid *D*	±		±	
Best estimate and uncertainty for the mass of the graduated cylinder		±		
Best estimate and uncertainty for the mass of the graduated cylinder and liquid *D*		±		
Best estimate and uncertainty for the volume of liquid *D*		±		
Best estimate and uncertainty for the mass of liquid *D*		±		
Density of liquid *D*				
Minimum density of liquid *D*				
Maximum density of liquid *D*				
Best estimate and uncertainty of the density of liquid *D*		±		

COMPLETE IN YOUR NOTEBOOK

QUESTIONS

1. Are the densities of any of the liquids, *A, B, C,* or *D* the same within experimental uncertainty?

2. Are the densities of any of the liquids *A, B, C,* or *D* different?

3. Could any of the liquids be the same?

4. Are any of the liquids different?

FOLLOW-UP QUESTIONS

1. If you had a larger or smaller graduated cylinder, how would this have affected the density you determined?

2. If you had used a different volume of the liquid, how would this have affected the density you determined?

3. How would the experimental results be different if this experiment were done in Victoria or in Banff? Explain your reasoning.

4. How would using a graduated cylinder that was not clean or dry affect the density you found?

5. In a research lab, a graduated cylinder is not likely to be a chemist's first choice for making precise, small, volumetric measurements. Suggest other chemical apparatus that would reduce the uncertainty in measuring liquid volumes.

CONCLUSION

State the results of Objectives 2 and 3.

Investigating the Chemical Properties of Four Liquids

In Experiment 3D, you measured the densities of four liquids to determine whether the liquids were the same or different. You probably found that densities of all four liquids were the same within experimental uncertainty. This means that density alone cannot be used to distinguish among these liquids.

Modern analysis of liquids can involve very sophisticated instrumentation. The gas chromatograph, along with the mass spectrometer, is used to analyze urine samples of athletes to determine whether illegal drugs have been taken.

OBJECTIVES

1. to recognize macroscopic changes

2. to compare some chemical properties of four liquids in order to determine whether the liquids are the same or different

MATERIALS

Apparatus	Reagents
4 test tubes (13 mm × 100 mm)	blue litmus paper
	red litmus paper
test-tube stand or rack	cobalt(II) chloride paper
safety goggles	zinc
medicine dropper	manganese(IV) oxide
lab apron	aluminum
wash bottle containing distilled water	liquids A, B, C, and D in dropper bottles

CAUTION: Remember A, B, C, and D are unknowns; whether they are hazardous or not, it is always a good practice to minimize your contact with unknown chemicals. Some of these chemicals are corrosive to skin, eyes, or clothing. Wear safety goggles and gloves when handling the chemicals. Wash spills and splashes off with plenty of water. Call your teacher.

PROCEDURE

1. Put on your lab apron and safety goggles.

2. Label four test tubes A, B, C, and D, or arrange them in a test-tube rack from left to right so you know which test tube contains A, etc.

3. Add two droppersful of each liquid (A, B, C, or D) to the appropriate test tube.

4. Tear a piece of red litmus paper into four pieces and put one piece in each test tube. Record your observations in your copy of Table 1.

5. Pour the liquids into the sink, put the test paper in the wastebasket, rinse the test tubes three times with tap water and three times with distilled water. The test tubes need not be dried.

6. Repeat Step 3 with the cleaned test tubes.

7. Tear a piece of blue litmus paper into four pieces and put one piece in each of the test tubes. Record your observations in Table 1.

8. Repeat Step 5.

9. Repeat Step 3.

10. Tear a piece of cobalt(II) chloride paper into four pieces and put one piece in each of the test tubes. Record your observations in Table 1.

11. Repeat Step 5.

12. Repeat Step 3.

13. Add one piece of zinc, Zn, to each test tube, wait at least two minutes, and record your observations in Table 1.

14. Pour the liquids into the sink, put the remaining zinc in the used zinc container, and clean the test tubes as in Step 5.

15. Repeat Step 3.

16. Add a piece of aluminum, Al, to each test tube, wait at least two minutes, and record your observations in Table 1.

17. Pour the liquids into the sink, put the remaining aluminum in the used aluminum container, and clean the test tubes as in Step 5.

18. Repeat Steps 2 and 3.

19. Add a small scoop of manganese(IV) oxide (equivalent to a grain of rice) to each test tube, wait at least two minutes, and record your observations in Table 1.

20. Pour the liquids and manganese(IV) oxide into the sink and clean the test tubes as in Step 5.

21. Before you leave the laboratory, wash your hands thoroughly with soap and water; use a fingernail brush to clean under your fingernails.

CAUTION: Keep the test paper pieces out of your mouth; they are poisonous.

CAUTION: Manganese(IV) oxide is poisonous. Do not get it in your mouth; do not swallow any.

REAGENT DISPOSAL

Rinse all solutions down the sink with copious amounts of water. Place all solids in the designated waste containers.

POST LAB DISCUSSION

Use the observations you made on the properties of the four liquids to determine whether the liquids are the same or different.

DATA AND OBSERVATIONS

Table 1

	LIQUID A	LIQUID B	LIQUID C	LIQUID D
Red litmus paper				
Blue litmus paper				
Cobalt(II) chloride paper				
Zinc				
Aluminum				
Manganese(IV) oxide				

QUESTIONS

1. Do liquids *A* and *B* have any properties alike? If so, name them.

2. Do liquids *A* and *B* have any properties that are different? If so, name them.

3. Could *A* and *B* be the same liquid? Why or why not?

4. Could any two of the liquids be the same?

FOLLOW-UP QUESTIONS

1. If any two of the liquids could be the same, explain why.

CONCLUSION

State the results of Objective 2.

Moles of Iron and Copper

The mole is a convenient unit for analyzing chemical reactions. The mole is equal to 6.02×10^{23} particles, or Avogadro's number of particles. More importantly, however, the mass of a mole of any compound or element is the mass in grams that corresponds to the molecular formula, or atomic mass. Simply stated, the atomic mass of copper is 63.5 u, which means that the mass of one mole of copper atoms is 63.5 g. Likewise, the molecular mass of water is 18.0 u, and the mass of one mole of water molecules is 18.0 g.

The mole is the common language in chemical reactions. In this experiment, you will observe the reaction of iron nails with a solution of copper(II) chloride and determine the number of moles involved in the reaction.

Iron and copper, along with gold, silver, lead, and antimony, were known in very early times. Iron and copper occur naturally in the earth's crust as oxides or sulfides. Chemical analysis and calculation of ore content is vital to the mining industry. Today an ore containing 3–4% copper is considered high-grade, while iron producers are little interested in ores containing less than 20–30% iron.

OBJECTIVES

1. to determine the number of moles of copper produced in the reaction of iron and copper(II) chloride

2. to determine the number of moles of iron used up in the reaction of iron and copper(II) chloride

3. to determine the ratio of moles of iron to moles of copper

4. to determine the number of atoms and formula units involved in the reaction.

MATERIALS

Apparatus

beakers (250 mL)	safety goggles
wash bottle	lab apron
stirring rod	plastic gloves
crucible tongs	sandpaper or
centigram balance	emery cloth
drying oven	face shield

Reagents

copper(II) chloride
2 iron nails
  (approx. 5 cm)
1M hydrochloric acid
distilled water

PROCEDURE

1. Find the mass of a clean, empty, dry 250 mL beaker. Record the mass to the nearest 0.01 g.

2. Add approximately 8 g of copper(II) chloride crystals to the beaker. Find the mass and record it in your notebook.

3. Add 50 mL of distilled water to the beaker. Swirl the beaker around to dissolve all of the copper(II) chloride crystals.

4. Obtain two clean, dry nails. If the nails are not clean, use a piece of sandpaper to make the surface of the nail shiny. Find the mass of the nails and record it in your notebook.

CAUTION: Copper(II) chloride is very poisonous and can kill you. Do not get it in your mouth. Do not swallow any.

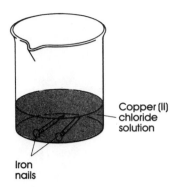

Copper (II) chloride solution

Iron nails

Figure 4B-1

5. Place the nails into the copper(II) chloride solution, as shown in Figure 4B-1. Leave them undisturbed for approximately 20 min. During that time, you should see the formation of copper in the beaker. At the same time, some of the iron will be used up.

6. Use the tongs to carefully pick up the nails, one at a time. Use distilled water in a wash bottle to rinse off any remaining copper from the nails before removing them completely from the beaker. (See Figure 4B-2.) If necessary, use a stirring rod to scrape any excess copper from the nails. Set the nails aside to dry on a paper towel.

Figure 4B-2 *Any copper remaining on the nails may be washed back into the beaker with the use of distilled water from a wash bottle.*

7. After the nails are completely dry, find the mass of the nails and record it in your notebook.

8. *Decant* means to pour off only the liquid from a container that is holding both solid and liquid. Carefully decant the liquid from the solid. (See Figure 4B-3.) Pour the liquid into another beaker so that in case you overpour, you can still recover the solid.

Figure 4B-3 *When decanting, it is helpful to direct the liquid into the second beaker along a stirring rod, as shown here.*

CAUTION: Hydrochloric acid is corrosive to skin, eyes, and clothing. When handling 1M hydrochloric acid, wear safety goggles, lab apron, and use a full face shield and gloves. Wash spills and splashes off your skin and clothing immediately using plenty of water. Call your teacher.

9. After decanting, rinse the solid again with about 25 mL of distilled water. Decant again. Repeat this step three or four more times.

10. Next, wash the solid with about 25 mL of 1M hydrochloric acid. Decant again; then, once more, clean the solid with 25 mL of distilled water.

11. After the final washing with water, place the copper in a drying oven to dry.

12. Allow the copper to become completely dry, then find the mass of the beaker plus the copper and record it in your notebook.

13. Clean up all of your materials. Before you leave the laboratory, wash your hands thoroughly with soap and water; use a fingernail brush to clean under your fingernails.

REAGENT DISPOSAL

Rinse all solutions down the drain with plenty of water. Place solids in the designated waste containers.

POST LAB DISCUSSION

In this experiment, you have reacted some of the iron from the nail at the same time as you have produced some copper. In order to find the moles of each of these substances, you will need to divide the mass of the iron used or the copper produced by the molar mass. You can also determine the moles of copper(II) chloride that you started with by dividing the mass of the copper(II) chloride by the molar mass. By multiplying by Avogadro's number, you will be able to determine the total number of atoms involved in the reaction. Finally, you will determine the ratio of moles of iron used to moles of copper produced.

DATA AND OBSERVATIONS

Before the reaction:

Mass of empty, dry beaker

Mass of beaker + copper(II) chloride

Mass of two iron nails

After the reaction:

Mass of two iron nails

Mass of beaker + copper (dry)

QUESTIONS AND CALCULATIONS

1. Find the following masses by doing the appropriate subtractions:
   a. mass of iron used in the reaction
   b. mass of copper(II) chloride used
   c. mass of copper produced

2. Find the number of moles of the following.
   a. moles of iron used
   b. moles of copper produced

3. Find the number of atoms of each of the substances involved in the reaction.
   a. atoms of iron used
   b. atoms of copper produced

4. Calculate the ratio of moles of copper produced to moles of iron used.

5. Was there any evidence that some of the copper(II) chloride was left in the beaker? Explain.

FOLLOW-UP QUESTIONS

1. Suppose that you have an unlimited supply of copper(II) chloride to react with iron. How many moles of copper would be produced by reacting 34.0 g of iron with the copper(II) chloride solution?

2. How many moles of iron would have been used up if 45.0 g of copper were to be produced?

3. How many atoms of copper would be involved in problem 2?

4. How many atoms of iron would be involved in problem 2?

5. How many grams of copper would be produced if 456 g of iron were reacted?

CONCLUSION

State the results of Objective 3.

Determining the Empirical Formula of a Compound

A compound, you will recall, is a substance composed of two or more elements that have been chemically united. In this experiment you will form an iron-oxygen compound by chemically uniting the element iron with the element oxygen. You will use steel wool, which is primarily iron, and react it with the oxygen in the air. (Remember that air is about 20% oxygen.)

The reaction of iron with oxygen is very common; you are probably familiar with this process in the form of rusting. Rusting is a slow process and, under normal lab conditions, the steel wool might take several years to rust. Therefore, to speed up the rusting process, you will dip the steel wool in an ammonium chloride solution, which is a catalyst for the reaction. A *catalyst* is a substance that speeds up a chemical reaction without being consumed in the reaction. For example, a catalyst is used on the inner surfaces of continuous-clean ovens, where the catalyst allows spilled food particles to react with oxygen and burn off at a faster rate. Another application of catalysts can be found in the exhaust systems of cars that run on unleaded gasoline. These exhaust systems use catalytic converters containing a specialized, honeycombed piece of metal. As the hot exhaust gases pass over the catalyst, some of the pollutants (harmful compounds) are decomposed into nitrogen and oxygen gases.

You will observe that, even with the aid of a catalyst, the rusting process still takes time. The experiment cannot be completed in one lab period—in fact, you may not be able to complete the experiment for a week or so. Some forethought is necessary on your part so that you can plan your activities. By the end of the experiment (Part III) you will have collected data that will enable you to determine the empirical formula of the compound which has formed.

OBJECTIVES

1. to form a compound from the elements iron and oxygen

2. to observe the effect of a catalyst on a chemical reaction

3. to determine the empirical formula of the compound produced in this chemical reaction

MATERIALS

Apparatus

ring stand
ring support
lab burner
crucible
crucible tongs
water soluble marker
pipestem triangle
heat resistant mat
centigram balance
safety goggles
lab apron

Reagents

steel wool, fine
1M ammonium chloride
    solution

PROCEDURE

Part I (First Day)

1. Put on the safety goggles and lab apron.

2. Obtain a clean, dry crucible (without a lid) and accurately determine its mass. Enter this value in your copy of Table 1.

3. Place a clump of steel wool on the balance pan and add or remove steel wool until you have 3.00 g.

4. Compress the 3.00 g of steel wool into a tight ball and place it in your crucible. Reweigh the crucible and contents, and enter the relevant information in your data table.

5. Take the crucible and contents to the "dunking station" that your instructor has set up. Here you will find the ammonium chloride solution in a large beaker.

6. Remove the ball of steel wool from the crucible and, using crucible tongs, gently submerge the steel wool in the ammonium chloride solution. Wait until the steel wool is thoroughly soaked, then remove it and carefully squeeze out any excess solution.

7. Replace the moistened steel wool in the crucible. Label the crucible with a piece of masking tape or a water soluble marker, indicating your name and class.

8. Place your crucible, uncovered, in the designated storage location. Now the waiting begins!

CAUTION: Ammonium chloride solution is corrosive. Keep it off your skin and out of your eyes. Wash away spills and splashes with plenty of water.

Part II (Next Several Days)

1. Over the next week, check your crucible each day to observe any changes.

2. Each day, use a medicine dropper to add a few drops of ammonium chloride solution so that the steel wool is remoistened.

3. Continue these activities for as long as your teacher advises. The time required usually varies between four and seven days. Since Part II requires only a few minutes during each class, you can expect to carry on with activities other than this experiment during the waiting period.

Part III (Final Day)

1. Retrieve your crucible from the storage location. Remove the masking tape label, if any.

2. Set the crucible in a heating apparatus, as shown in Figure 4C-1. The crucible will sit inside a pipestem triangle which rests on a ring support.

3. Heat the crucible and contents with the lab burner adjusted to a high temperature. The outside of the crucible will glow a dull red when it becomes very hot. Continue to heat the crucible at red heat for at least ten more minutes, then turn off the burner.

CAUTION: Objects that have been heated may appear to be cold. Serious burns can result.

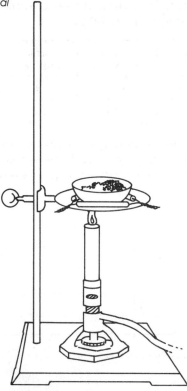

4. Let the crucible cool so that you can touch it. **CAUTION:** The ring stand and accessories can burn you even after several minutes. If you are in doubt about the ring stand, you can test how hot it is by touching it with a piece of wet paper towel.

5. Determine the mass of the crucible and contents (a compound) and record the relevant information in your data table.

6. Clean up your materials according to the reagent disposal instructions, and wash out and dry the crucible.

7. Before you leave the laboratory, wash your hands thoroughly with soap and water; use a fingernail brush to clean under your nails.

REAGENT DISPOSAL

The ammonium chloride solution can be rinsed down the sink with large amounts of water. The crucible's contents can be placed in a garbage can.

POST LAB DISCUSSION

In order to find the empirical formula of the compound produced, you need to know how many moles of iron and oxygen atoms reacted. Since you know the mass of iron reacted (you must assume here that all 3.0 g reacted), you can convert "mass of iron" into "moles of iron". The mass of oxygen reacted can be determined by examining Table 1 and applying some common sense: mass of compound – mass of iron = mass of oxygen. Now, the mass of oxygen atoms can be converted to moles of oxygen atoms. (Note: The atomic mass of O is 16.0, not 32.0.)

The next step towards determining the empirical formula is to calculate the ratio

$$\frac{\text{moles of O atoms}}{\text{moles of Fe atoms}}$$

Finally, if this mole ratio contains decimals, convert it into a whole-number ratio. An example is given in the chart which follows.

	MOLES	MOLE RATIO	RATIO DOUBLED	RATIO TRIPLED
Element X	2.42	1	2	3
Element Y	6.46	2.67	5.33	8.01

You double, triple, etc., the mole ratio until you end up with a value very close to a whole number. In the example being discussed, the whole-number ratio is 3:8. Hence, the empirical formula of the compound would be X_3Y_8.

DATA AND OBSERVATIONS

Table 1

BEFORE THE REACTION	
Mass of crucible + iron (steel wool)	
Mass of crucible	
Mass of iron	
AFTER THE REACTION	
Mass of crucible + compound	
Mass of crucible	
Mass of compound (iron + oxygen)	

COMPLETE IN YOUR NOTEBOOK

QUESTIONS AND CALCULATIONS

1. Calculate the number of moles of iron atoms that reacted.

2. Determine the mass of oxygen atoms that reacted.

3. Calculate the number of moles of oxygen atoms that reacted.

4. Calculate the smallest whole-number ratio of oxygen atoms to iron atoms.

5. Write the empirical formula for the compound.

6. Give three reasons for heating the crucible and its contents.

7. Look up the ion charges for iron and oxygen, and predict two possible formulas for iron oxide.

8. How does your experimentally determined formula compare with your predicted formulas?

FOLLOW-UP QUESTIONS

1. Catalysts are used to speed up reactions, and *inhibitors* are used to slow down reactions.
   a. Give an example of a chemical reaction in which the use of a catalyst would be desirable.
   b. Give an example of a chemical reaction in which the use of an inhibitor would be desirable.

CONCLUSION

State the results of Objective 3.

Formula of a Hydrate

Many salts that have been crystallized from a water solution appear to be dry, but when they are heated, large amounts of water are given off. The crystals often change color when the water is released. This suggests that water is a part of their crystal structure. These compounds are called *hydrates*, meaning that they contain water. When these compounds are heated strongly in a crucible, the water is driven off, leaving an *anhydrous* compound (without water). Usually, the amount of water present in a compound is in a whole-number mole ratio. One common example of a hydrate is copper(II) sulfate. The formula of the hydrate is $CuSO_4 \cdot 5H_2O$. The formula of the anhydrous form of the compound is simply $CuSO_4$. The formula of the hydrate indicates that five moles of water are combined with one mole of the copper(II) sulfate.

Granules of calcium chloride ($CaCl_2$) are often used to take moisture out of the air of damp rooms. They do this by forming the hydrate $CaCl_2 \cdot 6H_2O$. Chemical drying agents such as calcium chloride are called *dessicants*.

In this experiment, you will be given an unknown hydrate and asked to find the percent of water in the hydrate. This calculation will help you to determine the formula of the hydrate.

OBJECTIVES

1. to determine the percent of water in an unknown hydrate

2. to determine the moles of water present in each mole of the unknown substance

3. to use the molecular mass to find the empirical formula of the hydrate

MATERIALS

Apparatus		**Reagents**
lab burner	centigram balance	5 g of a hydrate
crucible and cover	desiccator	distilled water
crucible tongs	medicine dropper	
pipestem triangle	safety goggles	
ring stand and ring	lab apron	

PROCEDURE

1. Put on your safety goggles and lab apron. You will be using the lab burners during this experiment. Use them cautiously.

2. Place a clean, dry crucible with a cover in a pipestem triangle mounted on an iron ring. Leave the cover slightly off so that the heating will drive off any water that remains in the crucible. (See Figure 4D-1.) Heat with the burner for two to three minutes to make sure that the crucible is dry.

3. From this point on, you should not touch the crucible with your hands. Use only the crucible tongs. Allow the crucible to cool for about three minutes, then find the mass of the empty crucible and the cover. Record the mass in your copy of Table 1.

4. Place enough of the hydrate that you are assigned into the crucible so that it is one-fourth to one-third full. Find and record the mass of the crucible, cover, and hydrate.

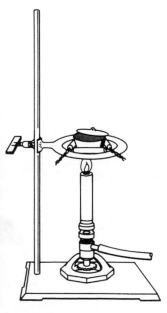

Figure 4D-1

5. Place the crucible, with the cover slightly off, on the pipestem triangle and begin heating. Gradually increase the heat until the bottom of the crucible is a dull red. Maintain this temperature for five minutes.

6. Turn off the burner and bring the crucible, with the cover, to a desiccator for cooling. Allow the crucible to cool for about five minutes, then find and record the mass of the crucible, cover, and contents.

7. Reheat the crucible for another five minutes to make sure that all of the water is driven off. Again, cool it in the desiccator, then find and record the mass. If the masses that you determine in Steps 6 and 7 do not agree within 0.03 g, check with your instructor to see if you need to continue the heating/mass-determination process.

8. Once your masses agree and the crucible is cool, add a few drops of distilled water to the crucible. Note any changes in the substance in Table 1.

9. If enough time remains, repeat the experiment with another hydrate.

REAGENT DISPOSAL

Place all solids in the designated waste containers.

POST LAB DISCUSSION

Your instructor will give you the mass of one mole of the anhydrous salt. This should help you in determining the empirical formula of the hydrate. In order to find the mass of water in your sample of hydrate, you will simply subtract the mass of the anhydrous compound from the mass of the hydrate. Using this value, you can then find the mass of water that would be present in one mole of the hydrate. Once you know the mass of water present in one mole of the hydrate, you can calculate the number of moles of water in one mole of anhydrous salt by dividing by the molar mass of water.

Adding water at the end of the experiment rehydrates the compound. In some compounds, there is a noticeable change in texture or color when the water is added. The hydrate should appear as it did before you heated it.

DATA AND OBSERVATIONS

Table 1

	TRIAL ONE	TRIAL TWO
Mass of empty crucible and cover		
Mass of crucible, cover and hydrate		
Mass after first heating		
Mass after second heating		
Mass of one mole of the anhydrous salt (from your teacher)		

COMPLETE IN YOUR NOTEBOOK

For both trials, describe any changes that you observed when adding water to the crucible.

QUESTIONS AND CALCULATIONS

1. For both trials, calculate the number of moles of the anhydrous salt that you prepared. (Your teacher will give you the molar mass of the anhydrous salt.)

2. For both trials, calculate the number of moles of water removed by heat from your sample of hydrate.

3. For both trials, calculate the moles of water per mole of the anhydrous salt.

4. For both trials, calculate the percent of water in the hydrate.

5. What is the empirical formula of the hydrate in each trial?

FOLLOW-UP QUESTIONS

1. Can you suggest reasons why the procedure used in this experiment might not be appropriate for all hydrates?

2. A substance was found to have the following percentages:

   Zinc 23%
   Sulfur 11%
   Oxygen 22%
   Water 44%
   What is the empirical formula of this compound?

3. If a sample of 2.56 g of this substance were heated in a crucible as in this experiment, calculate the mass of anhydrous compound that would remain in the crucible.

CONCLUSION

State the results of Objective 3.

Investigating Mass Changes in Chemical Reactions

In the industrial manufacture of chemicals, it is important that the chemists involved know how much product to expect from a given reaction. In such reactions the substances reacting (the *reactants*) and those being produced (the *products*) are closely monitored.

In this experiment, you will investigate a fundamental law of chemical reactions. You will examine a reaction under controlled conditions to find out how much change in mass results. The reactants will be placed in a flask which is sealed to prevent any gain or loss of matter. The mass of the flask and its contents will be measured before and after the reaction.

OBJECTIVES

1. to observe a chemical reaction in a sealed flask

2. to determine the change in mass that occurs during a chemical reaction

MATERIALS

Apparatus

Erlenmeyer flask (250 mL)
rubber stopper for flask
2 test tubes (13 mm × 100 mm)
test-tube rack
crucible tongs
centigram balance
lab apron
safety goggles

Reagents

one of the following pairs of
  0.1M solutions:
1. A. barium chloride
   B. sodium sulfate
2. A. lead acetate
   B. potassium iodide
3. A. iron(III) nitrate
   B. potassium thiocyanate
4. A. calcium chloride
   B. sodium carbonate

CAUTION: *These salts, especially barium chloride, are poisonous. Keep your hands away from your face until after you have washed thoroughly and have left the laboratory.*

PROCEDURE

1. Put on your safety goggles and lab apron.

2. Obtain a test tube that will fit inside your flask as in Figure 5A-1. Label this test tube *A*.

3. Obtain a second test tube identical to the first test tube. Label it *B*.

4. Half fill test tube *A* with solution *A* and half fill test tube *B* with solution *B*.

5. Pour solution *B* into the flask.

6. Carefully lower test tube *A* into the flask, using a pair of crucible tongs if necessary. (If any of solutions *A* and *B* are allowed to mix you will have to start over.)

7. Place the stopper on the flask. At this point your assembled apparatus and contents should look like that depicted in Figure 5A-1.

8. Determine the mass of your assembled apparatus and record this value in your copy of Table 1.

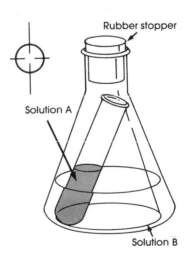

Figure 5A-1 *Apparatus assembled and ready for the reaction to start*

9. After making certain that the stopper is secure, gently turn your apparatus upside down, allowing solutions *A* and *B* to mix and react.

10. Place the apparatus upright on the balance and measure its mass again. Record this value in Table 1.

11. Use your data to calculate the mass gained or lost during the reaction and record this value on Table 2, which will be on the chalkboard. Indicate a positive value for a gain and a negative value for a loss.

12. Copy Table 2 into your notebook when all members of the class have recorded their results.

13. Clean up according to the reagent disposal instructions. Use a test-tube brush to get glassware clean.

14. Before leaving the laboratory, wash your hands thoroughly with soap and water; use a fingernail brush to clean under your fingernails.

REAGENT DISPOSAL

All solutions and precipitates should be poured into the designated container.

POST LAB DISCUSSION

When the class results are examined, keep in mind that there will always be some uncertainty in any measurement. The overall results should allow you to recognize any patterns and to draw some conclusions.

DATA AND OBSERVATIONS

Table 1   Results for Lab Station _____

Identity of solution *A*	
Identity of solution *B*	
Mass of apparatus and contents before reaction	
Mass of apparatus and contents after reaction	

COMPLETE IN YOUR NOTEBOOK

Table 2   Class Results

LAB STATION	SOLUTION *A*	SOLUTION *B*	MASS CHANGE (+ OR –) (g)
1			
2			
3			
. . .			

COMPLETE IN YOUR NOTEBOOK

COMPLETE IN YOUR NOTEBOOK

QUESTIONS

1. Why is it important that the flask be sealed for this experiment, even after the flask is returned to an upright position?

2. What observations lead you to believe that a chemical reaction occurred inside the flask?

3. In general, what overall mass change results from a chemical reaction?

FOLLOW-UP QUESTIONS

1. Suppose that a reaction was carried out in an open flask and the final mass was significantly greater than the initial mass. What would you conclude?

2. If a reaction was carried out in an open flask and the final mass was significantly less than the initial mass, what would you conclude?

3. What is "the law of conservation of mass" for chemical reactions? If necessary, use a reference book to find out.

CONCLUSION

State the results of Objective 2.

Investigating a Type of Chemical Reaction

In this experiment you will investigate several reactions of the same type and learn to write an equation for the reaction based on your observations. Once you discover how to write the equation for one reaction of a certain type, the rest will be much easier, because they are all similar. You will use the principle that all elements contained in the reactants (and only those elements) must appear in the products. You will also be able to practise balancing equations.

The sulfuric, hydrochloric, and phosphoric acids used in this experiment are called *mineral acids* because they come from mineral rather than organic sources. More sulfuric acid is produced worldwide each year than any other chemical.

OBJECTIVES

1. to identify a type of chemical reaction
2. to learn how to write an equation for a reaction using the observed macroscopic properties and the principle of conservation of elements
3. to practise balancing equations
4. to observe that chemical reactions of the same type are different in some ways

MATERIALS

Apparatus

2 test tubes (25 mm × 150 mm)
test-tube rack
one-hole stopper, containing
   a glass tube with a right-angle
   bend to fit the test tube
rubber tubing, 30 cm long,
   to fit the glass tubing
graduated cylinder (or variable
   volume dispenser)
beaker (150 mL)
lab apron
safety goggles
full face shield
plastic gloves

Reagents

distilled water
limewater, $Ca(OH)_2$
1M HCl (hydrochloric acid)
1M H_2SO_4 (sulfuric acid)
1M H_3PO_4 (phosphoric acid)
1M $HC_2H_3O_2$ (acetic acid)
Na_2CO_3 (sodium carbonate)
$SrCO_3$ (strontium carbonate)
K_2CO_3 (potassium carbonate)
$CuCO_3$ (copper(II) carbonate)
$CaCO_3$ (calcium carbonate)

CAUTION: Some of the acids you will be using are corrosive to skin, eyes, and clothing. Some of the other solutions are irritating to skin and eyes. Some of the solutions are poisonous. When handling these liquids, wear safety goggles, gloves, lab apron, and use a full face shield. Wash spills and splashes off your skin and clothing immediately using plenty of water. Call your teacher.

PROCEDURE

1. Put on your laboratory apron, safety goggles, face shield, and plastic gloves.

2. Add a small scoop of sodium carbonate (an amount equivalent to the size of a pea) to a test tube fitted with a stopper and a rubber tube, as in Figure 5B-1.

3. Add limewater to a second test tube until it is one-third full. Then insert the rubber tubing into the bottom of the test tube containing limewater.

4. Obtain 100 mL of 1 M hydrochloric acid in a 150 mL beaker.

5. Add 15 mL of hydrochloric acid to the test tube containing sodium carbonate and quickly put the stopper attached to the rubber tube in the test tube. (Figure 5B-1 shows how your setup should look at this point.)

Figure 5B-1

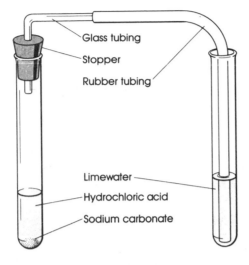

Glass tubing
Stopper
Rubber tubing

Limewater
Hydrochloric acid
Sodium carbonate

6. Record your observations in your copy of Table 1 in your notebook.

7. Pour the remaining substances in each test tube into the sink. Rinse each test tube with tap water three times and with distilled water three times.

8. Repeat Step 2 using strontium carbonate in place of sodium carbonate.

9. Repeat Steps 3-7 and record your observations in Table 1.

10. Repeat Steps 2-7 using potassium carbonate.

11. Repeat Steps 2-7 using calcium carbonate.

12. Repeat Steps 2-7 using copper(II) carbonate.

13. Rinse your beaker and graduated cylinder with tap water three times and with distilled water three times before proceeding to the next step.

14. Repeat Steps 2-12 using sulfuric acid in place of hydrochloric acid.

15. Repeat Steps 2-12 using phosphoric acid in place of hydrochloric acid.

16. Repeat Steps 2-12 using acetic acid in place of hydrochloric acid.

17. Before you leave the laboratory, wash your hands thoroughly with soap and water; use a fingernail brush to clean under your fingernails.

REAGENT DISPOSAL

Rinse all solutions except $CuCO_3$ down the drain with plenty of water. Place the $CuCO_3$ in the designated waste container.

POST LAB DISCUSSION

You should be able to write the formulas for the reactants in each of the reactions. Your observations can be used to identify one of the products in the reaction. You should recall the principle that every element included in the reactants should appear in the products. Discuss possible products for the first experiment with your lab partner and write and balance an equation. Ask your teacher if that equation is correct.

DATA AND OBSERVATIONS

Table 1

SUBSTANCE	HYDROCLORIC ACID	SULFURIC ACID	PHOSPHORIC ACID	ACETIC ACID
Sodium carbonate				
Strontium carbonate				
Potassium carbonate				
Calcium carbonate				
Copper(II) carbonate				

QUESTIONS

1. What do the bubbles indicate?

2. What do all of the reactions have in common?

FOLLOW-UP QUESTIONS

1. Write a general equation for this type of reaction similar to those in Section 5-7 of the textbook.

2. How is the reaction of sodium carbonate with acetic acid different from the reaction of sodium carbonate with hydrochloric acid?

3. Write a balanced equation for each of the 20 reactions. If no reaction occurs, write N.R.

4. When no reaction is observed, a very slow reaction may be taking place. Design an experiment that would detect a very slow reaction.

CONCLUSION

Identify the types of reactions you observed in this experiment.

Types of Chemical Reactions

There are many varieties of chemical reactions, some of them difficult to classify. However, the majority of chemical reactions fit into one of four main categories:

a. Synthesis: $A + B \rightarrow AB$
   (Two substances combine to form a new substance.)

b. Decomposition: $AB \rightarrow A + B$
   (The opposite of synthesis; one substance decomposes or breaks apart to form two new substances.)

c. Single Replacement: $AB + X \rightarrow A + XB$
   (A single change of partners results.)

d. Double Replacement: $AB + XY \rightarrow AY + XB$
   (Similar to single replacement, but a double exchange of partners occurs.)

In this experiment, you will first observe examples of each of the four types of chemical reactions. Next, you will write chemical equations that support your observations. Finally, you will classify each reaction as synthesis, decomposition, single replacement, or double replacement.

OBJECTIVES

1. to observe a variety of chemical reactions

2. to interpret and explain observations with balanced chemical equations

3. to classify each reaction as one of the four main types

MATERIALS

Apparatus	Reagents
lab burner	copper wire (bare)
6 test tubes	iron nail
(13 mm × 100 mm)	0.5M copper(II) sulfate solution
test-tube clamp	copper(II) sulfate pentahydrate
medicine dropper	water
wood splints	0.5M calcium chloride solution
crucible tongs	0.5M sodium carbonate solution
steel wool	mossy zinc
safety goggles	2M hydrochloric acid solution
lab aprons	hydrogen peroxide solution (6%)
	manganese(IV) oxide

CAUTION: *Most of these solutions are poisonous, corrosive, or irritants. When handling these solutions, wear your goggles, face shield, laboratory apron, and plastic gloves. Wash any spills and splashes immediately with plenty of water. Call your teacher.*

PROCEDURE

1. Put on your safety goggles and lab apron.

2. Make observations before, during, and after each reaction. Record your observations in your copy of Table 1 in your notebook.

REACTION 1

3. Adjust a burner flame to high heat.

4. Using crucible tongs, hold a 6 cm length of bare copper wire in the hottest part of the flame for a few minutes.

REACTION 2

5. Clean an iron nail with a piece of steel wool so that the surface of the nail is shiny.

6. Place the nail in a test tube and add copper(II) sulfate solution so that one half of the nail is covered.

7. After approximately 15 min, remove the nail and note any changes in both the nail and the solution. (You should move on to Reactions 3 and 4 while you are waiting.)

REACTION 3

8. Put some solid copper(II) sulfate pentahydrate in a test tube so that it is one third full.

9. Using a test-tube clamp, hold the test tube and contents at an angle away from yourself and your classmates. Heat the test tube, moving it back and forth gently over a burner flame.

10. Continue heating until no further change is observed. (Save the contents for Reaction 4.)

REACTION 4

11. Allow the test tube and contents from Reaction 3 to cool.

12. Use a medicine dropper to add 2 or 3 drops of water to the test tube.

REACTION 5

13. Fill a test tube one quarter full with calcium chloride solution. Fill a second test tube one quarter full with sodium carbonate solution.

14. Pour the calcium chloride solution into the test tube containing sodium carbonate solution.

REACTION 6

15. Place a piece of mossy zinc in a test tube.

16. Add hydrochloric acid solution to the test tube until the mossy zinc is completely covered.

REACTION 7

17. Half fill a test tube with hydrogen peroxide solution.

18. Add a small amount of manganese(IV) oxide. (*Note*: Manganese(IV) oxide acts as a catalyst in this reaction.)

19. Test the gas evolved by placing a glowing (not a burning) splint into the mouth of the test tube.

20. Before you leave the laboratory, wash your hands thoroughly with soap and water; use a fingernail brush to clean under your nails.

REAGENT DISPOSAL

Place all liquid and solid waste into the designated containers.

POST LAB DISCUSSION

To predict the products of a reaction, it is helpful to examine the chemical formulas of the reactants. Therefore, your first task is to determine which chemicals reacted in each case, then to write chemical formulas for these reactants.

Next, using a combination of logic and observations, predict the products for each reaction. Finally, balance each equation so that the number of atoms is conserved.

Classifying the reactions requires you to match each equation with one of the four types that was described in the introduction.

DATA AND OBSERVATIONS

When making up the data table, leave spaces between each reaction.

Table 1

		OBSERVATIONS	
REACTION	BEFORE	DURING	AFTER
1			
2			
3			
4			
5			
6			
7			

QUESTIONS

1. In Reaction 1, with which substance in the air did the copper react?

2. In Reaction 2, changes occurred in both the nail and the solution. What do the changes in the solution indicate?

3. What evidence did you see that chemical changes took place in Reactions 3 and 4?

4. In Reaction 5, one of the products is sodium chloride (table salt), which, as you know, is highly soluble in water. What, therefore, would be the product that would account for the precipitate which formed?

5. How could you test the gas released in Reaction 6 to confirm its identity?

6. a. What does the glowing splint test suggest about the identity of the gas evolved in Reaction 7?
   b. The formula for hydrogen peroxide is H_2O_2. Two products are formed in Reaction 7, one of them a common gas which you know from Question 6. a., and the other a common liquid. What is the most likely identity of this common liquid?

FOLLOW-UP QUESTIONS

1. In some industrial processes, solutions have impurities removed by single replacement reactions. In electrolytic zinc processes, for instance, impurities of cadmium in the form of $CdSO_4$ are removed from the electrolyte by the addition of zinc dust. Write a balanced equation for this reaction.

2. Write the balanced equation for the electrolysis of water. What type of reaction is this?

CONCLUSION

For each of the seven reactions in this experiment, write a balanced equation and classify it as a synthesis, decomposition, single replacement, or double replacement reaction.

Investigating the Differences in Activity of Metals

One of the types of reactions studied in Chapter 5 is the reaction of a metal with an acid to produce hydrogen and a compound of the metal. In Part I of this experiment you will use your observations to determine the relative *activities* of several metals. In Part II you will examine the relative activities of four acids.

There are obvious differences in the chemical activities of metals (and acids). Sodium and potassium are so reactive that they must be stored under oil to keep them from air and water vapor. Iron is less reactive, but still rusts in moist air. Gold is so unreactive that it keeps its shine.

OBJECTIVES

1. to make observations of a type of reaction

2. to write equations for chemical reactions

3. to practise balancing equations for a chemical reaction

4. to determine the relative activity of a metal

5. to learn how to identify and control important factors in an experiment

6. to learn that all acids of equal concentrations do not react alike

MATERIALS

Apparatus	Reagents
test-tube rack	zinc
4 test tubes	magnesium
(25 mm × 150 mm)	iron
4 beakers (150 mL)	copper
safety goggles	$1M$ hydrochloric acid, HCl
lab apron	$1M$ sulfuric acid, H_2SO_4
plastic gloves	$1M$ acetic acid, $HC_2H_3O_2$
full face shield	$1M$ phosphoric acid, H_3PO_4

PROCEDURE

Part I   Comparison of Metal Activities

1. Put on your laboratory apron, safety goggles, full face shield, and plastic gloves.

2. Label the test tubes Fe, Zn, Cu, and Mg.

3. Add a small amount of each metal (a piece or an amount between the size of a grain of rice and a pea) to each of the respective test tubes.

4. Obtain about 60 mL of $1M$ HCl and pour 15 mL (enough to about half-fill a test tube) into each test tube.

HAZARD

CAUTION: Some of the acids used in this experiment are corrosive to skin, eyes, and clothing. When handling such acids, wear safety goggles, full face shield, gloves, and lab apron. Wash spills and splashes off your skin and clothing immediately using plenty of water. Call your teacher.

5. Wait at least five minutes and record your observations in your copy of Table 1 in your notebook. Rank the metals in order of decreasing activity, with the most active ranked as 1 and the least active 4.

6. Pour the liquids in waste containers supplied by your teacher. Put the leftover metals in the designated waste container, and rinse the test tubes three times with tap water.

7. Repeat Steps 2-6 with sulfuric acid.

8. Repeat Steps 2-6 with phosphoric acid.

9. Repeat Steps 2-6 with acetic acid.

Part II   Comparison of Acid Activities

1. Put a piece of magnesium in each of the four test tubes.

2. Add about 15 mL of each of the four acids simultaneously to the test tubes containing magnesium (one acid to each test tube). Compare the rate of reaction of magnesium with each of the $1M$ acids. Record your observations in your copy of Table 2 in your notebook.

3. Before you leave the laboratory, wash your hands thoroughly with soap and water; use a fingernail brush to clean under your fingernails.

REAGENT DISPOSAL

Decant the acids from the metals. Rinse all solutions down the sink with copious amounts of water. Place all solids in the designated waste containers.

POST LAB DISCUSSION

The reaction of a metal with an acid is just one indication of its activity. Other reactions can be considered as well. In this experiment you made qualitative observations of reactions. The experiment also could be done quantitatively.

In deciding how to rank the activity of the metals, the other factors in the experiment may have to be considered. Acids of equal concentrations do not all react the same with a given metal. The properties of acids will be studied in Chapter 20, but this experiment shows one of the differences among acids.

If no observable reaction occurs, you can write N. R., which stands for *no reaction*. It is possible that a reaction is taking place, but too slowly to be observed in the time available, and that if you wait longer a reaction can be observed. It is also possible that a reaction will not occur no matter how long you wait. Being able to write a balanced equation for a reaction does not necessarily mean that reaction will take place.

DATA AND OBSERVATIONS

Part I Comparison of Metal Activities

Table 1

	ZINC	MAGNESIUM	COPPER	IRON
Hydrochloric acid				
Sulfuric acid				
Phosphoric acid				
Acetic acid				

COMPLETE IN YOUR NOTEBOOK

COMPLETE IN YOUR NOTEBOOK

Part II Comparison of Acid Activities

Table 2

	HYDROCHLORIC ACID	SULFURIC ACID	PHOSPHORIC ACID	ACETIC ACID
Magnesium				

COMPLETE IN YOUR NOTEBOOK

QUESTIONS

1. Using the results of all the experiments, rank the metals in order of decreasing activity.
2. Write balanced equations for all 16 reactions. If no observable reaction took place, write N. R., which stands for *no reaction*.

FOLLOW-UP QUESTIONS

1. Compare the activity series you obtained from this experiment with the one given in the textbook in Section 5-7. Suggest an explanation for any differences.

CONCLUSION

State the results of Objective 4 for the metals tested.

Moles and Mass in a Reaction

The reaction of a carbonate with an acid is an example of a common chemical reaction. One particular example is the reaction of acetic acid, or vinegar, with sodium hydrogen carbonate, or baking soda. This reaction produces carbon dioxide gas and water. A similar reaction is used by geologists to test rocks for the presence of limestone, or calcium carbonate. A few drops of hydrochloric acid are placed on a sample of rock. If bubbles of gas can be observed, then it is assumed that the rock contains limestone.

The reaction of sodium hydrogen carbonate with hydrochloric acid is a convenient reaction to use in studying relationships in chemical equations. It is convenient because the reaction is fairly rapid and produces three products, one of which is a gas and another of which vaporizes at a fairly low temperature. The final product is sodium chloride, another common chemical, which we know as "salt."

In Part I of this experiment, you will be using an excess of hydrochloric acid, with sodium hydrogen carbonate as the limiting reactant. The excess hydrochloric acid solution can be easily boiled away, leaving only sodium chloride in the reaction vessel. In Part II, you will verify the final mass of the product.

Chemical arithmetic is important. It tells chemical engineers how much of each ingredient to mix to get the desired product. The production of major chemicals is measured in the millions of tonnes each year. Mistakes involving calculations of such large amounts could cost a lot of money. With rare chemicals, a few grains may be worth hundreds of dollars. Here, too, calculations are essential.

OBJECTIVES

1. to observe the reaction between hydrochloric acid and sodium hydrogen carbonate

2. to calculate the number of moles of sodium hydrogen carbonate and relate that value to the number of moles of sodium chloride that are produced in the reaction

3. to calculate the moles of hydrochloric acid used in the reaction, as well as the moles of water and carbon dioxide produced

4. to convert the mole calculation into units of mass

MATERIALS

Apparatus

centigram balance
lab burner
graduated cylinder
  (100 mL)
ring stand and ring
wire gauze with
  ceramic centre
spatula or spoon
dropping pipet

beaker tongs or clamp
2 beakers (100 mL)
hot plate (for class)
fume hood (for class)
plastic gloves
lab apron
safety goggles
full face shield

Reagents

sodium hydrogen
  carbonate, $NaHCO_3$
$3M$ hydrochloric acid,
  HCl

PROCEDURE

Part I Reaction of HCl and NaHCO₃ (Day 1)

1. Put on your lab apron, safety goggles, full face shield, and gloves.

2. Obtain a 100 mL beaker and identify it with your name. Be sure that it is clean and dry. From this point on, you should pick up the beaker with clean tongs. This way you will avoid adding any additional mass because of what might be on your hands.

3. Find the mass of the dry beaker. Record it in your notebook.

4. Place about three grams of sodium hydrogen carbonate in the beaker. Find the mass of the beaker and the contents and record it in your notebook.

5. Place about 15 mL of 3 M hydrochloric acid in another 100 mL beaker. Using a pipet, slowly add about 10 mL of the acid to the beaker containing the sodium hydrogen carbonate. It is important that you add the acid slowly so that the reaction does not force some of the reactants out of the beaker. Continue adding acid until the bubbling stops. Do not add any more acid than is necessary.

6. Place your beaker on the warming tray in the fume hood. Dispose of the leftover acid as your instructor directs.

7. Before you leave the laboratory, wash your hands thoroughly with soap and water; use a fingernail brush to clean under your fingernails.

CAUTION: Hydrochloric acid is corrosive to skin, eyes, and clothing. When handling hydrochloric acid, wear safety goggles, lab apron, full face shield, and gloves. Wash spills and splashes off your skin and clothing immediately using plenty of water. Call your teacher.

Part II Determining the Mass of NaCl Produced (Day 2)

1. Put on your lab apron and safety goggles.

2. Measure the mass of the beaker plus dry solid. Record the mass in your notebook.

3. Place a wire gauze on top of a ring, and attach it to a ring stand. Set the beaker on the gauze. Using a burner, heat the beaker and its contents for three minutes.

4. Allow the beaker to cool. Then measure the mass of the beaker and its contents. Record the mass in your notebook.

5. If the mass from Step 4 does not agree, within experimental uncertainty, with the mass from Step 2, repeat Steps 3 and 4 until a constant mass is obtained.

5. Wash out the beaker. Before you leave the laboratory, wash your hands thoroughly with soap and water; use a fingernail brush to clean under your fingernails.

REAGENT DISPOSAL

All solutions can be rinsed down the sink with plenty of water.

POST LAB DISCUSSION

In the reaction of sodium hydrogen carbonate and hydrochloric acid, three products are formed: carbon dioxide, water, and sodium chloride. The only product that remains in the beaker after heating is sodium chloride. You will need to determine the balanced equation for the reaction before you can calculate the amounts of carbon dioxide and water that were formed in the reaction. The formula for sodium hydrogen carbonate is $NaHCO_3$, and the formula for hydrochloric acid is HCl.

In order to calculate the number of moles involved in the reaction, you will need to know the molar masses of the substances involved. The number of moles can be calculated by dividing the mass by the molar mass.

DATA AND OBSERVATIONS

Part I   Reaction of HCl and $NaHCO_3$ (Day 1)

Mass of beaker
Mass of beaker + $NaHCO_3$

Part II   Determining the Mass of NaCl Produced (Day 2)

Mass of beaker + dry solid (after the reaction)
Final mass of beaker and contents (after heating)

QUESTIONS AND CALCULATIONS

1. Calculate the masses of
   a. sodium hydrogen carbonate;
   b. sodium chloride.

2. Calculate the number of moles of
   a. sodium hydrogen carbonate;
   b. sodium chloride.

3. Write a balanced chemical equation for the reaction.

4. According to the equation, what is the ratio of moles of sodium hydrogen carbonate to moles of sodium chloride?

5. How does your answer to item 4 compare to the results that you obtained in item 2?

6. Using the value that you obtained for the number of moles of sodium chloride produced, calculate the number of moles of carbon dioxide and the moles of water that would have been produced.

7. Using the value that you obtained for the number of moles of sodium chloride produced, calculate the number of moles of hydrochloric acid that would have been used up in the reaction.

8. What are some possible sources of error in this experiment?

FOLLOW-UP QUESTIONS

1. A similar reaction occurs between limestone (calcium carbonate) and hydrochloric acid. Write a balanced equation for this reaction.

2. If 3.00 g of limestone reacted, what masses of the following would be produced?
   a. calcium chloride
   b. carbon dioxide
   c. water

3. Write a balanced equation for the reaction of vinegar (acetic acid, CH_3COOH) with baking soda.

CONCLUSION

Write a balanced chemical equation for the reaction and under each chemical formula state the number of moles either reacted or produced.

Calculations with a Chemical Reaction

The "recipe" for a chemical reaction is the balanced chemical equation. In the simplest example of $2H_2 + O_2 \rightarrow 2H_2O$, the recipe states that 2 mol of hydrogen molecules plus 1 mol of oxygen molecules will produce 2 mol of water molecules. Moles are the common language of chemical equations. However, there are no balances that measure amounts in moles. Balances measure amounts in grams. In the above example, we can use the molar masses of hydrogen, oxygen, and water to change the equation to say that 4.0 g of hydrogen will combine with 32.0 g of oxygen to form 36.0 g of water.

Often in chemical reactions, the amounts of substances are known or can be easily measured with a balance. Sometimes, the substances are dissolved in water, forming a solution. Solution concentrates are very often expressed in "molarity," abbreviated M. A $1.00M$ solution contains exactly 1.00 mol of a substance per litre of solution. If you need to know the number of moles of the substance in a certain volume, you can multiply the volume in litres by the molarity. For example, if you wanted to know how many moles of sodium chloride were present in 0.500 L of a $0.250M$ solution, you would multiply as follows:

$$0.500 \text{ L} \times 0.250 \text{ mol/L} = 0.125 \text{ mol}$$

Methyl salicylate is sold in dilute solution as the flavoring agent used in wintergreen Lifesavers. The compound is prepared from methanol and salicylic acid. Calculations show this reaction to be 72% efficient. Such efficiency calculations are commonplace for all industrial chemical processes, because the calculations indicate how much product will be obtained compared to the amount that the balanced equation predicts.

In this experiment, you will be observing the reaction between calcium chloride and sodium carbonate. Both substances are soluble in water, so the reaction will be produced by combining solutions of the two substances. The products of the reaction are calcium carbonate and sodium chloride. The sodium chloride is soluble, so it will remain in solution. The calcium carbonate is insoluble, so it will form a precipitate, which can then be collected and dried to determine the mass of product produced.

OBJECTIVES

1. to observe the reaction between solutions of calcium chloride and sodium carbonate, forming insoluble calcium carbonate

2. to calculate the number of moles of each of the starting materials present in the solutions

3. to determine the reactant that is in excess

4. to determine the theoretical amount of calcium carbonate that could be produced

5. to compare the theoretical amount to the actual amount of calcium carbonate and calculate the percent yield

MATERIALS

Apparatus

centigram balance
graduated cylinder
  (100 mL)
funnel
filter paper
wash bottle
2 beakers (250 mL)

stirring rod with
  rubber scraper
ring stand and
  ring support
safety goggles
lab apron
drying oven

Reagents

$0.60\,M$ sodium carbonate
  solution, Na_2CO_3
$0.40\,M$ calcium chloride
  solution, $CaCl_2$
distilled water

PROCEDURE

1. Put on your laboratory apron and safety goggles.

2. Obtain a clean 250 mL beaker.

3. Pour approximately 75 mL of sodium carbonate solution into the graduated cylinder. Record the volume to the nearest 0.5 mL in your notebook. Pour the sodium carbonate solution into the beaker.

4. Carefully rinse the graduated cylinder two or three times with distilled water. Then pour approximately 50 mL of calcium chloride solution into the graduated cylinder. Again, record the volume in your notebook. Pour the calcium chloride into the beaker. Describe the resulting reaction in your notebook. Stir the contents of the beaker for about one minute, then allow the solid to settle.

5. While waiting for the solid to settle, find the mass of a piece of filter paper. Determine the mass to the nearest 0.01 g and record the amount in your notebook.

6. Set up a funnel and the filter paper of known mass as shown in Figure 6B-1. Use a 250 mL beaker under the funnel.

CAUTION: *Wash spills and splashes off your skin and clothing with plenty of water. Wear your safety goggles to keep spills and splashes out of your eyes.*

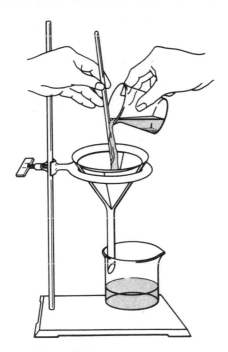

Figure 6B-1

7. Wet the filter paper with a small amount of distilled water. Now pour the contents of the beaker slowly into the funnel. Be careful as you

pour, so that none of the solid flows out of the filter paper or funnel. Use the rubber scraper to remove as much of the solid from the beaker as possible. Rinse the inside of the beaker with some distilled water to remove any more solid. Rinse the beaker two or three times.

8. Once all of the solid is on the filter paper and the liquid has all drained through into the beaker, carefully remove the filter paper from the funnel and unfold it onto a paper towel. Dry the precipitate on the filter paper using a drying oven or whatever other device your teacher may suggest.

9. Begin doing the calculations.

10. After it is thoroughly dried, find the mass of the precipitate and filter paper and record it in your notebook.

11. Before you leave the laboratory, clean up all of the materials and wash your hands thoroughly with soap and warm water. Use a fingernail brush to clean under your fingernails.

REAGENT DISPOSAL

Rinse all solutions down the sink with copious amounts of water. Place the solid residue in the designated waste container.

POST LAB DISCUSSION

Before you can begin the calculations, it is important that you know the chemical equation that correctly describes the reaction you have seen. In this reaction, the starting materials are calcium chloride and sodium carbonate. The products of the reaction are calcium carbonate and sodium chloride. You will need to look up the formulas.

The substance left on the filter paper is the precipitate calcium carbonate. By subtracting the mass of the filter paper from the mass of the filter paper plus the solid, you can obtain the mass of calcium carbonate produced.

Percent yield will tell you the percent of product obtained compared to the theoretical yield. You can calculate the percent yield by using this formula:

$$\text{Percent yield} = \frac{\text{actual amount (grams)}}{\text{theoretical amount (grams)}} \times 100$$

DATA AND OBSERVATIONS

Volume of sodium carbonate solution
Volume of calcium chloride solution
Describe what happens after mixing the two solutions.
Mass of dry filter paper
Mass of filter paper + dry solid

QUESTIONS AND CALCULATIONS

1. Calculate the following values:
   a. moles of sodium carbonate used
   b. moles of calcium chloride used
   c. mass of calcium carbonate produced
   d. moles of calcium carbonate produced

2. Write a balanced chemical equation for the reaction that you observed in this experiment.

3. Determine which of the reactants was in excess in this reaction.

4. Calculate the amount of calcium carbonate that should theoretically form from the amount of the limiting reactant.

5. Calculate the percent yield in your reaction.

6. Predict what would happen to the percent yield (greater than, less than, or no change) if the following occurred:
   a. the solid was not completely dry
   b. the balance measured all values over by 0.12 g
   c. you mixed up the volumes of the two liquids

FOLLOW-UP QUESTIONS

1. Suppose you wanted to add just enough $0.40\,M$ calcium chloride solution to 75.0 mL of $0.60\,M$ sodium carbonate solution for all of the sodium carbonate and calcium chloride to react.
   a. What volume of $0.40\,M$ calcium chloride solution would be required?
   b. What mass of calcium carbonate would be produced (assuming a 100% yield)?
   c. What mass of sodium chloride would be produced (assuming a 100% yield)?

2. How would you be able to recover the sodium chloride from the solution?

3. A similar reaction occurs when barium chloride solution is mixed with sodium carbonate solution. Write a balanced equation for the reaction.

4. Calculate each of the following for the reaction that occurs when 56.0 mL of $0.50\,M$ barium chloride solution are mixed with 78.0 mL of $0.75\,M$ sodium carbonate solution:
   a. moles of barium chloride added
   b. moles of sodium carbonate added
   c. mass of barium carbonate produced, if the yield is 78%

CONCLUSION

Write a balanced chemical equation for the reaction and state the results of Objective 5.

The Mass of a Reaction Product: Prediction Using Stoichiometry vs. Experimental Determination

Predictions backed up by laboratory measurement are used to determine many things. These include how much iron is in a barge of iron ore, how much sulfur dioxide is in polluted air, or whether a new batch of fertilizer contains all of the potassium, phosphorus, and nitrogen listed on the label.

In many industrial processes one of the reactants is used in excess to make sure that the other reactant is completely consumed. The reactant in excess is the least expensive reactant or the one that is easiest to isolate and reclaim.

In Part I of this experiment, you will calculate the number of millilitres of 1.00 M HCl required to react with the amount of sodium carbonate in your beaker. You will then add that amount plus an excess of ten percent to make sure all of the sodium carbonate reacts.

The mass of the product can be calculated using the principles of stoichiometry and the knowledge of which reactant is in excess. The product will then be isolated and the mass measured to determine whether it agrees with the predicted mass, within experimental uncertainty (Part II).

OBJECTIVES

1. to review types of reactions
2. to review writing and balancing an equation
3. to use the principles of stoichiometry to calculate the amount of one reactant that will completely react with another reactant
4. to review the use of percentages in order to calculate the amount to add to have a ten percent excess
5. to use the principles of stoichiometry and limiting reactants to predict the amount of a product
6. to review the use of significant digits in calculations

MATERIALS

Apparatus

centigram balance
beaker (150 mL or 250 mL)
graduated cylinder
hot plate (for class use)
safety goggles
lab apron
plastic gloves
full face shield
fume hood

Reagents

sodium carbonate
1 M HCl

PROCEDURE

Part I   Reaction of HCl and Na$_2$CO$_3$ (Day 1)

1. Put on your laboratory apron, safety goggles, plastic gloves, and face shield.

2. Measure the mass of a clean, dry beaker marked with your name, and record the data in your notebook.

3. Add between 3 g and 5 g of sodium carbonate to the beaker.

4. Measure the combined mass of the beaker and sodium carbonate and record the data in your notebook.

5. Do Calculations #4a.–e. in your notebook.

6. Check your calculations for volume needed of 1M HCl with your teacher, and if approved, add that amount of 1M HCl to the beaker slowly, using a graduated cylinder. Record the approved volume in your notebook.

7. Record your observations in your notebook.

8. Check to make sure your beaker is marked with your name, and place it on the hot plate in the fume hood.

9. Measure the mass of a beaker labeled *Class I* and record the data in your notebook.

10. Before you leave the laboratory, wash your hands thoroughly with soap and water; use a fingernail brush to clean under your fingernails.

CAUTION: Hydrochloric acid is corrosive to skin, eyes, and clothing. When handling hydrochloric acid, wear safety goggles, full face shield, gloves, and lab apron. Wash spills and splashes off your skin and clothing immediately using plenty of water. Call your teacher.

Part II   Determining the Mass of the Product (Day 2)

1. Put on your laboratory apron and safety goggles.

2. Examine the substance in your beaker and record your observations in your notebook.

3. Measure the mass of the beaker and contents, and record the data in your notebook.

4. Measure the mass of the beaker labeled *Class I* and its contents, and record the data in your notebook.

5. Before you leave the laboratory, wash your hands thoroughly with soap and water; use a fingernail brush to clean under your fingernails.

REAGENT DISPOSAL

All materials can be rinsed down the sink with copious amounts of water.

POST LAB DISCUSSION

After all your classmates measured the mass of the beaker labeled *Class I* in Part I of the experiment, 200 mL of 1M HCl were added to it. This beaker was then placed on the hot plate in the fume hood. The mass of the beaker was measured in Part II after the 1M HCl evaporated. You can use these data to answer items 8 and 9 in Questions and Calculations.

DATA AND OBSERVATIONS

Part I   Reaction of HCl and Na₂CO₃ (Day 1)

Mass of clean, dry beaker

Mass of beaker and sodium carbonate

Volume of 1M HCl to be added, in mL

Observations during and after adding 1M HCl to the beaker containing sodium carbonate

Mass of beaker labeled *Class I*

Part II   Determining the Mass of the Product (Day 2)

Observations of beaker and contents

Mass of beaker and contents

Mass of beaker labeled *Class I*

QUESTIONS AND CALCULATIONS

1. What is the formula for sodium carbonate?
2. What is the formula for hydrochloric acid?
3. Write the balanced equation for the reaction of sodium carbonate with hydrochloric acid.
4. Express each answer with the correct number of significant digits.

   a. Calculate the mass of sodium carbonate in your beaker.
   b. Calculate the number of moles of sodium carbonate in your beaker.
   c. Calculate the number of moles of HCl required to just react with the sodium carbonate in your beaker.
   d. Calculate the volume in millilitres of 1M HCl required to just react with the sodium carbonate in your beaker.
   e. Calculate the volume in millilitres of 1M HCl required for a ten percent excess.
   f. Calculate the mass of the product in the beaker using the principles of stoichiometry and limiting reactant.

5. Calculate the mass of the product in your beaker at the end of the experiment.

6. What is the formula for the product that remains in your beaker?

7. Is the predicted mass of the product the same as the measured mass within experimental uncertainty?

8. Within experimental uncertainty, is the mass of the beaker labeled *Class I* the same before and after 200 mL of 1M HCl has been evaporated from it?

9. What remains in the beaker labeled *Class I* when 1M HCl is evaporated from it? Explain your answer.

10. What is the purpose of the beaker labeled *Class I*?

FOLLOW-UP QUESTIONS

1. If 200 mL of tap water are added to a 250 mL beaker with a known mass, and the water is evaporated, what will remain in the beaker?

2. If the predicted mass of the product in your experiment and the measured mass are not the same within experimental uncertainty, analyze the experiment for causes.

3. Evaluate the causes to determine which is the most probable one.

4. What is the shape of crystals of the product?

5. Have you seen crystals like these before? If so, where?

CONCLUSION

State the results of Objective 5, and compare your prediction with the measured mass of the product in the experiment.

Investigating which Reactant is in Excess

The yield of a chemical process can usually be improved by finding more favorable conditions. One method often employed when economically feasible is to add an excess of one or more reactants, thus improving the conversion of some other (usually more expensive) chemical to the desired product.

When a reaction occurs, an equation for the reaction can be written to indicate the chemical changes that are taking place. For example, you learned in a previous experiment that zinc reacts exothermically with hydrochloric acid to produce zinc chloride and hydrogen gas.

$$Zn(s) + 2HCl(aq) \rightarrow ZnCl_2(aq) + H_2(g) + energy$$

The balanced equation indicates that on a microscopic level one atom of Zn reacts with two molecules of HCl to produce one molecule of $ZnCl_2$ and one molecule of H_2. This also means that one mole of Zn reacts with two moles of HCl to produce one mole of $ZnCl_2$ and one mole of H_2.

When these two reactants are combined, the reaction will continue to occur until one reactant is used up. At this time the other reactant also may be used up. If not, the reactant that remains is said to be in *excess*, because more of that reactant was present than the amount required to react.

In Part I of this experiment, you will measure the amount of each reactant carefully and predict which reactant will be in excess. In Part II, you will verify your predictions macroscopically.

OBJECTIVES

1. to make careful measurements of the amounts of each reactant

2. to calculate the number of moles of each reactant

3. to predict which reactant is in excess

4. to relate macroscopic observations to microscopic events

5. to use drawings to relate microscopic events; to write chemical equations that represent those microscopic events

6. to learn how to measure the volume of a liquid using a buret

MATERIALS

Apparatus

test tube (18 mm × 150 mm)
beaker (150 mL)
buret
centigram balance
forceps
safety goggles
lab apron
plastic gloves
full face shield

Reagents

zinc pieces
3*M* HCl

PROCEDURE

Part I   Reaction of Zn and HCl (Day 1)

1. Put on your laboratory apron, safety goggles, plastic gloves, and face shield.

2. Determine the mass of a clean, dry 18 mm × 150 mm test tube and record your data in your notebook.

3. Add one piece of zinc to the test tube and determine the mass of the test tube and zinc. Record your data in your notebook.

4. Read the volume of the HCl in the buret to the nearest 0.1 mL and record the reading in your notebook.

5. Add between 5 mL and 20 mL of 3 M HCl to the test tube and record the new reading in your notebook.

6. Record your observations in your notebook.

7. Make a drawing of the test tube and its contents in your notebook and label all the substances present.

8. Store the test tube in a beaker so it remains upright.

9. Before you leave the laboratory wash your hands thoroughly with soap and water; use a fingernail brush to clean under your fingernails.

CAUTION: Hydrochloric acid is corrosive to skin, eyes, and clothing. When handling hydrochloric acid, wear safety goggles, full face shield, gloves, and lab apron. Wash spills and splashes off your skin and clothing immediately using plenty of water. Call your teacher.

Part II   Determining the Excess Reactant (Day 2)

1. Put on your lab apron, safety goggles, plastic gloves, and face shield.

2. Observe your test tube and contents and record your observations in your notebook. Make another drawing of the test tube and label the contents.

REAGENT DISPOSAL

Decant the acid from the zinc metal. Rinse all solutions down the sink with copious amounts of water. Place the zinc in the designated waste container.

POST LAB DISCUSSION

If you correctly predicted that zinc would be in excess, then there should be some solid zinc remaining in your test tube. If you correctly predicted there would be HCl in excess, then there should be no zinc remaining in the test tube.

DATA AND OBSERVATIONS
Part I   Reaction of Zn and HCl (Day 1)

Mass of clean, dry test tube

Mass of test tube and zinc

Initial buret reading for $3M$ HCl

Final buret reading for $3M$ HCl

Observations of test tube containing Zn after addition of HCl

Part II   Determining the Excess Reactant (Day 2)

Observations of test tube and contents

QUESTIONS AND CALCULATIONS

1. Calculate the mass of zinc added to the test tube.

2. Calculate the number of moles of zinc added to the test tube.

3. Calculate the volume of $3M$ HCl added to the test tube.

4. Calculate the number of moles of HCl added to the test tube.

5. Predict which reactant will be in excess.

6. Based on your macroscopic observations of the test tube and contents, which reactant is in excess? Explain.

7. Was the prediction you made in item 5 of your calculations correct? Explain.

FOLLOW-UP QUESTIONS

1. Calculate the theoretical yield of zinc chloride.

2. Design an experiment to isolate and measure the actual yield of zinc chloride.

CONCLUSION

State the results of Objective 3, and compare your prediction to your macroscopic observations.

Predicting and Measuring the Mass of a Reactant in Excess

Hydrochloric acid is a normal component of digestive juices but in excess, it can cause discomfort. Intensive study for a test, too little sleep, an excess of drink, and too much pizza (factors not unknown to students) can produce this condition, known as "heartburn." Pharmaceutical companies produce antacids that neutralize the excess acid.

In Part I of this experiment, you will react a known amount of zinc with a measured amount of HCl. Some of the zinc will remain unreacted. The amount of zinc in excess will be calculated using *stoichiometry*. The unreacted zinc will be isolated, and the mass will be measured to determine whether it agrees with the predicted excess within experimental uncertainty.

In Part II, the remaining zinc will be retained in the test tube by decanting the liquid. The remaining zinc will still contain small amounts of the liquid. The zinc will be purified by rinsing with distilled water at least three times. This procedure will remove 99 percent of the soluble substances.

OBJECTIVES

1. to review types of reactions

2. to review writing and balancing an equation

3. to apply the principles of stoichiometry to a familiar chemical reaction

4. to predict the amount of zinc in excess

5. to isolate, purify, and measure a substance

6. to review the use of significant digits in calculations

7. to analyze experimental results to determine a cause for unexpected results

MATERIALS

Apparatus

test tube (18 mm × 150 mm)
centigram balance
buret
wash bottle containing
   distilled water
beaker (150 mL or 250 mL)

burner
test tube holder
safety goggles
lab apron
plastic gloves
full face shield

Reagents

$1.50\,M$ HCl
zinc

PROCEDURE

Part I   Reaction of Zn and HCl (Day 1)

1. Put on your laboratory apron, safety goggles, full face shield, and gloves.

2. Determine the mass of a clean, dry 18 mm × 150 mm test tube and record the data in your notebook.

3. Add at least 1.5 g of zinc to the test tube, measure the mass, and record the data in your notebook.

4. Fill the buret with 1.5 M HCl. The level of the HCl should be below the top marking on the buret.

5. Read and record the initial buret reading in your notebook.

6. Add between 10 mL and 15 mL of 1.50 M HCl to the test tube using the buret. Read and record the last measurement in your notebook.

7. Record your observations in your notebook.

8. Store the test tube in a beaker.

9. Before you leave the laboratory, wash your hands thoroughly with soap and water; use a fingernail brush to clean under your fingernails.

Part II Determining the Mass of Excess Zn (Day 2)

1. Put on your lab apron and safety goggles.

2. Examine your test tube from Day 1 and record your observations.

3. Decant the liquid into a clean, dry beaker.

4. Pour the liquid into the waste chemical jar.

5. Rinse the contents of the test tube three times using 10 mL of distilled water each time. Decant the water into the sink.

6. Using your burner, heat the test tube and excess zinc gently until all of the water is evaporated.

7. Cool the test tube.

8. Measure the mass of the test tube and zinc and record the data in your notebook.

9. Before you leave the laboratory, wash your hands thoroughly with soap and water; use a fingernail brush to clean under your fingernails.

REAGENT DISPOSAL

Rinse all solutions down the sink with plenty of water. Place the solids in the designated waste container.

POST LAB DISCUSSION

If the mass you predict for the excess zinc does not agree with the measured mass, you should check your calculations. In this reaction, zinc is in excess, so the number of moles of HCl must be used to calculate the number of moles of zinc reacted. The mole ratio between HCl and zinc is obtained from the balanced equation. After calculating the number of moles of zinc reacted, you can find the number of moles of excess zinc by subtracting. You can then convert the number of moles of excess zinc to grams.

DATA AND OBSERVATIONS

Part I   Reaction of Zn and HCl (Day 1)

Mass of test tube

Mass of test tube and zinc

Initial reading of 1.50M HCl

Last reading of 1.50M HCl

Mass of test tube and zinc after decanting, washing, and drying

Observations of test tube containing Zn after addition of HCl

Part II   Determining the Mass of Excess Zn (Day 2)

Mass of test tube and zinc

CALCULATIONS

1. Express each calculated value with the correct number of significant digits.
   a. Calculate the mass of zinc before adding the HCl.
   b. Calculate the number of moles of zinc in the test tube before the reaction started.
   c. Calculate the volume of 1.50M HCl added.
   d. Calculate the number of moles of 1.50M HCl added.
   e. Calculate the number of moles of zinc reacted.
   f. Calculate the number of moles of zinc in excess.
   g. Calculate the mass of zinc in excess.

2. Calculate the mass of the zinc isolated, purified, and measured at the end of the experiment.

3. Is the mass of zinc in excess that was predicted using stoichiometry the same as the mass of the isolated and purified zinc that was measured experimentally?

4. Use your knowledge of significant digits to determine if the experimental mass and the predicted mass are the same within experimental uncertainty.

FOLLOW-UP QUESTIONS

1. If the predicted and measured mass of the excess zinc are not the same within experimental uncertainty, analyze what may have caused the difference.

2. Evaluate the analyzed causes to select the most probable cause(s).

CONCLUSION

State the results of Objective 4, and compare your prediction to the measured mass of unreacted zinc.

The Gas Laws

Before battery-operated lamps were available, miners used calcium carbide acetylene gas lamps. Precise regulation of a drip of water onto the calcium carbide liberated acetylene gas, which was ignited to produce a bright white flame. Careful calculations involving the gas laws were necessary to determine the proper rate of generation of the gas.

For more than 100 years, the kinetic molecular theory has served as the foundation for explaining the physical behavior of gases. According to this theory, gases are composed of atoms or molecules that are in constant straight-line motion. The molecules of a confined gas collide with the walls of the container, as well as with each other. The collisions are assumed to be perfectly elastic — that is, no energy is gained or lost in the process. When molecules collide with the walls of a container, they exert a force on those walls. The force is directly related to the velocity at which the molecules strike the walls. The combined force of all molecular collisions with the walls divided by the total area that is being struck is the pressure that is exerted by the gas.

In the seventeenth century, Robert Boyle investigated the relationship between the volume of a confined gas and the pressure it exerted upon its container. He found that these variables were related as an inverse function. He expressed this function using the formula $P \times V = k$ (for a constant number of moles at constant temperature). This relationship can be explained in terms of the kinetic molecular theory. As the volume of the gas is decreased, more collisions occur per unit area of the container walls, thus increasing pressure. Similarly, when the volume is increased, fewer collisions occur per unit area, and a subsequent drop in pressure is observed.

More than 100 years later (in 1787), Jacques Charles observed a relationship between the volume of a gas and its temperature. He found that, as a sample of gas was heated, its volume increased. In terms of the kinetic molecular theory, as a gas is heated, its molecules move at a greater velocity and are capable of occupying a larger volume. Charles's work led to the formulation of the absolute temperature scale, a measuring system based on a more direct relationship between molecular motion and temperature.

In this experiment, you will duplicate the results observed by Boyle (Part I) and Charles (Part II). A confined gas volume will be subjected to stresses in pressure and temperature. The resulting changes in volume will be recorded. You will then plot these results and extrapolate the graph to find the volume that corresponds to zero on the absolute temperature scale.

OBJECTIVES

1. to observe the effect of increasing pressure on the volume of a confined gas

2. to observe the effect of increasing temperature on the volume of a confined gas

3. to plot a volume-temperature graph from the collected data and extrapolate the graph to find the volume of a gas at absolute zero

MATERIALS

Apparatus

gas piston-cylinder
assembly with block
supports
60 cm³ syringe with
end cap
metric ruler
5 weights
2 utility clamps
ring stand and ring
wire gauze

beaker (600 mL)
thermometer
inserted into rubber
stopper
laboratory balance
kilogram scale (for class)
laboratory burner
safety goggles
lab apron

PROCEDURE

Part I   Boyle's Law

1. Put on your laboratory apron and safety goggles.

2. Measure the barometric pressure of the room and record this value in your notebook.

3. Obtain a gas piston-cylinder with block supports. Separate the piston-cylinder component, shown in Figure 7A-1, from the rest of the assembly. Then remove the piston from the cylinder, and measure the internal diameter of the cylinder. Record the measurement in your notebook.

4. Measure the mass of the piston plus the upper support block. (See Figure 7A-2.) Record this value in your notebook.

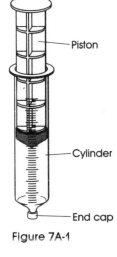

Figure 7A-1

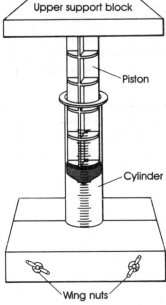

Figure 7A-2 *Assembled gas cylinder-piston system.*

5. Remove the cylinder end cap and fill the cylinder to a volume of 30 cm³ with air.

6. Replace the cap and assemble the support system as illustrated in Figure 7A-2. (Note: Firmly tighten, but do not strip, the wing nuts.)

CAUTION: Due to the instability of the stack, one member of the lab team should continually support the bricks.

7. Label five weights *A* to *E*. Determine the mass of each weight using the kilogram scale. DO NOT use the laboratory balance. Record these values in your copy of Table 1.

8. Place weight *A* on the upper support block of the gas piston. Record the volume of confined gas in your copy of Table 2.

9. Increase the number of weights, one at a time, and record each subsequent gas volume in Table 2. Continue until a maximum of five weights have been stacked.

Part II   Charles's Law

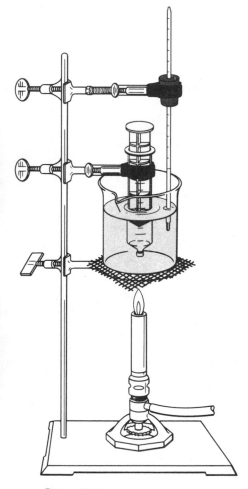

Figure 7A-3

1. Remove the end cap of a 60 cm³ syringe and fill the cylinder to a volume of 20 cm³ with air.

2. Replace the cap and secure the syringe within a utility clamp. NOTE: The volume scale should not be obscured by the clamp.

3. Obtain a thermometer inserted into a stopper.

4. Add approximately 400 mL of water at room temperature to a 600 mL beaker.

5. Assemble the apparatus as shown in Figure 7A-3. Lower the syringe far enough into the water so that at least 30 cm³ of air in the syringe will be below the water surface. Lower the thermometer to a point at which the bulb is about even with, or slightly above, the midpoint of the column of air in the syringe, in order to obtain a temperature that accurately represents that of the contained air. Secure the thermometer in place with a utility clamp placed around the rubber stopper. The syringe and the thermometer should not touch each other, and neither should touch any part of the beaker.

6. Wait several minutes and record the gas volume and solution temperature in your copy of Table 3. Gradually heat the water bath.

7. For every 20°C rise in water temperature, record the gas volume and temperature in Table 3. Continue until the boiling temperature is reached and record the final volume of the air in the cylinder in Table 3.

POST LAB DISCUSSION

In Part I, the total force acting upon the confined air volume when no weight is on the block is equal to the sum of the atmospheric pressure and the weight of the upper support block and piston. The downward force (weight) exerted by an object is equal to the product of its mass and the acceleration due to gravity (9.81 m/s²). To determine the contribution of the block and piston assembly, the weight of this unit must be divided by the surface area in contact with the confined air volume. Since the internal diameter of the cylinder has been measured, the area in contact with the piston may then be derived using the formula $A = \pi r^2$.

$$\text{System pressure acting upon gas in cylinder (no weight)} = \text{Atmospheric pressure} + \frac{\text{Mass of piston-block assembly} \times 9.81 \text{ m/s}^2}{\text{Effective piston area} \times \text{m}^2/10^4 \text{ cm}^2} \times \frac{10^{-3} \text{ kPa}}{\text{Pa}}$$

Once the force exerted by each weight (mass × acceleration due to gravity) is determined, this value must be divided by the surface area in contact with the confined air volume to obtain the weight's effective system pressure. The sum of the appropriate brick pressures is then added to the total "no weight" pressure to obtain the total pressure acting upon the system.

To properly illustrate the relationship between temperature and volume, the Celsius temperatures (t) in Part II must be converted into kelvin temperatures.

$$T = t + 273$$

Once the conversion is complete, the temperature may be plotted against volume. The resulting graph may be extrapolated to find the volume occupied by a gas at zero kelvins. It should be remembered that the gas laws describe the behavior of an ideal gas. Among other things, an ideal gas is assumed to consist of molecules that occupy zero volume, and this will be reflected in the temperature-volume plot.

DATA AND OBSERVATIONS

Part I   Boyle's Law

Barometric pressure (kPa)

Internal diameter of cylinder (cm)

Internal radius of cylinder (diameter/2)

Area of cylinder/piston interface (cm²)

Mass of piston-block assembly (kg)

Weight of piston-block assembly (kg·m/s²)

Pressure exerted by piston-block assembly (kPa)

Sum of barometric and piston-block pressure (kPa)

Table 1

WEIGHT	MASS (kg)	WEIGHT (kg·m/s²)	PRESSURE (kPa)
A			
B			
C			
D			
E			

Table 2

NUMBER OF WEIGHTS	VOLUME OF CONFINED AIR (cm³)	TOTAL PRESSURE (kPa)	k = PV
0			
1			
2			
3			
4			
5			

Part II Charles's Law

Table 3

TEMPERATURE (°C)	VOLUME OF CONFINED AIR (cm³)	TEMPERATURE (K)

COMPLETE IN YOUR NOTEBOOK

QUESTIONS

1. On graph paper provided by your teacher, plot the system pressure against the volume of contained gas (from Table 2).

2. What type of relationship does this graph illustrate? Explain.

3. On another sheet of graph paper provided by your teacher, plot the kelvin temperature against the volume of confined gas (from Table 3).

4. What type of relationship does this graph illustrate? Explain.

5. Extrapolate the graph to find the volume at zero kelvins.

6. Why must the zero kelvin value be obtained by extrapolation instead of direct observation?

FOLLOW-UP QUESTIONS

1. If a helium-filled balloon is released at the Earth's surface, what is its eventual fate? Why?

2. Aerosol spray cans should never be thrown into fires or disposed of in incinerators. Explain.

CONCLUSION

State the results of Objectives 1 and 2.

Measuring and Reporting the Molar Volume of a Gas

A variety of gases are commercially prepared by the chemical process industries. For instance, oxygen and hydrogen gases are produced as a result of the electrolysis of water. One use of these gases is as a rocket fuel for the space shuttle. Another gas, chlorine, is manufactured from an aqueous solution of common salt (sodium chloride). Its derivatives are used for water sterilization, and as bleaching agents in pulp and paper and household laundry detergents. Thus, the manufacture, collection and measurement of gases are important and deserve special consideration.

Chemists are concerned not only with the identities of the chemicals in a reaction, but also with the relative amounts of these chemicals. The chemists need to be able to count the number of molecules that are both reacting and being produced. When solids and liquids are measured, it is usually convenient to determine their masses and calculate their respective moles of molecules. While the mass of a gas cannot easily be measured, the volume occupied by a gas is a convenient measurement. This volume is affected by the temperature, pressure and number of molecules of the gas. As the moles of molecules of gas increase, the volume increases; as the temperature increases, the volume increases; as the pressure increases, the volume decreases.

The volume of a gas occupied by one mole of a substance at a given temperature and pressure is called its *molar volume*. Furthermore, Avogadro's hypothesis implies that, regardless of the type of gas, the molar volumes of gases are the same if their temperatures and pressures are the same. Consequently, it is important to remember that reporting the molar volume of a gas is meaningless unless its temperature and pressure are also included.

In this laboratory exercise, you will determine the molar volume of hydrogen gas. You will react a known mass of magnesium metal with a nonlimiting supply of hydrochloric acid and collect the generated hydrogen gas over water in a gas-collection tube. The evolved gas will rise to the top of the water-filled tube, displacing an equal volume of water. The chemical reaction will be:

$$Mg(s) + 2HCl(aq) \rightarrow MgCl_2(aq) + H_2(g)$$

While the hydrogen gas is forming, a small amount of water vapor also forms above the water in the tube. However, for simplicity's sake, we will treat the amount of water vapor formed as negligible.

OBJECTIVES

1. to collect over water a volume of hydrogen gas produced by the reaction between magnesium and hydrochloric acid

2. to calculate the number of moles of hydrogen gas produced

3. to measure the volume of hydrogen gas produced at room temperature and pressure

4. to calculate and report the volume occupied by one mole of hydrogen gas at room temperature and pressure

MATERIALS

Apparatus

barometer (for class)
thermometer (for class)
ring stand
utility clamp
gas-collection tube
beaker (400 mL)
graduated cylinder
   (10 mL)
analytical balance
   (optional)
safety goggles
plastic gloves

full face shield
lab apron
large graduated
   cylinder, battery jar,
   or large plastic
   bucket
ruler with millimetre
   scale
1-hole rubber stopper
   (to fit gas-collection
   tube)

Reagents

magnesium ribbon
copper wire
6M HCl

PROCEDURE

1. Put on your lab apron, safety goggles, full face shield, and plastic gloves.

2. Record the barometric pressure and the room temperature.

3. Your teacher will supply you with the mass of 1.00 m of magnesium ribbon. Record the value in your notebook.

4. Obtain a piece of magnesium ribbon approximately 5 cm long. Measure the length of the ribbon to the nearest 0.1 cm. Record this value in your notebook. NOTE: If an analytic balance is available, measure the mass of the ribbon directly, to the nearest 0.1 mg, and record the mass in your notebook.

5. Obtain a piece of fine copper wire approximately 15 cm in length. Roll the magnesium ribbon into a small ball and encase it in a cage of copper wire. Be sure to leave several centimetres of the copper wire extended from the cage. This "handle" will allow the ball of magnesium to be anchored at the stoppered end of a gas-collection tube. (See Figure 7B-1.)

Figure 7B-1

6. Assemble a ring stand and utility clamp apparatus that will support the gas-collection tube. (See Figure 7B-2.)

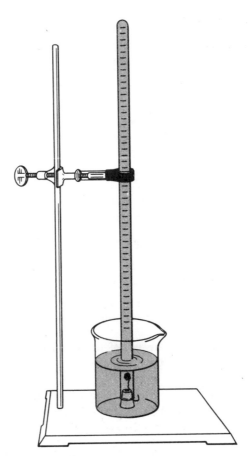

CAUTION: *Hydrochloric acid is corrosive to skin, eyes, and clothing. When handling hydrochloric acid, wear safety goggles, full face shield, lab apron, and gloves. Wash spills and splashes off your skin and clothing immediately using plenty of water. Call your teacher.*

7. Add approximately 300 mL of room-temperature tap water to a 400 mL beaker. If room-temperature water is not available, it may be prepared by mixing volumes of hot and cold tap water.

8. Carefully pour about 10 mL of 6M HCl into the collection tube.

9. Incline the tube slightly and continue filling with tap water from the 400 mL beaker. While pouring the tap water, try to rinse down any acid that may have remained on the tube sides. Avoid agitating the bottom acid layer.

10. While holding the copper handle, insert the encased magnesium about 4 cm into the tube. Hook the handle over the edge of the tube and secure the wire by inserting a 1-hole rubber stopper into the tube end. (See Figure 7B-1.) The tube should be filled to capacity, so that the stopper displaces several millilitres of tap water.

11. Cover the stopper hole with your finger. Invert the tube and submerge the stoppered end in the 400 mL beaker containing the remaining tap water. Secure the apparatus with a utility clamp. Position the tube so that the stoppered mouth is just above the bottom of the beaker. (See Figure 7B-2.) Since the acid is more dense than the water, it will diffuse through the tube and eventually react with the magnesium.

12. Once the reaction has stopped, wait about five minutes for the solution to cool to room temperature. Gently tap the tube with your finger to remove bubbles clinging to the tube sides.

13. With your gloves on, cover the stopper hole with your finger and transfer the tube into a large container filled with water. Raise or lower the tube until the level of liquid inside the tube is equal to the level outside the tube as in Figure 7B-3. Record the volume to the nearest 0.1 mL in your notebook.

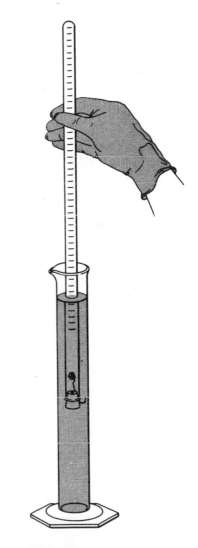

Figure 7B-3 *When the water level in the gas-collection tube is the same as that in the cylinder, the pressure of the gas in the tube is equal to the pressure of the atmosphere.*

14. Discard the tube contents and rinse all apparatus with tap water.

15. Before you leave the laboratory, wash your hands thoroughly with soap and water; use a fingernail brush to clean under your fingernails.

REAGENT DISPOSAL

Place the copper wire in the designated container for reuse. Pour the contents of the gas-collection tube down the drain.

POST LAB DISCUSSION

The balanced equation for the single displacement reaction carried out in this laboratory exercise is:

$$Mg(s) + 2HCl(aq) \rightarrow H_2(g) + MgCl_2(aq)$$

Since the coefficients of magnesium and hydrogen are the same, the reaction involves an equal number of moles of each substance. To obtain the number of moles of magnesium, and the number of moles of hydrogen, use the mass of magnesium ribbon that reacted and the molar mass of magnesium.

The above number of moles of hydrogen occupy a certain volume depending on the temperature and pressure (you have measured the volume at room temperature and pressure). Your last task is to determine the molar volume of hydrogen gas, that is, the volume that one mole of hydrogen would occupy at your conditions of temperature and pressure. The calculation involves a simple mole ratio. To find the new volume:

$$V_{new} = V_{old} \times \frac{moles\ (new)}{moles\ (old)}$$

Example: If at a certain temperature and pressure 0.00174 mol of H_2 occupy 40.0 mL, then the molar volume would be:

$$V_{new} = 0.0400\ L \times \frac{1.00\ mol}{0.00174\ mol} = 23.0\ L$$

DATA AND OBSERVATIONS

Barometric pressure (Step 2), kPa

Room temperature (Step 2), K

Mass of 1.00 m of Mg ribbon (Step 3), g

Length of Mg ribbon used (Step 4), m

Volume of collected gas (Step 13), mL

QUESTIONS AND CALCULATIONS

(Refer to Post Lab Discussion as necessary.)

1. Calculate the mass of Mg used. (If mass is obtained directly by using an analytical balance, a calculation is not needed.)

2. Calculate the number of moles of
   a. Mg used;
   b. H_2 produced.

3. Calculate the molar volume of H_2.

4. How would the volume of hydrogen gas produced differ if 10 cm of magnesium ribbon had been used?

5. Would changing the molarity of the hydrochloric acid affect the final results? Explain.

6. a. Compare the molar volume you obtained to that of another lab group in your class.
   b. How should these molar volumes compare?

FOLLOW-UP QUESTIONS

1. In this experiment hydrogen gas was collected over water in a tube. Find out why certain gases such as $HCl(g)$ and $NH_3(g)$ should not be collected over water.

2. Oxygen gas has a molecular mass that is approximately 16 times that of hydrogen gas. Based on your experimental results and Avogadro's hypothesis, predict the molar volume of oxygen gas at your experimental conditions of temperature and pressure.

CONCLUSION

State the results of Objective 4.

The Standard Molar Volume of a Gas

Gases are very important in industry, and a knowledge of molar volumes is necessary for calculations involving gases. Of the top ten chemicals produced annually in North America, five are gases (nitrogen, ammonia, oxygen, ethylene, and chlorine). It has been noted that the molar volume being calculated in this experiment is almost equal to the volume of three standard-sized basketballs.

Equal volumes of all gases, measured at the same temperature and pressure, contain equal numbers of particles. This assumption was proposed by Amadeo Avogadro, an Italian chemist, in 1811. Stanislao Cannizzaro, another Italian chemist, came upon Avogadro's hypothesis nearly 50 years after it had been proposed. He saw that this hypothesis pointed a way to finding the molar masses of gaseous elements and compounds. If equal volumes of gases contain equal numbers of particles, then the masses of those gas volumes should be in the same ratio as the masses of their constituent particles.

The volume of gas chosen for comparison was the volume occupied by one mole of a substance. However, the volume occupied by a mole of gas depends on the temperature and pressure of the gas. Therefore a standard temperature and pressure were chosen. Standard temperature and pressure (STP) are 273 K and 101.3 kPa. At STP the volume occupied by one mole of a gas is the *standard molar volume*.

In this laboratory exercise, you will determine the standard molar volume of a gas. You will react a known mass of magnesium metal with a nonlimiting supply of hydrochloric acid and collect the generated hydrogen gas over water in a gas-collection tube. The evolved gas will rise to the top of the water-filled tube, displacing an equal volume of water.

Since the collected hydrogen gas will be saturated with water vapor and at conditions other than standard, adjustments must be made to the observed volume. The total pressure of the gas mixture is equal to the sum of the component pressures of each gas:

$$P_t = P_{H_2} + P_{H_2O}$$

Algebraically, we can rearrange the equation and obtain:

$$P_{H_2} = P_t - P_{H_2O}$$

The gas-collection tube is adjusted so that the internal gas pressure equals the exterior atmospheric pressure, $P_t = P_{atm}$. Then, given the P_{H_2O}, the above equation can be solved for the actual pressure exerted by hydrogen gas.

This pressure value, the observed volume, and the ambient temperature can then be substituted into the combined gas laws to obtain the volume that would be occupied by this gas at STP. The number of moles of hydrogen can be calculated from the amount of magnesium used to generate it. The standard molar volume can then be calculated using the number of moles of hydrogen gas and the volume that would be occupied by the gas at STP.

OBJECTIVES

1. to collect over water a volume of hydrogen gas produced by the reaction between magnesium and hydrochloric acid.

2. to determine the partial pressure of hydrogen gas

3. to convert the observed volume of hydrogen gas to the corresponding volume at STP

4. to calculate the volume occupied by one mole of hydrogen gas at STP

MATERIALS

Apparatus

barometer (for class)
thermometer (for class)
ring stand
utility clamp
gas-collection tube
beaker (400 mL)
graduated cylinder
  (10 mL)
1-hole rubber stopper
  (to fit gas-collection
  tube)

large graduated
  cylinder, battery jar
  or large plastic
  bucket
metric ruler
analytical balance
  (optional)
safety goggles
plastic gloves
full face shield
lab apron

Reagents

magnesium ribbon
copper wire
6M HCl

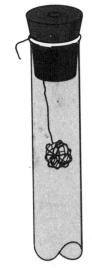

Figure 7C-1

PROCEDURE

1. Put on your laboratory apron, safety goggles, full face shield, and plastic gloves.

2. Record the barometric pressure and the room temperature in your notebook.

3. Your teacher will supply you with the mass of 1.00 m of magnesium ribbon. Record the value in your notebook.

4. Obtain a piece of magnesium ribbon approximately 5 cm long. Measure the length of the ribbon to the nearest 0.1 cm. Record this value in your notebook. (Note: If an analytical balance is available, measure the mass of the ribbon directly, to the nearest 0.1 mg, and record the mass in your notebook.)

5. Obtain a piece of fine copper wire approximately 15 cm in length. Roll the magnesium ribbon into a small ball and encase it in a cage of copper wire. Be sure to leave several centimetres of the copper wire extended from the cage. This "handle" will allow the ball of magnesium to be anchored at the stoppered end of a gas-collection tube. (See Figure 7C-1.)

6. Assemble a ring stand and utility clamp apparatus that will support the gas-collection tube. (See Figure 7C-2.)

7. Add approximately 300 mL of room-temperature tap water to a 400 mL beaker. If room-temperature water is not available, it may be prepared by mixing volumes of hot and cold tap water.

8. Carefully pour about 10 mL of 6M HCl into the collection tube.

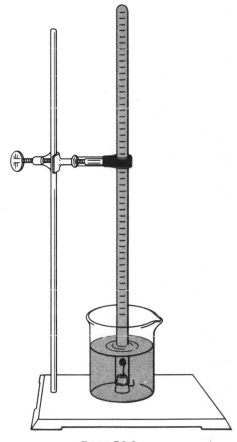

Figure 7C-2

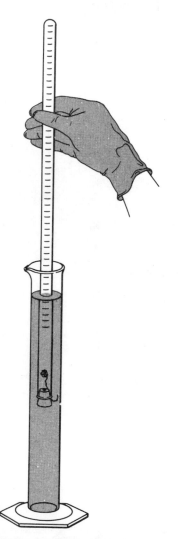

Figure 7C-3 *When the water level in the gas-collection tube is the same as that in the cylinder, the pressure of the gas in the tube is equal to the pressure of the atmosphere.*

9. Incline the tube slightly and continue filling with tap water from the 400 mL beaker. While pouring the tap water, try to rinse down any acid that may have remained on the tube sides. Avoid agitating the bottom acid layer.

10. While holding the copper handle, insert the encased magnesium about 4 cm into the tube. Hook the handle over the edge of the tube and secure the wire by inserting a 1-hole rubber stopper into the tube end. (See Figure 7C-1.) The tube should be filled to capacity, so that the stopper displaces several millilitres of tap water.

11. Cover the stopper hole with your finger. Invert the tube and submerge the stoppered end in the 400 mL beaker containing the remaining tap water. Secure the apparatus with a utility clamp. Position the tube so that the stoppered mouth is just above the bottom of the beaker. (See Figure 7C-2.) Since the acid is more dense than the water, it will diffuse through the tube and eventually react with the magnesium.

12. Once the reaction has stopped, wait about five minutes for the solution to cool to room temperature. Gently tap the tube with your finger to remove bubbles clinging to the tube sides.

13. With your gloves on, cover the stopper hole with your finger and transfer the tube into a large container filled with water. Raise or lower the tube until the level of liquid inside the tube is equal to the level outside the tube as in Figure 7C-3. Record the volume to the nearest 0.1 mL in your notebook.

14. Discard the tube contents and rinse all apparatus with tap water.

15. Before you leave the laboratory, wash your hands thoroughly with soap and water; use a fingernail brush to clean under your fingernails.

REAGENT DISPOSAL

Save any unused magnesium ribbon and copper wire. Rinse all solutions down the sink with copious amounts of water. Place all solid wastes into the designated waste containers.

POST LAB DISCUSSION

The balanced equation for the single displacement reaction carried out in this laboratory exercise is:

$$Mg(s) + 2HCl(aq) \rightarrow H_2(g) + MgCl_2(aq)$$

Since the coefficients of magnesium and hydrogen are the same, the reaction involves an equal number of moles of each substance. To obtain the number of moles of magnesium, and the number of moles of hydrogen, use the mass of magnesium ribbon that reacted and the molar mass of magnesium.

To calculate the partial pressure of hydrogen gas, the total system pressure and the partial pressure of water vapor must be known. In Step 13, the system pressure was equated with atmospheric pressure; therefore the initial barometer reading is equal to the total system pressure. The partial pressure of water vapor at the observed temperature can be obtained from the table of vapor pressures of water in Appendix 6.

Using the combined gas laws, calculate the volume occupied by the H_2 gas at STP (273 K and 101.3 kPa). Use this volume and the number of moles of hydrogen calculated earlier to find the standard molar volume of hydrogen.

DATA AND OBSERVATIONS

Barometric pressure (kPa)

Room temperature (K)

Mass of 1.00 m of Mg ribbon (g)

Length of Mg ribbon used (m)

Volume of collected gas (mL)

CALCULATIONS

(Refer to the Post Lab Discussion as necessary.)

1. What was the mass of Mg used? (If the mass was obtained directly by using an analytical balance, a calculation is not needed.)

2. How many moles of H_2 were produced?

3. What was the corrected pressure of H_2 gas?

4. What was the volume of collected gas at STP?

5. What was the molar volume of H_2?

FOLLOW-UP QUESTIONS

1. How would the volume of hydrogen gas produced differ if 10 cm of magnesium ribbon had been used?

2. Would changing the molarity of the hydrochloric acid affect the final results? Explain.

3. What volume would one mole of any gas occupy at 202.6 kPa and 50°C?

4. How does Avogadro's hypothesis relate to the results obtained in this experiment?

5. Calculate the percent of error in your experimental value for the volume of one mole of gas at STP, assuming that 22.4 L is the correct value.

CONCLUSION

State the results of Objectives 2, 3, and 4.

The Charge on an Electron

A zinc ion is charged 2+, indicating that it has lost two electrons. For a zinc ion to become a neutral zinc atom, the ion must gain two electrons. This process occurs in a zinc electroplating reaction. In this experiment, you will determine the number of zinc atoms involved in an electroplating reaction and the total amount of electrical charge required for that reaction. From those two values, you will be able to determine the amount of electrical charge required for one zinc atom to react. Knowing that two electrons are needed to complete the reaction, dividing by two will give the charge on one electron, the *elementary charge*.

Successful electroplating is not easy. The article must be thoroughly clean and free from grease. Other factors playing a role are the concentration of the solution, the temperature, and a current related to the size of the article. Improper conditions result in a rough, flaky, unattractive coating.

OBJECTIVES

1. to measure electric charge with an ammeter and a clock

2. to determine the number of zinc atoms plated on one electrode and dissolved from the other electrode

3. to determine, experimentally, the charge on one atom of zinc

4. to determine the charge carried by one electron

MATERIALS

Apparatus

ammeter, 0–1 A
  range
centigram balance
3 alligator clip
  wire leads
4 D-cell batteries
2 zinc electrodes
  (3.0 cm × 10 cm
  × 0.1 cm)

steel wool
clock with second
  hand
beaker (250 mL)
2 beakers (large)
lab apron
safety goggles

Reagents

225 mL zinc sulfate
  electroplating solution
denatured ethanol

Negative electrode   Positive electrode

ZnSO₄ solution

Figure 8A-1

PROCEDURE

1. Put on your lab apron and safety goggles.

2. Clean the electrodes thoroughly by rubbing them with steel wool; mark one positive and the other negative.

3. Find the mass of each electrode and enter the values in your notebook.

4. Place the electrodes in a 250 mL beaker on opposite sides, bending the tops over the rim of the beaker (see Figure 8A-1). The electrodes are not to touch one another.

5. Add 225 mL of the zinc sulfate solution to the beaker.

6. Set up, but do not connect, the ammeter and the two electrodes in a series circuit with the power source. Be certain to connect the positive side of the ammeter and the positive electrode to the positive post of the power source (see Figure 8A-2).

Figure 8A-2

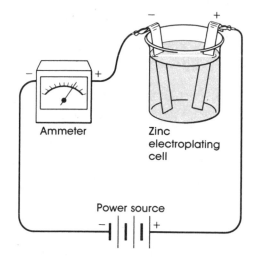

Ammeter   Zinc electroplating cell

Power source

7. Have your teacher check your set-up.

8. When ready to begin making ammeter and time readings, connect the power source and adjust the current until the ammeter reads about 0.70 A. Read the ammeter and record the reading every minute for at least 20 min. The ammeter measures the electrical current flowing through the circuit. Enter both time and ammeter readings in your copy of Table 1 in your notebook.

9. If the current changes by more than 0.05 A, an adjustment will be necessary. Wait until you have completed the timed reading and then adjust the current until the ammeter reading is again about 0.70 A.

10. After the last timed reading, disconnect the power source, ammeter, and electrodes. The zinc sulfate solution is to be saved for future use; return it to a container designated by your teacher.

11. Remove the electrodes very gently, being careful not to touch any part of the electrodes that were in the plating solution. Rinse the electrodes by slowly and gently moving them up and down in a large beaker of warm water. Rinse the electrodes again, in the same manner, in a large beaker of denatured ethanol. Alcohol is used because it dries very quickly. Let the electrodes dry completely.

12. Find the mass of each of the electrodes and enter the values in your notebook.

13. Before you leave the laboratory, wash your hands thoroughly with soap and water; use a fingernail brush to clean under your fingernails.

CAUTION: Denatured ethanol contains toxic additives and is highly flammable. Do not get any in your mouth and do not swallow any. Before using, be sure all flames in the laboratory are extinguished.

889

REAGENT DISPOSAL

Pour any leftover ethanol into the designated waste container. Save the zinc sulfate solution for reuse or pour it down the drain, according to your teacher's instructions. Zinc electrodes and scrap zinc may be saved for reuse or else wrapped solidly in old newspaper and put in the wastebasket.

POST LAB DISCUSSION

In this experiment, the electrical charge moving through the electroplating cell caused zinc atoms to adhere (plate) to the negative electrode and dissolve from the positive electrode. The zinc atoms plated on the negative electrode came from the electroplating solution that contained zinc ions. The zinc atoms that dissolved from the positive electrode became zinc ions in the solution. The number of atoms being plated should equal the number dissolving; consequently, the change in mass of each electrode should be the same. In order to find the actual number of atoms involved at each electrode, you will have to divide the change in mass by the mass of one zinc atom.

The total electric charge required for the reaction is determined in three steps. First, determine the average current in amperes. Next, calculate the total time, in seconds, that the circuit was connected. Finally, multiply the average current by the time in seconds to give the total charge in ampere-seconds.

Knowing the total number of atoms involved and the total charge required to react those atoms, you may now calculate the charge on one zinc atom in this reaction. Divide the total charge by the number of atoms. Complete the calculation for both electrodes. Knowing that two electrons are involved for each zinc atom or ion that reacts, the charge carried by an electron can now be calculated. Divide the charge per atom determined in the previous calculations by two. Again, complete the work for both electrodes. Your answer will be the number of ampere-seconds carried by one electron, or the elementary charge.

DATA AND OBSERVATIONS

Initial mass of negative electrode

Initial mass of positive electrode

Final mass of negative electrode

Final mass of positive electrode

Table 1

TIME (MINUTES)	CURRENT (AMPERES)	TIME (MINUTES)	CURRENT (AMPERES)
1		14	
2		15	
3		16	
4		17	
5		18	
6		19	
7		20	
8		21	
9		22	
10		23	
11		24	
12		25	
13			

CALCULATIONS

1. Find the total charge by doing the following calculations.

   a. Determine the average current in amperes.
   b. Determine the total time in seconds.
   c. Calculate the total charge (current × time).

2. Find the change in mass of each of the two electrodes with the appropriate subtractions.

3. Find the number of zinc atoms reacted at each electrode.

4. Find the charge in ampere-seconds per atom for each of the reactions.

5. Find the charge in ampere-seconds per electron for each of the reactions.

FOLLOW-UP QUESTIONS

1. If one coulomb equals one ampere-second, how do the values you obtained for the charge on an electron compare to the value determined by Millikan?

2. Using the value from your text for the mass of one electron and the values you obtained for the charge on an electron, calculate the charge to mass ratio for an electron. Is it small or large?

3. Using the values obtained in the experiment, calculate the charge carried by one mole of electrons.

CONCLUSION

State the results of Objective 4.

Radioactivity

Unstable nuclei spontaneously emit radiation, and so are said to be radioactive. The "radiation" may consist of particles, rays, or both. The radiation emitted by naturally occurring radioactive isotopes (radioisotopes) includes alpha (α) particles, beta (β) particles, and gamma (γ) rays. Alpha particles are the same as helium nuclei ($^4_2$He). Beta particles are high-speed electrons, emitted from the nucleus. Gamma rays are a form of electromagnetic radiation, more energetic than other forms, such as X rays, ultraviolet light, and visible light. Naturally occurring radioisotopes normally emit gamma radiation only in the process of alpha or beta emission. A number of artificially produced radioisotopes, however, emit gamma radiation alone.

When a radioisotope emits an alpha or beta particle, its atomic number changes, and it becomes an isotope of a different element. Such a process may be referred to as disintegration or *decay*. The emission of gamma radiation by a nucleus lowers its energy and makes it more stable, but does not change its atomic number.

Carbon-14, a naturally occurring radioactive isotope, emits a beta particle (at a velocity approaching that of light) and becomes a stable isotope of nitrogen.

$$^{14}_6C \rightarrow \ ^{14}_7N + \ ^0_{-1}e$$

Carbon-14 is utilized in determining the age of certain archeological objects (radiocarbon dating). Its use is applicable to carbon-containing objects that originated in living organisms within the past 60 000 years.

The radioisotope strontium-90 has long been associated with the hazards of fallout from nuclear explosions in the atmosphere. This radioactive isotope may be incorporated into biological systems and produce cancer. In humans, Sr-90 is incorporated mainly into bones and teeth. Strontium-90 undergoes alpha decay into the more stable krypton-86 as indicated below.

$$^{90}_{38}Sr \rightarrow \ ^{86}_{36}Kr + \ ^4_2He$$

Radioactive emissions can be detected by a device called a Geiger counter. As charged particles strike the instrument's argon-filled Geiger tube, some of the gas atoms are ionized. This creates a short burst of current, which produces an audible "click" or visible meter deflection. In Part I of this experiment, you will utilize a Geiger counter to determine the relative amounts of radioactivity from several natural and synthetic radiation sources.

Radiation given off by a nucleus interacts with its surroundings. The interaction process causes the radiation to slow down, and eventually, stop. Sources of significant radiation, such as nuclear reactors, are usually surrounded by materials that absorb the radiation, thus shielding people from exposure to it. In Part II of this experiment, you will evaluate the effectiveness of various thicknesses of cardboard, aluminum, and lead in absorbing beta radiation.

The behavior of ionizing particles, such as alpha and beta particles, can be observed within a cloud chamber (Part III). A cloud chamber is a container filled with a substance in vapor form. As the ionizing particles pass through the vapor, they leave a visible trail. The vapor in the cloud chamber is supersaturated, which means that there is more vapor present than the chamber would normally hold at a given temperature. As a result, droplets of the vapor will readily condense on anything that can serve as a condensation nucleus (for example, ions, dust particles, and crystals).

When the ionizing particles pass through the vapor, they interact with the atoms of the substance, producing ions. These ions act as condensation nuclei and their paths become visible.

The study of nuclear science has led to means of destroying or prolonging life. On the one hand, investigations of changes occurring in the uranium nucleus led to the development of atomic and hydrogen bombs. On the other, nuclear reactors fuelled with uranium now produce electricity, while chemicals "labeled" with radioactive atoms are used to locate tumors in the body.

OBJECTIVES

1. to operate a Geiger counter and test various objects for radioactive emissions

2. to determine the effectiveness of selected materials in absorbing beta radiation

3. to observe and compare the trajectories of alpha and beta radiation using a cloud chamber

MATERIALS

Apparatus	**Reagents**
Geiger tube	ethanol
Geiger counter	dry ice
ruler	10 cardboard sheets
ring stand	10 aluminum sheets
utility clamp	10 lead sheets
flashlight	radioactive samples
cloud chamber	beta emitter mounted
tongs	for cloud chamber
safety goggles	alpha emitter mounted
lab apron	for cloud chamber
gloves	other radioactive
	samples (as supplied
	by your teacher)

PROCEDURE

Part I   Measuring Radioactive Emissions

1. Put on your lab apron, safety goggles, and gloves.

2. Carefully secure a Geiger tube within a clamp attached to a ring stand, as in Figure 9A-1. DO NOT OVERTIGHTEN THE CLAMP!

3. Assemble the apparatus as shown in Figure 9A-1. The Geiger tube should be approximately 10 cm from the ring stand base.

4. Turn on the Geiger counter and allow it to "warm up" for several minutes. NOTE: Transistorized counters do not require a warm-up period.

5. Measure the radiation in counts per minute (cpm) and record it in your copy of Table 1 as the background count.

6. Place a rock containing a radioactive ore on a sheet of paper on the ring stand base. Record the counts per minute in Table 1.

CAUTION: The Geiger tube is fragile; too tight a clamp will crush it and could send sharp fragments in all directions.

CAUTION: Many radioactive materials can cause harm if not properly handled. Use tongs; do not touch the ore sample.

7. Repeat this measurement with a luminous watch face, lantern mantle, or other radioactive samples supplied by your teacher. Use tongs to handle all samples. Record these results in Table 1.

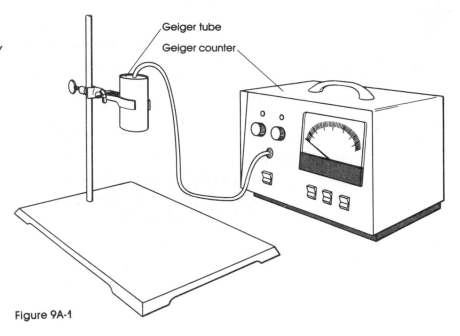

Figure 9A-1

Part II   Absorption of Beta Radiation

1. Using tongs, place a beta emitter on the ring stand base. Adjust the height of the Geiger tube so that the Geiger counter registers maximum meter deflection. Record this value in your copy of Table 2 in your notebook.

2. Place a sheet of cardboard between the sample and Geiger tube. Record the radiation count. Increase the number of cardboard sheets, one at a time, and record each observed radiation value in Table 2. Continue until ten cardboard pieces have been used.

3. Repeat Step 2 using aluminum sheets.

4. Repeat Step 2 using lead sheets.

5. Subtract the background reading obtained in Part I from the data collected in Steps 2-4 and record the results as "Transmitted radiation" in Table 2.

Part III   Trajectories of Alpha and Beta Particles

CAUTION: Dry ice can freeze and burn your fingers quickly. Do not touch dry ice; use tongs.

1. Have the teacher soak the lining of an empty cloud chamber with ethanol.

2. Place the chamber on a block of dry ice and allow the device to cool for several minutes.

3. Shine a bright light into the chamber, as shown in Figure 9A-2. Record your observations for Part III in your notebook.

116   Experiment 9A   Laboratory Experiments

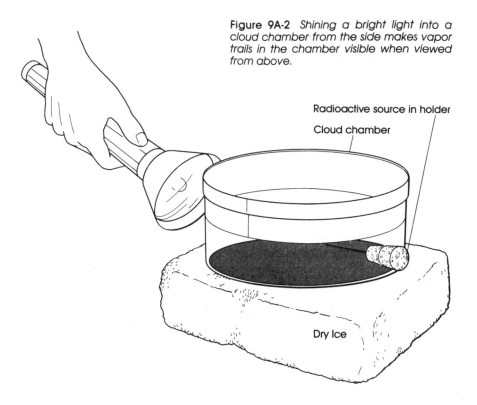

Figure 9A-2 *Shining a bright light into a cloud chamber from the side makes vapor trails in the chamber visible when viewed from above.*

Radioactive source in holder

Cloud chamber

Dry Ice

4. Insert an alpha source upon its holder into the chamber. (See Figure 9A-2.) Shine a bright light into the chamber and record your observations in your notebook.

5. Have the teacher resaturate the cloud chamber lining with ethanol and replace the alpha source with a beta source. Record your observations in your notebook.

6. Before you leave the laboratory, wash your hands thoroughly with soap and water; use a fingernail brush to clean under your fingernails.

REAGENT DISPOSAL

Pour any leftover ethanol into the designated waste container. Allow the dry ice to sublime. Aluminum sheets may be saved for reuse or discarded in wastebasket. Lead sheets should be saved for reuse; do not discard. Follow supplier's instructions for disposal of alpha and beta emitters. As for other radioactive sources: lantern mantles may be saved for reuse or discarded in the wastebasket — or used in a lantern. Watches should be returned to their owners. Ore samples should be saved for reuse.

POST LAB DISCUSSION

Even when operated in the absence of radioactive materials, the Geiger counter registers a consistent "background" count. This count results from the natural level of radiation in the environment. The largest contribution to the natural radiation level comes from cosmic rays. Lesser amounts are produced by traces of radioactive isotopes in the surrounding environment (buildings, rocks, and so on).

Primary cosmic rays are chiefly protons and larger positively charged atomic nuclei that enter Earth's atmosphere from outer space at very high speeds. They interact with components of the atmosphere, creating secondary cosmic rays. It is the secondary cosmic rays and the products of their interactions with the atmosphere that constitute the largest portion of the natural radiation level.

Each of the different forms of radiation demonstrates a specific penetrating capability. Due to their relatively large size and low energy, alpha particles can be stopped by a single sheet of cardboard. High-velocity beta particles can be affected by cardboard, but several sheets of aluminum are needed to absorb them completely. High-energy gamma radiation requires an even greater thickness of lead to absorb it.

When liquid ethanol was introduced into the cloud chamber, its vapor saturated the air space. As the temperature was lowered by direct contact with dry ice, a supersaturated condition was created. Dust, crystals, or ions present sites for ethanol condensation under such conditions. The paths of alpha and beta emissions were detected as the vapor condensed on the ions produced by the particles emanating from the radioactive source.

DATA AND OBSERVATIONS

Part I Measuring Radioactive Emissions

Table 1

SAMPLE	RADIATION LEVEL (cpm)
Background count	
Radioactive ore	
Luminous watch face	COMPLETE IN YOUR NOTEBOOK
Lantern mantle	

Part II Absorption of Beta Radiation

Table 2

SHEETS OF CARDBOARD	RADIATION LEVEL (cpm)	TRANSMITTED RADIATION (cpm)	SHEETS OF ALUMINUM	RADIATION LEVEL (cpm)	TRANSMITTED RADIATION (cpm)
0			0		
1			1		
2			2		
3			3		
4			4		
5	COMPLETE IN YOUR NOTEBOOK		5	COMPLETE IN YOUR NOTEBOOK	
6			6		
7			7		
8			8		
9			9		
10			10		

Table 2, cont'd

SHEETS OF LEAD	RADIATION LEVEL (cpm)	TRANSMITTED RADIATION (cpm)
0		
1		
2		
3		
4		
5		
6		
7		
8		
9		
10		

COMPLETE IN YOUR NOTEBOOK

Part III   Trajectories of Alpha and Beta Particles

Initial observations:

Make a sketch of the cloud chamber for each type of particle, alpha and beta, similar to those shown. Also describe the observed trajectories.

Description of alpha trajectories

Description of beta trajectories

Alpha

Beta

QUESTIONS

1. Explain why the background level of radiation is dependent upon location.

2. Which of the samples in Part I exhibited the highest level of radioactivity? Why?

3. Is it possible to observe a trail in the cloud chamber prior to the introduction of the radioactive source? Explain.

4. Which of the two types of emissions paths was longer? Straighter?

5. Which material acted as the best shield against beta radiation? Give a reason for this observation.

6. Graph each set of "transmitted radiation" results (radiation level minus background count) obtained in Part II of this experiment.

FOLLOW-UP QUESTIONS

1. Explain how background radiation may account for biological species diversity.

2. Compare the way in which gamma radiation and fluorescent emissions are similar.

CONCLUSION

State the results of Objectives 1, 2, and 3.

Emission Spectroscopy

According to the Bohr atomic model, electrons orbit the nucleus within specific energy levels. These levels are defined by unique amounts of energy. Electrons possessing the lowest energy are found in the levels closest to the nucleus. Electrons of higher energy are located in progressively more distant energy levels.

If an electron absorbs sufficient energy to bridge the "gap" between energy levels, the electron may jump to a higher level. Since this change results in a vacant lower orbital, the configuration is unstable. The "excited" electron releases its newly acquired energy and falls back to its initial or ground state. Often, the excited electrons acquire sufficient energy to make several energy level transitions. When these electrons return to their ground state, several distinct energy emissions occur. The energy that electrons absorb is often of a thermal or electrical nature, and the energy that electrons emit when returning to ground state is electromagnetic radiation.

In 1900, Max Planck studied visible emissions from hot glowing solids. He proposed that light was emitted in "packets" of energy called quanta, and that the energy of each packet was proportional to the frequency of the light wave. According to Einstein and Planck, the energy of the packet could be expressed as the product of the frequency (v) of emitted light and Planck's constant (h).

$$E = hv$$

If white light passes through a prism or diffraction grating, its component wavelengths are bent at different angles. This process produces a rainbow of distinct colors known as a continuous spectrum. If, however, the light emitted from hot gases or energized ions is viewed in a similar manner, isolated bands of color are observed. These bands form characteristic patterns, unique to each element. They are known as bright line or emission spectra.

By analyzing the emission spectrum of hydrogen gas, Bohr was able to calculate the energy content of the major electron levels. Although the electron structure as suggested by his planetary atomic model has been modified according to modern quantum theory, his description and analysis of spectral emission lines are still valid.

In addition to the fundamental role spectroscopy played in the development of today's atomic model, this technique can also be used in the identification of elements. Since the atoms of each element contain unique arrangements of electrons, emission lines can be used as "spectral fingerprints." Even without a spectroscope, this type of identification is possible since the major spectral lines will alter the color of the flame.

RCMP forensic scientists use flame emission spectroscopy to determine the chemical composition of paint and glass chips found at the scene of a hit-and-run accident or other crime. In the following experiment, you will use a spectroscope to examine several continuous and bright line spectra (Parts I and II). You will then place solutions of metallic salts into a laboratory burner flame (Part III). The characteristic spectra associated with each metallic ion will be recorded and used to determine the identity of components in an unknown salt mixture.

OBJECTIVES

1. to understand the relationship between atomic structure and emission spectroscopy

2. to use a spectroscope and observe several sources of continuous and bright line spectra

3. to observe the characteristic emission lines associated with electrical and thermal excitation

4. to identify the components of an unknown mixture of salts by a flame emission test

MATERIALS

Apparatus

student spectroscope
ring stand with
  utility clamp
low-wattage
  incandescent light
  source
fluorescent light
  source
laboratory burner
safety goggles
lab apron

high-voltage power
  supply (to be used
  by teacher only)
helium, hydrogen,
  mercury, and neon
  spectrum tubes (to
  be used by
  teacher only)
6 nichrome or
  platinum wire loops

Reagents

barium chloride
calcium chloride
lithium chloride
sodium chloride
strontium chloride
mixture of unknown
  salts
distilled water

PROCEDURE

Part I   Introduction to the Student Spectroscope

1. Put on your lab apron and safety goggles.

2. Obtain a student spectroscope and examine the spectrum emitted by a low-wattage incandescent light source. Record your observations in your notebook, in a drawing similar to Figure 10A-3.

3. Now aim the spectroscope at a fluorescent light source. Compare this spectrum with the spectrum observed in Step 1. Record your observations in your notebook in a drawing similar to Figure 10A-4. In addition, provide a written summary of your observations.

Part II   Spectrum Analysis of Gases

1. Since the high voltages required for this part of the experiment may present an electrical hazard, you should not touch the spectrum tube or high-voltage assembly. Your teacher will load the spectrum tube and assemble the high-voltage power supply as shown in Figure 10A-1.

2. Once the power supply is turned on, aim the spectroscope at the glowing tube. Record the position of the bright emission lines in your copy of Table 1.

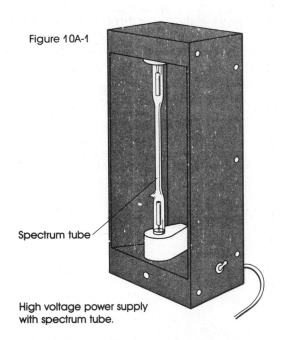
Figure 10A-1

Spectrum tube

High voltage power supply
with spectrum tube.

3. Once the entire class has recorded this spectrum for a given gas, your teacher will turn off the power supply and change the spectrum tubes. Repeat Step 2 for each of the gas samples and record your observations in Table 1.

Part III   Spectrum Analysis of Salts

CAUTION: Do not overtighten the utility clamp.

CAUTION: Do not bring the spectroscope too close to the flame. It may melt or catch fire.

1. Secure the spectroscope within a utility clamp and attach this assembly to a ring stand.

2. Ignite a laboratory burner. Adjust the burner so that the flame is almost invisible.

3. Position the spectroscope so that it is at the same level as the nonluminous portion of the flame. The end of the spectroscope should be about 5 cm from the burner flame as shown in Figure 10A-2.

Figure 10A-2

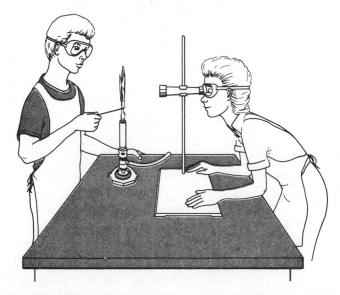

4. Moisten a test wire loop with distilled water. Insert the loop into its appropriate salt, and withdraw several crystals.

5. While one lab partner is viewing the flame through the spectroscope, the other partner should place the salt-coated loop into the nonluminous portion of the burner flame. Record the identity of the salt and its observed spectrum in your copy of Table 2. Replace the loop into its appropriate salt.

6. Repeat Steps 4 and 5, using other salts of known identity. To prevent contamination of the samples, be sure to replace each loop into its appropriate salt as soon as the test is completed. If a loop does become contaminated, insert the loop into the burner flame until all the salt has been burned off.

7. Obtain a mixture of salts of unknown identity from your teacher. Using this sample, repeat Steps 4 and 5. Record the probable identity of the unknown salts in Table 2.

8. Before you leave the laboratory, wash your hands thoroughly with soap and water; use a fingernail brush to clean under your fingernails.

CAUTION: These salts, especially barium chloride, are poisonous. Keep your hands away from your face until after you have washed thoroughly and have left the laboratory.

REAGENT DISPOSAL

Dispose of the barium chloride and any mixtures containing it according to your teacher's instructions.

All other salts and mixtures may be dissolved in water and poured down the drain, or wrapped solidly in old newspaper and put in the wastebasket.

POST LAB DISCUSSION

When electrical energy flows through the tungsten filament of an incandescent light bulb, the filament will emit light energy. Since this visible emission contains many wavelengths too closely spaced to be distinguishable, the emission will appear as a continuous spectrum. Although the spectra from the incandescent and fluorescent light sources appear continuous, they will contain unique amounts of specific colors.

When gas particles absorb electrical energy, their electrons jump to and fall back from specific energy levels. The characteristic colors and brightness associated with these transitions are dependent upon the specific identity of the gas and its unique electron arrangement. Gases such as mercury and neon emit a light bright enough for commercial illumination.

When ionic solids are vaporized within a flame, the metallic ions may absorb sufficient energy to emit a bright line spectra. Often these spectra contain a yellow-orange line associated with the presence of a sodium contaminant. This line must be subtracted from the observed spectrum to give a reliable emission fingerprint for the uncontaminated substance.

DATA AND OBSERVATIONS

Part I   Introduction to the Student Spectroscope

Figure 10A-3   *Incandescent spectrum (Part I, Step 2)*

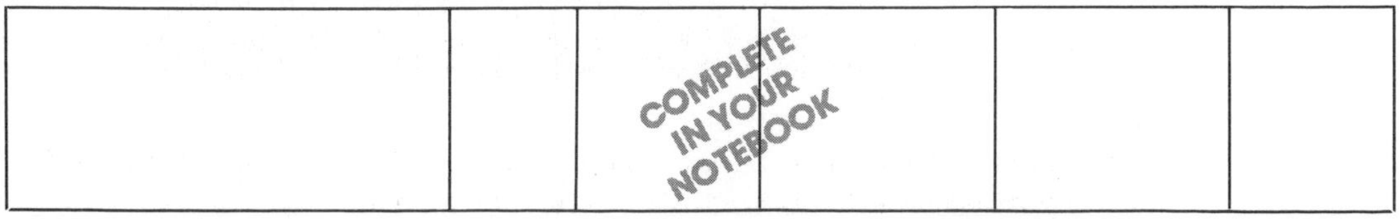

		COMPLETE IN YOUR NOTEBOOK		

Part II   Spectrum Analysis of Gases

Table 1

	RED	ORANGE	YELLOW	GREEN	BLUE	VIOLET
spectrum tube						
helium						
hydrogen						
mercury						
neon						

Part III   Spectrum Analysis of Salts

Table 2

METAL ION	RED	ORANGE	YELLOW	GREEN	BLUE	VIOLET
barium						
calcium						
lithium						
sodium						
strontium						
unknown						

QUESTIONS

1. Compare the spectra produced by incandescent and fluorescent sources.

2. Did a specific bright line occur in all or most of the flame tests? If so, what was the identity of the substance causing this emission?

3. How might the difference in the brightness of spectral lines be explained?

4. What was the identity of the components of the unknown salt mixture?

FOLLOW-UP QUESTIONS

1. How can the frequency of emitted light be used to determine the energy difference between electron levels?

2. Prior to its discovery on Earth, helium's existence was first confirmed in the sun. Explain how this was possible.

CONCLUSION

State the results of Objective 4.

The Periodic Table

In 1869, aware of the need to organize elements in a meaningful way, Dmitri Mendeleev developed a classification scheme based upon increasing molar mass. Elements that demonstrated similar patterns of chemical behavior were placed into one of eight groups. Members of these groups were displayed in vertical columns of his periodic table. Even though his chart was incomplete, Mendeleev was able to predict the properties of elements yet to be discovered. Over the next two years, Mendeleev published modified versions of his original periodic table.

Today's periodic table accommodates at least 49 additional elements. Although the scheme is based upon increasing atomic number, the arrangement of elements within the chart is similar in organization to the table published by Mendeleev in 1871. Trends in the chemical and physical properties of elements may be seen as a periodic function of electron configuration.

In the three parts of this exercise, you will examine several properties of elements and observe how these properties may be interpreted in respect to periodic law. Your knowledge of the modern periodic table and facts about the elements will then allow you to construct the periodic table published by Mendeleev in 1871.

OBJECTIVES

1. to understand the relationship between electron configuration and the location of an element within the periodic table

2. to examine and graph periodic trends in atomic radii and the first ionization energies

3. to construct the periodic table published by Mendeleev in 1871 according to a list of clues and your knowledge of the modern periodic table

MATERIALS

Apparatus

pencil
ruler
textbook

PROCEDURE

Part I   Electron Configuration and the Periodic Table

1. In your notebook, construct a chart similar to Figure 11A-1. Locate the upper section of the periodic table illustrated in the figure. For each of the elements listed, write its electron configuration within the appropriate box.

Part II Atomic Number, Atomic Radius, Ionization Energy, and the Periodic Table

1. On graph paper, construct a grid similar to Figure 11A-2. Using the data listed in Table 1, plot the atomic radius of each element against increasing atomic number. The atomic radii shown here are given in nanometres.

$$1 \text{ nm} = 1 \times 10^{-9} \text{ m}$$

2. Construct a second grid, similar to Figure 11A-3, on another sheet of graph paper. Plot the first ionization energy of each element against increasing atomic number on this grid.

Table 1

ELEMENT	ATOMIC NUMBER	ATOMIC RADIUS (nm)	FIRST IONIZATION ENERGY (kJ/mol)
hydrogen	1	0.037	1312
helium	2	0.05	2372
lithium	3	0.152	519
beryllium	4	0.111	900
boron	5	0.088	799
carbon	6	0.077	1088
nitrogen	7	0.070	1406
oxygen	8	0.066	1314
fluorine	9	0.064	1682
neon	10	0.070	2080
sodium	11	0.186	498
magnesium	12	0.160	736
aluminum	13	0.143	577
silicon	14	0.117	787
phosphorus	15	0.110	1063
sulfur	16	0.104	1000
chlorine	17	0.099	1255
argon	18	0.094	1519
potassium	19	0.231	418
calcium	20	0.197	590

Part III Other Characteristics of Elements and the Periodic Table

1. The positions of the 67 elements found on Mendeleev's 1871 version of the periodic table are coded below for Figure 11A-4. The clues are taken from various places throughout your text (*Heath Chemistry*). You will be expected to use your text as a reference in using the clues given to identify the coded elements. Its index will be very useful in your search. Identify each element and write the name in the correct position in your copy of Figure 11A-4 in your notebook.

1A has a single electron in the $1s$ sublevel.
1B derived its name from the Latin word for stone *lithos*.
1C can be collected as a silver liquid in the electrolysis of table salt.
1D has a first ionization energy of 418 kJ/mol.
1E has a density of 8.96 g/cm³.
1F is the first alkali metal with a completed $3d$ sublevel.

1G was originally identified by its Latin name, *argentum*.

1H is an alkali metal located in period 6 of the modern periodic table.

1I derived its name from the Latin word for dawn, *aurora*.

2A was used as a target substance in the experiments by Irène Joliot-Curie.

2B is an alkaline earth metal located in period 3.

2C is the metallic component of the substance limestone.

2D is a transition metal with 30 protons.

2E is represented by the symbol Sr.

2F possesses a nuclear charge of +48.

2G is an alkaline earth metal found in period 6 of the modern periodic table.

2H is a liquid metal, originally called *hydrargyrum*.

3A has a single electron in the $2p$ sublevel.

3B is a lightweight metal with a molar mass of 26.98 g.

3C is a transition metal with an atomic number of 39.

3D is a metal represented by the symbol In.

3E is the first member of the rare earth metals.

3F is found in group 13 and period 6 of the modern periodic table.

4A is the element whose common isotopic form is the basis of the atomic mass unit.

4B has a second ionization energy of 1577 kJ/mol.

4C is located between scandium and vanadium on the modern periodic table.

4D is represented by the symbol Zr.

4E derives its symbol from the Latin word *stannum*.

4F is a very dense metal with an atomic mass of 207.2 u.

4G is the second member of the actinide series.

5A is the most abundant element in the atmosphere.

5B has 3 electrons in the $3p$ sublevel.

5C is a byproduct of fossil-fuel oxidation and represented by the symbol V.

5D is a period 4 nonmetal known since 1650.

5E is a member of both group 5 and period 5 of the modern periodic table.

5F was originally called *stibium*.

5G is located in period 6 of the modern periodic table, beneath niobium.

5H is a metal with atomic number 83.

6A is the most abundant element in Earth's crust.

6B is a member of group 16, known during the time of the Roman empire.

6C is the first member of group 6 on the modern periodic table.

6D is represented by the symbol Se.

6E has 42 protons within its nucleus.

6F is a halogen whose crystals sublime.

6G was originally called wolfram.

6H is the fourth member of the actinide series.

7A has an atomic radius of 0.099 nm.

7B is represented by the symbol Mn.

7C forms a diatomic gas with a molar mass of 160 u.

7D has a molar mass of 127.6 g.

8A is a group 8 metal known during the time of the Roman empire.

8B is an element named after the German word for Satan.

8C has an average atomic mass of 59 u.

8D is located between iron and osmium on the modern periodic table.

8E has a nuclear charge of +45.

8F has an atomic mass of 106.4 u.

8G has 114 neutrons within its nucleus.

8H is named after the Latin word for rainbow, *iris*.

8I is an inert metal often used in electrodes and has an atomic number of 78.

DATA AND OBSERVATIONS

Part I Electron Configuration and the Periodic Table

Figure 11A-1 *Representative elements of periods 1-4*

Group 1									Group 18
1 H									2 He
	Group 2			Group 13	Group 14	Group 15	Group 16	Group 17	
3 Li	4 Be			5 B	6 C	7 N	8 O	9 F	10 Ne
11 Na	12 Mg	TRANSITION ELEMENTS		13 Al	14 Si	15 P	16 S	17 Cl	18 Ar
19 K	20 Ca			31 Ga	32 Ge	33 As	34 Se	35 Br	36 Kr

Representative Elements of Periods 1–4

Part II Atomic Number, Atomic Radius, Ionization Energy, and the Periodic Table

Figure 11A-2 *Atomic radius graph*

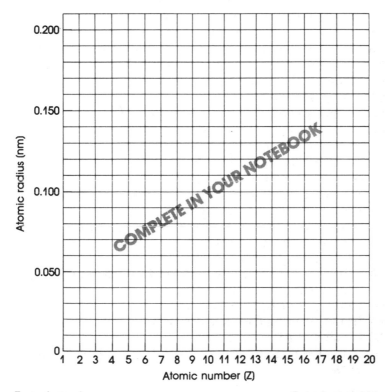

COMPLETE IN YOUR NOTEBOOK

Figure 11A-3 *Ionization energy graph*

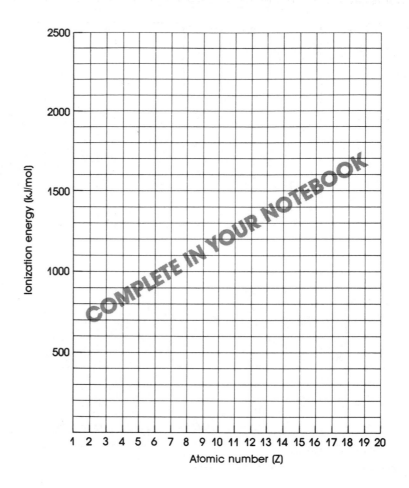

Figure 11A-4

Mendeleev's Periodic Table of Elements (1871)

Columns (or groups)

COMPLETE IN YOUR NOTEBOOK

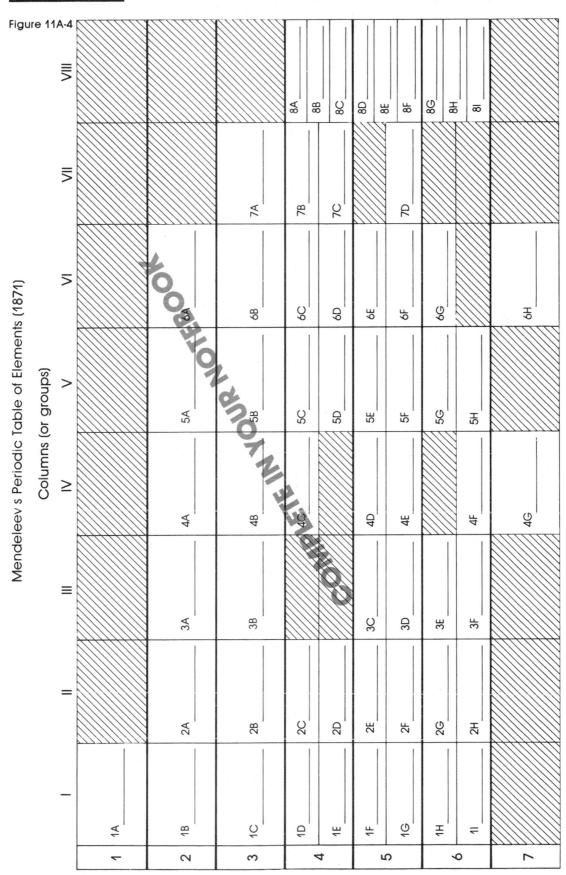

Rows (or periods)

QUESTIONS

1. Examine the placement of electron configurations in Figure 11A-1. What relationship can be seen in an element's placement within a group and its electron configuration?

2. Examine the graph of atomic radius plotted against increasing atomic number (Figure 11A-2). Can a periodic tendency be observed? If so, describe the indicated trend.

3. Which group appears to have members of the largest atomic radii for a given period? Which group has the smallest radii?

4. Examine the graph form of ionization energy plotted against increasing atomic number (Figure 11A-3). Can a periodic tendency be observed? If so, describe the indicated trend.

FOLLOW-UP QUESTIONS

1. No members of group 18 of the modern periodic table can be found on Mendeleev's classification chart. Suggest a reason for their absence.

2. What factor may account for the observed trend in atomic radii as one proceeds across the period?

CONCLUSION

State the results of Objectives 1 and 2.

Differences Between Ionic and Covalent Compounds

A compound is defined as the chemical combination of two or more elements. A chemical bond is the "glue" that holds atoms of different elements together. Bonds can be classified into two general types: *ionic* and *covalent*. Ionic bonds generally occur between a metallic atom and a nonmetallic atom. The ionic bond involves the transfer of electrons from the metallic atom to the nonmetallic atom, resulting in a charge difference. The positively charged metal ion is then attracted to the negatively charged nonmetal ion. Covalent bonding generally occurs between atoms that are nonmetallic and it involves the sharing of electrons.

Properties such as melting point, boiling point, solubility, electrical conductivity, and odor are some of the properties that can help you distinguish ionic from covalent compounds. In this experiment, you will observe several properties of some ionic and covalent compounds and attempt to recognize some patterns among the properties. It is important to understand that the patterns are generalizations that do not necessarily apply to all ionic and covalent compounds.

Whatever holds us together—skin and muscle and bones—must be strong enough to withstand the daily stresses and strains the body normally encounters. At the heart of this "stickiness" of matter are electrical forces of attraction. The atoms are able to reorganize their electrons in one way to form ionic compounds and in another to form covalent compounds.

OBJECTIVES

1. to identify compounds as either primarily ionic or primarily covalent from the name and formula

2. to observe and record the solubility, melting time, and electrical conductivity of several ionic and covalent compounds

3. to recognize patterns among some of the properties that will help to distinguish ionic compounds from covalent compounds

MATERIALS

Apparatus

centigram balance
glazed paper
6 test tubes
  (18 mm × 150 mm)
test-tube rack
6 stoppers, for test
  tubes
hot plate
beaker (250 mL)
graduated cylinder
safety goggles
lab apron

Reagents

benzoic acid, C_6H_5COOH
magnesium chloride, $MgCl_2$
paradichlorobenzene, $C_6H_4Cl_2$
potassium iodide, KI
sodium nitrate, $NaNO_3$
sucrose, $C_{12}H_{22}O_{11}$
methanol

CAUTION: *Magnesium chloride is poisonous; do not get any in your mouth.*

CAUTION: *Paradichlorobenzene is poisonous and flammable. In high concentrations its vapors can irritate the eyes.*

PROCEDURE

1. Put on your lab apron and safety goggles.

2. Obtain six pieces of glazed paper and label each piece with the name of one of the six solids that you will test. (Methanol is a liquid.) Using the balance, put two grams of each substance on the appropriate piece of paper and divide the two grams into two equal piles.

3. Obtain six test tubes, six stoppers, and a test-tube rack. Label the test tubes 1-6 to correspond to the numbers in Tables 1 and 2.

4. Begin heating approximately 150 mL of water in a 250 mL beaker on a hot plate. This will be used to determine the solubility of each substance (Step 6) in hot water.

5. Place 5 mL of water at room temperature in each of the test tubes. Then put 1 g of each of the solids into the appropriate test tube. Stopper the tubes and shake them to dissolve the solids as much as possible. Shake for one to two minutes. If the substance dissolves, it is soluble; if not, it is insoluble. Record the results in your copy of Table 1 in your notebook.

6. Put any test tubes containing substances that did not dissolve in room-temperature water into the beaker of hot water for two or three minutes. Again, shake the contents. Record the solubilities in Table 1.

7. Rinse the test tubes and stoppers. (See Reagent Disposal, below.)

8. Place 5 mL of methanol in each of the test tubes. Then put 1 g of each of the solids into the appropriate test tube. Stopper the test tubes and shake them for one or two minutes. Record the solubilities in Table 1.

9. Rinse the test tubes and stoppers.

10. Clean up all of the materials and wash your hands thoroughly with soap and water; use a fingernail brush to clean under your fingernails. The remainder of the lab will be done as a demonstration by your teacher.

11. Watch as your teacher demonstrates the melting time of the solids. Melting time is the amount of time necessary to melt a certain quantity of a solid. This does not give an accurate value for the melting point, but will enable you to see differences among the compounds. Record the melting times in Table 1.

12. Again, watch as your teacher demonstrates the electrical conductivity of solutions of the solids. Electrical conductivity can be tested by using a conductivity tester. Electrodes are placed into a solution and the tester is turned on. If the solution conducts electricity, the light bulb will light. If the solution does not conduct electricity, the light will not go on. If the light bulb is dim, the solution is considered to be a poor conductor. Record the results in Table 1.

CAUTION: Methanol is very poisonous. Do not get it in your mouth or eyes; do not swallow any.

CAUTION: Methanol is flammable. Before using it, be sure all burners and other flames in the laboratory are extinguished.

REAGENT DISPOSAL

Sodium nitrate, or any mixtures or solutions containing it, can be dissolved in water and poured down the drain. Any test tubes containing methanol should be placed in the designated waste container.

All other solids may be wrapped in old newspaper and put in the wastebasket.

Follow your teacher's instructions for disposing of paradichlorobenzene and any mixtures or solutions containing it.

POST LAB DISCUSSION

You have just recorded several properties of some ionic and covalent compounds. Up until now, you have not identified the substances as ionic or covalent. Ionic compounds are generally made up of metallic and nonmetallic elements, with the metal giving up electrons to the nonmetals. Covalent compounds are generally made up of atoms that are nonmetallic, with the atoms sharing electrons. In addition, the differences in electronegativity between the atoms involved can help to determine the ionic character of the bonds. Sodium chloride is an ionic compound because sodium is a metal that gives up an electron to chlorine, a nonmetal. The electronegativities of sodium and chlorine, respectively, are 0.96 and 3.00, having a difference of 2.04. Carbon dioxide is a covalent compound, because the elements carbon and oxygen share electrons in bonding. The electronegativities of carbon and oxygen are 2.56 and 3.37, having a much smaller difference of 0.81.

You will need to refer to your textbook or another reference to help you in determining whether the compounds used in this experiment are ionic or covalent. It is important to emphasize that some of the results of the experiment may not reflect particular patterns.

DATA AND OBSERVATIONS

Table 1

SUBSTANCE	SOLUBILITY IN			MELTING TIME	ELECTRICAL CONDUCTIVITY OF SOLUTION
	WATER AT ROOM TEMP.	HOT WATER	METH-ANOL		
1					
2					
3					
4					
5					
6					

COMPLETE IN YOUR NOTEBOOK

QUESTIONS

1. Determine whether each of the compounds is ionic or covalent. Refer to your textbook or another reference to check your prediction. Summarize the answers in your copy of Table 2 in your notebook.

Table 2

NAME OF SUBSTANCE	FORMULA	IONIC OR COVALENT
1		
2		
3		
4		
5		
6		

COMPLETE IN YOUR NOTEBOOK

2. Look at the results carefully. Are there any patterns that you have observed in the property of solubility? Explain.

3. Similarly, look at the other properties. What can you say about each of the other properties—melting time and electrical conductivity—in relation to the ionic or covalent character of the compounds?

FOLLOW-UP QUESTIONS

1. Predict the following:
   a. solubility of sodium iodide in water
   b. melting time of sodium iodide
   c. electrical conductivity of a glucose solution

2. Using the information in your textbook or another reference, draw a sketch of the bonding in
   a. paradichlorobenzene
   b. methanol
   c. sucrose

CONCLUSION

State the results of Objective 3.

Model Building with Covalent Molecules

Most of our learning is in two dimensions. We see pictures in books and on walls and chalkboards. We often draw representations of molecules on flat paper. Two-dimensional representations include *electron dot structures* and *structural formulas*. In electron dot structures, a pair of "dots" (which represents a pair of electrons) is used to represent a single covalent bond. The hydrogen molecule is shown as H:H. In structural formulas, a single covalent bond is represented by a straight line. The hydrogen molecule is H-H. Although such "models" help us in understanding the structure of molecules, flat models do not give us the three-dimensional view that is necessary to truly visualize most molecules. In this experiment, you will build three-dimensional molecular models and then compare them with the corresponding structural formulas.

In covalent molecules there are single, double, and triple bonds between atoms. In some cases, the molecules are in a chainlike arrangement. At other times, the atoms arrange themselves in a ringlike structure. Still other molecules are in the form of branched chains.

Sometimes a group of atoms may form more than one structure. Thus, a given molecular formula might represent more than one compound. For example, C_2H_6O represents both ethyl alcohol and dimethyl ether, compounds with different structural formulas and quite different properties. Substances that have the same chemical formula but different structures are called *structural isomers*.

Scientists who are responsible for determining the structure of molecules often start with molecular model kits like the ones you will use in this experiment. Complicated molecules such as DNA (deoxyribonucleic acid) are most often shown in three-dimensional models. Without these models, we would not understand how the atoms of the molecule interact.

Ball and stick models give us an approximate picture of molecules. Although these models are extremely useful, they have drawbacks. The construction of a complicated model is tedious and expensive, with the result fragile. In recent years, chemists have been able to obtain better models of molecules by using increasingly sophisticated computer graphics programs.

OBJECTIVES

1. to construct models of some simple and more complicated covalent molecules

2. to draw structural formulas that show the shape of the molecules

3. to construct more than one structure for some of the molecules represented

MATERIALS

Apparatus

molecular model kit

PROCEDURE

1. Obtain a molecular model kit and remove the contents. Separate the contents based on the atoms that are represented. The chart on the next page will help you in identifying the atoms:

ATOM	NUMBER OF BONDING SITES (EITHER HOLES OR EXTENSIONS)
hydrogen chlorine bromine iodine fluorine	1
oxygen sulfur	2
nitrogen	3
carbon	4

In most kits, different colors represent different elements. Record in your notebook the color that corresponds to each element. If there are no instructions included in your kit, ask your teacher to assign colors to the elements listed in the preceding chart. Record them in your notebook.

2. Make models of the following molecules. There is only one structural isomer of each one. To confirm this, try making the atoms combine in some other way and you will find that once you turn the molecule around, it will be identical to the original structure. When you are satisfied that you have the correct structure, sketch it in your notebook.

   a. water, H_2O
   b. methane, CH_4
   c. methanol, CH_4O
   d. carbon tetrachloride, CCl_4
   e. ammonia, NH_3
   f. hydrazine, N_2H_4
   g. hydrogen sulfide, H_2S
   h. nitrogen tri-iodide NI_3

3. For the following molecular formulas, there can be more than one arrangement of the atoms. For each one, try to find as many different structural isomers as you can. Draw a structural formula for each of the isomers in your notebook.

   a. butane, C_4H_{10}
   b. propanol, C_3H_8O
   c. pentane, C_5H_{12}
   d. dibromoethane, $C_2H_4Br_2$

4. All of the preceding molecules include only single bonds. In the following group of molecules there are single, double, and triple bonds. Make each structure, then determine if any other isomers exist. Finally, draw the structural formula for each of the molecules in your notebook.

   a. carbon dioxide, CO_2
   b. nitrogen, N_2
   c. oxygen, O_2
   d. ethyne, C_2H_2
   e. hydrogen cyanide, HCN
   f. carbon disulfide, CS_2
   g. methanal (formaldehyde), CH_2O

5. Continue building molecules as your teacher suggests. Sketch each of the models or draw the structural formulas in your notebook.

POST LAB DISCUSSION

The models that you have constructed can help you in visualizing molecules as they exist in three dimensions. The more you work with models and sketches, the more comfortable you will feel with new structures, even the more complicated molecules. Although it is not always efficient to use models for symbolizing molecules, it helps to be familiar with them so that, as you draw molecular structures, you will have a mental image of their three-dimensional structure as well.

DATA AND OBSERVATIONS

Your observations in this experiment are best not put in table form as you do not know in advance how many structures there are for each substance. Just list the compounds and then draw all of the structures you find for that compound.

QUESTIONS

1. How many different isomers can you construct for a. butane, b. pentane ?

2. The name propanol indicates that the compound is a member of the alcohol family, a class of compounds that contain the hydroxyl group (O directly attached to H, -O-H). Review the structures that you sketched for propanol. How many have a hydroxyl group? (These are isomers of propanol.) Any structures remaining are not isomers of propanol, and belong to a completely different class of compound. How many do you have?

3. Draw structural formulas for the following:

   a. Cl_2
   b. HBr
   c. H_2O_2
   d. C_2H_4

CONCLUSION

What is the advantage of representing molecules by means of three-dimensional models?

Properties of Metals

Metals make up the majority of the elements in the periodic table. Some metals are highly reactive, such as those of Groups I and II. Other metals are relatively nonreactive, such as gold and silver.

There are some common properties of metals, such as electrical conductivity and the tendency to give up electrons in chemical reactions, forming positive ions. Other properties are distinctive for each individual metal. Some families of metals are very similar, such as the metals in the sodium family.

In the three parts that make up this experiment, you will be working with several common metals. You will be comparing and contrasting some of the properties of these metals.

OBJECTIVES

1. to observe the appearance of several common metals, including magnesium, iron, aluminum, copper, and zinc

2. to determine the relative hardness of the metals

3. to determine the relative malleability of the metals

4. to determine the relative electrical conductivity of the metals

5. to determine the relative reactivity of the metals in water and acids

MATERIALS

Apparatus

small file
razor blade, knife, or
  nail
emery cloth or fine
  sandpaper
battery (6 V)
light bulb and socket
3 wires with alligator
  clips

10 test tubes
  (18 mm × 150 mm)
test-tube rack
graduated cylinder
  (100 mL)
safety goggles
lab apron
full face shield
plastic gloves

Reagents

thin strips of the
  following metals:
  zinc, copper,
  magnesium,
  aluminum, and
  iron
small pieces of the
  same metals
1M hydrochloric acid
distilled water

PROCEDURE

Part I   Some Physical Properties of Metals

1. Put on your lab apron and safety goggles.

2. Obtain a small strip of zinc, copper, magnesium, aluminum, and iron.

3. Record the appearance of the metals in your copy of Table 1 in your notebook. Note the color, lustre, texture, etc.

4. Use a piece of emery cloth or sandpaper to shine the surface of each of the metals. Note any changes in the appearance of the metals as a result of sanding in Table 1.

5. Use a knife, nail, or razor blade (as your teacher directs), and then a file, to determine the relative hardness of each of the metals. First, try to cut the metal with the knife, nail, or razor blade. Be very careful when "cutting"; be sure to wear your safety goggles. Then try to file the metals. Based on the ease of cutting and filing, list the metals in order of decreasing hardness in Table 1.

6. Malleability is the ability of a metal to be shaped. In order to determine the relative malleability, try to bend the strips of metal back and forth. The most malleable metals will bend back and forth very easily and will not break after repeated bending. Record the relative malleability of the metals in Table 1.

Part II Relative Electrical Conductivities of Metals

1. Set up a battery, a light bulb and socket, and wires as shown in Figure 13A-1. Check to make sure that the bulb is working by connecting the light bulb directly to the battery, as shown in Figure 13A-2.

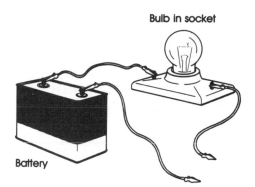

Figure 13A-1 *Setup for conductivity tests.*

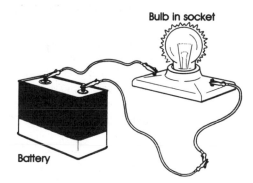

Figure 13A-2 *Check to show that the bulb works.*

2. Test the electrical conductivity of each of the metals by connecting the strip of metal as shown in Figure 13A-3. Determine the relative conductivity of the metals by observing the brightness of the bulb. Record your results in your copy of Table 2.

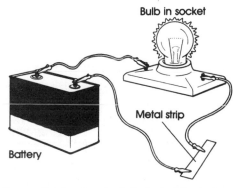

Figure 13A-3 *Conductivity test: If the bulb lights, the metal conducts electricity.*

Part III   Relative Reactivities of Metals

CAUTION: Hydrochloric acid is corrosive to skin, eyes, and clothing. When handling hydrochloric acid, wear safety goggles, full face shield, gloves, and lab apron. Wash spills and splashes off your skin and clothing immediately using plenty of water. Call your teacher.

1. Put on your full face shield and plastic gloves.

2. Set up five test tubes in a test tube rack. Place 15 mL of distilled water in each of the tubes.

3. Place a small piece of one of the metals into each of the test tubes. Observe and record any immediate reaction. Wait ten minutes to observe any changes. Record these changes in your copy of Table 3.

4. While you are waiting, set up another five test tubes and place 15 mL of 1M hydrochloric acid in each of the tubes. Place a small piece of each of the metals in the test tubes. Record any immediate reaction and any changes after ten minutes in Table 3.

5. Observe as your teacher shows the reaction of the five metals in 3M nitric acid. This demonstration will be done in the fume hood. Record the results in Table 3.

6. Clean up all of the materials. Before you leave the laboratory, wash your hands thoroughly with soap and water. Use a fingernail brush to clean under your fingernails.

REAGENT DISPOSAL

All leftover metals may be saved for reuse, or wrapped in newspaper and put in the wastebasket, according to your teacher's instructions. Check with your teacher about disposal of hydrochloric acid and any mixtures or solutions containing it.

POST LAB DISCUSSION

When metals react with acid, a gas is usually produced. For each metal that reacts with an acid, you will be asked to write a chemical equation. One example of the reaction of a metal with an acid is shown as follows:

$$Pb + 2HCl \rightarrow PbCl_2 + H_2$$

lead + hydrochloric acid → lead(II) chloride + hydrogen

DATA AND OBSERVATIONS

Part I   Some Physical Properties of Metals

Table 1

METAL	APPEARANCE	APPEARANCE AFTER SANDING	RELATIVE HARDNESS	MALLEABILITY
zinc				
copper				
magnesium		COMPLETE IN YOUR NOTEBOOK		
aluminum				
iron				

Part II   Relative Electrical Conductivities of Metals

Table 2

RELATIVE CONDUCTIVITY (BEST TO WORST, 1-5)	Zn	Cu	Mg	Al	Fe

Part III   Relative Reactivities of Metals

Table 3

	Zn	Cu	Mg	Al	Fe
Reaction with water immediately					
after ten minutes					
Reaction with 1M HCl immediately					
after ten minutes					
Teacher demonstration of reaction with 3M HNO₃					

QUESTIONS

1. Based on the results of this experiment, which metal would you choose to perform the indicated task? Explain your answers.
   a. pipes for your house plumbing
   b. lightweight camping equipment
   c. structural support in a large building
   d. electrical wires

2. For the reaction between each metal and hydrochloric acid, write a balanced chemical equation.

3. Which of the metals showed a reaction in water? Write an equation for the reaction that occurred.

FOLLOW-UP QUESTIONS

1. Many of the metals commonly used in a variety of applications are alloys. What is the advantage of using an alloy of iron, rather than iron itself, for the manufacture of automobiles?

2. Refer to your textbook to predict the results of this laboratory experiment with gold and silver:

	GOLD	SILVER
appearance		
hardness		
malleability		
reaction with water		

3. What are some common uses for magnesium alloys?

CONCLUSION

Describe the ranges of differences in the various properties of the metals you observed in this experiment.

Photochemistry

Under ordinary circumstances, most molecules possess insufficient energy to undergo a reaction. An additional source of energy must be supplied to initiate a chemical change. Although heat is the most common source, electricity and electromagnetic radiation also may trigger the reaction process.

Visible light, a small segment of the electromagnetic spectrum, consists of high-velocity energy packets known as *quanta* or *photons*. When photons collide with photosensitive substances, they may supply enough energy to activate a reaction. Common examples of these light-induced reactions include photosynthesis, photovoltaic effects (in solar collectors), and photographic processes.

Monochrome (black and white) photographic film consists of a transparent plastic strip impregnated with crystals of silver halide. When a photon strikes a crystal, it causes an embedded ion halide to liberate an electron. The electron migrates to a crystal surface, attracting an oppositely charged, Ag^+ ion. The subsequent formation of a neutral silver atom can act as a catalyst for the reduction of other Ag^+ ions. Although adequate exposure to light will produce satisfactory results, additional electrons may be supplied when a photographic developer solution is brought into contact with exposed film.

Since the entire film would eventually turn black, the underexposed grains of the silver halide must be removed. Treatment with sodium thiosulfate (hypo) binds the silver ion into a silver thiosulfate complex.

$$AgBr(s) + 2S_2O_3^{2-}(aq) \rightarrow Ag(S_2O_3)_2^{3-}(aq) + Br^-(aq)$$

The silver thiosulfate complex is water-soluble and can be removed by a water rinse.

Architectural and mechanical drawings are often reproduced by the process of blueprinting. Utilizing the photosensitivity of iron salts, paper soaked in ferrous ammonium sulfate/potassium ferricyanide solution is placed beneath a monochrome diagram. When exposed to light, reactant regions produce the characteristic blue color. Regions masked from direct exposure remain white, producing a white-on-blue-background copy. Since the unexposed iron salts are water-soluble, the blueprint image may be fixed by a simple water wash.

A very important photochemical reaction using light from the sun occurs in many cities. It is the formation of smog. Smog formation involves hundreds of compounds, with over 1000 identified chemical species reacting in the atmosphere of heavily polluted cities.

OBJECTIVES

1. to observe the effects of visible light on crystals of silver chloride and on a complex iron salt

2. to print a positive image onto laboratory-prepared photographic paper

3. to observe the effects of developer, stop bath, and sodium thiosulfate solution

4. to duplicate a diagram utilizing the blueprint process

MATERIALS

Apparatus

4 small test tubes
test-tube rack
aluminum foil
forceps
2 high-contrast
  monochrome
  negatives
mechanical drawing
glass plate

2 petri dishes
  (10 cm diameter)
wax pencil
filter paper
paper towels
safety goggles
lab apron
plastic gloves
full face shield

Reagents

$0.1M$ AgNO$_3$
$0.1M$ NaCl
$0.1M$ K$_3$Fe(CN)$_6$
$0.1M$ Fe(NH$_4$)$_2$(SO$_4$)$_2$
$0.1M$ HCl
hypo solution
  (Na$_2$S$_2$O$_3$)
commercial developer
  solution

PROCEDURE

Part I   Preliminary Investigations of Photosensitive Reactions

CAUTION: Silver nitrate is poisonous, and it is corrosive to skin and eyes. When handling silver nitrate, wear safety goggles, gloves, and lab apron. Wash spills and splashes off your skin with plenty of water. Call your teacher.

CAUTION: Ferrous ammonium sulfate is poisonous. Do not get it in your mouth; do not swallow any.

1. Put on your lab apron, safety goggles, and full face shield.

2. Set up four test tubes labeled A to D. Perform Steps 3 and 4 in diffuse lighting.

3. To tubes A and B, add five drops of AgNO$_3$. Next add five drops of NaCl to each of these tubes. Record your observations in your copy of Table 1 in your notebook.

4. To tubes C and D, add five drops of potassium ferricyanide. Next add five drops of ferrous ammonium sulfate to each of these tubes. Record your observations in Table 1.

5. Wrap tubes A and C in aluminum foil, so that no light can penetrate the solutions. Place all four tubes in a rack and expose them to direct sunlight.

6. After five minutes, unwrap the foil-covered tubes. Examine the contents of each tube. Record your observations in Table 1.

Part II   Making a Photographic Print

CAUTION: Silver nitrate is poisonous, and it is corrosive to skin and eyes. When handling silver nitrate, wear safety goggles, gloves, and lab apron. Wash spills and splashes off your skin with plenty of water. Call your teacher.

1. Obtain a piece of filter paper, approximately 8 cm × 4 cm, and place it in a petri dish.

2. In diffuse lighting, soak the surface of the filter paper with five drops of AgNO$_3$. In a similar manner, add five drops of NaCl.

3. Using forceps, remove the treated filter paper from the dish and blot it dry between two pieces of paper toweling. Place the strip in a dark area.

4. Prepare three additional strips of photosensitive paper by repeating Steps 1 through 3. Store two of the four photosensitive paper strips in a dark area for use in Part III.

5. Place a high-contrast monochrome negative on each of the two remaining treated strips. Place this combination in direct sunlight and cover it with a glass plate to secure it from movement. (See Figure 13B-1.)

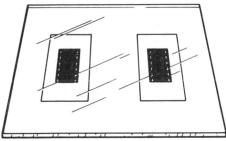

Figure 13B-1

6. Wait five minutes, then remove the materials from direct sunlight. Separate the negatives from the treated filter paper. Record your observations in your notebook.

7. Put 5 mL of hypo solution into a clean, dry petri dish. Using forceps, immerse one of the newly produced "prints" in this solution.

8. Wait one minute and remove the print. Carefully rinse the print with tap water and blot it dry.

9. Again place both prints in direct sunlight. At the end of the laboratory period, examine the prints. Record your observations in your notebook.

CAUTION: The composition of the developer you will use is a trade secret. It could contain components that are corrosive, or poisonous, or allergenic, or more than one of these. Therefore, wear safety goggles, full face shield, and gloves. Wash spills and splashes off your skin and clothing immediately using plenty of water. Call your teacher.

Part III   Making a Photographic Print with Developer

1. Put on your full face shield and plastic gloves.

2. Using a wax pencil, mark the exterior of a petri dish with the letter *D*. Put 5 mL of developer solution into this dish.

3. Mark a second dish with the letter *S* and place 5 mL of 0.1*M* HCl into this dish.

4. Place a coin in the middle of each of the remaining photosensitive strips prepared in Part II. Place the coin-strip combinations in direct sunlight.

5. Wait one minute and remove the materials from direct sunlight. Immerse both exposed strips in the developer solution in petri dish *D*. Record your observations in your notebook.

6. Wait 30 s, then transfer one of the prints into the acid solution in petri dish *S*.

7. Wait an additional two minutes, then compare the two prints. Record your observations in your notebook.

8. You can remove your face shield.

CAUTION: Hydrochloric acid is corrosive to skin, eyes, and clothing. When handling 0.1M acid, wear safety goggles and gloves. Wash spills and splashes off with plenty of water. Call your teacher.

Part IV   Making a Blueprint

1. In diffuse lighting, place ten drops of potassium ferricyanide into a clean, dry petri dish. Add ten drops of ferrous ammonium sulfate.

CAUTION: Ferrous ammonium sulfate is poisonous. Do not get it in your mouth; do not swallow any.

2. Obtain a piece of filter paper, approximately 8 cm × 4 cm. Using forceps, immerse the paper in the iron salt solution.

3. Wait ten seconds. Using forceps, remove the paper and place it between two pieces of paper toweling. Blot it dry.

4. Place the diagram to be copied over the treated paper. Place the combination in direct sunlight. Secure the system by placing a glass plate over the papers.

5. Wait five minutes, then remove the materials from direct sunlight. Separate the original diagram from the blueprint copy. Rinse the copy with tap water and blot it dry. Record your observations in your notebook.

6. Before leaving the laboratory, wash your hands thoroughly with soap and water; use a fingernail brush to clean under your fingernails.

REAGENT DISPOSAL

Return any wastes containing silver compounds to the designated waste container. All other solutions may be washed to waste with plenty of water unless your teacher instructs you to save for reuse.

POST LAB DISCUSSION

The precipitate formed in the reaction between $AgNO_3$ and $NaCl$ demonstrated a photosensitive nature. When allowed to impregnate paper, the exposed crystals produced a static record of their reaction with light. Since the pattern of light and dark observed on the print was an inverse image of the silver deposited on the negative, a reversed print, or "positive," was produced.

When a developer solution was added to the exposed silver halide crystals, an increase in the rate of silver deposition was observed. Upon the addition of a weak acid, development was halted.

When the print was fixed and rinsed, the soluble silver complex was removed from the filter paper. Once this complex was removed, the paper lost its photosensitivity while retaining the original silver image. Unfixed images, on the other hand, were still surrounded by light-sensitive silver halide that continued to react and deposit metallic silver.

As light activated the iron salt blueprint paper, a water-insoluble compound was produced. Its blue color stained the treated paper in regions where light penetrated the original diagram. Areas masked by diagrammatic lines contained unreacted water-soluble salts. A tap water rinse removed these unreacted salts, fixing the blueprint.

DATA AND OBSERVATIONS

Part I   Preliminary Investigations of Photosensitive Reactions

Table 1

	OBSERVATIONS (STEPS 3 AND 4)	OBSERVATIONS (STEP 6)
Tube A		
Tube B		
Tube C		
Tube D		

QUESTIONS

1. Describe the effect of light on both the silver halide crystals and the iron salt solution.

2. What happened to the development process when the print prepared in Part III was immersed in $0.1 M$ HCl? Explain.

3. After examining the prints obtained in Part II, explain why it was necessary to use a high-contrast negative.

4. Account for the changes observed when the photographic prints were examined at the end of the laboratory period.

5. Suggest several methods for increasing the amount of silver deposition.

6. Were the diagrammatic lines of the blueprint duplicate pure white? Give a reason for this observation.

7. "Stop bath" is a solution used to halt the development process. Is it acidic or alkaline? Explain.

FOLLOW-UP QUESTIONS

1. Would you expect all visible colors of the same intensity to deposit equal amounts of metallic silver? Why?

2. Unexposed photographic film that has been placed near a radioactive source will demonstrate silver deposition. Explain.

CONCLUSION

State the results of Objective 3.

High-Tech Chemistry

The silicon crystal has played an essential role in the evolution of our high-technology society. Composed of a repeating geometric arrangement of silicon atoms, the crystal possesses a structure similar to that found in diamonds. Each of silicon's four outermost electrons forms a covalent bond with a neighboring silicon atom. The electrons forming these bonds are restricted in their movement, and therefore they are referred to as localized electrons.

When certain impurities are introduced into the crystal matrix, changes in the electrical conductivity occur. Crystals doped with arsenic atoms having mobile electrons produce n-type semiconductors. When gallium is allowed to diffuse into a silicon crystal, it creates electron deficiencies or "holes" that may be filled by a mobile electron to produce p-type semiconductors. Doped semiconductor materials are assembled into basic electronic components such as diodes and transistors.

Most electronic devices today use semiconductors. A semiconductor has a conductivity on the range between that of an insulator and a good conductor. Most common semiconductors involve crystals of germanium or silicon. Electronic devices using semiconductors in the form of transistors are smaller, require less power, produce less heat, and last much longer than the older vacuum tubes.

Semiconductor materials also may be assembled into *photovoltaic cells.* When the crystals in these cells are struck by photons, they release electrons. These electrons migrate through the semiconductor layer and travel through an external circuit. The electricity generated by this process may be used directly or stored for later use.

As part of this investigation, you will assess the electrical output of a photovoltaic cell. The electricity generated by this cell will then be used to furnish energy for the following reaction:

$$2H_2O(l) + 2Cl^-(aq) \rightarrow 2OH^-(aq) + H_2(g) + Cl_2(g)$$

The indicator phenolphthalein will be used to detect the presence of the OH^- ions that are produced. Phenolphthalein turns pink in the presence of OH^- ions. The solar cell then will be used to charge a simple lead storage cell.

OBJECTIVES

1. to construct molecular models of semiconductor crystals

2. to examine and compare a vacuum tube, a transistor, and an integrated circuit

3. to perform a chemical reaction using energy generated by a photovoltaic cell

4. to store electrical energy generated by a photovoltaic cell in a lead storage cell

5. to investigate several of the properties of optical fibers

MATERIALS

Apparatus

centigram balance
stereo microscope
molecular model set
modified models
  representing arsenic
  and gallium
photovoltaic cell
transistor
exposed integrated
  circuit
vacuum tube
2 beakers (100 mL)
medicine dropper

2 insulated copper
  wires (20 cm length)
adhesive tape
voltmeter
light source
plastic optical fibers
safety goggles
lab apron
plastic gloves
full face shield
graduated cylinder
  (100 mL)

Reagents

$1M$ H_2SO_4
saturated NaCl
  solution
phenolphthalein
  solution
2 bare copper wires
  (10 cm length)
2 lead strips

PROCEDURE

Part I Models of Semiconductors

1. Obtain a molecular model set. Locate the atoms containing four bonding holes, oriented in a tetrahedral fashion. These spheres will be used to represent silicon atoms.

2. Begin assembling a crystalline matrix of pure silicon. Each atom must be bonded to four identical atoms. Form as many interconnected atoms as possible. Continue until all the available silicon atoms are incorporated into the structure.

3. Select a silicon atom that has made four covalent bonds. Sketch this atom, its bonds, and the location of its four nearest neighbors in your notebook.

4. Obtain a modified sphere that contains five bored holes. This sphere will be used to represent an arsenic atom.

5. Without disassembling the entire model, remove the silicon atom used in Step 3 from the matrix. Substitute the arsenic atom for the removed silicon and reform the bonds. Add a bonding peg of ½ length to the vacant hole left in the arsenic sphere.

6. Sketch this atom, its bonds, its unpaired electron, and the location of its four nearest neighbors in your notebook.

7. Obtain a modified sphere that contains only three bored holes. This sphere will be used to represent a gallium atom.

8. Without disassembling the entire model, substitute the gallium atom for the arsenic atom. Complete as many bonds as possible. Use a bonding peg of ½ length to represent the unpaired silicon electron.

9. Sketch this atom, its bonds and the location of its four nearest neighbors in your notebook.

10. Disassemble the model and return the spheres and bonding pegs to their appropriate container.

Part II   Comparing Vacuum Tubes, Transistors, and Integrated Circuits

1. Carefully examine a vacuum tube. Note the electrodes and any wire grids found within the tube. Draw a rough sketch of this unit in your notebook.

2. Examine a transistor. Draw a rough sketch of this semiconductor device in your notebook.

3. Obtain an exposed integrated circuit. Place the circuit on the stage of a stereo microscope and examine the chip under the highest possible magnification. Draw a rough sketch of your observations in your notebook.

4. Using a centigram balance, obtain the masses of the vacuum tube, transistor, and integrated circuit. Record your data in your notebook.

Part III   Obtaining Energy from a Photovoltaic Cell

1. Put on your lab apron and safety goggles.

2. Obtain a photovoltaic cell and examine its structure. Using two pieces of insulated copper wire, connect the exposed leads of the cell to a voltmeter.

3. Place the cell in direct sunlight. Record the voltage measurement in your notebook. Cover the face of the cell with your hand, allowing no light to fall on its photoactive surface. Record the voltage measurement in your notebook.

4. Wind a length of bare copper wire around a pencil. Pull tightly on the wire forming a tight coil. Remove the pencil and repeat with a second length of copper wire.

5. Place approximately 75 mL of a saturated NaCl solution into a clean, dry 100 mL beaker. Add several drops of phenolphthalein solution.

6. Attach one wire lead from the photovoltaic cell to each of the bare coils. Place both coils into the solution. Do not allow the coils to touch (See Figure 14A-1.)

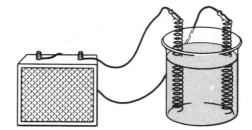

Figure 14A-1

7. Position the cell so that its photosensitive surface is in direct lighting. Examine the solution for any changes in appearance. Gently agitate each copper coil. Record your observations in your notebook.

8. Obtain two lead strips. Connect a bare end of an insulated wire length to each of the strips. Connect the other end of each wire to a voltmeter.

9. With your gloves on, place approximately 20 mL of a $1M$ H_2SO_4 solution in a clean, dry 100 mL beaker. Place the two lead strips into this solution. Make sure that the strips do not touch each other. Observe the voltage and if necessary wait until it falls to zero.

10. Disconnect the wires at the voltmeter and attach them to the photovoltaic cell. Place the cell in direct sunlight and wait several minutes.

11. Disconnect the wires at the photovoltaic cell and reconnect them to the voltmeter. Record your observations in your notebook.

12. Before you continue the lab, wash your hands thoroughly with soap and water; use a fingernail brush to clean under your fingernails.

CAUTION: Sulfuric acid is corrosive to the skin, eyes, and clothing. When handling it, wear safety goggles, full face shield, apron, and gloves. Wash spills and splashes off your skin and clothing immediately, using plenty of water. Call your teacher.

Part IV   Investigating Optical Fibers

1. Obtain several strands of optical fibers and examine their structure. Align their ends and wrap the strands into a tight bundle. Use a piece of tape to secure the bundle.

2. Aim the aligned end of the fiber bundle at a bright light source.

3. Examine the free ends of the fibers. Does bending the fibers affect the transmitted light? Record your observation in your notebook.

CAUTION: To prevent burns and the risk of fire, do not get too close to the light source.

REAGENT DISPOSAL

Save any copper wire or lead strips for possible reuse, as directed by your teacher. Discard the sodium chloride and phenolphthalein mixture down the sink with plenty of water. Return the sulfuric acid to the designated waste container.

POST LAB DISCUSSION

The electrical energy generated by the solar cell in Part III caused a measurable deflection of the voltmeter needle. When introduced into a saturated NaCl solution, this electrical energy decomposed water, producing OH^- ions. Phenolphthalein within the solution reacted to this increase in hydroxide ion concentration by undergoing its indicative color change.

The energy generated by solar cells is produced during hours of sunlight. This energy must be stored in some physical or chemical form until it is needed. The assembled lead cell, similar to that found in a car storage battery, is capable of storing this energy as shown by its acquired voltage potential.

DATA AND OBSERVATIONS

Part II   Comparing Vacuum Tubes, Transistors, and Integrated Circuits

Table 1

Mass of vacuum tube

Mass of transistor

Mass of integrated circuit

Part III   Obtaining Energy From a Photovoltaic Cell

Voltage in direct sunlight

Voltage with hand covering cell

Voltage with two lead strips in H_2SO_4

QUESTIONS AND CALCULATIONS

1. What difference was observed between the pure silicon crystal and the arsenic-doped crystal?

2. What difference was observed between the pure silicon crystal and the gallium-doped crystal?

3. If we assume that the integrated circuit contains 3×10^3 miniaturized transistors, what is the mass of a single integrated circuit transistor?

4. What number of integrated circuit transistors has the same mass as a single vacuum tube?

FOLLOW-UP QUESTIONS

1. Although "holes" cannot migrate through crystalline structures, semiconductors behave as if this occurs. Explain.

2. Describe some possible new uses for photovoltaic cells and optical fibers that have not already been discussed.

CONCLUSION

Summarize the results for each part of this experiment.

Volatility and Surface Tension of Liquids

You may already have learned that liquids are substances that have a definite volume, and take the shape of the container. The molecular explanation for the behavior of liquids is a bit complicated. Liquid molecules are close together, in comparison to gas molecules. Liquid molecules can move around freely, unlike the molecules of solids, which are fixed in position. The fact that liquids take the shape of the container is explained by the constant movement of the molecules. The fact that liquids have a definite volume is explained by the fact that the molecules are close together.

Volatility is a property that is related to the rate at which a substance evaporates. Evaporation takes place only at the surface of the liquid, and can take place at any temperature. If a substance is highly volatile, the substance will evaporate easily.

Surface tension is another important property of liquids. The greater the surface tension of a liquid, the more closely the molecules of the liquid are attracted to one another. The high surface tension of water allows some insects to travel on its surface. The *meniscus* in a graduated cylinder also is caused by the high surface tension of water. The water adheres to the sides of the cylinder and causes the meniscus. (See Figure 15A-1.)

In the home, soaps and detergents are used to lower the surface tension of water. Basically, this means that the water is made "wetter" and can do a better job of removing grease and dirt.

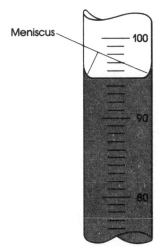

Figure 15A-1

OBJECTIVES

1. to determine the relative volatilities of several liquids

2. to explain the differences in vapor pressure among the liquids tested

3. to determine the relative surface tensions of several liquids

4. to explain the differences in surface tension among the liquids

MATERIALS

Apparatus	**Reagents**
4 watch glasses	small dropper bottles containing:
5 test tubes	acetone
test tube rack	methanol
spatula	2-propanol
stopwatch or watch	distilled water
with second hand	1% sodium chloride solution
2 small pieces of	1% soap solution
absorbent cotton	1% liquid detergent solution
safety goggles	1% powdered detergent solution
lab apron	sulfur powder

PROCEDURE

Part I   Determining Relative Volatilities of Liquids

CAUTION: Acetone, methanol, and 2-propanol are all flammable liquids. Be certain that there are no flames in the lab when you are using these liquids.

1. Put on your lab apron and safety goggles.

2. Place four clean and dry watch glasses on the lab table. Get your stop watch ready to keep time.

3. Obtain dropper bottles of acetone, methanol, 2-propanol, and distilled water. With the help of a partner, put one drop of each liquid on its own watch glass at the same time, and begin timing. In order to determine the relative volatility, record the amount of time (in minutes and seconds) that it takes for one drop of the liquid to completely evaporate from the watch glass. Record the amount of time for each of the liquids to evaporate in your copy of Table 1.

4. 2-Propanol is the chemical name for rubbing alcohol, a common household chemical. Using a piece of absorbent cotton, wet the back of your hand with the 2-propanol. Wave your hand around. Record any observations in your notebook.

5. In a similar fashion, wet the back of your hand with distilled water. Again, wave your hand around. Record your observations in your notebook.

Part II   Determining Relative Surface Tensions

1. Carefully clean five test tubes. Rinse each test tube several times with tap water, then rinse with distilled water to remove any traces of soap or other substances.

2. Set up the five test tubes in a test tube rack. Label the test tubes with the numbers 1-5. Place 10 mL of each solution to be tested in the test tubes as indicated:
   test tube 1: distilled water
   test tube 2: 0.1% sodium chloride solution
   test tube 3: 0.1% soap solution
   test tube 4: 0.1% liquid detergent solution
   test tube 5: 0.1% powdered detergent solution

3. With a spatula, place a very small amount of sulfur powder into each of the test tubes. Gently tap the side of each test tube. What happens to the sulfur powder? What differences do you note for each liquid? Gradually increase the tapping to help you determine the relative surface tensions of the liquids. Record your observations in your notebook.

4. Clean up all the materials, following instructions for reagent disposal.

5. Before leaving the laboratory, wash your hands thoroughly with soap and water, using a fingernail brush to clean under your fingernails.

REAGENT DISPOSAL

Pour down the drain any sulfur mixed with water or other named solutions. Acetone, methanol, and 2-propanol should each be diluted with at least ten times its original volume of water and poured down the drain. Save any leftover sulfur for reuse, or else wrap it in newspaper and put it in the wastebasket, as your teacher directs.

POST LAB DISCUSSION

In the experiment, you determined the relative volatilities of the liquids involved. In addition, you noted the difference in cooling on the back of your hand as two of the liquids evaporated. The cool feeling on the back of your hand is similar to the soothing effect of an alcohol bath for a person who is very hot. In the following questions, you will be asked to explain why the cooling effect takes place. It is important to recognize that whenever a change of state takes place, there is an energy change. If the change in state is rapid, the resulting energy change is rapid as well.

In your investigation of surface tension, you noted the differences among the liquids by observing the movement of the sulfur in the solution. Sulfur powder is denser than the liquids, so it will ultimately sink, once the surface tension is broken. The ability of a liquid to "wet" a solid is dependent on the surface tension of the liquid and the adhesive forces between the liquid and the solid.

DATA AND OBSERVATIONS

Part I   Determining Relative Volatilities of Liquids

Table 1

	TIME IN MINUTES AND SECONDS FOR ONE DROP TO EVAPORATE
Acetone	
Methanol	
2-Propanol	
Distilled water	

QUESTIONS

1. Explain what is happening to the molecules when a liquid evaporates and forms molecules of gas.

2. It takes energy for a substance to evaporate. In terms of energy, explain why your hand feels cooler when the 2-propanol evaporates compared to when the distilled water evaporates.

3. If you were to put some acetone on the back of your hand, what would you expect to feel? Explain your answer.

4. Does sodium chloride have any effect on the surface tension of water? Explain your answer.

5. In addition to dissolving grease and oil, soaps reduce the surface tension of water. Why is this important in cleaning?

FOLLOW-UP QUESTIONS

1. At a given temperature, would you expect the vapor pressure of acetone to be greater or less than the vapor pressure of water? Explain your answer.

2. In terms of the attractive forces between molecules, explain the differences between water and acetone.

3. Perfumes are composed of substances that have a strong pleasing odor and volatile liquids. What might be the purpose of using volatile liquids in perfumes?

4. The water strider is an insect that can walk on the surface of water in lakes and ponds. What would happen to the population of water striders if a pond were polluted with a great deal of detergent pollution? Explain your answer.

CONCLUSION

State the results of Objectives 1 and 2.

Particle Arrangement in Crystalline Solids

Solids represent a condensed state of matter characterized by restricted movement of particles. Although component particles may vibrate, they remain at fixed positions. When the ions, atoms, or molecules occupying these positions form a repeating geometric pattern, the solid is a crystal. The unit cell is the simplest repetitive unit of crystalline solids. Closest-packed cells contain the maximum number of particles per given volume.

Chemists construct three-dimensional models to help visualize the structure of crystals. In this experiment, you will assemble models representing various unit cells and crystalline structures. You will then use these models as a source of information in answering questions.

OBJECTIVES

1. to construct models of the three unit cells most often associated with metals

2. to construct a model of the sodium chloride lattice

3. to construct a model of the crystalline structure of graphite and diamond

4. to explain the properties of solids as they relate to their crystalline structure

MATERIALS

Apparatus

36 plastic foam spheres (5 cm diameter)
13 plastic foam spheres (2.5 cm diameter)
38 pieces of chenille wire (2.5 cm length)
4 pieces of chenille wire (5 cm length)
hydrocarbon model set

PROCEDURE

Part I   Models for Three Different Unit Cells

1. Using 5 cm plastic foam spheres and 2.5 cm lengths of chenille wire, assemble the layers required for body-centred cubic packing as shown in Figure 15B-1. Be sure to leave a space of about 0.8 cm between the spheres.

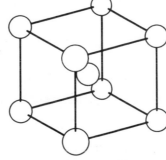

Figure 15B-1   *Body-centred unit cubic cell*

2. Place the single sphere in the central depression of the bottom layer. Now add the top layer so that its spheres align directly above those of the bottom layer. Set the model aside.

3. Using 5 cm spheres and 2.5 cm lengths of chenille wire, assemble the three layers required for face-centred cubic packing as shown in Figure 15B-2.

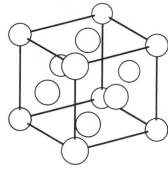

Figure 15B-2 *Face-centred unit cubic cell*

4. Set the bottom layer flat on a level surface. Place the middle layer on the first so that the spheres rest in the spaces between the corner spheres of the bottom layer. Now add the third layer so that its spheres align directly above those in the first layer. Set the model aside.

5. Using the 5 cm spheres and 2.5 cm lengths of chenille wire, assemble the layers required for hexagonal closest packing as shown in Figure 15B-3.

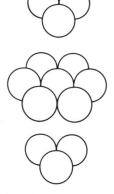

Figure 15B-3 *Layers for hexagonal closest packing*

6. Set the bottom layer flat on a level surface. Place the middle layer on the first so that the centre sphere fits closely into the depression of the bottom layer. You might have to rotate the middle layer until this is achieved. Now add the top layer so that it aligns over the central sphere of the middle layer and also directly above the spheres in the bottom layer. Set the model aside.

7. Compare the structures in the assembled unit cells. Select one sphere in each structure. Determine the number of spheres that touch the sphere you selected. Remember— the crystal extends farther than the number of spheres in your model. Record the number of nearest neighbors for each model in your copy of Table 1.

8. Rearrange the model assembled in Step 6 so that the top layer is not directly over the bottom layer, but is rotated 60° with respect to it.

9. Rotate this model slightly and look for four spheres forming a square facing you. Now remove the top layer of the model assembled in Step 4 and place it against the four spheres you located. Identify this crystal arrangement and record your response in your notebook.

Part II   A Model for a Sodium Chloride Lattice

1. Reconstruct the face-centred cubic packing model as assembled in Part I, Step 4, using the 5 cm spheres.

2. Insert 13 2.5 cm spheres into the spaces between the spheres of each layer. Since chloride ions have a diameter of approximately twice that of sodium ions, we will represent chloride ions with 5 cm spheres and sodium ions with 2.5 cm spheres.

3. Examine the crystalline lattice. Identify the number of sodium ions surrounding each chloride ion and vice versa and record it in your notebook.

Part III   Models for Graphite and Diamond

1. Disassemble all crystal models. Using 5 cm spheres and 2.5 cm lengths of chenille wire, assemble two models of a graphite layer segment as shown in Figure 15B-4. Be sure to leave a space of about 1.5 cm between the spheres.

Figure 15B-4 *Graphite layer*

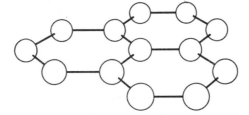

2. Place one layer approximately 5 cm directly above the other layer. Using the 5 cm lengths of chenille wire, join the layers by inserting wires between any four exterior pairs of corresponding carbon atoms. The bond lengths between layers should be about 3.5 cm. Set the model aside.

3. Select a carbon atom from the hydrocarbon model set. Insert four bonding sticks oriented in a tetrahedral fashion. Attach another carbon sphere to the exposed ends of each bond stick.

4. To each of the four end spheres, attach three bond sticks in tetrahedral fashion. Continue expanding the structure.

5. Compare the structures assembled in Steps 2 and 4. In your notebook, describe physical properties you might associate with these forms. Disassemble the models and place the parts in the storage containers.

POST LAB DISCUSSION

The differences in macroscopic properties of graphite and diamond are attributed to differences in their crystalline arrangement. The reinforced tetrahedral structure of diamond contains a three-dimensional network of covalent bonding. Graphite's hexagonal arrangement has its covalent bonds within the plane of the hexagon. Layers remain cross-linked by the relatively weak van der Waals forces.

DATA AND OBSERVATIONS

Part III Models for Three Different Unit Cells

Table 1

UNIT CELL	NUMBER OF NEAREST SPHERES
body-centred cubic	
hexagonal closest packed	
face-centred cubic	

QUESTIONS

1. What is the maximum number of spheres of one size that can contact a central sphere?

2. In one type of cubic packing, the spheres occupy about two-thirds of the space, and in the other they fill about three-fourths of the space available.

   a. Identify the cells.
   b. Which is more dense?
   c. In which cell does each atom form the larger number of bonds?

3. Account for the stability of the high-density sodium chloride crystal.

FOLLOW-UP QUESTIONS

1. Metallic iron crystallizes in the body-centred cubic form called α-ferrite below 906°C. Above this temperature, the stable form is γ-ferrite, which is face-centred cubic. At 1401°C, the crystal form changes back to the body-centred solid called σ-ferrite.

   a. What is the coordination number of iron in each of these forms?
   b. Suggest a reason for the transition that occurs at 906°C in terms of numbers of available bonding electrons.

2. Suppose you have a crystal *XY* with the sodium chloride structure. *X* has a 2+ charge, and *Y* has a 2– charge, but the two are the same size as Na^+ and Cl^-.

   a. Would *XY* have a higher or lower melting point than NaCl?
   b. Suggest an actual ionic substance with the above characteristics and look up its melting point to support your prediction.

3. The structure of diamond makes it a very hard material. Using a reference book, make a list of uses for industrial diamonds.

4. Graphite is a component of some lubricating greases, and can be obtained in powder form in a tube to squirt in a sticking lock to free it. Explain how the structure of graphite gives it these lubricating properties.

CONCLUSION

State the results of Objective 4.

Polar and Non-polar Solutes and Solvents

In Experiment 12A, you studied the differences between ionic and covalent compounds by investigating such characteristics of solutions as solubility, melting point, and electrical conductivity. As a result, you discovered that ionic compounds have higher melting points than covalent compounds. You also found that solutions of ionic compounds are good conductors of electricity, whereas solutions of covalent compounds are poor conductors. Finally, you learned that ionic compounds tend to be more soluble in water, while covalent compounds tend to be more soluble in methanol. In the case of solubility, you also noted one obvious exception to this trend: sucrose (table sugar), a covalent compound, is highly soluble in water but only slightly soluble in methanol. From these results, it appears that not all covalent compounds are soluble in the same type of solvent.

People engaged in the drycleaning industry have learned that different stains on garments sometimes require different approaches to cleaning. A drycleaner will often ask a customer for information about a given stain, then make a cleaning decision based on that information. In many cases, the nature of the stain (solute) will determine the drycleaning solvent to be used.

Covalent compounds can be further classified as *polar* or *non-polar*. Although, as a result of the sharing of electrons between component atoms, all covalent compounds are bonded, this sharing is not necessarily an *equal* sharing of electrons. As a result, one side of a neutral molecule can end up with a net negative charge, while the other side is left with a net positive charge. (See Figure 16A-1.) It is this type of covalent compound which is said to be polar. It is more common than the non-polar type.

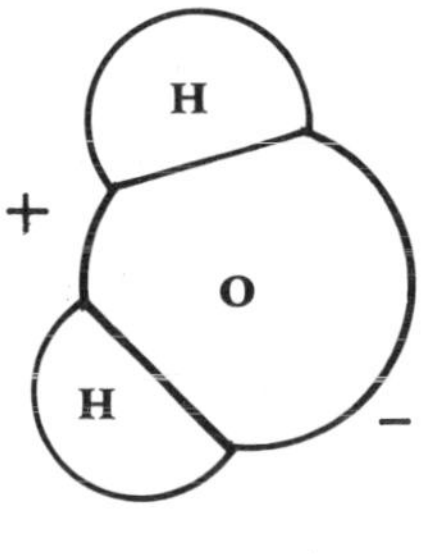

The classification of a covalent compound as polar or non-polar requires information about electron-sharing tendencies and molecular shapes. Since such a detailed study of compounds is beyond the scope of this experiment, you will simply be informed as to the classification of the compounds you will be using. It is important to remember that both the solute and the solvent have characteristics that can affect solubility. Therefore, in this experiment you will test the solubilities of a variety of solutes in a variety of solvents. The solutes to be tested are ionic, polar covalent, and non-polar covalent, while the solvents to be tested are polar covalent and non-polar covalent. (There are no typical ionic solvents.) In Part I you will be doing solubility tests on known solutes, and in Part II you will be testing the solubility of unknown solutes. In Part III you will be mixing liquids to study their solubilities.

Figure 16A-1

OBJECTIVES

1. to determine the type of solvent that generally dissolves ionic compounds

2. to determine the type of solvent that generally dissolves polar covalent compounds

3. to determine the type of solvent that generally dissolves non-polar covalent compounds

4. to investigate the effect of adding a polar liquid solute to a non-polar liquid solvent

MATERIALS

Apparatus
6 test tubes
(13 mm × 100 mm)
6 stoppers to fit test tubes
test-tube rack
tweezers
safety goggles
lab apron

Reagents
sodium chloride (table salt) crystals
sucrose (table sugar) crystals
iodine crystals
3 unknown solid solutes
paint thinner (or varsol)
glycerin

PROCEDURE

Part I   Solubility Tests on Known Solutes

CAUTION: Paint thinner is poisonous. Do not get any in your mouth.

1. Put on your lab apron and safety goggles.

2. Obtain 6 clean, dry test tubes and place them in a test-tube rack so that you have two rows of test tubes with three test tubes in each row.

3. Half fill one set of three test tubes with water at room temperature, and half fill the other set of three test tubes with paint thinner. Your test tubes should now form a grid that is similar to the grid in Table 1.

4. In the first pair of test tubes (one containing water, the other containing paint thinner) add enough crystals of salt with a pair of tweezers to cover the bottom of the test tubes.

5. Stopper one of these test tubes, then invert it to agitate the mixture. Turn the test tube over several times until you are convinced that no further change will take place. Carefully examine the inside of the test tube for crystals that may get trapped on the walls. Repeat this agitation process for the second test tube, then record your observations for both test tubes in your copy of Table 1 in your notebook. (Record whether or not the solute dissolves.)

CAUTION: Some of these unknown solutions can harm skin and clothing. Wash off spills and splashes with plenty of water. Call your teacher.

6. Repeat Steps 3 and 4 with crystals of sugar in the second pair of test tubes.

7. Repeat Steps 3 and 4 with an iodine crystal in the remaining pair of test tubes. (Note: One iodine crystal gives better results than several crystals.)

8. Clean up your apparatus according to the reagent disposal instructions.

Part II   Solubility Tests on Unknown Solutes

1. Repeat Part I of this experiment, but refer to Table 2 and test the solubilities of unknown solutes *A*, *B*, and *C*.

Part III   Mixing Two Liquids

1. Fill a clean test tube one quarter full with water, then add twice as much paint thinner as water to the same test tube.

2. Stopper the open end of the test tube and agitate the liquids as in Part I.

3. Examine what happens to the liquids after agitation, and record your observations in your copy of Table 3.

4. Add one iodine crystal to the test tube and agitate the contents. Make a labelled sketch of your test tube and its contents. Include this sketch in your observations.

5. Using a second test tube, repeat Steps 1 to 4, but use glycerin in place of paint thinner. Glycerin is also known as glycerol, or, as you will learn in organic chemistry, 1, 2, 3 – propanetriol. It is a polar liquid.

6. Clean up all apparatus according to the reagent disposal instructions.

7. Before you leave the laboratory, wash your hands thoroughly with soap and water; use a fingernail brush to clean under your nails.

REAGENT DISPOSAL

Pour the contents of all test tubes into the container designated by your instructor. Wash out the test tubes with water, using a test tube brush if necessary.

POST LAB DISCUSSION

It is obvious from the results in Table 1 that certain types of solutes will dissolve only in certain types of solvents. Although there are exceptions to the results obtained in this experiment, you should now be able to propose a general rule for the type of solvent that will dissolve each type of solute.

DATA AND OBSERVATIONS

Part I   Solubility Tests on Known Solutes

Table 1   Known Solutes with Known Solvents

	SOLUTES		
SOLVENTS	SALT (NaCl) (IONIC)	SUGAR ($C_{12}H_{22}O_{11}$) (POLAR COVALENT)	IODINE (I_2) (NON-POLAR COVALENT)
Water (Polar covalent)			
Paint thinner (Non-polar covalent)			

Part II   Solubility Tests on Unknown Solutes

Table 2   Unknown Solutes with Known Solvents

	SOLUTE		
SOLVENT	A	B	C
Water (Polar covalent)			
Paint thinner (Non-polar covalent)			

Part III   Mixing Two Liquids

Table 3

COMBINATIONS OF LIQUIDS	COVALENT TYPES	RESULTS
Water and paint thinner		
Water and glycerin		

COMPLETE IN YOUR NOTEBOOK

QUESTIONS

1. a. What general trend appears in Table 1 with regard to which type of solute dissolves in which type of solvent?
    b. This general solubility trend is sometimes expressed as "Like dissolves like." Explain this expression.

2. a. Attempt to classify each of the unknown solutes from Part II as ionic, polar covalent, or non-polar covalent.
    b. What problem do you encounter in making this classification?
    c. Explain what further tests you would perform to remove any doubts about your classification.

3. a. Compare the results from Part III with the general solubility trends observed in Part I.
    b. Using a reference, explain the meaning of the term "immiscible", then use this word to describe results from Part III.

4. How did the addition of iodine crystals help in identifying the layers of liquids in the water-paint thinner combination?

5. Explain how many layers you would expect to see if water, paint thinner, and glycerin were combined in one test tube.

FOLLOW-UP QUESTIONS

1. Explain which solvent from this experiment you would use to remove road salt stains from a pair of jeans.

2. Some people use gasoline (a non-polar covalent compound) to clean grease stains from clothing. Although it is an effective solvent for grease, explain why gasoline should *never* be used for this purpose. Suggest a suitable alternate solvent.

CONCLUSION

What general rule can be followed when choosing a type of solvent for a particular solute?

Preparation of Standard Solutions and Use of a Spectrophotometer to Measure the Concentration of an Unknown Solution

One of the most important skills a chemistry student must acquire is knowing how to prepare a solution of a substance with a precise volume and molarity. In a wide variety of laboratories, including medical, teaching, research, manufacturing, and testing laboratories, solutions of known concentration are constantly required. Another important skill is to be able to measure the concentration of an unknown solution quickly and easily.

In Part I of this experiment, you will prepare a solution of cobalt(II) nitrate hexahydrate, $(Co(NO_3)_2 \cdot 6H_2O)$, having a molarity of $0.160 M$. In Part II you will make several solutions of lower concentration by making appropriate dilutions. Then in Part III the solutions will be placed in an instrument called a spectrophotometer which will be used to determine their color intensities. Finally, you will use a spectrophotometer to analyze an unknown solution in order to determine its molarity.

A spectrophotometer makes use of the fact that in a given colored solution, light of a particular frequency is absorbed. When a suitable frequency is selected, the light is passed through the solution (which should be in a special type of tube having walls of uniform thickness which is designed for this purpose) and detected by a photo cell. The intensity of the light is shown by a needle on a dial and can be read either as absorbance or as percent transmittance. The value of this reading depends on the concentration of the colored material in the solution.

The spectrophotometer may be set up in advance by your instructor, or selected students may be asked to do it. (The instructions below refer to a Bausch and Lomb Spectronic 20® spectrophotometer. If your instrument is a different one, your teacher will advise you of any modifications to the procedure.) The procedure is as follows:

1. Turn on the instrument by the left-hand knob. Allow it to warm up for 15 min.
2. Select an appropriate wavelength to use by rotating the dial on the top of the instrument. In this experiment, use 510 nm.
3. With the receptacle lid closed, adjust the left-hand knob on the front of the instrument until the needle reads 0% transmittance.
4. Place a cuvette three quarters full of distilled water in the receptacle on top and close the lid. Adjust the right-hand knob on the front of the instrument until the needle reads 100% transmittance. The spectrophotometer is now ready for use.

The following are some important points to note regarding use of this instrument:

(a) Make sure the receptacle lid is always closed before taking any readings, since stray light will affect the results.

(b) Don't touch any of the knobs unless specifically instructed by your teacher to recheck the 0% and 100% transmittance calibration.

(c) The scale may have a mirror behind it — make sure the needle and its mirror image are lined up with one another before taking the reading to ensure greater accuracy.

(d) If you are using the special tubes for the spectrophotometer, make sure that the lines marked on them line up with the mark on the receptacle.

Your teacher may instruct you to read either of the two scales (percent transmittance or absorbance) or both. There are advantages and disadvantages to each type of reading. The percent transmittance scale is uniform and therefore easier to read, but the calibration graph produced will be a curve, and a graph must be drawn in order to obtain the concentration of the unknown. The absorbance scale is more difficult to read; it increases as you go from right to left, and the size of the unit changes across the scale. However, the resulting calibration graph will usually be a straight line in the range of concentrations used; therefore, the concentration of an unknown may be obtained by calculation as well as from the graph.

OBJECTIVES

1. to prepare a standard solution of known concentration of cobalt(II) nitrate

2. to prepare various dilutions of the standard solution

3. to measure the percent transmittance, or absorbance, or both, of the solutions using a spectrophotometer, and to construct a calibration graph from the data

4. to obtain the concentration of an unknown solution using the calibration graph

MATERIALS

Apparatus

beaker (100 mL)
centigram balance
volumetric flask (100.0 mL)
funnel
wash bottle
5 test tubes (18 mm × 150 mm)
test-tube rack
graduated cylinder (10 mL)
graduated cylinder (25 mL)

pipet
spectrophotometer
5 cuvettes
   (Use 13 mm × 100 mm test tubes
   instead if necessary.)
safety goggles
lab apron

Reagents

cobalt(II) nitrate hexahydrate
  $(Co(NO_3)_2 \cdot 6H_2O)$
solution of above substance
  of unknown concentration

PROCEDURE

Part I   Preparation of a Standard $Co(NO_3)_2$ Solution

CAUTION: Cobalt(II) nitrate is moderately toxic. Do not get any in your mouth.

1. Before coming to the laboratory, calculate the mass of cobalt(II) nitrate hexahydrate $(Co(NO_3)_2 \cdot 6H_2O)$ needed to make 100.0 mL of a $0.160M$ solution. Check with other students or your teacher to make certain that you have calculated the correct mass before proceeding.

2. Put on your lab apron and safety goggles.

3. Measure the mass of a clean, dry 100 mL beaker, then transfer the precise amount of $Co(NO_3)_2 \cdot 6H_2O$ (calculated in Step 1 above) to the beaker.

4. Dissolve the compound in about 50 mL of water.

5. Transfer the solution to a 100.0 mL volumetric flask by means of a funnel, then wash the beaker several times with small amounts of water, adding the washings to the flask. Be careful not to add so much water that you go beyond the mark. (*Note:* If you do not have a 100.0 mL volumetric flask, use a 100 mL graduated cylinder instead.)

6. Remove the funnel, and add water from a wash bottle until the volume is exactly at the 100.0 mL mark. (Add the water drop by drop when you are close.)

7. Stopper the flask, and shake to ensure thorough mixing. You now have a 0.160M solution.

Part II Preparation of Dilute Solutions of $Co(NO_3)_2$

1. Obtain 5 test tubes (18 mm × 150 mm) and place them in a rack. Label them *A* to *E*.

2. In test tube *A*, place approximately 10 mL of your stock solution (0.160M).

3. Prepare a diluted solution by placing 12.0 mL of the stock solution in a 25 mL graduated cylinder and adding water until the solution is up to the 16.0 mL mark. Transfer this solution to test tube *B*.

4. Repeat Step 3 using 8.0 mL of stock solution and making it up to 16.0 mL. (If the graduated cylinder is wet from previous washings, rinse it out with about 4 mL of your stock solution first, and discard the rinsing liquid.) Transfer the diluted solution to test tube *C*.

5. In the same manner prepare a dilution with 4.0 mL of stock solution made up to 16.0 mL for test tube *D*, and 2.0 mL of stock solution made up to 16.0 mL for test tube *E*.

6. Calculate the new molarities of the diluted solutions, and enter them in your copy of Table 1 in your notebook.

Part III Measuring the Concentration with a Spectrophotometer

1. Make sure you understand thoroughly how to use the spectrophotometer, as outlined in the introduction to this experiment.

2. Transfer solutions *A* to *E* into five cuvettes. (If cuvettes are not available, use 13 mm × 100 mm test tubes that are clean and scratch-free instead.) If the tubes are wet inside, rinse each with about 4 mL of the solution which will go in it, discard the rinsings, then fill each about three quarters full with the appropriate solution.

3. Make sure the tubes are clean and dry on the outside, place each in turn in the receptacle on top of the spectrophotometer, then close the lid. Read off the value of either the percent transmittance or the absorbance, or both, as directed by your instructor. Enter the values in Table 1.

4. Obtain a $Co(NO_3)_2$ solution of unknown concentration from the instructor and note any identifying letter or number on it. Fill a tube three quarters full as before. Read either percent transmittance or absorbance, depending on which scale you read for your standards. Enter this value in Table 1 as well.

5. Before you leave the laboratory, wash your hands thoroughly with soap and water; use a fingernail brush to clean under your nails.

REAGENT DISPOSAL

Rinse all solutions down the sink with plenty of water, unless your instructor asks you to save them.

POST LAB DISCUSSION

The accuracy of your answer for the concentration of the unknown solution will be a good measure of your experimental skill. It is important to have taken all your readings carefully and have double-checked them to be sure you had the correct values. Graphs must now be plotted carefully and accurately, using metric graph paper.

DATA AND OBSERVATIONS

Table 1

ORIGINAL MOLARITY	DILUTION	NEW MOLARITY	ABSORBANCE	PERCENT TRANSMITTANCE
0.160	—	0.160		
0.160	12 mL to 16 mL			
0.160	8 mL to 16 mL			
0.160	4 mL to 16 mL			
0.160	2 mL to 16 mL			
unknown	—	—		

COMPLETE IN YOUR NOTEBOOK

QUESTIONS AND CALCULATIONS

1. Calculate the molarity of the Co^{2+} ion in each of solutions 1–5. The new molarity is given by the molarity of the stock solution multiplied by the dilution factor (ratio of original volume to final volume).

2. Plot a graph of your results, using metric graph paper. Put concentration on the x-axis, using a scale of 1 cm = 0.01M, and absorbance on the y-axis, using a scale of 1 cm = 0.05 A. (If you recorded your results as percent transmittance, use 1 cm = 5% transmittance.)

3. Determine the concentration of your unknown solution by reading from your graph the concentration that is equivalent to the absorbance or percent transmittance you recorded. Be sure to state in your report which unknown you used if more than one was available.

4. Why does a volumetric flask have the shape it does?

5. Looking at your results and the shape of your graph, do you think your results could have been improved by the use of graduated pipets instead of graduated cylinders?

6. What is the advantage of reading the absorbance rather than the percent transmittance on the spectrophotometer?

7. Why is it a good idea to wash out the tubes with the solution you are using before refilling it to read in the spectrophotometer?

FOLLOW-UP QUESTIONS

1. In order to analyze the waste water containing Co^{2+} from a manufacturing process, 1.0 L of water was evaporated to 10.0 mL, then placed in a spectrophotometer tube. The absorbance was found to be 0.20 (63% transmittance). Using your calibration curve, calculate the number of milligrams of Co^{2+} in 1.0 L of waste water.

CONCLUSION

State the results of Objective 4.

Factors Affecting Solubility and Rate of Dissolving

Solutions are homogeneous mixtures containing a *solute* (the substance being dissolved) and a *solvent* (the substance doing the dissolving). Solutes and solvents can be any combination of solids, liquids, and gases. The most common solutions have liquid solvents. You can probably think of many solutions of this sort that you encounter regularly, such as fruit juices, soda pop, and salt water.

When a solute is dissolved by a solvent to form a solution, several characteristics of the process are of interest to chemists. One characteristic is the *rate of dissolving*, which depends upon the time required for a given amount of solute to dissolve in a given amount of solution. Another is *solubility*, a measure of the amount of solute that will dissolve in a given amount of solvent.

In Part I of this experiment, you will investigate the effect of temperature on the rate of dissolving of sodium chloride and potassium nitrate crystals in water. In Part II you will investigate the effect of temperature on the solubilities of these substances in water.

OBJECTIVES

1. to determine the effect of temperature on rate of dissolving

2. to determine the effect of temperature on solubility

3. to determine whether a relationship exists between solubility and rate of dissolving

MATERIALS

Apparatus

6 test tubes
(18 mm × 150 mm)
test-tube rack
test-tube holder
graduated cylinder (10 mL)
watch with second hand
or stopwatch
thermometer
3 beakers (250 mL)
2 glass stirring rods

plastic spoon
lab burner
ring stand and ring support
wire gauze with ceramic
centre
centigram balance
safety goggles
lab apron

Reagents

sodium chloride crystals
(NaCl)
potassium nitrate crystals
(KNO_3)
distilled water
ice cubes

PROCEDURE

Part I   Effect of Temperature on Rate of Dissolving

1. Put on your lab apron and safety goggles.

2. Use a lab burner to heat 150 mL of water to boiling. Set this water aside as your hot water bath. If you have a lab partner, one of you can proceed to Step 3 while the other monitors the boiling of the water.

3. Obtain one half spoonful of sodium chloride crystals and one half spoonful of potassium nitrate crystals on separate, labelled pieces of folded paper. Weigh out three 0.5 g samples of sodium chloride and three 0.5 g samples of potassium nitrate on six labelled pieces of folded paper.

4. Obtain six test tubes and label three of them A and three of them B, using a water soluble marker. Make sure you label them near the top. Set the empty test tubes in a test-tube rack.

5. Add 10 mL of distilled water to each of the six test tubes.

6. Set up a bath at room temperature by adding 150 mL of water to a second beaker. Set up a cold water bath by adding 150 mL of ice and water to a third beaker.

7. Set one A test tube and one B test tube in each of the three water baths. Allow these test tubes to sit in the water baths for 2 min to 3 min while you get organized for Step 8.

8. Record the temperature of the cold water bath in your copy of Table 1 in your notebook. Add a 0.5 g sample of the NaCl crystals to test tube A while it remains in the bath, and start timing. Quickly cover the test tube with a thumb and immediately tilt the tube back and forth once to remove any crystals which might have stuck to the sides. Using a stirring rod, stir the contents of the test tube at a steady rate and time how long it takes the crystals to dissolve.

9. Repeat Step 8 for a 0.5 g sample of KNO_3 in test tube B.

10. Repeat Steps 8 and 9 for the other two water baths. Reheat the hot water bath before use.

11. Clean up all test tubes according to the reagent disposal instructions. Save the three water baths as well as one test tube A and one test tube B for Part II of the experiment.

Part II   Effect of Temperature on Solubility

1. Readjust the temperatures of the three water baths from Part I. Reheat the hot bath and add more ice to the cold bath if necessary.

2. Obtain 3.0 g of NaCl and 3.0 g of KNO_3.

3. Add 10 mL of water to a clean test tube labelled A and 10 mL of water to one labelled B.

4. Set the test tubes in the cold water bath and wait for 2 min to 3 min. Record the water temperature in your copy of Table 2 in your notebook. Put the NaCl in test tube *A* and the KNO₃ in test tube *B*. Use two different, labelled stirring rods to stir each of the solutions for approximately two minutes. Record your observations in Table 2.

5. Move both test tubes to the water bath at room temperature, and stir for approximately two minutes. Record your observations.

6. Repeat Step 5 for the hot water bath.

7. Add another 1.0 g of each solute to its respective test tube in the hot water bath and stir for approximately two minutes. Record these observations in Table 2.

8. Clean up all your apparatus according to the reagent disposal instructions.

9. Before leaving the laboratory, wash your hands thoroughly with soap and water; use a fingernail brush to clean under your nails.

REAGENT DISPOSAL

All solutions, as well as any remaining solid sodium chloride or potassium nitrate, may be rinsed down the sink with copious amounts of water.

POST LAB DISCUSSION

A solution is considered to be saturated if it contains as much solute as can be possibly dissolved in a given amount of solvent at a given temperature. The solubility of a solid in a liquid is often expressed as the mass of solid dissolved in 100 mL of liquid to form a saturated solution.

The only factor that affects solubility is temperature. Other factors such as smaller solute particle size and stirring will cause a higher rate of dissolving, but they will not cause more solute to dissolve. Thus, solubility remains the same.

As you might expect, an increase in temperature can produce a higher rate of dissolving. However, when rates are compared between solids at different temperatures, some unexpected results are observed. One substance may dissolve faster than another at one temperature—but the reverse may be true at a different temperature. By examining your data in Table 1 and the information provided by Figure 16C-1, you can deduce a reason for this unusual phenomenon.

For the purposes of this experiment, rate of dissolving refers to the rate at which 0.5 g of solute dissolves in 10.0 mL of water at a specific temperature. Thus, rate of dissolving can be expressed as $\dfrac{1}{\text{time (s)}}$ or s^{-1}. For instance, if the time taken to dissolve is 40 s, the rate of dissolving is $\dfrac{1}{40 \text{ s}} = 2.5 \times 10^{-2} s^{-1}$.

DATA AND OBSERVATIONS

Part I Effect of Temperature on Rate of Dissolving

Table 1

		SODIUM CHLORIDE		POTASSIUM NITRATE	
BEAKER	**TEMPERATURE (°C)**	**TIME TO DISSOLVE SAMPLE (in s)**	**RATE OF DISSOLVING (in s^{-1})**	**TIME TO DISSOLVE SAMPLE (in s)**	**RATE OF DISSOLVING (in s^{-1})**
Cold					
Room Temp.	COMPLETE IN YOUR NOTEBOOK			COMPLETE IN YOUR NOTEBOOK	
Hot					

Part II Effect of Temperature on Solubility

Table 2

BEAKER	TEMPERATURE (°C)	SODIUM CHLORIDE	POTASSIUM NITRATE
Cold			
Room Temp.			
Hot	COMPLETE IN YOUR NOTEBOOK		COMPLETE IN YOUR NOTEBOOK
Hot (with more solute added)			

QUESTIONS AND CALCULATIONS

1. For Part I, calculate the rate of dissolving for each solute at each temperature. Enter this information in Table 1 in your notebook.
2. Refer to your data in Table 1 in answering the following questions.
   a. How does temperature appear to affect the rate of dissolving?
   b. How does the rate of dissolving of KNO_3 compare to that of NaCl at the highest temperature?
   c. How do these rates compare at room temperature?
   d. How do these rates compare at the lowest temperature?
3. Refer to your data in Table 2 in answering the following questions.
   a. How does temperature appear to affect solubility?
   b. How does the solubility of KNO_3 compare to that of NaCl at the lowest temperature?
   c. How do these solubilities compare at room temperature?
   d. How do these solubilities compare at the highest temperature?
4. At certain temperatures, KNO_3 has a higher rate of dissolving than NaCl, but at other temperatures the opposite is true. Suggest a reason for this phenomenon. (If necessary, consult Figure 16C-1.)
5. Does rate of dissolving depend on temperature or on solubility? Explain your answer.

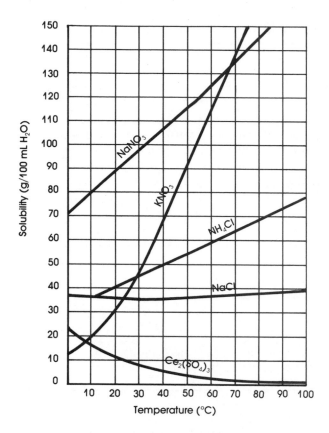

Figure 16C-1 *Each line illustrates the effect of temperature on the solubility of a different substance.*

FOLLOW-UP QUESTIONS

1. a. Other than temperature, what other factors increase the rate of dissolving?
   b. What effect do these additional factors have on solubility?

2. Cerium(III) sulfate, $Ce_2(SO_4)_3$, is an unusual substance in that its solubility *decreases* as the temperature increases. (See Figure 16C-1.) On the basis of this information and your experimental results, predict what will happen to the rate of dissolving as the temperature increases.

CONCLUSION

State the results of Objective 3.

Solubility Trends and Precipitate Formation

A precipitation reaction occurs when certain ions are allowed to interact in solution. The result of the interaction is that the force of attraction between a positive ion and a negative ion is so great that they join together to form a slightly soluble substance called a *precipitate*. Certain *lakes* (coloring pigments in inks and wallpapers) are produced by precipitation reactions.

Chemists often analyze a precipitation reaction by writing a series of equations that enables them to understand how the precipitate resulted. A *formula equation* shows all of the compounds involved in the reaction and also identifies the precipitate that forms. For example, when solutions of lead(II) nitrate and potassium iodide are mixed, a yellow precipitate results. The initial formula equation for the reaction would be

$$Pb(NO_3)_2(aq) + 2KI(aq) \rightarrow 2KNO_3 + PbI_2$$

One of these must be a solid (the precipitate).

Further tests are required to deduce that the precipitate here is lead(II) iodide, PbI_2. Therefore, the final formula equation should be written as

$$Pb(NO_3)_2(aq) + 2KI(aq) \rightarrow 2KNO_3(aq) + PbI_2(s)$$

The next equation used to analyze the reaction is a *complete ionic equation* which shows all compounds other than the precipitate in their dissociated form:

$$Pb^{2+}(aq) + 2NO_3^-(aq) + 2K^+(aq) + 2I^-(aq) \rightarrow 2K^+(aq) + 2NO_3^-(aq) + PbI_2(s)$$

A close examination of the above ionic equation reveals that K^+ ions and NO_3^- ions do not change in the reaction. Hence, they are known as *spectator ions*. When you eliminate all spectator ions from the ionic equation you are left with the *net ionic equation*:

$$Pb^{2+}(aq) + 2I^-(aq) \rightarrow PbI_2(s)$$

This net ionic equation shows only those ions which were actually involved in the reaction.

In this experiment, you will mix several solutions together; some will form precipitates and some will not. One of your tasks will be to deduce the identity of the precipitates by carefully examining all of your results. Having identified the precipitates, you will analyze the precipitation reaction by writing formula, complete ionic, and net ionic equations.

OBJECTIVES

1. to mix several pairs of solutions together and then note whether any precipitates form

2. to deduce, from the experimental results, which combinations of ions form precipitates

3. to write a balanced formula equation for each precipitation reaction

4. to write a complete ionic equation for each precipitation reaction

5. to determine and write the net ionic reaction for each precipitation reaction

MATERIALS

Apparatus

6 small test tubes
   (10 mm × 75 mm)
test-tube rack
6 medicine droppers
glass square
   (10 cm × 10 cm)
safety goggles
lab aprons

Reagents

one or more sets of 6 solutions

CAUTION: Several of these solutions are poisonous. Do not get any in your mouth; wash any spills and splashes immediately with plenty of water. Call your teacher.

PROCEDURE

1. Put on your safety goggles and lab apron.

2. Obtain a sample of each solution in each of the 6 small test tubes, filling each test tube one quarter full and labelling it. Use one medicine dropper for each solution, to avoid contaminating the others. Place the samples in the test-tube rack at your lab station.

3. Place a drop of one solution on the glass square and, using the appropriate dropper, add a drop of second solution to it. A piece of paper with a grid drawn on it can be placed under the glass so that several tests can be done at a time.

4. If a precipitate forms, record this result in the copy of Table 1 in your notebook by placing "ppt" in the appropriate square. If no precipitate forms, simply mark a dash (—) in the square.

5. Repeat Steps 2 and 3 until all possible combinations of solutions have been tested.

6. Follow the reagent disposal instructions, then rinse out all equipment and dry the glass square. Test another set of solutions (repeat Steps 1 to 4) if time permits.

7. Before you leave the laboratory, wash your hands thoroughly with soap and water; use a fingernail brush to clean under your nails.

REAGENT DISPOSAL

Wash all solutions down the sink with copious amounts of water.

POST LAB DISCUSSION

In each square of the data table which shows that a precipitate forms, you will notice that there are two possible compounds that could be the precipitate. It is up to you, through a series of logical deductions based on all the data in the table, to determine the identity of the precipitate in each case.

If, for example, a precipitate was recorded in the Na^+, SO_4^{2-}/Al^{3+}, Cl^- square, then the precipitate would be either $NaCl$ or $Al_2(SO_4)_3$. Before you can conclusively choose either of these compounds, you will need to examine the possibilities in the other squares.

DATA AND OBSERVATIONS

The table below is only a sample table. The actual solutions will depend on the set that is provided by your teacher.

Table 1

		(6) Al^{3+}, Cl^{-}	(5) Ba^{2+}, NO$_3^{-}$	(4) Ba^{2+}, Cl^{-}	(3) Sr^{2+}, NO$_3^{-}$	(2) Al^{3+}, SO$_4^{2-}$	(1) Na^{+}, SO$_4^{2-}$
(1)	Na^{+}, SO$_4^{2-}$						
(2)	Al^{3+}, SO$_4^{2-}$						
(3)	Sr^{2+}, NO$_3^{-}$						
(4)	Ba^{2+}, Cl^{-}						
(5)	Ba^{2+}, NO$_3^{-}$						
(6)	Al^{3+}, Cl^{-}						

COMPLETE IN YOUR NOTEBOOK

QUESTIONS

1. What observations led you to believe that precipitates formed?

2. How many precipitation reactions did you observe?

3. How many *different* precipitates did you observe?

4. Construct a table summarizing your results similar to Table 2, which shows those combinations of ions that formed precipitates and those that did not.

Table 2

THIS NEGATIVE ION	PLUS THESE POSITIVE IONS	FORMED
e.g. S^{2-}	Na^{+}, Ca^{2+}	no precipitate
S^{2-}	Cu^{2+}	precipitate

5. For each different precipitation, write the following:
   a. balanced formula equation
   b. complete ionic equation
   c. net ionic equation

FOLLOW-UP QUESTIONS

1. Compare your table from Question 4 above to the solubility table located in Appendix 2. Describe any similarities or differences in results.

CONCLUSION

State the results of Objective 5.

An Introduction to Qualitative Analysis

The term "qualitative analysis" in chemistry refers to a set of procedures used to identify a particular ion or ions in a given sample when it is not necessary to find out the quantity of any ion present. (Hence the term "qualitative" rather than "quantitative" is used.)

If the number of ions that could be in a sample is large, then the scheme to be followed in order to identify a particular ion correctly becomes very complex. A large number of reagents, many of which may give no result, is required. The quantities and concentrations of reagents involved are critical, since in many cases the separation of two ions depends on relatively small differences in solubility. For these reasons a comprehensive treatment of qualitative analysis is beyond the scope of this lab manual, but it is worthwhile for you to see the methods involved and to acquire enough knowledge of some reactions to enable you to identify some unknowns.

In Part I of this experiment you look at a scheme for identifying different metal ions belonging to Group 2 of the periodic table (the alkaline earth metals), magnesium, calcium, strontium, and barium. Then in Part II you will look at a scheme for identifying four different anions, namely carbonate, sulfate, chloride, and iodide. In each case, after carrying out your reactions, you will be given at least one unknown containing one ion to be identified.

OBJECTIVES

1. to carry out tests on the ions Mg^{2+}, Ca^{2+}, Sr^{2+}, and Ba^{2+} that enable each to be identified separately, and to use these tests to identify an unknown

2. to carry out tests on the ions SO_4^{2-}, CO_3^{2-}, Cl^-, and I^- that enable each to be identified separately, and to use these tests to identify an unknown

MATERIALS

Apparatus	Reagents	
20 test tubes	$0.1M$ $Mg(NO_3)_2$	$0.1M$ NaCl
(13 mm × 100 mm)	$0.1M$ $Ca(NO_3)_2$	$0.1M$ NaI
test-tube rack	$0.1M$ $Sr(NO_3)_2$	$0.1M$ $AgNO_3$
lab apron	$0.1M$ $Ba(NO_3)_2$	$1M$ HNO_3
safety goggles	$0.02M$ K_2CrO_4	$6M$ NH_3
	$0.1M$ $(NH_4)_2C_2O_4$	solution containing
	$0.1M$ Na_2SO_4	unknown cation
	$0.1M$ NaOH	solution containing
	$0.1M$ Na_2CO_3	unknown anion

PROCEDURE

Part I Qualitative Analysis of Group 2 Elements

1. Put on your lab apron and safety goggles.

2. Place 2 mL of $0.1M$ $Mg(NO_3)_2$, $Ca(NO_3)_2$, $Sr(NO_3)_2$, and $Ba(NO_3)_2$ respectively in four 13 mm × 100 mm test tubes.

3. To each tube add 2 mL of $0.02M$ K_2CrO_4, and observe in which tubes a precipitate occurs. Note also the amount of precipitate as light or heavy, and whether it formed immediately or after a short time had elapsed. Record your observations in your copy of Table 1 in your notebook.

4. Repeat Steps 2 and 3, using 2 mL of $0.1M$ $(NH_4)_2C_2O_4$ as the added reagent. Record your observations in Table 1.

5. Repeat Steps 2 and 3, using 2 mL of 0.1 M Na_2SO_4 as the added reagent. Again, record what you observe.

6. Repeat Steps 2 and 3, using 2 mL of $0.1M$ $NaOH$ as the added reagent. Record your observations.

7. Obtain an unknown solution containing only one cation, and carry out separate reactions on 2 mL of the sample with 2 mL of each of the four reagents. Identify the cation from your results.

8. Dispose of all the contents of your test tubes according to the reagent disposal instructions. Wash the test tubes, and reuse them in Part II.

CAUTION: Barium compounds are poisonous. Do not get any in your mouth. Do not swallow any.

CAUTION: Chromates are poisonous, and are skin irritants. Do not get any in your mouth; do not swallow any. Wash away any spills and splashes with plenty of water.

CAUTION: Oxalates are poisonous. Do not get any in your mouth. Do not swallow any.

Part II   Qualitative Analysis of Selected Anions

1. Place 2 mL of $0.1M$ Na_2CO_3, Na_2SO_4, $NaCl$, and NaI respectively in four 13 mm × 100 mm test tubes.

2. To each tube, add 2 mL of $1M$ HNO_3. Observe the results, and record them in your copy of Table 2.

3. Repeat Step 1, then add to each tube 2 mL of $0.1M$ $Ba(NO_3)_2$ and note and record in which tubes a precipitate was formed.

4. To the tubes containing precipitates, add 1 mL of $1M$ HNO_3. Observe and record the results.

5. Repeat Step 1, then add to each test tube 2 mL of $0.1M$ $AgNO_3$. Note in which test tubes a precipitate results, and record your results in Table 2.

6. Divide the contents of each test tube containing a precipitate in half, placing each half in a separate test tube.

7. To one set of precipitates add 1 mL of $1M$ HNO_3. Observe the results and record them in Table 2.

8. To the other set of precipitates add 1 mL of $6M$ NH_3, and observe and record the results.

9. Obtain a sample containing a single unknown anion. Carry out each test that you used for the known anions, and observe the results. Identify the anion from your results.

10. Wash your hands thoroughly with soap and water before leaving the laboratory; use a fingernail brush to clean under your fingernails.

CAUTION: Nitric acid is corrosive. Keep it off your skin and out of your eyes. Wash away any spills and splashes with plenty of water.

CAUTION: Silver nitrate is poisonous, and corrosive to skin and eyes. It will result in brown stains on your skin if you spill any on yourself. If this occurs, wash with sodium thiosulfate solution, then with plenty of water. Call your teacher.

CAUTION: Ammonia solution is corrosive. Keep it off your skin and out of your eyes. Avoid breathing its fumes. Wash away any spills and splashes with plenty of water.

REAGENT DISPOSAL

Test tubes containing silver compounds, barium compounds, and chromates should be emptied into the designated waste containers. All other waste material may be safely rinsed down the sink with copious amounts of water.

POST LAB DISCUSSION

The reactions in Part I are all straightforward precipitation reactions. It is important to observe how much precipitate formed, and whether it formed immediately or took somewhat longer to become evident. In some cases these differences are needed to make a definite identification of an unknown.

An important part of the procedure for Part II is adding HNO_3 to see whether the precipitate formed will dissolve in acid. It is quite easy to distinguish between two ions of which both give a precipitate with the same reagent, but one dissolves in acid and the other doesn't.

The $6M$ NH_3 is used to help identify precipitates formed with Ag^+. Some precipitates can dissolve as a result of the formation of the silver diammine ion, $Ag(NH_3)_2^+$; this reaction aids in their identification.

DATA AND OBSERVATIONS

Organize your data and observations in tables similar to the following. It would be a good idea to have these in your notebook before coming to the laboratory.

Part I   Qualitative Analysis of Group 2 Elements

Table 1

REAGENTS	0.1 M SOLUTIONS OF GROUP 2 CATIONS (AS NITRATES)				
	Mg^{2+}	Ca^{2+}	Sr^{2+}	Ba^{2+}	UNKNOWN # ____
0.02M K_2CrO_4					
0.1M $(NH_4)_2C_2O_4$					
0.1M Na_2SO_4					
0.1M NaOH					

Part II   Qualitative Analysis of Selected Anions

Table 2

REAGENTS	0.1 M SOLUTIONS OF ANIONS (AS Na SALTS)				
	CO_3^{2-}	SO_4^{2-}	Cl^-	I^-	UNKNOWN # ____
1M HNO_3					
0.1M $Ba(NO_3)_2$					
0.1M HNO_3 added to above					
0.1M $AgNO_3$					
1M HNO_3 added to above					
6M NH_3 added to precipitates from $AgNO_3$					

QUESTIONS

Part I   Qualitative Analysis of Group 2 Elements

1. Write net ionic equations for each combination in which a precipitate occurred.

2. State the identity of your unknown (along with its sample number). Give the reasoning you used to arrive at this conclusion.

Part II   Qualitative Analysis of Selected Anions

1. Write net ionic equations for each combination in which a precipitate formed or another reaction occurred.

2. Write net ionic equations for each situation in which the precipitate redissolved on the addition of HNO_3 or NH_3.

3. State the identity of your unknown (along with its sample number). Give the reasoning you used to arrive at this conclusion.

FOLLOW-UP QUESTIONS

1. Devise a sequence of reactions to follow (using filtering or centrifuging where necessary to remove precipitates) to identify an unknown containing two or more cations of Group 2 elements.

2. Devise a sequence of reactions to follow (using filtering or centrifuging where necessary to remove precipitates) to identify an unknown consisting of two or more of the anions tested in Part II.

3. Why are the reagents used to test for cations usually alkali metal salts or ammonium salts rather than salts of other metals?

4. Why are the reagents used to test for anions usually a nitrate of the cation that is reacting rather than other salts of that cation?

5. For fast and accurate identification of substances, major research or testing laboratories now use very sophisticated (and expensive) equipment. Find out the name of one of the instruments now used for analysis, and briefly describe its method of operation.

CONCLUSION

State in general terms the principles involved in developing a qualitative analysis scheme.

Thermodynamics

The formation or destruction of chemical bonds is always accompanied by an energy exchange between the reactant molecules and the immediate environment. The term ΔH is used to describe the resulting *enthalpy changes*. When atoms or ions form new bonds, energy is released into the environment and the reaction products possess lower enthalpy than the reactants. This energy release may be observed as a measurable increase in the temperature of the surroundings. *Exothermic* reactions are associated with negative ΔH values. Conversely, when chemical bonds are broken, energy must be absorbed from the environment and the products possess a higher enthalpy than the reactants. The ΔH value is positive. This is called an *endothermic* reaction, which is characterized by a measurable decrease in the temperature of the surroundings.

Germain Henry Hess, a Swiss-Russian chemist, examined heat transformations in reactions involving several steps. He found that the enthalpy changes for a series of reactions can be added together to describe the energy change for the overall reaction. Known as Hess's law, this relationship will be studied in this laboratory exercise.

In this experiment, by measuring the heat transformations generated from a sequence of reactions, you will obtain experimental evidence for the law of enthalpy additivity. Determinations and comparisons of the heat that evolved in the following three exothermic reactions will be performed in the three parts of the experiment, respectively:

$$NaOH(s) \rightarrow Na^+(aq) + OH^-(aq)$$
$$Na^+(aq) + OH^-(aq) + H^+(aq) + Cl^-(aq) \rightarrow H_2O + Na^+(aq) + Cl^-(aq)$$
$$NaOH(s) + H^+(aq) + Cl^-(aq) \rightarrow H_2O + Na^+(aq) + Cl^-(aq)$$

A simple calorimeter will be constructed using a plastic foam cup. Noticeable rises in water temperature will be used to calculate the ΔH value for each of the reactions.

OBJECTIVES

1. to construct a simple calorimeter

2. to determine the amount of heat energy released or absorbed in three separate reactions

3. to obtain experimental evidence for the additivity of reaction heats

CAUTION: Your thermometer is made of glass and can break, leaving sharp edges that cut. Handle your thermometer gently. For example, do not use it to crush a piece of ice. The glass around the mercury bulb is very thin. Mercury vapor and liquid are very poisonous. If your thermometer breaks, call your teacher.

MATERIALS

Apparatus

		Reagents
graduated cylinder	stirring rod	NaOH pellets
plastic foam cup	lab apron	distilled water
tongs or forceps	safety goggles	1.0M HCl
centigram balance	plastic gloves	0.5M HCl
thermometer	full face shield	1.0M NaOH
1 beaker (250 mL)	glazed paper (optional)	

PROCEDURE

Part I Heat of Solution of Solid Sodium Hydroxide

1. Put on your lab apron, safety goggles, plastic gloves, and full face shield.

2. Measure 100 mL of distilled water into a graduated cylinder and pour it into a clean, dry, plastic foam cup.

3. Obtain approximately 2 g of NaOH pellets. Record their mass to the nearest 0.01 g on glazed paper. Since NaOH absorbs water from the air, it is necessary to proceed to Steps 4 and 5 as soon as the mass of the pellets has been found.

4. Measure and record the temperature of the water in the calorimeter to the nearest 0.1°C.

5. Add the NaOH pellets to the water and constantly check the solution temperature. Use a stirring rod to gently stir the solution until all the solid has dissolved.

6. Record the highest solution temperature reached in your copy of Table 1 in your notebook. Place the solution in the designated waste container and rinse all apparatus with distilled water.

CAUTION: Sodium hydroxide pellets are very corrosive to the skin, eyes, and clothing; if even one gets in your mouth or is swallowed, it will cause serious damage. Wear safety goggles, full face shield, and gloves. Do not touch a pellet, even while wearing gloves; use tongs. If any pellets are spilled, call your teacher. Do not attempt to pick up or move spilled pellets. Immediately wash pellets and residues of pellets off your skin or clothing, using plenty of water. Call your teacher.

Part II Heat of Reaction between Hydrochloric Acid and Sodium Hydroxide Solution

1. Measure 50 mL of a 1.0M hydrochloric acid solution into a graduated cylinder. Carefully pour this solution into a clean, dry, plastic foam cup.

2. Measure 50 mL of 1.0M sodium hydroxide solution into a graduated cylinder. Carefully pour it into a 250 mL beaker.

3. Record the temperature of each solution to the nearest 0.1°C. Use the same thermometer for both readings, but be sure to rinse it with distilled water between measurements.

4. Pour the sodium hydroxide into the plastic foam cup containing the hydrochloric acid solution. Using a stirring rod, stir the solution gently. Record the highest temperature reached in your copy of Table 2. Discard the solution down the sink with plenty of water and rinse all apparatus with distilled water.

CAUTION: Hydrochloric acid is corrosive to the skin, eyes, and clothing. When handling 1M acid, wear safety goggles and gloves. Immediately wash spills and splashes off your skin and clothing, using plenty of water. Call your teacher.

Part III Heat of Reaction between Hydrochloric Acid and Solid Sodium Hydroxide

1. Measure 100 mL of 0.5M hydrochloric acid into a graduated cylinder. Pour the solution into a clean, dry, plastic foam cup.

2. Obtain 2 g of NaOH pellets. Record their mass to the nearest 0.01 g in your copy of Table 3.

CAUTION: Sodium hydroxide solution is corrosive to the skin, eyes, and clothing. When handling 1M solutions, wear safety goggles and gloves. Immediately wash spills and splashes off your skin and clothing, using plenty of water. Call your teacher.

3. Measure and record the temperature of the hydrochloric acid solution to the nearest 0.1°C in your copy of Table 3.

4. While monitoring the solution temperature, add the NaOH pellets to the HCl. Using a stirring rod, gently stir the solution until all the solid has dissolved.

5. Record the highest solution temperature reached in Table 3. Discard the solution down the sink with plenty of water.

6. Before you leave the laboratory, wash your hands thoroughly with soap and water; use a fingernail brush to clean under your fingernails.

REAGENT DISPOSAL

Return any leftover NaOH or HCl solutions to the designated containers for each, along with the NaOH solution from Part I. Solutions from Parts II and III consisted simply of salt solution, and can safely be washed away.

POST LAB DISCUSSION

The heat liberated by each of the three reactions was released into the calorimeter environment. Since the quantity of heat absorbed by the plastic foam cup or transferred to the atmosphere is negligible, you can assume that all evolved energy was absorbed by the solution. To convert the observed rise in solution temperatures into heat values, the collected data for each reaction must be substituted into the following equation:

$$\text{heat of reaction} = \text{temperature change}(\Delta t)$$
$$\times \text{ mass of solution } (m) \times \text{specific heat of solution}(c)$$

The mass of the solution can be calculated from its final volume if its density is known. Since the solutions in this experiment are dilute aqueous solutions, their densities can be taken to be the same as that of water, 1.0 g/mL. The specific heat (c) of a dilute aqueous solution can be taken to be the same as that of water, 4180 J/kg·K.

Since the heats of reaction are commonly expressed as heat per *mole*, an additional calculation is needed. The heat of reaction per mole of NaOH can be obtained by dividing the heat given off in a reaction by the number of moles of NaOH that reacted.

The energy value obtained in Part I represents the energy of solution for one mole of NaOH(s). The value represented for Part II represents the heat of reaction for one mole of $H^+(aq)$ and one mole of $OH^-(aq)$. Part III can be considered to be the sum of the reactions occurring in Parts I and II. Its heat of reaction should therefore equal the heat of solution of NaOH(s) plus the heat of reaction of $H^+(aq)$ and $OH^-(aq)$.

DATA AND OBSERVATIONS

Part I   Heat of Solution of Solid Sodium Hydroxide

Table 1

Original temperature of water (t_1)	
Final temperature of solution (t_2)	
Temperature change $(t_2 - t_1 = \Delta t)$	
Mass of 100 mL of water	
Heat evolved by reaction	
Mass of NaOH(s)	
Moles of NaOH	
Energy per mole of NaOH	
ΔH_1 (kJ/mole) NaOH	

Part II   Heat of Reaction between Hydrochloric Acid and Sodium Hydroxide Solution

Table 2

Original temperature of HCl(aq)	
Original temperature of NaOH(aq)	
Average original temperature (t_1)	
Final temperature of solution (t_2)	
Temperature change $(t_2 - t_1 = \Delta t)$	
Total mass of solution (assume 1 mL = 1 g)	
Heat evolved by reaction	
Molarity of NaOH solution	
Volume of NaOH solution	
Moles of NaOH	
Energy per mole of NaOH	
ΔH_2 (kJ/mole) NaOH	

Part III Heat of Reaction between Hydrochloric Acid and Solid Sodium Hydroxide

Table 3

Original temperature of HCl(aq) (t_1)	
Final temperature of solution (t_2)	
Temperature change ($t_2 - t_1 = \Delta t$)	
Mass of HCl (assume 1 mL = 1 g)	
Heat evolved by reaction	
Mass of NaOH(s)	
Moles of NaOH	
Energy per mole of NaOH	
ΔH_3 (kJ/mole) NaOH	

QUESTIONS AND CALCULATIONS

1. Compare the calculated enthalpy change of each of the three reactions.

2. Write the net ionic equations for the reactions in Part II and Part III.

3. How does the value of ΔH_3 differ from the sum of ΔH_1 and ΔH_2?

4. Calculate the percent deviation between ΔH_3 and the sum of ΔH_1 and ΔH_2. Assume ΔH_3 to be correct.

5. Suggest several reasons for the observed percent difference.

6. Suppose you doubled the mass of NaOH used in Part I. How would this affect the number of joules released in this reaction? What would be the effect on ΔH_1?

FOLLOW-UP QUESTIONS

1. The dissolving of ammonium nitrate in water is a highly endothermic process. How could this fact be utilized in the development of a cold pack used to treat athletic injuries?

CONCLUSION

State the results of Objective 3.

Heat of Fusion

According to the kinetic molecular theory, all molecules are in constant random motion. If energy is absorbed by a particle, its molecular velocity will increase. Temperature is a measure of the average kinetic energy or the amount of heat per particle of a substance.

The *specific heat* of a substance is the energy in joules required to raise the temperature of one kilogram of a material one kelvin. For example, the specific heat of water has been determined to be 4.180×10^3 J/kg·K. To calculate a change in heat associated with a change in temperature, the following equation is used:

$$\text{Heat} = (\text{kg substance}) \times (\text{temperature change in K}) \times (\text{specific heat})$$

In solids, the motion described by the kinetic molecular theory is restricted to molecular vibration. If particles at the surface of a solid obtain sufficient energy, they escape. Ice requires 3.34×10^5 J/kg to liberate particles from a crystalline matrix. The relatively large quantity of energy required for this change in state is called the *heat of fusion*. The change in heat associated with this change of state can be determined using the following equation:

$$\text{Heat} = (\text{kg substance}) \times (\text{heat of fusion})$$

The high heat of fusion of water helps modify the weather around the Great Lakes in Ontario. Heat released through fusion on the Great Lakes has the same effect as a giant heater and keeps the area warmer throughout the winter. Siberia in Russia lies about as far north as Southern Ontario, but the absence of large lakes results in a much colder winter (and a much warmer summer).

In this exercise, you will determine experimentally the heat of fusion of ice. Energy released by warm water will be absorbed by pieces of melting ice. The melted ice will then rise in temperature until the solutions reach an equilibrium temperature. If you assume that all the energy released as the warm water cools is absorbed by the melting ice, you can determine the amount of energy involved in each transformation. From these values, you will be able to calculate the heat of fusion of ice.

OBJECTIVES

1. to calculate the energy released from a mass of cooling water

2. to calculate the energy absorbed by a mass of melted ice

3. to utilize the collected data to determine the heat of fusion of ice

MATERIALS

Apparatus		**Reagents**
centigram balance	ring stand and ring	several ice cubes,
plastic foam cup	lab burner	snow, or crushed ice
beaker (600 mL)	stirring rod	distilled water
thermometer	safety goggles	
wire gauze with	lab apron	
ceramic centre		

PROCEDURE

1. Put on your lab apron and safety goggles. You will be using the lab burners during this experiment. Use them cautiously.

2. Find the mass of a clean, empty, dry plastic foam cup. Record this value to the nearest 0.01 g in your copy of Table 1 in your notebook.

3. Add approximately 200 mL of distilled water to a 600 mL beaker.

4. Set up the wire gauze and ring on the ring stand. Place the beaker and contents on this assembly. Light and adjust your burner to a low flame. Gently heat the beaker until the distilled water is about 40°C. Turn off the lab burner.

5. Add the heated water to the plastic foam cup until the cup is about half full. Find the mass of the cup and contents and record this value in Table 1.

6. Measure the temperature of the water and record this value in Table 1.

7. Select two medium-sized ice cubes and blot their surfaces dry with a piece of paper toweling. Carefully place the ice cubes into the plastic foam cup. Using a stirring rod, gently stir the ice and water mixture.

8. Once the ice cubes have completely melted, insert the thermometer into the solution and determine the temperature of the water. Record this value in Table 1. Remove the thermometer and mix the contents with a stirring rod. Continue monitoring the solution temperature until it remains at a fixed value. Record this temperature in Table 1.

9. Place the plastic foam cup and its contents on a centigram balance. Find this new mass and record it in Table 1.

CAUTION: Your thermometer is made of glass and can break, leaving sharp edges that cut. Handle your thermometer gently. Do not use it to crush or stir ice. If the thermometer breaks, call your teacher. Mercury liquid and vapors are poisonous.

POST LAB DISCUSSION

Once the data are collected, a series of simple calculations will allow you to determine the heat of fusion of ice. Since specific heat is given in J/kg·K, all mass measurements must be converted to kilograms.

DATA AND OBSERVATIONS

Table 1

Mass of cup in kg	
Mass of cup + heated water in kg	
Mass of heated water in kg	
Temperature of heated water	
Initial temperature of mixture	
Final temperature of mixture	
Temperature difference in K	
Mass of cup + contents in kg	
Mass of added ice in kg	

CALCULATIONS

1. Calculate the amount of heat lost, in joules, by the warm water solution.

2. Determine the amount of heat absorbed, in joules, as the melted ice warmed to the equilibrium temperature.

3. Determine the amount of heat, in joules, that was absorbed during the melting process.

4. Calculate the heat of fusion for ice.

FOLLOW-UP QUESTIONS

1. What factors might account for deviations between your calculated heat of fusion value and the value given in the Prelab Discussion?

2. In the process which is the reverse of the one considered in this experiment (that is, water in the form of a liquid changing to ice), heat is given off. (The amount of heat of solidification is the same as the heat of fusion, but is given off instead of absorbed.) In a refrigerator, when water is frozen into ice cubes, where does the released heat go?

CONCLUSION

State the results of Objective 3.

Factors Affecting Reaction Rate

For a given set of conditions, every chemical reaction occurs at a characteristic rate. Chemical engineers are often interested in discovering ways to increase the rates of slow reactions, particularly when they are important to industrial processes. In industry, the general goal is to produce a top-quality material as quickly, efficiently, and cheaply as possible under the constraints of environmental and safety considerations.

The rate of a chemical reaction is determined by a large number of factors. Some reactions will take place very slowly under any conditions, while others are extremely rapid under any conditions. Most reactions can be affected by changing the conditions under which the reactions take place.

A chemical reaction occurs when the reacting particles have an effective collision that results in the formation of new particles. If the number of effective collisions can be controlled, then the rate of the reaction can be controlled. Some of the ways that can be used to change the number of collisions include changing the concentrations of the reactants, changing the surface area of the reactants, or changing the speed at which the particles are moving. The speed at which particles are moving is affected by temperature changes.

In order to observe the effect of each change, this experiment is divided into three parts. Each part varies only one condition: concentration of one reactant (Part I), surface area of one reactant (Part II), or temperature (Part III). Each of these factors will have an effect on the reaction rate, which you will measure.

Magnesium metal will be combined with hydrochloric acid in this experiment. The products of this reaction are hydrogen gas and magnesium chloride. The rate of the reaction is easily noted because the magnesium metal will be completely used up.

OBJECTIVES

1. to observe and record the effect of reactant concentration on the reaction rate

2. to observe and record the effect of reactant surface area on the reaction rate

3. to observe and record the effect of reactant temperature on the reaction rate

MATERIALS

Apparatus

3 beakers (250 mL)
4 test tubes
  (18 mm × 150 mm)
centigram balance
test tube rack
graduated cylinder
  (25 mL)
stirring rod
marking pen
stop watch or watch
  with second hand

thermometer
hot plate
sandpaper or emery
  cloth
scissors
metric ruler
safety goggles
lab apron
full face shield
plastic gloves

Reagents

0.5 M hydrochloric
  acid
1.0 M hydrochloric
  acid
3.0 M hydrochloric
  acid
6.0 M hydrochloric
  acid
magnesium ribbon
ice cubes

PROCEDURE

Part I Effect of Concentration on Reaction Rate

1. Put on your lab apron and safety goggles. In this experiment, you will be working with hydrochloric acid in several different concentrations.

2. Obtain a piece of magnesium ribbon from your teacher. Use the sandpaper to remove any coating from the outside of the metal. You will need a total of eleven pieces of magnesium that are each 1 cm long. Using the metric ruler and scissors, carefully cut an 11 cm strip of magnesium. Determine the mass of this strip using the balance. Record this value in your notebook. Now cut eleven pieces from the large strip of magnesium. It is important that each piece be exactly the same length so that the amount of magnesium does not change in each of the reactions. Divide the mass of the large strip by 11 to get the average mass of each 1 cm piece. Record this value in your notebook.

3. With a marking pen, label four test tubes with the appropriate concentration of acid to be added (6M, 3M, 1M, 0.5M).

4. Using a graduated cylinder, carefully measure 10 mL of each of the concentrations of acid and place in the appropriate test tube.

5. Starting with the lowest concentration first (0.5M), place the 1 cm piece of magnesium in the test tube containing the acid. Begin timing as soon as the magnesium comes into contact with the acid. Record the time it takes for all the magnesium to react in your copy of Table 1.

6. Repeat this procedure with each of the concentrations of acid. Calculate the average reaction rate by determining the grams of magnesium used per second. Record these values in Table 1.

7. Clean up according to the reagent disposal instructions.

CAUTION: Hydrochloric acid is corrosive to skin, eyes, and clothing. When handling the hydrochloric acid, wear safety goggles, lab apron, plastic gloves, and use a full face shield. Wash any spills or splashes immediately with plenty of water. Call your teacher.

Part II Effect of Surface Area on Reaction Rate

1. Relabel three test tubes as A, B, and C. Place 10 mL of 1.0M hydrochloric acid in each of the test tubes.

2. For this part of the experiment, you will need three 1 cm pieces of magnesium. Take one piece and use the scissors to cut the strip into as many slivers as possible. Be careful not to lose any of the slivers, as this will affect the results. Place the slivers in test tube A. In your copy of Table 2 in your notebook, record the time it takes for all of the magnesium to react. Take the second piece of magnesium. Fold and bend the piece so that it is rolled up as tightly as possible. Place the rolled magnesium into test tube B. Record the time it takes for the magnesium to react in Table 2.

3. The third piece will be left as is. Add this piece to test tube C. In Table 2, record the time that it takes for all the magnesium to react.

4. Rinse the test tubes and go on to Part III.

1.. Label four 250 mL beakers *A, B, C,* and *D.* Add about 150 mL of water to beaker *A.* Place this beaker on a hot plate and begin heating to a temperature close to the boiling point of water. Add 150 mL of hot tap water to beaker *B.* You will want water that is approximately 50°C. If you need to raise the temperature slightly, put beaker *B* on the hot plate. In beaker *C,* you will have 150 mL of room temperature water. Record the exact temperature in your notebook. In beaker *D,* you will have 150 mL of ice and water that is approximately 0°C.

2. Place 10 mL of 1.0*M* hydrochloric acid into each of four test tubes. Place one of the test tubes into each of the beakers so that the acid will reach the temperature of the water in the beaker. Use the thermometer to check that the temperatures of the acids in the test tubes match those of the water baths. Do not proceed until they match.

3. Measure and record in your notebook the temperature of each test tube. Then, as in Part I, place a 1 cm magnesium strip in each of the test tubes, and record the amount of time necessary for the reaction to go to completion in your copy of Table 3.

4. Clean up all the materials. Before leaving the laboratory, wash your hands thoroughly with soap and water; use a fingernail brush to clean under your fingernails.

REAGENT DISPOSAL

Return any unused magnesium metal to the designated container. HCl solutions left in the test tubes after the reaction has finished should be returned to another designated container for neutralization before being discarded down the sink.

POST LAB DISCUSSION

In this experiment, you examined the effects of concentration, surface area, and temperature on the reaction between hydrochloric acid and magnesium. A reaction occurs only when an effective collision takes place between the particles involved. You will be asked to explain, in molecular terms, how each of these factors can change the number of effective collisions. The following review may help you.

Surface area is the actual area of a substance that is exposed in the reaction. If you can visualize a cube that is one metre on each side, you should be able to see that the surface area is equal to six times the area on one face of the cube. Thus the surface area of the cube is six square metres. If the cube is cut in half once, there is an increase in surface area because in addition to the faces that were previously exposed, two more faces are exposed. Thus the total surface area of the two shapes would be eight square metres.

The temperature of a sample is described as a measure of the average kinetic energy of its particles. The higher the temperature, the higher the average kinetic energy. Kinetic energy depends on two factors: the mass and the speed of the particles. Since the mass of the particles does not change when heated, the increase in kinetic energy is due to the increased speed of the particles involved.

DATA AND OBSERVATIONS

Part I   Effect of Concentration on Reaction Rate

Mass of 11 cm strip of Mg _____

Average mass of 1 cm piece of Mg _____

Table 1

CONCENTRATION OF ACID	REACTION TIME (IN SECONDS)	REACTION RATE (g Mg/s)
0.5M		
1.0M		COMPLETE IN YOUR NOTEBOOK
3.0M		
6.0M		

Part II   Effect of Surface Area on Reaction Rate

Table 2

SHAPE OF MAGNESIUM STRIP	REACTION TIME (IN SECONDS)	REACTION RATE (g Mg/s)
Test tube A—slivers		
Test tube B—rolled		COMPLETE IN YOUR NOTEBOOK
Test tube C—flat		

Part III   Effect of Temperature on Reaction Rate

Table 3

TEMPERATURE (IN °C)	REACTION TIME (IN SECONDS)	REACTION RATE (g Mg/s)
Beaker A		
Beaker B		COMPLETE IN YOUR NOTEBOOK
Beaker C		
Beaker D		

QUESTIONS AND CALCULATIONS

1. On separate sheets of graph paper, construct two graphs. On one, graph the reaction rate vs. concentration of HCl data from Part I. On the other, graph the reaction rate vs. temperature data from Part III.

2. Complete in your notebook the following general statements about each of the factors that were investigated in the experiment:

   a. As concentration increases, reaction rate...
   b. As surface area increases, reaction rate...
   c. As temperature increases, reaction rate...

3. Look at your data from Part I. Does doubling the concentration of hydrochloric acid double the reaction rate? Explain your answer.

4. Look at your data from Part II. Which reaction rate was the fastest? Explain your answer.

5. Look at your data from Part III. Which reaction has the slowest rate? Explain why.

6. Use your graphs to predict the reaction rates and then calculate reaction times for each of the following:

   a. reaction of 1 cm magnesium strip with 4.0 M hydrochloric acid (all other conditions the same as Part I)
   b. reaction of 1 cm magnesium strip with 1.0 M hydrochloric acid at a temperature of 15°C (all other conditions the same as in Part III)

7. Does doubling the temperature double the rate of the reaction in Part III? Cite evidence to support your answer.

FOLLOW-UP QUESTIONS

1. Is it possible to vary the factors of concentration, surface area, and temperature in a way that would prevent a reaction from happening? Explain your answer in terms of effective collisions.

2. What effect would the addition of a catalyst have on this reaction?

3. Explain why you will be more successful in lighting a fire made from kindling wood than in lighting a log directly.

4. Explain why blowing on a smoldering fire may make it burn better.

CONCLUSION

State the results of Objectives 1, 2, and 3.

The Iodine Clock Reaction

It is very important for a chemist to understand the conditions that affect the rate of a chemical reaction. In chemical manufacturing processes, controlling the rate of a given reaction can make all the difference between an economical process and an uneconomical one. For instance, using catalysts is one method for getting reactions to speed up.

In the previous experiment (18A) you learned that the rate of a reaction is determined by several factors, namely temperature, the concentration of the reactants, and the surface area of the reactants (for a heterogeneous reaction). In this experiment you will carry out different reactions, but you will again investigate the effect of the concentration of reactants (Part I) and temperature (Part II) on reaction rate. In addition, in Part III you will examine the effect of the nature of the reactants, and in Part IV, the effect of a catalyst, on a reaction.

Part I involves a reaction that is sometimes called an *iodine clock reaction*. There are a number of different combinations of chemicals that give a reaction of this type. What happens, essentially, is that there are two different reactions: one in which iodine is produced (a slow reaction) and one in which the iodine produced in the first reaction is used up (a fast reaction). By carefully controlling the quantities of reactants, you can obtain a situation in which the reactant in the second reaction is used up first, allowing iodine to form at that point. At very low concentrations the iodine then combines with starch to suddenly give a deep blue-black color at a characteristic time for the conditions. Hence the term "iodine clock." The time taken after mixing until the point when the blue-black color appears is measured, and from this quantity the rate of the reaction can be determined. You will alter the conditions of concentration of reactants in Part I and temperature in Part II in order to determine their effect on reaction rate.

In Part III, you will observe how the nature of the reactants can affect the rate by reacting two different substances with the same reagent. Finally, in Part IV, you will observe the effect of adding a catalyst on the rate of a reaction, and you will look again at the effect of temperature.

OBJECTIVES

1. to observe and record the effect of changing the concentration of a reactant on the rate of a reaction

2. to observe and record the effect of changing the temperature of a system on the rate of a reaction

3. to observe and record the effect of the nature of the reactants on the rate of a reaction

4. to observe and record the effect of a catalyst on the rate of a reaction

EXPERIMENT 18B

MATERIALS

Apparatus

2 beakers (100 mL)
2 graduated cylinders
(10 mL)
10 test tubes
(18 mm × 150 mm)
thermometer
4 beakers (250 mL)
2 medicine droppers
ice
6 test tubes
(13 mm × 100 mm)
lab apron
safety goggles

Reagents

Solution A: 0.02M KIO$_3$ (potassium iodate)
Solution B: 0.002M NaHSO$_3$ (sodium bisulfite)
(also containing 4 g of starch and
12 mL of 1M H$_2$SO$_4$/L)
0.02M KMnO$_4$ (potassium permanganate)
0.1M FeSO$_4$ (iron(II) sulfate)
0.1M Na$_2$C$_2$O$_4$ (sodium oxalate)
0.1M MnSO$_4$ (manganese(II) sulfate)
1M H$_2$SO$_4$

PROCEDURE

Part I   Effect of Concentration

1. Put on your lab apron and safety goggles.

2. Obtain approximately 60 mL of Solution A (0.02M KIO$_3$) and 90 mL of Solution B (0.002M NaHSO$_3$ containing H$_2$SO$_4$ and starch) in 100 mL beakers.

3. In a 10 mL graduated cylinder place 10.0 mL of Solution A, using a medicine dropper to obtain the volume as accurately as possible. Transfer the solution to an 18 mm × 150 mm test tube in a rack.

4. In the same manner measure out 10.0 mL of Solution B and transfer it to another test tube. Use a different graduated cylinder and medicine dropper than for Solution A, and keep the same ones for each solution for subsequent parts of the procedure.

5. In order to measure the time needed for the reaction to occur, you will need a watch or clock with a sweep second hand, or preferably, a digital watch with a stopwatch function. One partner must record the time while the other partner mixes the solutions. Mix the solutions in one of the two test tubes, and record the time from the instant they first mix.

6. Very quickly pour the solution back and forth between the two test tubes three times to make sure they are thoroughly mixed, then wait for the completion of the reaction.

7. Record the time at the instant the deep blue-black color first appears.

8. In order to study the effect of changing the concentration of Solution A, half the class will now be assigned the values 9.0 mL, 7.0 mL, 5.0 mL, and 3.0 mL, and the other half the values 8.0 mL, 6.0 mL, 4.0 mL, and 2.0 mL. In each instance measure out the volume in the graduated cylinder, and add enough water to make it up to the 10.0 mL mark. Then transfer each dilution of Solution A to a test tube and mix it with 10.0 mL of solution B as before. For each, record the time taken for the color to appear in Table 1 in your notebook.

9. Record your results on the board in order to get class averages.

Part II   Effect of Temperature

1. In this part of the procedure you will keep the concentration constant, and vary the temperature, both above and below room temperature. In order that the observed reaction times lie in a suitable range, Solution *A* will be at only half the concentration of the original solution.

2. Make up 4 sets of each of solutions *A* and *B*, with 5.0 mL of Solution *A* and 5.0 mL of water in one set of 4 test tubes, and 10.0 mL of Solution *B* in the other 4 test tubes.

3. Make 4 water baths (in 250 mL beakers) at temperatures of 5°C, 15°C, 25°C, and 35°C or 10°C, 20°C, 30°C, and 40°C, depending on which set of temperatures your teacher assigns you. Use ice to obtain the temperatures below room temperature, and hot water from a tap or kettle to obtain the temperatures above room temperature. The beakers should be about two thirds full, so that the solutions in the test tubes are well beneath the water in the baths.

4. Place one test tube containing diluted Solution *A* and another containing Solution *B* in each water bath, and leave them for 10 min to allow them to adjust to the temperature required.

5. Try to maintain the temperatures in the water baths within 0.5°C of the temperatures assigned, to make comparisons with other groups in the class more meaningful.

6. When the temperatures are at the correct value, and the tubes have been in for enough time, mix each pair of solutions in one test tube by pouring them back and forth three times. Then place that test tube back in the water bath. In Table 2, record the time from the instant the solutions are mixed to the first appearance of the blue-black color. Do this for each pair of solutions at each temperature.

7. Record your results on the board in order to get class averages.

Part III   Effect of the Nature of the Reactants

1. Place 3 mL of freshly prepared $0.1M$ $FeSO_4$ in a 13 mm × 100 mm test tube. Add 1 mL of $1M$ H_2SO_4, then add 5 drops of $0.02M$ $KMnO_4$, shaking after each drop.

2. Place 3 mL of $0.1M$ $Na_2C_2O_4$ in a 13 mm × 100 mm test tube. Add 1 mL of $1M$ H_2SO_4 and 5 drops of $0.02M$ $KMnO_4$.

3. Compare the lengths of time taken for the purple color to disappear in each test tube. (Leave them in the test-tube rack while you go on to Part IV.) Record your data in Table 3.

CAUTION: Potassium permanganate ($KMnO_4$) solution is a strong irritant and will stain skin and clothing. Wash any spills and splashes with plenty of water.

CAUTION: Sulfuric acid (H_2SO_4) is very corrosive. Do not get any on your skin, in your eyes, or on your clothing. Wash any spills and splashes with plenty of water, and call your teacher.

Part IV Effect of a Catalyst

1. In this part, you will be studying the same reaction as in Part III, Step 2, but using different temperatures and a catalyst. To each of four 13 mm × 100 mm test tubes add 3 mL of 0.1M Na$_2$C$_2$O$_4$ and 1 mL of 1M H$_2$SO$_4$.

2. Leave two of the test tubes in the rack at room temperature, and place the other two in a water bath at about 50°C.

3. To only one test tube at each temperature, add 3 drops of 0.1M MnSO$_4$ as a catalyst.

4. Then to all four tubes add 5 drops of 0.02M KMnO$_4$.

5. Record your data in Table 4, then compare the time taken to reach a colorless solution with and without the catalyst in each case. Also compare the times at room temperature with those at 50°C.

6. Clean up and put away all materials, following the instructions for reagent disposal.

7. Before leaving the laboratory, wash your hands thoroughly with soap and water; use a fingernail brush to clean under your fingernails.

REAGENT DISPOSAL

All solutions remaining after reaction may be safely rinsed down the sink with plenty of water. Your teacher will tell you what to do with the left-over original solutions.

POST LAB DISCUSSION

The blue-black color observed in Parts I and II occurs as a result of two separate reactions. Initially, the iodate ion, IO$_3^-$, reacts with the bisulfite ion, HSO$_3^-$, giving iodide ion, I$^-$, and sulfate ion, SO$_4^{2-}$, as follows:

$$IO_3^-(aq) + 3HSO_3^-(aq) \rightarrow I^-(aq) + 3SO_4^{2-}(aq) + 3H^+(aq)$$

The bisulfite ions are present in lower concentration and are, therefore, used up first. When this happens, the IO$_3^-$ ions then react with I$^-$ ions in the presence of H$^+$ ions to give molecular iodine, I$_2$:

$$IO_3^-(aq) + 5I^-(aq) + 6H^+(aq) \rightarrow 3I_2(aq) + 3H_2O(l)$$

In the presence of starch, iodine forms the intense blue-black color as a result of the iodine molecules being trapped in the long starch molecules. The appearance of this color indicates that the first reaction is complete and the second one has begun to take place.

The uncertainty involved in measuring the time taken for the reaction could easily be ±2 s unless you are very careful. Thus the interpretation of results will be more meaningful if the class averages at a particular concentration or temperature are considered. Measuring the time taken for a reaction to be completed is not the same as measuring its rate, but there is an inverse relation between them: rate is proportional to the reciprocal of time. Consequently, in interpreting the results you will calculate the rate in terms of reciprocal seconds (s^{-1}) and plot graphs of the rate against concentration or temperature.

The reactions occurring in Part II are given by:

$$5Fe^{2+}(aq) + MnO_4^-(aq) + 8H^+(aq) \rightarrow 5Fe^{3+}(aq) + Mn^{2+}(aq) + 4H_2O(l)$$

and $\quad 2MnO_4^-(aq) + 5C_2O_4^{2-}(aq) + 16H^+ \rightarrow 2Mn^{2+}(aq) + 10CO_2(g) + 8H_2O(l)$

The second equation is also the one for the reaction occurring in Part IV.

DATA AND OBSERVATIONS

Part I   Effect of Concentration

Table 1

VOLUME OF KIO_3 (mL)	10.0	9.0	7.0	5.0	3.0
Time for reaction (s)	COMPLETE	IN YOUR	NOTEBOOK		

(If you were assigned the other values of 8.0, 6.0, 4.0, 2.0, use these instead.)

Part II   Effect of Temperature

Table 2

TEMPERATURE (°C)	5.0	15.0	25.0	35.0
Time for reaction (s)	COMPLETE IN YOUR NOTEBOOK			

(If you were assigned the other values of 10°C, 20°C, 30°C, 40°C, use these instead.)

Part III   Effect of the Nature of the Reactants

Table 3

	TIME FOR REACTION
$Fe^{2+} + MnO_4^- + H^+$	
$C_2O_4^{2-} + MnO_4^- + H^+$	COMPLETE IN YOUR NOTEBOOK

Part IV   Effect of a Catalyst

Table 4

	TEMPERATURE	TIME (s)	TEMPERATURE	TIME (s)
With Mn^{2+} catalyst	Room Temp.		50°C	
Without Mn^{2+} catalyst	Room Temp.		50°C	

QUESTIONS AND CALCULATIONS

Part I   Effect of Concentration

1. Calculate the concentration of KIO_3 in the final mixture for each of your dilutions. Remember that the original $[KIO_3]$ was $0.02M$, and that the original dilution, when mixed with 10 mL of Solution B, gave a total volume of 20 mL in each case.

2. Calculate the rate of the reaction (in s^{-1}) for each case.

3. Plot a graph of your results, with rate plotted against $[KIO_3]$.

4. Repeat these calculations with the class averages, and plot the results on the same sheet of graph paper as for question 3. Remember to label your results and the class averages.

5. Considering any uncertainties in time for the reaction, what type of graph results?

6. Referring to the collision theory of reaction rates, state why you would expect the change of rate with concentration that you observed.

Part II   Effect of Temperature

1. Calculate the rate of the reaction at each temperature (in s^{-1}) by taking the reciprocal of the time elapsed.

2. Calculate the factor by which the rate changed for each 10°C interval in temperature.

3. Plot a graph of the results, with rate plotted against temperature.

4. Repeat these calculations using the class averages, and plot the results on the same graph paper.

5. Referring to the collision theory of reaction rates, state why you would expect the change of rate with temperature that you observed.

Part III   Effect of the Nature of the Reactants

1. Which reaction occurred at a faster rate?

2. Explain the reason for this result by comparing what is involved in changing Fe^{2+} to Fe^{3+} to what is involved in changing $C_2O_4^{2-}$ to $2CO_2$.

Part IV   Effect of a Catalyst

1. The Mn^{2+} acts as a catalyst in this reaction. By what factor did the rate increase (at each temperature) when the catalyzed reaction is compared to the uncatalyzed reaction?

2. By what factor did the rate increase for the different temperatures used in each case?

FOLLOW-UP QUESTIONS

1. Look up the meaning of the term "autocatalysis" in a reference book. Explain why this term would apply to the catalyzed reaction you studied in Part IV.

2. Different versions of the iodine clock reaction use different chemicals from those used here. From a reference book, find one other combination of chemicals that gives a reaction such as this one, in which iodine is suddenly formed after a certain time lapse.

3. Enzymes are catalysts made of protein which are necessary for almost every reaction occurring in living cells. Find out why the rates of these reactions increase with increasing temperature only up to about 37°C (body temperature), then decrease above that temperature.

CONCLUSION

State how the rate of a chemical reaction is affected by the following: (a) altering the concentration of reactants, (b) altering the temperature, and (c) adding a catalyst.

Measuring Reaction Rate Using Volume of Gas Produced

The previous two experiments (18A and 18B) demonstrated the effect of various factors on the rate of a chemical reaction. In these experiments the time required to complete the reaction was measured, and a reaction rate was calculated from that quantity. It is often very important, however, for a chemist to know at a particular moment in a reaction just what the rate is at that time, in order to monitor how the reaction is proceeding. This information can be obtained in a variety of ways. For instance, if a gas is produced in a closed container, then continuous monitoring of the pressure will indicate the rate. If a color is produced or used up, monitoring of the color intensity with a spectrophotometer will indicate the rate. If a gas is produced and allowed to escape from the system, the decrease in mass over various time intervals can also show how the reaction rate is progressing. This latter method can easily be demonstrated if you have an electronic balance. When a flask containing hydrochloric acid is placed on the pan of an electronic balance and marble chips are dropped in, the decrease in mass with time will give a measure of the rate at which CO_2 is produced. Yet another method of monitoring the rate of a reaction involving gases is to measure the volume of gas produced by displacing water from a gas measuring tube. It is this method that will be used in this experiment.

Ordinary household bleach is an aqueous solution of sodium hypochlorite, NaClO, containing a little more than 5% NaClO by mass. The bleaching action is caused by the hypochlorite ion, ClO^-. Under normal circumstances the hypochlorite ion breaks down slowly to give oxygen gas and the chloride ion, Cl^-:

$$2ClO^-(aq) \quad \rightarrow \quad 2Cl^-(aq) + O_2(g)$$

To speed this reaction to a measurable rate a catalyst is required. In this experiment, the catalyst will be provided by the addition of cobalt(II) nitrate solution to the bleach. A black precipitate of cobalt(III) oxide will form, and this substance will act as the catalyst in the decomposition of ClO^-. The volume of oxygen produced will be measured at 30 s intervals by displacing water from a gas measuring tube (also called a *eudiometer*). From the results, you can plot a graph of volume produced versus time. You will also calculate the average rate of evolution of oxygen in mL/min. The experiment will be repeated at other temperatures and concentrations of ClO^-, and the effect of these changes on the rate observed.

OBJECTIVES

1. to measure the volume of a gas produced from a reaction mixture at regular time intervals during the reaction

2. to interpret the results and obtain the overall rate of reaction

3. to observe how the rate changes at different temperatures and concentrations

MATERIALS

Apparatus

Erlenmeyer flask (250 mL)
one-hole stopper with glass
   tubing (to fit above flask)
rubber tubing
trough
50 mL gas measuring tube
   (eudiometer)
buret stand and clamp

graduated cylinder (25 mL)
graduated cylinder (10 mL)
thermometer
ice
lab apron
safety goggles

Reagents

sodium hypochlorite solution
   (bleach) (5.25%)
0.10M cobalt(II) nitrate,
   $Co(NO_3)_2$

PROCEDURE

1. Put on your lab apron and safety goggles.

2. Refer to the diagram (Figure 18C-1) to help in understanding how to set up the apparatus.

Figure 18C-1

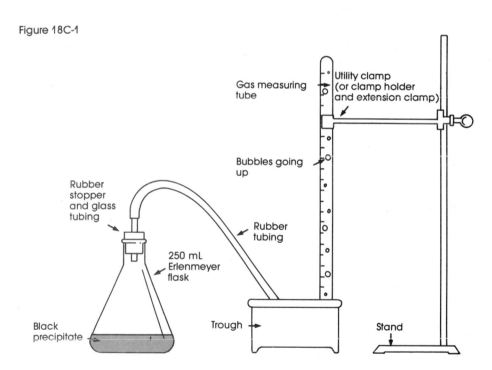

3. Fill the gas measuring tube with water, and invert it into the trough (half filled with water), without letting any water come out. Hold it in the vertical position with the buret clamp attached to the stand.

4. Join the rubber tubing to the top of the glass tube which goes through the stopper on the flask. Place the other end into the neck of the gas measuring tube. (If your trough has an outside attachment for tubing, use that, and position the gas measuring tube above the hole at the bottom of the trough.)

5. Measure out 15 mL of bleach solution into the 25 mL graduated cylinder, then pour it into the Erlenmeyer flask.

CAUTION: Sodium hypo-
chlorite (bleach) is very
caustic, and harmful to
skin, eyes, and clothing.
Wash any spills or splashes
on your skin or clothes
with plenty of water. Call
your teacher.

6. Measure out 5 mL of 0.10M cobalt(II) nitrate solution into the 10 mL graduated cylinder.

7. Pour the cobalt nitrate solution into the flask and *immediately* place the stopper and tube on it. Record the time of mixing.

8. Note the formation of a black precipitate of cobalt(III) oxide, Co_2O_3. From now on you must swirl the flask gently but continually. This is necessary to dislodge bubbles of oxygen from the catalyst's surface. If you stop swirling the rate will decrease, so the amount of swirling must be kept uniform throughout this and subsequent steps of the Procedure.

9. Record the total volume of oxygen that has collected in the gas measuring tube every 30 s until a volume of 50 mL has been obtained.

10. Repeat Steps 5 to 9, but have the reactants at a temperature 10°C above room temperature before mixing them. You can accomplish this by placing both the flask and the graduated cylinder in a water bath for 10 min, then mixing the reactants into the flask and putting it back into the water bath. Use hot water from a tap or kettle, and adjust to the required temperature with cold water.

11. Repeat Step 10, but bring the reactants to a temperature 10°C below room temperature by using ice.

12. Repeat Steps 5 to 9 at room temperature, but add 20 mL of water to the bleach solution before mixing, so that the overall concentrations on mixing will be halved in comparison with the original experiment.

13. Repeat Steps 5 to 9 at room temperature, but this time add 60 mL of water to the bleach solution before mixing, so that the overall concentrations after mixing are one quarter of their original values.

14. Repeat the experiment at any other concentration or temperature if requested to do so by your teacher.

15. Clean up all your materials, following the instructions for reagent disposal.

16. Before you leave the laboratory, wash your hands thoroughly with soap and water; use a fingernail brush to clean under your fingernails.

REAGENT DISPOSAL

After collecting 50 mL of oxygen in each trial, pour the waste solution containing the black Co_2O_3 into the designated container.

POST LAB DISCUSSION

The reaction in which the Co^{2+} ion reacts with the ClO^- ion is given by this equation:

$$2Co^{2+}(aq) + ClO^-(aq) + 2H_2O(l) \rightarrow Co_2O_3(s) + 4H^+(aq) + Cl^-(aq)$$

This reaction has to occur before the Co_2O_3 can start catalyzing the bleach, so do not be surprised if you found that no oxygen was given off during the first 30 s or 60 s.

When you plot your results, you may find that the rate is not uniform. One cause might be that large bubbles sometimes come through just as you take a measurement. Another might be that the concentration of the bleach decreases as the reaction proceeds. The trend relating reaction rate with changing temperature and concentration will nevertheless be readily apparent.

DATA AND OBSERVATIONS

Record your data and observations in five tables similar to the following. It would be a good idea to copy them into your notebook before coming to the laboratory. Place them in such a way that they can be extended if necessary, as you do not know how many readings will be required to reach 50 mL. It is possible that in some situations up to 20 readings will be needed (10 min) before the 50 mL mark is reached.

CONDITIONS: TEMPERATURE = BLEACH CONCENTRATION = TIME (s)	VOLUME OF O_2 (mL)
0	
30	
60	
90	
. . .	

QUESTIONS AND CALCULATIONS

1. Plot the graphs for each trial on a single sheet of graph paper, plotting volume of oxygen produced versus time elapsed. Label each graph with the conditions under which the results being graphed were obtained.

2. For each trial, calculate the overall rate of production of oxygen by dividing the volume of 50 mL by the time taken to produce that amount, in minutes. (The average rate will therefore be expressed in mL/min.)

3. Compare the calculated values of the rates with the temperatures used. By what factor did the rate change with a 10°C increase in temperature? By what factor did the rate change with a 10°C decrease in temperature?

4. Compare the calculated values of the rates at the different concentrations of bleach. By what factor did the rate change when the concentration of the bleach was halved? By what factor did the rate change when the concentration of the bleach was quartered?

FOLLOW-UP QUESTIONS

1. Bleach is made by the action of chlorine gas on sodium hydroxide, NaOH:

$$Cl_2(g) + 2OH^-(aq) \rightarrow Cl^-(aq) + ClO^-(aq) + H_2O(l)$$

However, if an acid is added to bleach, the reverse process occurs:

$$Cl^-(aq) + ClO^-(aq) + 2H^+(aq) \rightarrow Cl_2(g) + H_2O(l)$$

Why should you never mix bleach with any cleaner or other household product which may contain acid?

2. Special cleaning agents such as those used for cleaning mold and mildew off bathroom tiles may contain 10% sodium hypochlorite. Predict how the shape of the rate curve with this concentration will differ from that of regular strength bleach.

CONCLUSION

State the results of Objective 3.

Investigating Chemical Equilibrium

Most chemical reactions appear to proceed to completion. Under certain conditions, however, the products may have sufficient energy to reform reactants in a reverse reaction. When forward and reverse reaction rates are equal, a state of equilibrium is established. Although both reactions continue to occur, the net concentration of each substance remains the same.

Le Chatelier's principle allows us to predict the effects of a stress placed on an equilibrium system. The stress produces a shift in concentrations that may be recognized by changes in the macroscopic properties of the system.

The reactions presented in this investigation demonstrate observable reversibility. Under changing conditions, the systems will respond to counteract any stress placed upon the equilibrium state. A variation in a precipitate provides the observable evidence that a shift has occurred in the equilibrium concentrations.

You will study five different equilibrium systems involving ions in solution. The first system, studied in Part I, is the conversion of the indicator thymol blue from its blue form to its yellow form. The extent to which the forward reaction is favored depends upon the concentration of hydrogen ions in solution:

$$\text{thymol blue (blue form)} + H^+ \rightleftharpoons \text{thymol blue}^+ \text{ (yellow form)}$$

The second reaction (Part II) involves the light yellow iron(III) ion, Fe^{3+}, and thiocyanate ion, SCN^-, which forms the colored complex $FeSCN^{2+}$:

$$Fe^{3+}(aq) + SCN^-(aq) \rightleftharpoons FeSCN^{2+}(aq)$$

The third system (Part III) involves the hydrated cobalt(II) ion, $Co(H_2O)_6^{2+}$, which can be converted to the chlorinated complex ion, $Co(H_2O)_4Cl_2$.

$$Co(H_2O)_6^{2+}(aq) + 2Cl^-(aq) \rightleftharpoons Co(H_2O)_4Cl_2(aq) + 2H_2O(l)$$

You will study the effects on this system of changing the temperature. Your data should allow you to predict whether the forward or reverse reaction is exothermic.

The fourth system (Part IV) involves the equilibrium between the yellow chromate ion, CrO_4^{2-}, and the orange dichromate ion, $Cr_2O_7^{2-}$. You will study the effect of adding H^+ and OH^- to this equilibrium, and also the effect of adding Ba^{2+} to it.

The last system (Part V) involves an equilibrium between hydrated copper(II) ion, $Cu(H_2O)_4^{2+}$, and the tetramminocopper(II) ion, $Cu(NH_3)_4^{2+}$, in which the water molecules have been replaced with NH_3 molecules. The effect of acid and of NH_3 on this equilibrium will be examined.

OBJECTIVES

1. to recognize the macroscopic properties of five chemical systems at equilibrium

2. to observe shifts in equilibrium concentrations as stresses are applied to the systems

3. to observe a shift in equilibrium concentrations associated with changes in temperature

4. to explain the observations obtained by applying Le Chatelier's principle

MATERIALS

Apparatus

5 test tubes
   (13 mm × 100 mm)
test tube rack
graduated cylinders
   (100 mL, 10 mL)
1 beaker (250 mL)
2 beakers (100 mL)

2 Erlenmeyer flasks
   (250 mL)
beaker tongs
ring stand and ring
wire gauze
laboratory burner

safety goggles
lab apron
full face shield
plastic gloves
fume hood (required for
   Part III)

Reagents

0.1M HCl
0.1M NaOH
0.2M FeCl$_3$
0.2M KSCN
0.2M KCl
6.0M NaOH
0.1M K$_2$Cr$_2$O$_7$
0.1M K$_2$CrO$_4$
1.0M HCl
0.1M Ba(NO$_3$)$_2$

0.2M Fe(NO$_3$)$_3$
CoCl$_2$·6H$_2$O
6.0M HCl
0.04% thymol blue
   solution
distilled water
0.1M CuSO$_4$
1.0M NaOH
1.0M NH$_3$

PROCEDURE

Part I   Equilibrium Involving Thymol Blue

1. Put on your lab apron and safety goggles.

2. Obtain 2 clean, empty, dry 250 mL Erlenmeyer flasks. Add approximately 100 mL of distilled water and 1 mL of thymol blue solution to each flask. Record the color of this solution in your notebook.

3. To the first flask add a single drop of 0.1M HCl. Swirl the contents of the flask and continue the drop-by-drop addition until a definite color change is observed. The second flask will serve as a control. Compare the solution colors. Record the new color and the number of drops required for this change in your copy of Table 1 in your notebook.

4. Continue the drop-by-drop addition of 0.1M HCl to the first flask until a second color shift occurs. Compare with the control and record the new color change and number of drops required for this change in Table 1.

5. Now add 0.1M NaOH drop by drop in the first flask until a definite color change is observed. Record the color change and number of drops required in your data table.

6. Continue the drop-by-drop addition of 0.1M NaOH until the color changes again. Record the color change and number of drops required in Table 1.

CAUTION: Hydrochloric acid is corrosive to skin, eyes, and clothing. When handling this acid, wear a full face shield and plastic gloves in addition to your safety goggles and lab apron. Wash any spills or splashes immediately with plenty of water. Call your teacher.

Part II   Equilibrium Involving Thiocyanatoiron(III) Ion

1. Place 1 mL of 0.2M FeCl$_3$ into a 250 mL beaker. Using a graduated cylinder, measure a 1 mL portion of 0.2M KSCN. Record the color of each solution in your notebook.

2. Add the measured portion of $0.2M$ KSCN solution to the beaker containing the $0.2M$ FeCl$_3$. Swirl the mixture and record the color in your notebook. Add enough distilled water to the solution to dilute the intense color to a light amber color (approximately 80 mL).

3. Pour 5 mL of this solution into each of 5 separate test tubes labeled A to E. Test tube A serves as a control.

4. For each of the following reactions (steps 5–8) record the results in your copy of Table 2. To record the "stress" involved, state which ion in the original equilibrium changed concentration, and whether this change was an increase or a decrease.

5. To test tube B, add 10 drops of $0.2M$ KCl.

6. To test tube C, add 10 drops of $0.2M$ Fe(NO$_3$)$_3$.

7. To test tube D, add 10 drops of $0.2M$ KSCN.

8. To test tube E, add 10 drops of $6.0M$ NaOH.

Part III   Equilibrium Involving Cobalt(II) Complexes

1. Place a pea-sized sample (approximately 0.3 g) of CoCl$_2$·6H$_2$O into each of two 100 mL beakers.

2. To the first beaker, add 10 mL of $6.0M$ HCl.

3. To the second beaker, add 10 mL of distilled water. Note the colors of the solutions in both beakers and record this information in your notebook.

4. Gradually add distilled water to the solution in the first beaker until a definite color change occurs. Record your observations in your copy of Table 3.

5. Place the first beaker on a ring stand with a ring and wire gauze in the fume hood. Adjust the laboratory burner to a very low flame and heat gently. When a definite color change is observed, shut off the burner. Using tongs, remove the beaker from the ring stand. Record the resulting color in Table 3.

6. Add approximately 50 mL of cold tap water to a clean 250 mL beaker. Carefully place the warm beaker and contents from Step 4 upright into this cold water bath. Record any additional changes in color or intensity in Table 3.

Part IV   Equilibrium Involving Chromate and Dichromate Ions

1. Place 10 drops of $0.1M$ K$_2$CrO$_4$ and 10 drops of $0.1M$ K$_2$Cr$_2$O$_7$ in different 13 mm × 100 mm test tubes.

2. Add to each, in alternation, $1M$ NaOH drop by drop until a color change occurs in one of the test tubes.

3. To the same test tubes add $1M$ HCl in the same manner until a color change is observed.

4. Repeat Steps 1 to 3, but add the $1M$ HCl first until a color change is observed; then add $1M$ NaOH. Record all your results in your copy of Table 4.

5. Place 10 drops of $0.1M$ K_2CrO_4 in a 13 mm × 100 mm test tube. Add 2 drops of $1M$ NaOH. Then add $0.1M$ $Ba(NO_3)_2$ solution drop by drop until a change is noted.

CAUTION: Barium compounds are poisonous. Do not get any in your mouth. Do not swallow any.

6. Add $1M$ HCl solution drop by drop to the test tube from Step 5 until a change occurs.

7. Place 10 drops of $0.1M$ $K_2Cr_2O_7$ in a 13 mm × 100 mm test tube. Add 2 drops of $1M$ HCl, then add 10 drops of $0.1M$ $Ba(NO_3)_2$ drop by drop.

8. Add $1M$ NaOH solution drop by drop to the test tube from Step 7 until a change is noted. Record all your results in Table 4.

9. Place 10 drops of $0.1M$ K_2CrO_4 in one test tube and 10 drops of $0.1M$ $K_2Cr_2O_7$ in another test tube. Add 10 drops of $0.1M$ $Ba(NO_3)_2$ to each. Observe the results, and record them in Table 4.

Part V   Equilibrium Involving Copper(II) Complexes

1. Place 2 mL of $0.1M$ $CuSO_4$ in a 13 mm × 100 mm test tube.

2. Add 3 drops of $1M$ NH_3 and observe the result.

3. Continue adding $1M$ NH_3 until another change occurs.

4. Add $1M$ HCl drop by drop until a change occurs. Record your observations in your copy of Table 5.

CAUTION: Copper compounds are poisonous. Do not get any in your mouth. Do not swallow any.

5. Clean up all of your materials. Before you leave the laboratory, wash your hands thoroughly with soap and water; use a fingernail brush to clean under your fingernails.

CAUTION: Ammonia solution is corrosive. Keep it off your skin and out of your eyes. Avoid breathing its fumes. Wash any spills and splashes with plenty of water.

REAGENT DISPOSAL

All test tubes from Part IV (containing chromates, dichromates, and barium compounds) should be placed in the designated container. All other solutions may safely be rinsed down the sink with plenty of water.

POST LAB DISCUSSION

The equilibrium system in Part I can be affected by the addition of any reagent supplying H^+ or OH^-. Recall that the H^+ ions are characteristic of acids and OH^- ions are characteristic of bases. The addition of an acid should favor the conversion into the lighter colored form of the indicator.

Another factor to consider in explaining your observations is the fact that H^+ will react with OH^- to form water molecules. As a result of the formation of water, the concentrations of H^+ and OH^- in the equilibrium reaction are reduced.

In reviewing your data from Part II, it is important to note that the formation of $FeSCN^{2+}$ is heavily favored over the reverse decomposition reaction. Diluting the solution with water allows you to observe small changes in the equilibrium more readily. In explaining your observations of this equilibrium, remember that spectator ions do not participate in the net reaction.

In Step 6 of Part II, you noted the formation of a precipitate. In this case, the precipitate is $Fe(OH)_3$. In explaining your results, remember that the formation of this precipitate reduces the Fe^{3+} concentration of the solution.

For the reaction in Part III, recall that increasing the temperature of an equilibrium reaction favors the endothermic reaction. From your observations, you should be able to predict which of the two reactions is endothermic.

The equilibrium in Part IV can be represented by the equation

$$2CrO_4^{2-}(aq) + 2H^+(aq) \rightleftharpoons Cr_2O_7^{2-}(aq) + H_2O(l)$$

The presence of $H^+(aq)$ in the equilibrium explains how it is that adding H^+ and OH^- is able to affect the position of this equilibrium. The other equilibrium involved in Part IV is the one in which Ba^{2+} ions react with CrO_4^{2-} ions to give solid $BaCrO_4$:

$$Ba^{2+}(aq) + CrO_4^{2-}(aq) \rightleftharpoons BaCrO_4(s)$$

Whether or not a precipitate could be observed here depends on the position of the first equilibrium involving CrO_4^{2-} and $Cr_2O_7^{2-}$.

The equilibrium in Part V initially involves the formation of OH^- ions in NH_3 solution:

$$NH_3(aq) + H_2O(l) \rightleftharpoons NH_4^+(aq) + OH^-(aq)$$

The OH^- ions then react with $Cu^{2+}(aq)$ to give a precipitate of $Cu(OH)_2$:

$$Cu^{2+}(aq) + 2OH^-(aq) \rightleftharpoons Cu(OH)_2(s)$$

When more NH_3 was added, NH_3 molecules replaced H_2O molecules in $Cu^{2+}(aq)$:

$$Cu(H_2O)_4^{2+}(aq) + 4NH_3 \rightleftharpoons Cu(NH_3)_4^{2+}(aq) + 4H_2O(l)$$

H^+ ions can react with NH_3 to give NH_4^+; therefore, the equilibrium shifts in response to this change.

DATA AND OBSERVATIONS

Organize your data and observations in tables similar to the following. It would be a good idea to have these in your notebook before coming to the laboratory.

Part I   Equilibrium Involving Thymol Blue

Table 1

REAGENT ADDED	STRESS (ION ADDED)	COLOR OBSERVATION	DIRECTION OF EQUILIBRIUM SHIFT
HCl (Step 3)			
HCl (Step 4)			
NaOH (Step 5)			
NaOH (Step 6)			

Part II   Equilibrium Involving Thiocyanatoiron(III) Ion

Table 2

REAGENT ADDED	STRESS (ION ADDED)	OBSERVATION	DIRECTION OF EQUILIBRIUM SHIFT
KCl (test tube *B*)			
Fe(NO₃)₃ (test tube *C*)			
KSCN (test tube *D*)			
NaOH (test tube *E*)			

Part III   Equilibrium Involving Cobalt(II) Complexes

Table 3

	STRESS	OBSERVATION	DIRECTION OF EQUILIBRIUM SHIFT
Step 3			
Step 4			
Step 5			

Part IV   Equilibrium Involving Chromate and Dichromate Ions

Table 4

		0.1*M* K₂CrO₄		0.1*M* K₂Cr₂O₇	
Steps 2 and 3	Initial Color				
	1*M* NaOH added				
	1*M* HCl added				

		0.1*M* K₂CrO₄		0.1*M* K₂Cr₂O₇	
Step 4	Initial Color				
	1*M* HCl added				
	1*M* NaOH added				

		INITIAL COLOR	+ 1*M* NaOH	+ 0.1*M* Ba(NO₃)₂	+ 1*M* HCl
Steps 5 and 6	0.1*M* K₂CrO₄				

		INITIAL COLOR	+ 1*M* HCl	+ 0.1*M* Ba(NO₃)₂	+ 1*M* NaOH
Steps 7 and 8	0.1*M* K₂Cr₂O₇				

		0.1*M* K₂CrO₄	0.1*M* K₂Cr₂O₇
Step 9	Add 0.1*M* Ba(NO₃)₂		

Part V Equilibrium Involving Copper(II) Complexes

Table 5

	0.1M CuSO$_4$	+ 3 DROPS NH$_3$	+ MORE NH$_3$	1M HCl ADDED
Appearance		COMPLETE IN YOUR NOTEBOOK		

QUESTIONS

1. In Part I, how would increasing the molarity of the NaOH solution from 0.1M to 0.2M affect the number of drops required for the observed color changes?

2. Apply Le Chatelier's principle to explain the results obtained when 6.0M NaOH was introduced into the iron(III) thiocyanate ion equilibrium system.

3. If the hydrated cobalt(II) ion complex was refrigerated, what would you predict as the color of the refrigerated solution?

4. Look at the equilibrium equation for the reaction involving the hydrated cobalt(II) ion complex. From your lab results, which reaction is endothermic? Cite evidence for your answer.

5. Predict how the addition of sodium chloride, NaCl, would affect the hydrated cobalt(II) ion equilibrium. Explain your prediction in terms of Le Chatelier's principle.

6. Write the balanced equation for the reaction of $Cr_2O_7^{2-}$ with OH^-.

7. Explain the reasons for the equilibrium shifts observed in Steps 1 to 4 of Part IV.

8. Compare the relative solubilities of $BaCrO_4$ and $BaCr_2O_7$.

9. Explain why no precipitate formed in $K_2Cr_2O_7$ in Step 7 of Part IV, while some did form in Step 9.

10. Explain the cause of the color change observed when HCl was added to the complex ion $Cu(NH_3)_4^{2+}$ in Part V.

FOLLOW-UP QUESTIONS

1. When Ag^+ ions are added to the red $FeSCN^{2+}$ ions in Part II, the color disappears, and a white precipitate of AgSCN forms. Explain why Fe^{3+} can be used as an indicator in a reaction to determine the concentration of an unknown solution of Ag^+ by reacting it with a solution of KSCN of known concentration.

2. A student discovers that after doing Part IV of this experiment, several of the test tubes are coated with a yellow precipitate that does not wash off easily. Devise a chemical method of removing this material.

CONCLUSIONS

1. State the effect on the position of an equilibrium of a change in concentration of a reactant or product.

2. State the effect on the position of an equilibrium of a change in temperature.

The Quantitative Relationship Involving Concentrations of Reactants and Products at Equilibrium

In many chemical reactions at equilibrium, from chemical manufacturing processes to reactions between pollutant gases in the atmosphere, scientists need to know how the concentrations of reactants and products are related to one another. This experiment will investigate that relationship.

In Experiment 19A you investigated the equilibrium reaction in which the iron(III) ion reacted with the thiocyanate ion to give the thiocyanato-iron(III) complex ion:

$$Fe^{3+}(aq) + SCN^-(aq) \rightleftharpoons FeSCN^{2+}(aq)$$

The $FeSCN^{2+}$ ion gives a deep blood-red color, which may appear orange in more dilute solutions. Here the reaction will be investigated quantitatively. In Part I, different initial concentrations of $Fe^{3+}(aq)$ will have $SCN^-(aq)$ added to them. In Part II, the equilibrium concentration of $FeSCN^{2+}(aq)$ will be measured by means of a spectrophotometer. From these data, the equilibrium concentrations of all three ions will be obtained, and the results will be used to see whether any constant relationship exists among the values.

OBJECTIVES

1. to prepare various dilutions of Fe^{3+} ion and to react them with SCN^- ion

2. to measure the concentration of $FeSCN^{2+}$ ion produced by means of a spectrophotometer

3. to use a spectrophotometer to discover a constant mathematical relationship among the concentrations of reactants and products at equilibrium

MATERIALS

Apparatus

5 test tubes
  (18 mm × 150 mm)
graduated cylinder (10 mL)
graduated cylinder (25 mL)
3 beakers
test-tube rack
5 spectrophotometer tubes
  (or 13 mm × 100 mm test tubes)
spectrophotometer
lab apron
safety goggles

Reagants

$0.200 M$ $Fe(NO_3)_3$ (acidified)
$0.0020 M$ KSCN

PROCEDURE

Part I Reaction of SCN⁻ with Various Dilutions of Fe³⁺

1. Put on your lab apron and safety goggles.

2. Obtain in separate beakers approximately 30 mL of $0.0020M$ KSCN and 20 mL of $0.200M$ $Fe(NO_3)_3$.

3. Place the five 18 mm × 150 mm test tubes in a rack and label them A to E. (Note: The test tubes should be clean and dry.)

4. Measure 5.0 mL of $0.200M$ $Fe(NO_3)_3$ in a 10 mL graduated cylinder and transfer it to test tube A.

5. Measure 10.0 mL of the $Fe(NO_3)_3$ solution into a 25 mL graduated cylinder. Add water to make it up to the 25 mL mark, then transfer it to a clean, dry beaker to mix.

6. Using your 10 mL graduated cylinder, transfer 5.0 mL of this diluted solution to test tube B. (If the cylinder is wet, rinse it with about 2 mL of your solution first.) Then measure 10 mL of the diluted solution, again in the 10 mL cylinder, and pour it into the 25 mL cylinder (it can be wet). Make up to 25 mL with water.

7. Repeat Step 6 with this new, diluted solution, but place the 5 mL portion in test tube C, and continue similar dilutions of 10 mL to 25 mL to get 5 mL portions in test tubes D and E.

8. To each test tube add 5.0 mL of $0.0020M$ KSCN.

The following flowchart may help to clarify the dilution procedures:

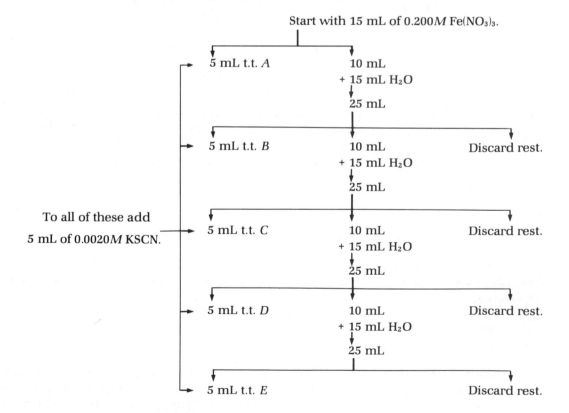

Part II   Measuring the Concentration of FeSCN²⁺ with a Spectrophotometer

1. If necessary, refer to the introduction to Experiment 16B to refresh your memory as to how the spectrophotometer should be set up and used. The wavelength for this experiment is 590 nm.

2. Obtain 5 spectrophotometer tubes and place them in the rack. (Use clean, scratch-free 13 mm × 100 mm test tubes if the other special ones — cuvettes — are not available.) Transfer each of Solutions A to E to these tubes, first washing them with 2 mL of the solution if they are wet. Fill the tubes about three quarters full.

3. Read the absorbance for each solution and record the value in your copy of Table 1 in your notebook. Note that for this experiment you will be calculating the concentration from your readings, so you must read absorbance rather than percent transmittance.

4. Before leaving the laboratory, wash your hands thoroughly with soap and water; use a fingernail brush to clean under your nails.

REAGENT DISPOSAL

Wash all solutions down the sink with plenty of water.

POST LAB DISCUSSION

The data you have obtained in this experiment will now permit you to calculate the concentrations of each ion present at equilibrium. Your task will then be to determine whether a mathematical relationship exists among these concentration values.

DATA AND OBSERVATIONS

Table 1

TEST TUBE NUMBER	INITIAL [Fe³⁺]	INITIAL [SCN⁻]	ABSORBANCE
1			
2			
3			
4			
5			

(The initial $[Fe^{3+}]$ and initial $[SCN^-]$ can be calculated before you come to the laboratory. See Calculations, item 1.)

CALCULATIONS

1. Calculate the initial $[Fe^{3+}]$ and initial $[SCN^-]$ in each of the mixed solutions. Remember to account not only for the dilution factor for Fe^{3+} involved in each successive test tube (10 mL going to 25 mL), but also for the subsequent dilution of 5 mL to 10 mL for each ion when the solutions are mixed. As noted earlier, you could do these calculations before coming to the laboratory.

2. In calculating $[FeSCN^{2+}]$ in each test tube, some assumptions must be made. It is impossible to make up a set of test tubes of standard concentration of $FeSCN^{2+}$ to compare against, since the equilibrium reaction will always come into play, and the position of the equilibrium will shift on dilution of the mixture. For these reasons, no calibration graphs can be drawn, so you will have to assume that the absorbance measured is proportional to the $[FeSCN^{2+}]$.

   In obtaining a standard concentration for comparison of results, you must assume that in test tube A, in which $0.200 M$ Fe^{3+} is mixed with $0.002 M$ SCN^-, there is so much excess Fe^{3+} that essentially all the SCN^- will be used up. You can therefore state that the initial $[SCN^-]$ will be equal to the equilibrium $[FeSCN^{2+}]$ in test tube A. This test tube therefore becomes the standard for comparison of the absorbances measured in the experiment.

   Calculate the equilibrium $[FeSCN^{2+}]$ in each tube from the following equation:

   $$[FeSCN^{2+}] \text{ (test tube } x) = [FeSCN^{2+}] \text{ (test tube } A) \times \frac{\text{Absorbance (test tube } x)}{\text{Absorbance (test tube } A)}$$

   Note that the assumption that all the SCN^- will be used up in test tube A implies that the equilibrium $[SCN^-] = 0$. This will give no meaningful results for any quantitative relationships in that test tube, but it does enable you to get meaningful results in the remaining four.

3. For test tubes B to E, calculate the equilibrium $[Fe^{3+}]$ and equilibrium $[SCN^-]$ by subtracting the equilibrium $[FeSCN^{2+}]$ from the initial $[Fe^{3+}]$ and initial $[SCN^-]$ respectively. (Mole ratio in equation $= 1:1:1$.)

4. In order to see whether there is any mathematical relationship between these equilibrium concentrations, calculate the value of each of the following expressions for each of test tubes B to E. (Your instructor may suggest alternate or additional expressions to try.)

   a. $\dfrac{[FeSCN^{2+}][Fe^{3+}]}{[SCN^-]}$

   b. $\dfrac{[FeSCN^{2+}]}{[Fe^{3+}][SCN^-]}$

   c. $[Fe^{3+}][SCN^-][FeSCN^{2+}]$

   d. $\dfrac{[Fe^{3+}] + [SCN^-]}{[FeSCN^{2+}]}$

5. Calculate the ratio of the largest value to the smallest value for each of expressions (a) to (d) above. The expression that gives the smallest ratio will be the one that is the most constant. It is unrealistic to expect any expression to give values which come out exactly the same, considering the assumptions that were made, and the errors that will be present with so many volume measurement readings.

FOLLOW-UP QUESTIONS

1. The most constant expression in question 5 is called the equilibrium constant expression (K_{eq}). Describe the form of the equilibrium constant expression (K_{eq}) in terms of equilibrium concentrations of reactants and products. How are these concentrations related?

2. Referring to the fact that equilibrium reactions have an equilibrium constant expression, explain why changing the concentration of a reactant or product causes an equilibrium shift in the direction predicted by Le Chatelier's principle.

CONCLUSION

What is your average value for the equilibrium constant for this reaction?

Determination of a Solubility Product Constant

When an ionic solid dissolves in water, it dissociates to give the positive and negative ions that make up the solid. These ions are hydrated, and are found in solution in the same relative proportion as in the solid. As more solid dissolves, the concentration of the ions increases. This build-up allows the reverse reaction, in which the ions crystallize out, to have a greater possibility of occurring. Eventually, a situation is reached in which the rate of dissolving is equal to the rate of crystallization. At this point, no more solid can dissolve, and the solution is said to be *saturated*. A state of equilibrium has been reached which can be recognized by a constant color for the solution (if it is colored), or by a constant mass left undissolved.

The solubility product constant, K_{sp}, for an ionic solid is given by the product of the concentration of the ions, each raised to the power of the coefficients in the dissolving reaction. For instance, the K_{sp} for silver chloride, $AgCl$, is given by

$$K_{sp} = [Ag^+][Cl^-]$$

For a substance such as lead iodide, PbI_2, the K_{sp} is given by

$$K_{sp} = [Pb^{2+}][I^-]^2$$

The K_{sp} expression gives the relationship between the ions in the saturated solution, and therefore their maximum possible concentration without causing precipitation. If solutions of suitable concentration of substances are available, it is possible to mix them to form a precipitate, then carry out appropriate dilutions until a point is reached at which no precipitate occurs. This process allows an approximate value to be determined for the K_{sp}.

In this experiment, you will mix solutions of lead nitrate and potassium iodide at a number of different dilutions, and watch for the first situation in which no precipitate occurs. You will then be able to state the K_{sp} at room temperature as a range of values. The test tubes in which a precipitate did occur will then be heated until the precipitate dissolves, in order that you may determine the K_{sp} at different temperatures.

OBJECTIVES

1. to prepare a number of solutions of each of Pb^{2+} and I^-, of differing concentrations

2. to mix combinations of the above solutions and note whether a precipitate occurs

3. to obtain an approximate value of the K_{sp} for PbI_2 at room temperature

4. to obtain the approximate K_{sp} for PbI_2 at temperatures higher than room temperature

MATERIALS

Apparatus

12 test tubes
  (18 mm × 150 mm)
2 test-tube racks
2 graduated cylinders
  (10 mL)
medicine dropper
beaker (400 mL)
2 beakers (100 mL)

laboratory burner
ring stand and ring
wire gauze
thermometer
water soluble marker
lab apron
safety goggles

Reagents

$0.010M$ $Pb(NO_3)_2$
$0.020M$ KI

CAUTION: Lead nitrate is very toxic. Do not get any in your mouth and do not swallow any. Avoid getting any on your skin, since it can be absorbed. Wash away any spills or splashes with plenty of water. Call your teacher.

PROCEDURE

1. Put on your lab apron and safety goggles.

2. Obtain in separate 100 mL beakers about 40 mL of each of $0.010M$ $Pb(NO_3)_2$ and $0.020M$ KI, and label the beakers.

3. Obtain twelve 18 mm × 150 mm test tubes and arrange them in two racks, each with 6 test tubes. Label each set A to F with your water soluble marker. Label them near the top, since they will be immersed in water later.

4. Into the first set of test tubes place 10.0 mL, 8.0 mL, 6.0 mL, 4.0 mL, 3.0 mL, and 2.0 mL of $0.010M$ $Pb(NO_3)_2$, respectively. Use your 10 mL graduated cylinder, and get the precise amount by adding or subtracting drops with a dropper.

5. Add an amount of water to each tube to make the volume in each up to 10.0 mL (that is, 0.0 mL, 2.0 mL, 4.0 mL, 6.0 mL, 7.0 mL, and 8.0 mL, respectively).

6. Repeat Steps 4 and 5 with the test tubes in the second rack, using $0.020M$ KI instead of $0.010M$ $Pb(NO_3)_2$.

7. Mix the contents of test tube A from the lead nitrate set with the contents of test tube A from the potassium iodide set, and replace the test tube in the rack.

8. Repeat Step 7 for each of the other 5 combinations.

9. Record in which test tubes a precipitate occurs in your copy of Table 1 in your notebook.

10. Add about 250 mL of water to a 400 mL beaker, and place the beaker on a wire gauze on a ring clamp attached to a stand.

11. Place each of the test tubes which contain a precipitate in the beaker, and begin heating slowly with a laboratory burner. (See Figure 19C-1.)

12. When the precipitate in each test tube dissolves, note the temperature of the water bath and record it in Table 1.

13. Before leaving the laboratory, wash your hands thoroughly with soap and water; use a fingernail brush to clean under your fingernails.

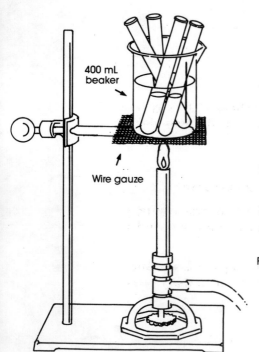

400 mL beaker

Wire gauze

Figure 19C-1

REAGENT DISPOSAL

Empty the contents of all test tubes into the designated waste container.

POST LAB DISCUSSION

The K_{sp} expression for lead iodide, $[Pb^{2+}][I^-]^2$, represents the equilibrium concentrations at the point where a precipitate just starts to form. When other concentration values are substituted in this expression it is called a *trial ion product* (or simply, *ion product*). When this trial ion product exceeds K_{sp}, a precipitate should form until the equilibrium concentrations are reached. If the trial ion product is less than or equal to K_{sp}, no precipitate should form. If you note the temperature at which a precipitate dissolves, the trial ion product for that sample becomes the K_{sp} at that temperature.

DATA AND OBSERVATIONS

Organize your data and observations in a table similar to the following. It would be a good idea to have the table ready in your notebook before coming to the laboratory.

Table 1

TEST TUBE #	A	B	C	D	E	F
Volume of $0.010M$ $Pb(NO_3)_2$ (mL)	10.0	8.0	6.0	4.0	3.0	2.0
Volume of water (mL) added	0.0	2.0	4.0	6.0	7.0	8.0
Volume of $0.020M$ KI (mL)	10.0	8.0	6.0	4.0	3.0	2.0
Volume of water added (mL)	0.0	2.0	4.0	6.0	7.0	8.0
Precipitate or no precipitate (at room temperature)						
Temperature at which precipitate dissolves (°C)						

COMPLETE IN YOUR NOTEBOOK

QUESTIONS AND CALCULATIONS

1. For each of test tubes *A* to *F*, calculate the $[Pb^{2+}]$ in the final mixed solution. In using the appropriate dilution factor, remember that the final volume in each case is the sum of the volumes of both the lead nitrate and the potassium iodide, i.e., 20 mL.

2. Repeat for $[I^-]$ in the final mixed solution in test tubes *A* to *F*.

3. Calculate the value of the trial ion product for each of test tubes *A* to *F* (given by $[Pb^{2+}][I^-]^2$).

4. State the range of values in which your experimental K_{sp} must lie. (This will be between the trial ion product of the last test tube giving a precipitate and the trial ion product of the first test tube not giving a precipitate.)

5. From the results of the temperature at which a precipitate dissolved, make up a table showing the temperature, the K_{sp} and the solubility in each case. (Since in each situation the $[I^-]$ was twice the $[Pb^{2+}]$, the solubility of PbI_2 is given simply by the $[Pb^{2+}]$ alone.)

6. What is the trend in the solubility as the temperature is increased?

7. Plot a graph of solubility (moles per litre) against temperature.

FOLLOW-UP QUESTIONS

1. If you were given a saturated solution of lead iodide and asked to determine the K_{sp} of PbI_2 from it, how would you proceed?

2. Will lead iodide be more or less soluble in a solution of $0.10 M$ KI than it will be in pure water? Explain your answer.

3. After doing this experiment, a student finds that the test tubes have a coating of yellow lead iodide on the inside which doesn't wash off easily. On the basis of your experimental results, suggest the best method for removing this coating.

4. Compare your K_{sp} value with that obtained from a chemical handbook or other reference book. Suggest some reasons for any difference.

CONCLUSION

State the results of Objective 3.

Applications of Solubility Product Principles

There are many instances in which a knowledge of solubility equilibria and solubility product values is important to a chemist. You were introduced to the study of qualitative analysis in Chapter 16 in a rather simple way. More detailed schemes for identifying a large number of different ions depend on a knowledge of K_{sp} values, and the common ion effect is often used to control the concentration of the reagents in order to exceed the K_{sp} for one ion and not another, thus effecting a separation.

One aspect of solubility equilibria with which you may already be familiar is the topic of water hardness. Essentially, hard water is water that does not allow soap to lather well because Ca^{2+} and Mg^{2+} ions are present in the water, though some other metal ions can also be involved. The Ca^{2+} and Mg^{2+} ions get into the water from the geological formations over which the water flows. Water found in limestone areas is more likely to be hard than water which contacts mainly granite. Thus, how much of a problem water hardness is depends greatly on where you live.

The reason why hard water does not allow soap to form suds very well is that the Ca^{2+} and Mg^{2+} ions react with the stearate ion, $C_{17}H_{35}COO^-$ (soap consists mostly of sodium or potassium stearates), forming an insoluble curd or scum. Thus, a lot of soap gets wasted, precipitating Ca^{2+} and Mg^{2+} before it can start to lather and help remove dirt.

There are two main types of hard water. *Temporarily hard water* contains $Ca(HCO_3)_2$ or $Mg(HCO_3)_2$, which can be removed by boiling. *Permanently hard water* contains mainly sulfates and chlorides of Ca^{2+} and Mg^{2+}, which cannot be removed by boiling; other means must be used. In Parts I and II of this experiment you will investigate temporarily and permanently hard water respectively, and investigate ways of removing the hardness.

One other important application of solubility equilibria and K_{sp} values is in analytical chemistry, in situations where the quantity of a dissolved ion needs to be determined. This is often done by precipitation, and in Part III of this experiment you will determine the $[Cl^-]$ in a sample of water (tap water, river water, lake water, or an unknown chloride solution) by titrating with a standard solution of silver nitrate. Sodium (or potassium) chromate can be used as an indicator. Since AgCl is less soluble than Ag_2CrO_4, it will be precipitated first. When all the chloride has been precipitated, Ag_2CrO_4 will be formed. It has a brick-red color (as opposed to white for the AgCl), so the first appearance of a brick-red color indicates that all the chloride has been precipitated.

OBJECTIVES

1. to demonstrate the formation of temporarily hard water, as well as how the hardness can be eliminated

2. to demonstrate the effect of permanently hard water, as well as how the hardness can be eliminated

3. to determine the concentration of Cl^- in a water sample by titrating with standard $AgNO_3$

MATERIALS

Apparatus

Erlenmeyer flask (250 mL)
Bunsen burner
ring stand
clamp
wire gauze
test-tube rack
8 test tubes (13 mm × 100 mm)
buret (50 mL)
stopper
pipet (25 mL) *or*
  graduated cylinder (25 mL)
2 beakers (250 mL)
filter funnel
lab apron
safety goggles

Reagents

saturated limewater
  (calcium hydroxide, $Ca(OH)_2$)
CO_2 supply
powdered pure soap *or*
  liquid soap
$0.4M$ $MgSO_4$
$0.4M$ $CaCl_2$
$2M$ Na_2CO_3
$0.100M$ $AgNO_3$
sample of water containing
  chloride ions
$0.10M$ Na_2CrO_4

PROCEDURE

Part I Temporarily Hard Water

1. Put on your lab apron and safety goggles.

2. Obtain 25 mL of saturated limewater solution and record its appearance in your copy of Table 1 in your notebook.

3. Bubble CO_2 gas into the solution from the cylinder provided or from the CO_2 gas generating flask and record the appearance of the solution in Table 1. Keep bubbling until the precipitate which forms at first dissolves again, and record the appearance of the solution.

4. Pour off about 5 mL of this solution into a 13 mm × 100 mm test tube (A).

5. Set up the flask on the stand, and heat with the Bunsen burner until the solution has boiled for 5 min. Observe the result.

6. Pour 5 mL of the flask's contents into a second test tube in the rack (B). Discard the remaining contents.

7. Place 5 mL of distilled water into a third test tube (C).

8. To each test tube add enough powdered pure soap to cover the surface of the liquid, or 1 drop of liquid soap.

9. Shake each test tube. Note the relative amount of lathering in each test tube, and record your observations in your copy of Table 2.

Part II Permanently Hard Water

1. Set up five 13 mm × 100 mm test tubes in a rack. Label them *A* to *E,* and add the following to each:

   A: distilled water
   B: 4 mL of $0.4M$ $MgSO_4$
   C: 4 mL of $0.4M$ $CaCl_2$
   D: 4 mL of $0.4M$ $MgSO_4$ + 1 mL of $2M$ Na_2CO_3
   E: 4 mL of $0.4M$ $CaCl_2$ + 1 mL of $2M$ Na_2CO_3

2. To each add enough pure soap powder to cover the surface of the liquid, or 1 drop of liquid soap. Note the appearance of each in your copy of Table 3.

3. Shake each test tube. In Table 3, record the relative amount of lathering in each test tube.

Part III   Determination of Chloride Ion Concentration in a Water Sample

1. Obtain approximately 100 mL of $0.100M$ silver nitrate solution, $AgNO_3$, in a 250 mL beaker. (Your teacher may suggest more or less of this, depending on the amount of chloride in your samples to be tested and how many measurements you are to make.)

2. Set up the buret with its clamp and stand, and pour about 10 mL of $AgNO_3$ into it, using a filter funnel. Rinse back and forth (use a stopper, not your finger!), and discard the rinsings through the tip into a 250 mL beaker. Use this beaker for all your silver wastes.

3. Refill the buret to the top, and drain enough into your silver wastes beaker that the tip is filled and free from air bubbles.

4. Your teacher will recommend using a 25 mL, 50 mL, or 100 mL sample of water, depending on the amount of chloride content in it. Transfer the specified amount to your Erlenmeyer flask, using either a 25 mL pipet or a graduated cylinder. Record the volume of the sample in your copy of Table 4.

5. Add 2 mL of $0.10M$ Na_2CrO_4 to the water sample.

6. Record the initial volume reading on the buret in Table 4, and run the $AgNO_3$ solution into the flask, swirling all the time. You should notice that, although a white precipitate is produced, the solution stays yellow because of the chromate ions.

7. As the titration continues you will notice a reddish color begin to form which disappears as the swirling continues. Slow down the rate at which you are adding the $AgNO_3$ at this point, until you are adding it drop by drop. Stop at the point where the contents of the flask show the first sign of a reddish color that remains.

8. Read the final volume in the buret, and calculate the volume used to precipitate all the Cl^- ions. Record both figures in Table 4.

9. Empty the contents of the flask into your beaker containing silver wastes.

10. Repeat Steps 3 to 9 once or twice more, with either the same water sample or a different one, as directed by your teacher.

11. Wash your hands thoroughly with soap and water before leaving the laboratory, using a fingernail brush to clean under your fingernails.

CAUTION: Silver nitrate is poisonous, and is corrosive to skin and eyes. It will result in brown stains on your skin if you spill any on yourself. If this occurs, wash with sodium thiosulfate solution, then with plenty of water. Call your teacher.

CAUTION: Sodium chromate is poisonous, and is an irritant to skin and eyes. Do not get any on your skin. If you do, wash it off with plenty of water.

REAGENT DISPOSAL

All the solutions from Parts I and II may be safely disposed of by being rinsed down the sink with copious amounts of water. Empty your beaker of silver wastes from Part III into the designated waste container. Return any unused silver nitrate solution to the container provided. Clean all glassware carefully.

POST LAB DISCUSSION

Calcium carbonate, $CaCO_3$, is only very slightly soluble in water:

$$CaCO_3(s) \rightleftharpoons Ca^{2+}(aq) + CO_3^{2-}(aq)$$

$$K_{sp} = [Ca^{2+}][CO_3^{2-}] = 4.8 \times 10^{-9}$$

This means that the solubility is about $7 \times 10^{-5}M$ or 7×10^{-3} g/L. However, when CO_2 dissolves in water, another equilibrium is set up:

$$CO_2(g) + H_2O(l) \rightleftharpoons H_2CO_3(aq) \rightleftharpoons H^+(aq) + HCO_3^-(aq)$$

The $H^+(aq)$ from this equilibrium combines with the CO_3^{2-} from the $CaCO_3$ equilibrium, forming more HCO_3^-. The removal of the CO_3^{2-} causes the solubility equilibrium for $CaCO_3$ to move to the right; in other words, more $CaCO_3$ dissolves. Eventually, a colorless solution of calcium bicarbonate, $Ca(HCO_3)_2$, forms. The dissolved Ca^{2+} ions cause the water to be hard because they can precipitate the stearate ions from soap.

If this solution of $Ca(HCO_3)_2$ is boiled, CO_2 gas comes out of solution. The result is the shifting of all the equilibria back to the left and the consequent precipitation of $CaCO_3$. This process naturally removes the hardness from the water, as the Ca^{2+} ions have been removed from the solution. Thus, this solution is *temporarily* hard.

Note that $Ca(HCO_3)_2$ does not exist in the solid phase. If you try to boil off the water to obtain the solid, then $CaCO_3$ will be formed. The same result occurs if the solution is allowed to evaporate over a long period: CO_2 and H_2O are removed, and $CaCO_3$ is deposited.

The use of CrO_4^{2-} in Part III as an indicator in the titration with Ag^+ to determine $[Cl^-]$ is an interesting application of solubility product principles. The K_{sp} for $AgCl$ is 1.8×10^{-10}, whereas that for Ag_2CrO_4 is 1.1×10^{-12}. If, in this experiment, you used a 50 mL sample, the $[CrO_4^{2-}]$ would have been $0.0040M$. The $[Ag^+]$ at which precipitation of Ag_2CrO_4 would just start to occur is therefore $1.7 \times 10^{-5}M$. However, if the $[Cl^-]$ in the sample of water had been $0.020M$, then the $[Ag^+]$ at which precipitation of $AgCl$ would have occurred would have been $9.0 \times 10^{-9}M$. Obviously, the $AgCl$ precipitates out first, and no Ag_2CrO_4 can be precipitated until all the Cl^- has been removed as $AgCl$. The appearance of the red color indicating that Ag_2CrO_4 has finally been formed means that the volume of Ag^+ used till that point was all used up for Cl^-. From this information the $[Cl^-]$ in the original sample can be calculated.

DATA AND OBSERVATIONS

Record your data and observations in tables similar to the following. It would be a good idea to have these in your notebook before coming to the laboratory.

Part I   Temporarily Hard Water

Table 1

Appearance of limewater solution	
Appearance when CO_2 initially bubbled in	
Appearance when CO_2 bubbled in for a longer time	

COMPLETE IN YOUR NOTEBOOK

Table 2

TEST TUBE #	CONTENTS	HEIGHT OF LATHER
A	Unboiled solution	
B	Boiled solution	COMPLETE IN YOUR NOTEBOOK
C	Distilled water	

Part II   Permanently Hard Water

Table 3

TEST TUBE #	CONTENTS	APPEARANCE	HEIGHT OF LATHER
A	Distilled H_2O		
B	$0.4M$ $MgSO_4$		
C	$0.4M$ $CaCl_2$	COMPLETE IN YOUR NOTEBOOK	COMPLETE IN YOUR NOTEBOOK
D	$0.4M$ $MgSO_4$ + $2M$ Na_2CO_3		
E	$0.4M$ $CaCl_2$ + $2M$ Na_2CO_3		

Part III   Determination of Chloride Ion Concentration in a Water Sample

Table 4

[AgNO₃] =	TRIAL 1	TRIAL 2	TRIAL 3 (IF NECESSARY)
Sample #			
Volume of water sample used (mL)			
Initial reading of AgNO₃ (mL)	COMPLETE IN YOUR NOTEBOOK		COMPLETE IN YOUR NOTEBOOK
Final reading of AgNO₃ (mL)			
Volume of AgNO₃ used (mL)			

QUESTIONS AND CALCULATIONS

Part I   Temporarily Hard Water

1. Explain the results that occurred when CO_2 was bubbled into the limewater solution.

2. Explain the results that occurred when the solution was boiled.

3. In which test tube were the fewest soapsuds formed? Why?

Part II   Permanently Hard Water

1. State what happened in test tubes D and E when the Na_2CO_3 solution was added. Give equations for the reactions.

2. Explain the results of adding soap to each test tube and shaking.

Part III   Determination of Chloride Ion Concentration in a Water Sample

1. Write the net ionic equation for the reaction that occurred.

2. For each determination, do the following:
   a. Calculate the number of moles of Ag^+ used (from the volume required and molarity).
   b. Calculate the number of moles of Cl^- present (from the number of moles of Ag^+ and the balanced equation).
   c. Calculate the $[Cl^-]$ present in mol/L (from the number of moles of Cl^- and the volume used).
   d. Calculate the $[Cl^-]$ in parts per million (ppm). (This is the same as the number of milligrams of Cl^- per litre.)

FOLLOW-UP QUESTIONS

1. Limestone consists of calcium carbonate, $CaCO_3$. Use your understanding of the equilibria shown in the Post Lab Discussion to explain how limestone caves have been formed, and why stalactites and stalagmites are often found in them. Use a reference book if necessary.

2. What is meant by the terms "kettle scale" and "boiler scale"?

3. A certain brand of automatic coffee machine has instructions saying "Important: With daily use this unit should be cleaned once a month with white vinegar." Explain the reason for this instruction.

4. Why would it be a good idea, in an area with permanently hard water, to add some washing soda (Na_2CO_3) to the water in a washing machine before adding the laundry detergent?

5. In the 1960s and 1970s laundry detergents contained large amounts of trisodium phosphate $(TSP, (Na_3PO_4))$. The use of this chemical has now been cut back. Find out the reason for this change.

6. A 25.0 mL sample of seawater was found to require 152 mL of $0.10 M$ $AgNO_3$ to precipitate all the chloride ion in a titration like that in Part III. Assuming that AgCl was the only substance precipitated, what is the $[Cl^-]$ in the seawater?

CONCLUSIONS

1. Describe how to eliminate temporary and permanent hardness of water.

2. Classify your water samples as being either high or low in chloride concentration, and relate this to whether a sample was of fresh or salt water.

Introduction to Acids and Bases

By the 1500s chemists recognized that certain substances shared a common property—a sour taste. These substances possessed other characteristic properties as well. They were given the collective name of "acids" from the Latin word *acidus*, meaning "sour". Another group of substances, called alkalis (or bases), were prepared from the ashes of wood. Bases had a slippery feel and were discovered to be effective cleaners.

When defining acids or bases, it is important to realize that there are two types of definitions—*operational* (or *laboratory*) definitions and *conceptual* definitions. An operational definition is a description of expected test results from a laboratory situation. A conceptual definition attempts to explain the operational definition.

Tests for acidity and alkalinity are commonplace today in such fields as gardening and swimming pool maintenance. For example, specialized acid-base test kits are available to home gardeners who wish to monitor the acidity or alkalinity of their soil. One component of such kits is a chemical indicator solution which will show a characteristic color, depending on the conditions of acidity.

In Part I of this experiment you will first test several unknown solutions of acids and bases and note some of their properties. The similarities of properties should enable you to write some operational definitions. Next, the identities of the unknown solutions will be revealed, and you will attempt to write conceptual definitions of acids and bases.

In the past, several conceptual definitions of acids and bases were proposed by chemists. What is certainly the most fundamental definition was suggested by Svante Arrhenius in the late 1800s. Arrhenius, one of Sweden's most famous chemists, was awarded the Nobel prize in chemistry in 1903 for his work with ionic solutions. It is quite likely that your conceptual definitions of acids and bases in this experiment will be similar to those of Arrhenius.

Part II of this experiment involves acid-base tests of household products. From the results you obtain and the information provided, you will be asked to classify the household products according to your operational and conceptual definitions of acids and bases.

OBJECTIVES

1. to become familiar with a variety of typical laboratory tests for acids and bases

2. to develop operational definitions of acids and bases

3. to develop conceptual definitions of acids and bases

4. to test a variety of household products and classify them as acids or bases

MATERIALS

Apparatus

6 small test tubes
  (10 mm × 75 mm)
6 medicine droppers
glass square (10 cm × 10 cm)
  or Corning Cell Wells 6 × 4
  or spot plate
test-tube rack
lab apron
safety goggles

Reagents

magnesium ribbon (6 cm)
phenolphthalein solution in a
  dropper bottle
methyl orange solution in a
  dropper bottle
blue litmus paper
red litmus paper
set of 6 unknown solutions
set of 6 household products
  (vinegar, Easy-Off® oven cleaner,
  household ammonia, lemon juice,
  7-Up®, milk of magnesia)

PROCEDURE

Part I   Tests of Unknown Solutions

CAUTION: Remember, A to F are unknowns; whether they are hazardous or not, it is always a good practice to minimize your contact with unknown chemicals. Some of these chemicals are corrosive to skin, eyes, or clothing. Wear safety goggles and gloves when handling them; wash away spills or splashes with plenty of water. Call your teacher.

1. Put on your lab apron and safety goggles.

2. Label your 6 test tubes A to F, then obtain corresponding samples of the 6 unknown solutions. The test tubes should be about one third full, so that you can reach each sample with a medicine dropper. Place the test tubes in a test-tube rack, and put a clean medicine dropper in each.

3. On a piece of paper the size of your glass square, construct a labelled grid similar to Table 1, with one exception: do not include the column for magnesium on the grid. Your grid will therefore have 6 rows and 4 columns. Instead of a glass square, you can use Corning Cell Wells #25820, which provide a 6 × 4 grid.

4. Place the glass square on top of the grid and place 1 or 2 drops of the phenolphthalein and methyl orange indicator solutions in the appropriate squares of the grid. Tear the red and blue litmus papers into small pieces and place these pieces in the appropriate squares.

5. Using the medicine dropper, add 1 or 2 drops of solution A to the phenolphthalein square of the grid. Record your observations in your copy of Table 1 in your notebook.

6. Add solution A to the methyl orange, blue litmus, and red litmus squares of the grid, and record the results.

7. Repeat Steps 5 and 6 for the other 5 unknown solutions.

8. Obtain a 3.0 cm length of magnesium ribbon and cut it into 6 pieces of approximately equal length. Place a piece of magnesium in each of the 6 test tubes and record your observations in your data table.

9. Clean up your apparatus according to the reagent disposal instructions.

10. Before you leave the laboratory, wash your hands thoroughly with soap and water; use a fingernail brush to clean under your fingernails.

Part II Tests of Common Household Products

1. Repeat Part I for the household products provided by your instructor. Record your observations in a copy of Table 2 in your notebook.

REAGENT DISPOSAL

Rinse all chemicals from the glass square, test tubes, and medicine dropper with copious amounts of water. To avoid plugging the drain, remove the rinsed pieces of litmus paper and magnesium, and place them in the designated waste container.

POST LAB DISCUSSION

You should be able to place each of the six unknown solutions into one of two groups, on the basis of Table 1. One property of acids is that they react with active metals such as magnesium. Knowing this, you will be able to determine which group is the acid group and which is the base group.

In Part II, you may have noticed that in some instances some of the indicators did not react as you might have expected. For now, you can think of the indicators as having different "sensitivities" to acids and bases, with the result that they will not always give positive results. As long as one of the tests showed a positive result, and provided that you did not get any conflicting results, you can classify a solution on the basis of that one result.

In order to develop conceptual definitions, you will require more information about the solutions tested. Relevant information such as chemical formulas and electrical conductivity will be provided by your instructor at an appropriate time.

DATA AND OBSERVATIONS

Part I Tests of Unknown Solutions

Table 1

UNKNOWN SOLUTION	CHEMICAL INDICATORS				MAGNESIUM METAL
	PHENOLPHTHALEIN	METHYL ORANGE	BLUE LITMUS	RED LITMUS	
A					
B					
C					
D					
E					
F					

Part II   Tests of Common Household Products

Table 2

HOUSEHOLD PRODUCT	CHEMICAL INDICATORS				MAGNESIUM METAL
	PHENOLPHTHALEIN	METHYL ORANGE	BLUE LITMUS	RED LITMUS	
Vinegar					
Easy Off® oven cleaner					
Household ammonia					
7-Up®					
Lemon juice					
Milk of magnesia					

COMPLETE IN YOUR NOTEBOOK

QUESTIONS

1. a. Examine the data in Table 1, and form groups of solutions on the basis of similar properties.
    b. Classify one of these groups as acids and the other as bases. (A hint was provided in the Post Lab Discussion.)

2. Write operational definitions for acids and bases based on the results of Part I of this experiment.

3. Using your results from Part II and your operational definition from Part I, classify the household products as acids or bases.

4. What, if any, general pattern exists with regard to the types of household products which are acids and those which are bases?

FOLLOW-UP QUESTIONS

1. a. Find out the chemical formula for each of the unknown solutions from your instructor, and classify them as acids or bases.
    b. Write conceptual definitions of acids and bases.

2. a. Find out the chemical formulas of the active ingredients in the household products from your instructor, and group them as acids or bases.
    b. How do your conceptual definitions explain your acid-base classifications of the household products?

3. a. Using a reference book, discover and write out the Arrhenius definitions of acids and bases.
    b. How do the Arrhenius definitions compare to your conceptual definitions?

4. Acid rain contains varying amounts of sulfuric acid and/or nitric acid.

    a. Predict the test results you might expect if you were to test a sample of acid rain using the procedure in this experiment.
    b. What should the chemical formulas of sulfuric acid and nitric acid have in common?
    c. From a reference book, discover and write out the chemical formulas for sulfuric acid and nitric acid.

CONCLUSION

State the results of Objective 3.

Brönsted-Lowry Acid and Base Equilibria

In Experiment 20A you were introduced to the topic of acids and bases, and you learned that an acid gives off H^+ ions in solution and a base gives off OH^- ions in solution. These statements are called the Arrhenius definitions for acid and base. They apply to aqueous solutions.

Another pair of definitions for acid and base has been proposed to take into account the fact that not all acid-base reactions occur in aqueous solution; they can occur in other solvents as well. These definitions are known as the Brönsted-Lowry definitions, after the scientists who first proposed them. According to the Brönsted-Lowry theory, an acid is defined as a proton donor, and a base is defined as a proton acceptor. Another part of this theory states that when an acid and a base react together, they produce another acid and another base. You can see that the Brönsted-Lowry definitions include the Arrhenius definitions, since H^+ is the same as a proton, and OH^- reacts with (accepts) a proton (H^+) when they neutralize one another.

Using HA to indicate an acid, and B^- to indicate a base, the equation for an acid-base reaction can be shown as follows:

$$HA + B^- \rightleftharpoons A^- + HB$$
$$\text{acid} \quad \text{base} \quad \text{base} \quad \text{acid}$$

A pair of substances such as HA and A^- or HB and B^- is called a *conjugate acid-base pair*. (A^- is the conjugate base of HA; HA is the conjugate acid of A^-.) If the reaction equilibrium shown above favors the products over the reactants, then HA must be a stronger acid than HB. (That is, HA has the greater tendency to give off protons.) Likewise, B^- is a stronger base than A^- (B^- has a greater tendency to accept protons).

An *acid-base indicator* is a weak acid or base that has a conjugate base or acid which is a different color. The $[H^+]$ at which the color changes varies from one indicator to another; thus, indicators can be used to determine the $[H^+]$ in a solution.

In this experiment you will use five different indicators which will be identified only by number. They will each be added to each of six unknown solutions containing a conjugate acid-base pair. Therefore, you will have eleven solutions to start with, including the indicators that are conjugate acid-base pairs. From the resulting thirty mixtures you will be able to deduce the relative strengths of all eleven as weak acids, and arrange them in order of decreasing strengths of acids (or increasing strengths of conjugate bases). The amounts of solution and indicator involved will vary depending on whether the experiment is performed with a glass plate (or spot plate) instead of test tubes. Using test tubes will require somewhat more of each to see results clearly, but in either case best results are obtained if the amount of indicator is about one quarter of the amount of solution. Your instructor will give you more precise directions.

OBJECTIVES

1. to obtain an understanding of the equilibria which involve acids and bases

2. to observe the color changes that occur with a number of different acid-base indicators in several different solutions

3. to arrange all the Brönsted-Lowry acids involved in this experiment in order of decreasing strength

MATERIALS

Apparatus	Reagents

glass plate
  or spot plate
  or 13 mm × 100 mm test
  tubes with rack
lab apron
safety goggles
	$1M$ HCL
	$1M$ NaOH
	6 solutions of different pH
	  (labelled HA_1/A_1^-, HA_2/A_2^-, etc.,
	  to HA_6/A_6^-)
	5 different indicator solutions
	  (labelled HIn_1/In_1^-, HIn_2/In_2^-,
	  etc., to HIn_5/In_5^-)

CAUTION: *The hydrochloric acid and sodium hydroxide solutions are corrosive to skin, eyes, and clothing. Wash any spills and splashes with plenty of water. Call your teacher.*

CAUTION: *Some of the unknowns in this experiment are strongly acidic or strongly basic. Treat them all as though they were hydrochloric acid or sodium hydroxide solutions, as described in the CAUTION statement above.*

CAUTION: *Some of the indicators used in this experiment consist of flammable solutions. Make sure there are no burners in the vicinity.*

CAUTION: *Some of the indicators used in this experiment are toxic. Do not get any in your mouth; do not swallow any. Wash any spills or splashes with plenty of water.*

PROCEDURE

1. Put on your lab apron and safety goggles.

2. On a sheet of white paper the size of your glass plate, mark off five regions, and label them HIn_1, HIn_2, etc., to HIn_5.

3. Place 4 drops of $1M$ HCl on each of these areas on the glass plate.

4. Add 1 drop of each indicator solution to the designated area, and record the color in your copy of Table 1 in your notebook. (These results give you the colors of the acid form of each indicator.) Rinse and dry the glass plate.

5. Repeat Steps 3 and 4, using $1M$ NaOH instead of HCl. (The results give the colors of the base forms of each indicator.)

6. Repeat Steps 3 and 4 with unknown solution HA_1/A_1^- and the five different indicators, and continue the process with all the other unknown solutions until you have recorded the color in all 30 possible combinations of unknown solution with unknown indicator.

7. Wash your hands thoroughly with soap and water before leaving the laboratory; use a fingernail brush to clean under your fingernails.

REAGENT DISPOSAL

Rinse all chemicals down the sink with plenty of water.

POST LAB DISCUSSION

The results with HCl and each indicator tell you what the color of the acid form of the indicator is, since HCl is a strong acid and will cause the indicator to accept a proton. The results with NaOH and each indicator tell you what the color of the base form of the indicator is, since NaOH is a strong base and will cause the indicator to donate a proton.

In order to interpret the results and deduce a list of acid strengths, consider the following example:

$$HA_1 + In_3^- \rightleftharpoons A_1^- + HIn_3$$

If in this combination the indicator HIn_3 is showing the color of its acid form, then HA_1 is a stronger acid than HIn_3, because HA_1 was able to donate a proton. In addition, In_3^- is a stronger base than A_1^-. On the other hand, if in the same example the mixture shows the color of the basic form of HIn_3, namely In_3^-, then HIn_3 is stronger than HA_1, and A_1^- is stronger than In_3^-. Note that the stronger acid and base always react to give the weaker acid and base.

You will often be using indicators in subsequent experiments. Some of them may be ones you used in this experiment. The important fact to realize about indicators is that they are weak acids just like any other weak acid, and are therefore subject to the shifting of the weak acid equilibrium. The only reason for which these weak acids were chosen as indicators is that the weak acid and conjugate base which constitute the indicator happen to have different colors.

DATA AND OBSERVATIONS

It would be a good idea to copy this table into your notebook before coming to the laboratory.

Table 1

	HIn_1/In_1^-	HIn_2/In_2^-	HIn_3/In_3^-	HIn_4/In_4^-	HIn_5/In_5^-
HCl					
NaOH					
HA_1/A_1^-					
HA_2/A_2^-					
HA_3/A_3^-					
HA_4/A_4^-					
HA_5/A_5^-					
HA_6/A_6^-					

QUESTIONS

1. Make up another table like the one showing your observations, but leave out HCl and NaOH. From your results, fill in each box with a statement about the relative strengths of the two acids involved; for instance, $HA_1 > HIn_3$, or $HIn_3 > HA_1$.

2. Arrange the eleven acids in a list, with the strongest at the top and weakest at the bottom. Then write an ionization equation for each by putting H^+ and the conjugate base on the right. Label each side of the list with a vertical arrow, one for increasing strength of acid and one for increasing strength of base.

FOLLOW-UP QUESTIONS

1. The five indicators used in this experiment were bromcresol green, bromthymol blue, indigo carmine, orange IV, and thymolphthalein. Use Appendix 4 to discover the pH range over which each indicator changes color.

2. Use the information from item 1 to identify each indicator used in the experiment.

3. The six unknown solutions were all at a whole number of pH units in the range 0–14. Try to work out the pH of each unknown solution. (For some of them you may not be able to determine the pH exactly, but you should be able to narrow it down to a choice of 2 integral pH values.)

4. One way of determining the pH of a particular solution is to use what is called a *universal indicator*, which consists of a mixture of different indicators that give a number of different color changes as the pH changes. From a reference book, find out the composition of a universal indicator.

CONCLUSION

State the results of Objective 3.

Acid-Base Titration

Titration is a laboratory technique that can be used to determine the concentration of certain substances. A standard solution of known molarity is titrated against (reacted with) a solution of unknown concentration. An indicator can signal the completion of the reaction and the concentration can be quantitatively determined.

Acid-base titrations involve the neutralization reaction between aqueous hydrogen and hydroxide ions. These ions combine to form the neutral water molecule:

$$H^+(aq) + OH^-(aq) \rightleftharpoons H_2O(l)$$

The indicator phenolphthalein will be used to show when the number of moles of acid equals the number of moles of base. This point is called the equivalence point.

Titration is one of the most common operations performed by the chemist. We all depend upon chemical analysis, and it is with this branch of chemistry that the average citizen is most likely to come into contact. Decisions involving huge sums of money, or even life and death, depend upon the accuracy and speed of chemical analysis, whether in hospital lab testing, environmental pollution monitoring, or crime detection.

OBJECTIVES

1. to titrate a hydrochloric acid solution of unknown concentration with standardized 0.50M sodium hydroxide

2. to titrate an acetic acid solution (vinegar) with standardized 0.50M sodium hydroxide

3. to utilize the titration data to calculate the molarity of the hydrochloric acid, and the molarity and percentage composition of the vinegar

MATERIALS

Apparatus

suction bulb	1 buret clamp and stand
2 delivery pipets (10 mL)	lab apron
2 Erlenmeyer flasks (250 mL)	safety goggles
1 buret	

Reagents

standardized NaOH solution (approx. 0.50M)	white vinegar
unknown HCl solution (approx. 0.50M)	phenolphthalein solution

PROCEDURE

Part I   Determination of Molarity of Hydrochloric Acid Solution

1. Put on your lab apron and safety goggles.

2. Obtain about 50 mL of the hydrochloric acid solution of unknown concentration and about 100 mL of the standardized NaOH solution. Your teacher will provide you with the exact molarity of the NaOH. Record this value in your copy of Table 1 in your notebook.

3. Using a suction bulb, pipet 10.0 mL of the HCl solution into a 250 mL Erlenmeyer flask, after rinsing your pipet with a small amount of HCl first.

4. Add 3 drops of phenolphthalein solution.

5. Rinse a clean buret with approximately 15 mL of the standardized NaOH solution. Drain the buret and refill with standardized NaOH solution. Record the initial volume of the NaOH in the buret in your copy of Table 1 in your notebook.

6. Gradually dispense some of the standardized NaOH solution into the titration flask. Swirl the flask constantly. (See Figure 20C-1.) Continue adding NaOH, noting any changes in the flask..

CAUTION: The NaOH solution is corrosive to skin, eyes, and clothing. Wash any spills or splashes immediately with plenty of water.

CAUTION: Phenolphthalein is poisonous and flammable. Do not get any in your mouth; keep well away from flame.

Figure 20C-1

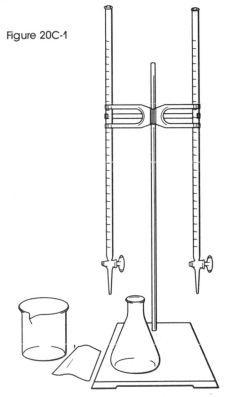

7. As the equivalence point is approached, a pinkish color will appear, and dissipate more slowly as the titration proceeds. Now add the NaOH drop by drop. Stop the titration when the addition of a single drop causes the solution to remain pinkish for 30 s. Record the volume of NaOH needed to reach the equivalence point in your copy of Table 1. The most accurate reading is one in which the solution is the faintest possible pink, but still remaining that color.

8. Repeat steps 3 through 7 using a second 10.0 mL sample of the HCl. Knowing the volume obtained in your first titration, you can be extra careful when you are within 1 mL of the previous value, and add the NaOH a drop at a time, shaking after each drop. This lessens the likelihood of your overshooting the mark.

9. If the two values differ widely, it would be a good idea to do one more titration if you have time.

Part II   Determination of Percentage Composition of Vinegar

CAUTION: The vinegar solution is mildly corrosive. Keep it off your skin and out of your eyes. Wash any spills and splashes immediately with plenty of water.

1. Obtain approximately 30 mL of white vinegar (acetic acid solution).

2. Using the same buret of NaOH as was used in Part I, do more titrations, but this time use 10.0 mL portions of vinegar instead of HCl. Follow exactly the same procedure as in Part I (Procedures 3 to 9). Record your observations in your copy of Table 2.

REAGENT DISPOSAL

Mix any leftover acids and bases together to neutralize, and pour down the sink with plenty of water. Do not return any solutions to their original containers.

POST LAB DISCUSSION

During the HCl titration, the hydroxide ions liberated from the standardized NaOH solution reacted in a 1-to-1 ratio with the H^+ ions from HCl to form neutral water molecules. When the concentration of both ion species were the same, the equivalence point was reached. Since the molarity and volume of the standardized NaOH is known, the total number of moles reacting can be calculated as shown in the following equation:

$$(\text{Volume}_{NaOH})\,(\text{Molarity}_{NaOH}) = \text{Reactant Moles}_{NaOH}$$
$$= \text{Reactant Moles}_{HCl}$$

Knowing the volume of HCl used originally, the molarity of the HCl can be calculated from the formula:

$$(\text{Molarity}_{HCl}) = \text{Moles}_{HCl} \div \text{Volume of HCl (in L)}$$

In Part II, calculate the molarity of the acetic acid in vinegar in the same manner as shown for HCl. In addition, calculate the percentage composition of the vinegar. This is given by:

$$\text{Percentage composition} = \frac{\text{mass solute}}{\text{mass solution}} \times 100\%$$

The mass of the acetic acid (CH_3COOH) is obtained from the number of moles times the molar mass. The mass of the solution is obtained from the measured volume of the solution times its density. For this experiment, you may assume that the density of the vinegar is 1.00 g/mL.

DATA AND OBSERVATIONS

Part I   Determination of Molarity of Hydrochloric Acid Solution

Table 1   Volume of NaOH Needed to Neutralize 10.00 mL of Unknown HCl

MOLARITY OF NaOH =	TRIAL 1	TRIAL 2	TRIAL 3 (IF NECESSARY)
Initial volume of NaOH (mL)			
Final volume of NaOH (mL)			
Volume of NaOH used			
Average volume of NaOH			

Part II   Determination of Percentage Composition of Vinegar

Table 2 Volume of NaOH Needed to Neutralize 10.00 mL of Vinegar

MOLARITY OF NaOH =	TRIAL 1	TRIAL 2	TRIAL 3 (IF NECESSARY)
Initial volume of NaOH (mL)			
Final volume of NaOH (mL)			
Volume of NaOH used			
Average volume of NaOH			

CALCULATIONS

1. Calculate moles of NaOH from the average volume used in Part I, and the given molarity.

2. Calculate moles of HCl present originally.

3. Calculate the molarity of the HCl solution.

4. Calculate moles of NaOH from the average volume used in Part II, and the given molarity.

5. Calculate moles of acetic acid present originally.

6. Calculate the molarity of the acetic acid solution.

7. Calculate the mass of acetic acid in 1 L of solution.

8. Calculate the percentage of acetic acid in the vinegar.

FOLLOW-UP QUESTIONS

1. While doing a titration, it is permissible to use a wash bottle to wash down any material that may have splashed higher up. This would appear to increase the volume of the acid in the flask. Why will it have no effect on the results?

2. What was the reason for rinsing out the buret with NaOH solution before starting the titrations?

3. By law, vinegar must be not less than 4% by mass acetic acid. Did your sample meet this specification?

CONCLUSION

State the results of Objective 3.

Hydrolysis — The Reaction of Ions with Water

When a base neutralizes an acid, the result of the reaction is the formation of a salt and water. You would expect, therefore, that a salt dissolved in water would be neither acidic nor basic; that is, its pH should be 7. However, some ions are known to undergo a reaction with water, in a process called *hydrolysis*. When a positive ion (cation) reacts with water, the process is called *cationic hydrolysis* and results in an acidic solution. When a negative ion (anion) reacts with water, the process is called *anionic hydrolysis* and results in a basic solution. In the case of some salts, both anion and cation hydrolyze; the resulting pH depends on which does so to the greater extent.

In this experiment, you will determine the pH of a large number of salt solutions in water. From the results you will deduce information about which ions have hydrolyzed. The type of hydrolysis is related to the relative strengths of the acid and base from which a given salt is formed. In addition, you will measure the pH of some salts of amphiprotic anions (anions which can either gain or lose a proton), and use the result to deduce which occurs to a greater extent, hydrolysis or further ionization, that is, whether $K_b > K_a$, or $K_b < K_a$. The pH of each solution will be determined by one of two methods: either adding some universal indicator solution, or using small strips of universal indicator paper. The method used will depend on which type of indicator your teacher has available. A universal indicator is a mixture of several different indicators which change color at different pH values, so that a sequence of color changes is observed over a large pH range. The sequence usually approximates the colors of the spectrum, with red at low pH, green near neutral, and blue or violet at high pH.

OBJECTIVES

1. to measure the pH of a large number of salts, and identify those which have undergone hydrolysis

2. to explain why hydrolysis occurs (or does not occur) in terms of relative strengths of the acid and base from which a given salt is made, and to write a net ionic equation for each hydrolysis

3. to deduce which is greater for some amphiprotic anions, the K_a for the further ionization of the ion, or the K_b for the hydrolysis of the ion

MATERIALS

Apparatus

20 test tubes (13 mm × 100 mm)
test-tube rack
safety goggles
lab apron

Reagents

0.1M solution of each of the following:

sodium acetate, $NaCH_3COO$
sodium chloride, $NaCl$
ammonium chloride, NH_4Cl
ammonium sulfate, $(NH_4)_2SO_4$
aluminum chloride, $AlCl_3$
calcium nitrate, $Ca(NO_3)_2$
iron(III) sulfate, $Fe_2(SO_4)_3$
sodium carbonate, Na_2CO_3
sodium phosphate, Na_3PO_4
potassium sulfate, K_2SO_4
potassium bromide, KBr
ammonium oxalate, $(NH_4)_2C_2O_4$
ammonium acetate, NH_4CH_3COO

ammonium carbonate, $(NH_4)_2CO_3$
potassium monohydrogen phosphate, K_2HPO_4
potassium dihydrogen phosphate, KH_2PO_4
sodium bicarbonate, $NaHCO_3$
potassium bisulfate, $KHSO_4$
sodium bisulfite, $NaHSO_3$
solutions of $Fe_2(SO_4)_3$, $FeCl_3$, and $Al_2(SO_4)_3$ that have been standing some months
universal indicator solution *or* universal indicator paper

PROCEDURE

1. Put on your lab apron and safety goggles.

2. Obtain twenty 13 mm × 100 mm test tubes. Into separate test tubes, place about 3 mL of each solution listed in the following data tables. Also, place either distilled water or tap water, whichever was used to make up the solutions, in the first tube as a control. Your teacher will tell you which to use. The substances listed in Table 2 are salts containing amphiprotic anions; hence, the results for them will be recorded somewhat differently.

3. To the solution in each tube, add *either* 5 drops of universal indicator solution, *or* a 1 cm strip of universal indicator paper, depending on the instructions of your teacher.

4. Note the color that each solution gives to the indicator. By consulting the color chart provided with the universal indicator, which correlates color with pH, estimate the pH of each solution.

5. Your teacher will have on display some solutions of iron(III) chloride (or iron(III) sulfate) and aluminum sulfate in stoppered flasks that have been left standing for a period of some weeks or months. Look at them carefully and record what you see.

6. Before you leave the laboratory, wash your hands thoroughly with soap and water; use a fingernail brush to clean under your nails.

CAUTION: Most of these solutions are poisonous, corrosive, or irritants. Wash any spills and splashes immediately with plenty of water. Call your teacher.

REAGENT DISPOSAL

Wash all solutions down the sink with copious amounts of water. Be careful not to let the small pieces of indicator paper block the sink; discard them in the wastepaper basket.

POST LAB DISCUSSION

Salts formed from a strong acid and a strong base do not undergo hydrolysis.

Anionic hydrolysis occurs when a salt is formed from a strong base and a weak acid. For example, consider a hypothetical weak acid HA. Its sodium salt will give Na^+ and A^- in solution. Weak acids must always satisfy the relationship between [HA], [H⁺], and [A⁻] as determined by the K_a expression and its corresponding value. When [A⁻] is present in appreciable quantities in solution and non-ionized HA is not present at all, the K_a expression cannot be at its correct value. The position of the equilibrium must therefore shift, with the ion A⁻ combining with the H⁺ from water to give non-ionized HA until the K_a value is satisfied. This process leaves OH⁻ behind, and the solution becomes basic.

Cationic hydrolysis of ammonium ion occurred in this experiment because ammonia is a weak base, and salts of ammonia with strong acids will hydrolyze, giving acidic solutions:

$$NH_4^+(aq) + H_2O(l) \rightleftharpoons NH_3(aq) + H_3O^+(aq)$$

Some ammonium salts used in this experiment were formed from a weak acid and ammonia. In these, the pH you observed depended on the relative strength of the acid compared to ammonia. You will do calculations to verify your results.

The other type of cationic hydrolysis involved metal ions having small diameter and a high charge (3+). Such ions are strongly attracted to water molecules, and in fact form hydrated ions in which the metal ion itself is surrounded by (usually) six water molecules. The water molecules align themselves with the negative oxygen ends of the molecule dipoles toward the positive metal ion. The attraction of the positive metal ion for the negative electron in the surrounding water molecules is so great that protons can be donated from the water molecules to give an acidic solution (pH less than 7). For example, the ion $Fe(H_2O)_6^{3+}$ can act as an acid:

$$Fe(H_2O)_6^{3+}(aq) + H_2O(l) \rightleftharpoons Fe(H_2O)_5OH^{2+}(aq) + H_3O^+(aq)$$

The K_a for this ionization is 6.0×10^{-3}, making $Fe(H_2O)_6^{3+}$ relatively strong as weak acids go, stronger than such weak acids as HF, HNO_2, and CH_3COOH. The ionization can proceed further, with $Fe(H_2O)_5OH^{2+}$ losing more protons, and giving $Fe(H_2O)_4(OH)_2^+$ and eventually $Fe(H_2O)_3(OH)_3$. The latter is formed as a precipitate in solutions of Fe^{3+} (aq) that have been left standing for a long time.

The five substances in Table 2 are salts of sodium or potassium with an amphiprotic anion, that is, an anion which can donate or accept a proton. There are two possible reactions involving these substances. The anion (represented here by the general formula HB⁻) can either hydrolyze back to the non-ionized acid H_2B by accepting a proton to give a basic solution, or donate a proton in becoming B^{2-} to give an acid solution. Which of these two reactions will occur to the greater extent will depend on the value of K_a for HB⁻ relative to K_b for HB⁻. If the K_a is larger, the solution will be acidic, but if the K_b is larger, the solution will be basic. The pH that you measured for the solution will therefore indicate whether the K_a or the K_b is larger. (You will check your results by calculation.) K_a values can be obtained from the table of acid ionization constants in Appendix 3. K_b can be calculated from the formula $K_b = \dfrac{K_w}{K_a}$ where $K_w = 1.00 \times 10^{-14}$. Here, K_a refers to the acid ionization constant for the conjugate acid of the anion HB⁻, namely H_2B.

DATA AND OBSERVATIONS

It would be a good idea to copy these tables into your notebook before coming to the laboratory.

Table 1

SOLUTION	COLOR OF UNIVERSAL INDICATOR	pH	TYPE OF HYDROLYSIS (ANIONIC, CATIONIC, BOTH, OR NEITHER)
$NaCH_3COO$			
$NaCl$			
NH_4Cl			
$(NH_4)_2SO_4$			
$AlCl_3$			
$Ca(NO_3)_2$			
$Fe_2(SO_4)_3$			
Na_2CO_3			
Na_3PO_4			
K_2SO_4			
KBr			
$(NH_4)_2C_2O_4$			
NH_4CH_3COO			
$(NH_4)_2CO_3$			

COMPLETE IN YOUR NOTEBOOK

Table 2

SOLUTION	COLOR OF UNIVERSAL INDICATOR	pH	TYPE OF REACTION (ANIONIC HYDROLYSIS OR FURTHER IONIZATION)
K_2HPO_4			
KH_2PO_4			
$NaHCO_3$			
$KHSO_4$			
$NaHSO_3$			

COMPLETE IN YOUR NOTEBOOK

COMPLETE IN YOUR NOTEBOOK

QUESTIONS AND CALCULATIONS

1. For each salt tested, state the acid and base from which it is obtained, and whether the acid and base are strong or weak. Then write the net ionic equation for the hydrolysis, if any occurs.
2. Note that some (ammonium) salts are formed from a weak acid and the weak base NH_3. For these, write a net ionic equation for each ion, then state from your results which is stronger, the acid or the base. Verify your result by calculating the K_b for the anion (as outlined in the Post Lab Discussion) and comparing it to the K_a for NH_4^+.
3. The substances K_2HPO_4, KH_2PO_4, $NaHCO_3$, $KHSO_4$, and $NaHSO_3$ all have an amphiprotic anion, that is, one which can either gain or lose a proton. Write two net ionic equations for each ion, one in which a proton is removed (the ion is acting as an acid), and one in which a proton is accepted in anionic hydrolysis (the ion is acting as a base).

4. For each of the substances in Question 3, state which reaction occurred to the greater extent on the basis of your observations of the pH. Then look up the K_a for each ion, and calculate each K_b (from K_w divided by the K_a of the conjugate acid). Verify that your calculations agree with your experimental observations.

5. What was the precipitate observed in solutions of Fe^{3+} salts that had been standing for a long time? Give equations showing how this precipitate is formed.

6. Repeat Question 5 for Al^{3+} salts.

FOLLOW-UP QUESTIONS

1. Many plants do not grow well in soil that is too acidic. A certain gardener wishes to increase the nitrogen content of the soil and has available potassium nitrate, KNO_3, and ammonium sulfate, $(NH_4)_2SO_4$, both of which are common fertilizers. Which one would be better for keeping the soil near neutral?

2. The chemical sodium phosphate, Na_3PO_4, is sold in stores as TSP (trisodium phosphate). It is commonly used as a cleaning agent. Explain why it could be expected to be useful for such a purpose.

3. Some types of baking powder consist of sodium bicarbonate, $NaHCO_3$, and calcium dihydrogen phosphate, $Ca(H_2PO_4)_2$. Explain the function of the $Ca(H_2PO_4)_2$ in the baking powder.

4. The precipitate that forms in solutions of Al^{3+} and Fe^{3+} salts removes these ions from the solution; therefore, the solution does not remain at the concentration at which it was originally made up. Suggest a material that could be added to the solution when it is initially prepared that would minimize the hydrolysis and therefore prevent precipitation. (Hint: Think of Le Chatelier's principle!)

5. Look at the equations that you have written for the hydrolysis of the NH_4^+ and CO_3^{2-} ions in $(NH_4)_2CO_3$. What two ions produced (one in each) will now react with one another? What effect will this have on the position of both equilibria?

6. It is very likely that in the First Aid kit in your laboratory there is a small vial containing ammonium carbonate. This vial is crushed when needed to revive anyone who has fainted. In light of your answer to Question 5, state what substance you think would be responsible for reviving the patient. (You may wish to experiment with this yourself. Ask your teacher if you may carefully waft the fumes from a bottle of solid ammonium carbonate towards your nose.)

CONCLUSION

Summarize, in general terms, what types of salts undergo hydrolysis, and what type of solution they produce.

Acid-Base Trends of Metal and Non-Metal Hydroxides

Oxides of elements are commonly encountered on a daily basis. Metal oxides, for instance, are important substances because O_2, the molecular form of oxygen found in air, is readily available and reacts well with most metals. For example, rust (Fe_2O_3) results when metallic iron reacts with the oxygen in the air.

Non-metal oxides also have an effect on people. Oxides of sulfur and nitrogen are produced by industrial processes and can be serious air pollutants.

The oxide of any element can be produced by combining that element with oxygen. The reaction equation is often a simple equation similar to this:

$$X \quad + \quad O_2 \quad \rightarrow \quad XO$$

$$\text{element} \qquad \text{oxygen} \qquad \text{oxide}$$

The above equation has not been balanced, since the formula of the oxide will depend on the ion charge of the element.

Although the reaction is easy to describe, the preparation of oxides poses a few problems. For instance, it can be difficult or hazardous to prepare some of the more interesting oxides such as MgO and SO_2. Therefore, in this experiment you will be provided with the oxides already prepared. In Part I, you will prepare hydroxide solutions of four metal oxides by adding water to them, then test the solutions for acidic and basic properties. In Part II, you will receive two already prepared solutions of non-metal oxides and test them for acidic and basic properties.

When an oxide reacts with water, a hydroxide is formed according to this general equation:

$$XO + H_2O \quad \rightarrow \quad XOH$$

Once again, note that the equation has not been balanced. A summary of the elements in this experiment, their oxides, and hydroxide solutions appears below:

Element	+	Oxygen	→	Oxide	;	Oxide	+	Water	→	Hydroxide Solution
2Mg	+	O_2	→	2MgO	;	MgO	+	H_2O	→	$Mg(OH)_2$
2Ca	+	O_2	→	2CaO	;	CaO	+	H_2O	→	$Ca(OH)_2$
2Zn	+	O_2	→	2ZnO	;	ZnO	+	H_2O	→	$Zn(OH)_2$
4Al	+	$3O_2$	→	$2Al_2O_3$	;	Al_2O_3	+	$3H_2O$	→	$2Al(OH)_3$
2S	+	$3O_2$	→	$2SO_3$	;	SO_3	+	H_2O	→	$SO_2(OH)_2$
N_2	+	$2O_2$	→	$2NO_2$	;	$2NO_2$	+	H_2O	→	$NO_2(OH) +$ $NO(OH)$

As you know, some substances are acids and are capable of reacting with bases. But there are certain substances (known as amphiprotic substances) which can react with acids or bases. An additional task you will have in Part III of this experiment is to test the hydroxide solutions for amphiprotic behavior.

OBJECTIVES

1. to test the acid-base properties of solutions of metal oxides

2. to test the acid-base properties of solutions of non-metal oxides

3. to determine what, if any, periodic trend exists in acid-base properties of oxide solutions

MATERIALS

Apparatus	Reagents
10 test tubes (13 mm × 100 mm)	universal indicator solution or wide-range pH paper
1 test tube rack	CaO powder
4 rubber stoppers	MgO powder
2 medicine droppers	ZnO powder
2 small beakers (50 mL)	Al_2O_3 powder
safety goggles	two prepared solutions (labelled A and B) of non-metal oxides
lab apron	6M HCl
	6M NaOH

PROCEDURE

Part I Preparing and Testing Solutions of Metal Oxides

CAUTION: Magnesium oxide is toxic. Do not get any in your mouth.

1. Put on your safety goggles and lab apron.

2. Add a small amount of each of the four powdered oxides to separate, labelled test tubes. The powder should just cover the bottom of a 13 mm × 100 mm test tube.

3. Half-fill the test tubes with distilled water, stopper them, and shake the contents for about two minutes. You will probably notice that slurries result, since the hydroxides formed here are only slightly soluble.

4. Add 2 or 3 drops of universal indicator solution to each slurry. (Wide-range pH paper can be used in place of universal indicator.) Record your results in a copy of Table 1 in your notebook.

Part II Testing Solutions of Non-metal Oxides

1. Solution A is a hydroxide solution of an oxide of sulfur; solution B is a hydroxide solution of an oxide of nitrogen. Half-fill two labelled test tubes with these solutions.

2. Test both solutions with universal indicator solution as in Part I. Include these results in Table 1 as well.

Part III Testing for Amphiprotic Behavior

1. Shake each test tube thoroughly again, then divide each slurry that resulted in Part I into two portions by pouring half of the sample into a clean test tube.

2. Obtain about 10 mL of 6 *M* HCl and 6 *M* NaOH in separate small beakers which have been labelled. Place a clean medicine dropper in each beaker.

3. Test one portion of each slurry by adding 6 *M* HCl drop by drop. Shake the test tube occasionally as you add the acid. Continue adding acid and shaking until no further changes occur. Note all changes in a table similar to Table 2 in your notebook. Pay close attention to what happens to the cloudiness of each slurry.

4. Test the other portion of each slurry by adding 6 *M* NaOH drop by drop. Shake the test tube occasionally as you add the base and record any changes in Table 2.

5. Before you leave the laboratory, wash your hands thoroughly with soap and water; use a fingernail brush to clean under your nails.

REAGENT DISPOSAL

Pour all solutions and slurries into the designated waste container.

POST LAB DISCUSSION

By studying your data tables, you will be able to determine which hydroxides are acidic, basic, neutral, or amphiprotic. Then, by examining the periodic table and noting the positions of the elements from which the hydroxides formed, you can determine whether any acid-base trends exist.

At this point, you may think it odd that a hydroxide of an element can act as an acid. Although many hydroxides behave as bases, the Brönsted-Lowry definition of an acid merely requires that a substance donate protons in a reaction. Consider the following equations involving a hypothetical hydroxide:

As a base: $X - O - H \rightarrow X^+ + OH^-$
    can accept a proton

As an acid: $X - O - H \rightarrow XO^- + H^+$
    can donate a proton

DATA AND OBSERVATIONS

Part I   Preparing and Testing Solutions of Metal Oxides

Part II   Testing Solutions of Non-metal Oxides

Table 1   Acid-Base Properties

HYDROXIDE SOLUTION TESTED	UNIVERSAL INDICATOR RESULTS	ACIDIC, BASIC, OR NEUTRAL
$Mg(OH)_2$		
$Ca(OH)_2$		
$Zn(OH)_2$		
$Al(OH)_3$		
$SO_2(OH)_2$		
$NO_2(OH)$		

COMPLETE IN YOUR NOTEBOOK

Part III   Testing for Amphiprotic Behavior

Table 2

HYDROXIDE SOLUTION TESTED	ADDITION OF ACID OR BASE	UNIVERSAL INDICATOR RESULTS		OTHER CHANGES
		BEFORE	AFTER	

QUESTIONS

1. Classify each of the six hydroxide solutions you examined as acidic, basic, neutral, or amphiprotic.

2. a. Write the formula for solution A ($SO_2(OH)_2$) in a different, more familiar form. (Hint: Put the elements in groups and place hydrogen at the beginning of the formula.)
   b. What is the acid name of this substance?

3. Repeat item 2 for solution B ($NO_2(OH)$).

4. Write chemical equations to explain how $Zn(OH)_2$ can react with an acid or a base. (Refer to the Post Lab Discussion.)

FOLLOW-UP QUESTIONS

1. a. Carbon dioxide gas, an oxide of carbon, is present in varying amounts in the atmosphere. Predict whether rainwater containing dissolved CO_2 would be acidic or basic.
   b. Consult a reference book to explain the effect of rainwater on limestone and marble (both $CaCO_3$).

2. a. Consult the *Heath Chemistry* textbook to help you explain how acid rain is formed from the pollutants SO_2 and NO.
   b. Lime (CaO) is sometimes used to neutralize the effects of acid rain. It can be dumped into affected lakes in order to raise the pH to acceptable levels. However, this rather drastic measure ignores the source of the problem. Find out some ways in which acid rain can be reduced at the source.

CONCLUSION

State the results of Objective 3.

Buffer Solutions of Weak Acids and Weak Bases

A buffer solution is a solution of special composition which is able to resist changes in pH that occur if small amounts of acid or base are added. Many important chemical reactions, especially enzyme reactions, will occur only over a small range in pH. Investigating such reactions requires the use of buffer solutions to maintain the pH in that range.

In Part I of this experiment, you will investigate the effect of the buffering of an acetic acid solution on the rate at which the acid reacts with solid calcium carbonate. In Part II, you will use acid-base indicators to determine which substances can give rise to buffers, and which cannot. In Part III, you will compare the relative abilities of two solutions at the same pH (one a prepared buffer, one unbuffered) to resist a change in pH when an acid or a base is added.

OBJECTIVES

1. to investigate the equilibria involving weak acids and bases, and how these equilibria may be altered

2. to discover the requirements for making a buffer solution

3. to determine the effectiveness of a buffer solution in neutralizing excess acid and base, in comparison with a non-buffered solution

MATERIALS

Apparatus

3 test tubes (18 mm × 150 mm)
3 test tubes (25 mm × 200 mm)
8 test tubes (13 mm × 100 mm)
test-tube rack
graduated cylinder (10 mL)
water soluble marker
centigram balance
lab apron
safety goggles

Reagents

$3M$ acetic acid, CH_3COOH
sodium acetate, $NaCH_3COO$
calcium carbonate, $CaCO_3$ (powder)
bromcresol green indicator
$0.1M$ HCl
NaCl
$0.1M$ ammonia, NH_3
phenolphthalein indicator
ammonium chloride, NH_4Cl
buffer solution pH 7 (prepared)
NaCl solution (any molarity)
$0.1M$ NaOH

PROCEDURE

Part I Effect of a Common Ion on [H₃O⁺] in a Weak Acid

1. Put on your lab apron and safety goggles.

2. Obtain three 18 mm × 150 mm test tubes in a rack, and label them *A*, *B*, and *C.* Place 10 mL of $3M$ CH_3COOH in each.

3. Place 2 g of $NaCH_3COO$ in test tube *B* and shake to dissolve. Place 4 g of $NaCH_3COO$ in test tube *C* and shake to dissolve. You will use Solutions *A*, *B*, and *C* in Step 6.

CAUTION: The acetic acid solution is mildly corrosive. Keep it off your skin and out of your eyes. Wash any spills and splashes immediately with plenty of water.

4. Obtain three 25 mm × 200 mm test tubes, and using a water soluble marker make a mark on each 10 cm from the bottom.

5. Place 0.5 g of powdered $CaCO_3$ in the bottom of each large test tube.

6. Add Solution A to the first large test tube, shake quickly. Note the time in seconds it takes for the foam to rise to the 10 cm mark. Repeat with Solutions B and C. Record your data in your copy of Table 1 in your notebook.

Part II   Detecting Common Ion Effect with Indicators

CAUTION: The hydrochloric acid solution is corrosive to skin, eyes, and clothing. Wash any spills and splashes off your skin and clothing immediately with plenty of water. Call your teacher.

CAUTION: The ammonia solution is mildly corrosive. Keep it off your skin and out of your eyes. Wash any spills or splashes immediately with plenty of water.

CAUTION: Phenolphthalein solution is flammable. Extinguish all flames in the area before using the solution.

1. Place 1 mL of $3M$ acetic acid in each of two 13 mm × 100 mm test tubes. Add water to half fill each test tube, then add 3 drops of bromcresol green indicator. Note the color in your copy of Table 2. Use the table of indicators in Appendix 4 to determine the range in which the pH of acetic acid must lie.

2. Add 0.5 g (a few crystals) of $NaCH_3COO$ as a source of the common ion CH_3COO^- to one of the test tubes, and shake to dissolve. Record the color in Table 2, and estimate the range in which the pH must lie.

3. Repeat Steps 1 and 2 using fresh test tubes, but place 5 mL of $0.1M$ HCl instead of acetic acid and water, in both tubes, and add 0.5 g (a few crystals of NaCl as a source of the common ion Cl^- to one of them.

4. Add 5 drops of $0.1M$ NH_3 solution to each of two small test tubes half full of water. Add 1 drop of phenolphthalein to each and note the color in Table 2. Use the table of indicators in Appendix 4 to determine the range of pH in which ammonia must lie.

5. To one of the tubes, add a few small crystals of NH_4Cl, as a source of the common ion NH_4^+, and record any color change in Table 2.

6. Repeat Steps 4 and 5 using fresh test tubes, but place 5 drops of $0.1M$ sodium hydroxide, NaOH, in both tubes, and add a few crystals of NaCl as a source of the common ion Na^+ to one of them.

Part III   Determining the Effectiveness of Buffers

CAUTION: the NaOH solution is corrosive to skin, eyes, and clothing. Wash any spills or splashes immediately with plenty of water.

1. Obtain 5 mL of NaCl solution in a 13 mm × 100 mm test tube. (Assume that the pH of the solution is 7.) Obtain 5 mL of the pH 7 buffer solution in a second 13 mm × 100 mm test tube. Add 2 drops of phenolphthalein indicator to each.

2. Add $0.1M$ NaOH solution drop by drop to each test tube. Count the number of drops required before a color change is observed, and record it in Table 3.

3. Repeat Step 1, but add 2 drops of bromcresol green indicator instead of the phenolphthalein. Record your observations in your data table.

4. Add $0.1M$ hydrochloric acid (HCl) solution drop by drop to each test tube. Count the number of drops required before a color change is observed, and record it in Table 3.

5. Before leaving the laboratory, wash your hands thoroughly with soap and water; use a fingernail brush to clean under your fingernails.

REAGENT DISPOSAL

Rinse all solutions down the sink with plenty of water.

POST LAB DISCUSSION

The reaction you observed in Part I is a reaction between calcium carbonate and the hydronium ions from the acid, according to the equation

$$CaCO_3(s) + 2H_3O^+(aq) \rightarrow Ca^{2+}(aq) + CO_2(g) + 3H_2O(l)$$

Since increased $[H_3O^+]$ will lead to a faster rate (as shown by the time for the foam to reach a particular height), the measured time will give an indication of the $[H_3O^+]$ present, and therefore of the equilibrium involving the non-ionized acetic acid molecules and also the acetate ions which accompany the H_3O^+.

In Part II, of the four solutions tested, two were acids (one weak and one strong) and two were bases (one weak and one strong). If a color change in the indicator occurred, it meant that an equilibrium must have existed, and the common ion added was able to change the position of the equilibrium.

The buffer solution used in Part III contained a weak acid and its conjugate base in approximately equal concentrations. The results showed its effectiveness in minimizing the effect on pH when a strong acid or base was added. The buffer solution did this by means of the types of equilibrium shifts studied in Parts I and II.

DATA AND OBSERVATIONS

You might find it useful to copy these tables into your notebook before coming to the laboratory.

Part I   Effect of a Common Ion on [H₃O⁺] in a Weak Acid

Table 1

SOLID REAGENT	SOLUTION ADDED	TIME FOR FOAM TO RISE 10 cm (s)
$CaCO_3$	CH_3COOH	
$CaCO_3$	CH_3COOH (aq) + 2 g $NaCH_3COO$	COMPLETE IN YOUR NOTEBOOK
$CaCO_3$	CH_3COOH (aq) + 4 g $NaCH_3COO$	

Part II   Detecting Common Ion Effect with Indicators

Table 2

SOLUTION	INDICATOR	COLOR	pH RANGE
CH_3COOH	bromcresol green		
$CH_3COOH + CH_3COO^-$	bromcresol green		
HCl	bromcresol green		
HCl + Cl⁻	bromcresol green	COMPLETE IN YOUR NOTEBOOK	
NH_3	phenolphthalein		
$NH_3 + NH_4^+$	phenolphthalein		
NaOH	phenolphthalein		
NaOH + Na⁺	phenolphthalein		

Part III   Determining the Effectiveness of Buffers

Table 3

SOLUTION	COLOR CHANGE TO PHENOLPHTHALEIN BY ADDING BASE	NO. OF DROPS OF BASE TO GIVE COLOR CHANGE	COLOR CHANGE TO BROMCRESOL GREEN BY ADDING ACID	NO. OF DROPS OF ACID TO GIVE COLOR CHANGE
NaCl Solution (unbuffered; assume pH 7)				
pH 7 Buffer Solution				

QUESTIONS AND CALCULATIONS

1. Which solution in Part I gave the slowest rate? Explain this result in terms of Le Chatelier's principle, as applied to the acetic acid ionization equilibrium.

2. Which of the two acids tested in Part II changed pH when a common ion was added? Explain why this result occurred.

3. Which of the two bases tested in Part II changed pH when a common ion was added? Explain why this result occurred.

4. Referring to your results in Part III, calculate the fraction of the volume of the buffer or the unbuffered solution that was required to cause the indicator to change color in each of the four situations studied. Assume that the volume of one drop is 0.05 mL.

FOLLOW-UP QUESTIONS

1. Which of the following pairs of solutions will constitute a buffer? (Use the table of acid strengths in Appendix 3 if necessary.)

   a. NH_3 and NH_4NO_3
   b. HNO_3 and $NaNO_3$
   c. KH_2PO_4 and K_2HPO_4
   d. KOH and KCl
   e. HNO_2 and $NaNO_2$

2. Blood must be maintained at a fairly constant pH of between 7.3 and 7.4. One of the principal buffers responsible for doing this consists of carbonic acid (H_2CO_3, from $CO_2(g)$ and H_2O) in equilibrium with the bicarbonate ion, HCO_3^-. If you breathe too deeply and rapidly, a condition known as hyperventilation may occur in which some muscles may become temporarily paralyzed because the pH of the blood becomes too high. Explain why the pH changes in this way, and why the condition can be corrected by exhaling into a paper bag and then breathing the exhaled air in again.

CONCLUSION

State in general terms what types of substances are needed to make a buffer.

Preparation and Standardization of Acid and Base Solutions, and Testing of Unknowns

A common laboratory procedure is to determine the concentration of an acid or base solution by titrating it against a solution of known concentration. In an earlier experiment (16B) you were introduced to the method of preparing a standard solution. In a subsequent experiment (20C) you performed an acid-base titration to determine the concentration of acetic acid in vinegar, having been given a sodium hydroxide solution of known molarity. In this experiment you will have to standardize the NaOH yourself.

You will first have to prepare a solution of an acid of known concentration by weighing out a sample and making it up to a known volume in a volumetric flask. To be suitable for such a use, a substance must be very pure and stable. Also, it must not absorb water from the air. A chemical such as this is called a *primary standard*. Sodium hydroxide cannot be used as a primary standard because it is difficult to obtain 100% pure, it readily adsorbs moisture from the air, and it reacts with the carbon dioxide in the air. A common primary standard for acid-base titrations is oxalic acid, which occurs in the crystalline form as the dihydrate $H_2C_2O_4 \cdot 2H_2O$ (or $(COOH)_2 \cdot 2H_2O$). This is the primary standard that you will use in Part I of this experiment. (It must be of analytical reagent purity.)

After preparing the solution of oxalic acid of known molarity, you will carry out a titration with sodium hydroxide solution in order to determine the molarity of the NaOH (Part II). This standardized NaOH can have a variety of uses, such as determining the molar mass of an unknown solid acid (Part III) or the molarity of an unknown acid solution (Part IV). Keep in mind that it is important to make all measurements with as much accuracy as possible.

In this experiment you will also have the opportunity to do some optional procedures which you will design yourself (Parts V and VI).

OBJECTIVES

1. to prepare a standard solution of oxalic acid and use it to standardize an unknown sodium hydroxide solution

2. to determine the molar mass of an unknown solid acid by titration with standardized NaOH solution

3. to determine the pH and molarity of an unknown acid solution and calculate the K_a from the results

4. to analyze a variety of other unknown solutions by titration

MATERIALS

Apparatus

centigram balance
beaker (100 mL)
beaker (250 mL)
funnel
volumetric flask (250 mL)
wash bottle
buret
pipet (25 mL)
suction bulb
pH meter (or universal indicator
    paper or solution)
stoppered bottle (500 mL)
label
stand
buret clamp
lab apron
safety goggles

Reagents

oxalic acid (crystals)
sodium hydroxide (NaOH)
    solution (approx. 0.1M)
phenolphthalein indicator
unknown solid acid
unknown weak acid solution
Optional Reagents
    soft drink
    apple, lemon, or
        grapefruit juice
    unknown HCl solution
    household ammonia
    limewater
    bromcresol green indicator
    solid sodium carbonate
    antacid tablet

PROCEDURE

Part I   Preparation of a Primary Standard Acid

CAUTION: Oxalic acid is poisonous. Do not get any in your mouth. Do not swallow any. Always use the suction bulb to withdraw the oxalic acid into the pipet.

1. Before coming to the laboratory, calculate the mass of oxalic acid, $H_2C_2O_4 \cdot 2H_2O$, that you will need to make up 250.0 mL of a 0.0500M solution.

2. Put on your lab apron and safety goggles.

3. Accurately determine the mass of an empty (clean and dry) 100 mL beaker and record it in Table 1 in your notebook.

4. Measure into the beaker the amount of oxalic acid that you have calculated you need and accurately determine the mass of the oxalic acid and the beaker. Record this figure in Table 1. Do not spend much time trying to get exactly the same mass as you calculated. The important thing is to record accurately the mass you do have, and to calculate the molarity from this mass. For example, the mass you use may give the solution a molarity of 0.0496M. This is perfectly acceptable, provided that you use this figure in your calculations.

6. Dissolve the oxalic acid in water, and pour the solution through a funnel into a 250 mL volumetric flask. Wash the beaker with water twice, and add these washings to the flask. Now add water to the flask until the level is up to the mark. (Use a wash bottle as you get close to the mark.) Stopper the flask, and shake to ensure that the solution is homogeneous. You now have your standard solution of oxalic acid.

Part II   Standardization of an Unknown NaOH Solution

1. Obtain a 500 mL bottle with a stopper and fill it with NaOH solution of unknown molarity. Label it with your name and class.

2. Add about 15 mL of the NaOH solution to a buret through a funnel, rinse it back and forth, then discard it through the tip into the sink.

3. Fill up the buret with more NaOH solution and allow some to drain in order to remove any air bubbles in the tip. Remove the funnel.

4. Using the suction bulb on the end of your pipet, withdraw about 5 mL of oxalic acid, rinse it around in the pipet, and discard it. Then withdraw 25 mL of the standard oxalic acid solution and transfer it to a 250 mL Erlenmeyer flask. The correct volume is delivered when you have touched the tip of the pipet to the side of the flask. Do not blow through the pipet. (*Note*: Depending on the shape and size of your pipet and volumetric flask, you may have to transfer the oxalic acid first to a clean, dry beaker since the pipet will not reach deep enough into the volumetric flask.)

5. Add 3 drops of phenolphthalein solution to the acid in the Erlenmeyer flask.

6. Read the initial volume of NaOH in the buret as accurately as you can, and record it in Table 2. Then open the valve on the buret. Allow the NaOH solution to run into the flask and swirl constantly to ensure thorough mixing.

7. After a time, you will notice a pink color that appears where the NaOH enters the liquid in the flask. When this color takes a longer time to disperse and disappear, slow down the rate of addition of NaOH until eventually you are adding it a drop at a time. Stop the titration when the faintest possible pink color stays in the flask for about 20 s. Read the final volume of the NaOH in the buret and record it in Table 2. (The difference between the initial reading and the final reading represents the volume of NaOH required to neutralize the oxalic acid.)

8. If you are at all in doubt as to whether you have a pale pink color, take the reading anyway, then add one more drop. If the color immediately becomes much darker, the reading you took was probably the most accurate result. This is called the *endpoint* of the titration. Discard the solution down the sink.

9. Pipet another 25 mL sample of oxalic acid into the flask and again add 3 drops of phenolphthalein. Refill the buret (if necessary) and repeat the titration. Run in NaOH to within 1 mL of the volume needed in the first titration, then add the solution a drop at a time, swirling after each drop, until you get the faint pink endpoint. Repeat the titration until you have two readings that agree to within 0.1 mL.

10. Store your labelled bottle of standardized NaOH (as instructed by your teacher) until the next laboratory period, when Parts III and IV will be done.

CAUTION: Sodium hydroxide solution is corrosive to skin, eyes, and clothing. When handling NaOH, wear safety goggles, full face shield, gloves, and lab apron. Wash spills and splashes off your skin and clothing immediately using plenty of water. Call your teacher.

CAUTION: Phenolphthalein solution is flammable. Make sure there are no burner flames in the vicinity.

CAUTION: You must assume that any unknowns you are dealing with could be poisonous. Do not get any in your mouth and do not swallow any.

Part III Determination of the Molar Mass of an Unknown Solid Acid

1. Obtain a vial containing an unknown solid acid from your teacher. Record the identifying number or letter in Table 3.

2. Weigh out about 0.75 g of the solid acid into a clean, dry beaker, and record the mass accurately in Table 3. It does not have to be exactly 0.75 g, as long as you know exactly how much you have.

3. Dissolve the acid in about 40 mL of water and transfer the solution to an Erlenmeyer flask. Rinse the beaker twice into the flask to ensure that all the acid solution is transferred. (The amount of water added does not affect the results.) Add 3 drops of phenolphthalein.

4. Run in NaOH from a buret as in Part II, measuring the volume required to reach the endpoint. Record this figure in Table 3.

5. Repeat Steps 2 to 4 until you get two readings in close agreement. (If you did not have exactly the same mass each time, check whether the results agree by determining the ratio of the volumes and comparing it with the ratio of the masses used. Alternatively, follow the calculations set out in the Questions and Calculations section to determine the molar mass of the acid, and see whether those results agree within experimental error.)

Part IV   Determination of K_a for an Unknown Monoprotic Weak Acid

1. Obtain approximately 100 mL of the unknown weak acid provided. Record any identifying number or letter in Table 4, if more than one unknown is available.

2. Measure the pH of the solution. The most accurate way of doing this is with a pH meter, if one is available in the lab. If so, your teacher will give instructions on its use and calibration. Otherwise, use universal indicator paper or solution to determine the pH.

3. Use the suction bulb on your pipet to deliver a 25.00 mL portion of the unknown acid into an Erlenmeyer flask. (Rinse the pipet with the acid first.) Add 3 drops of phenolphthalein.

4. Titrate with your standard NaOH solution as you did in Parts II and III, until you get two results agreeing, or until you run out of time.

OPTIONAL PROCEDURES

The following procedures are considered optional, to be done only if you are requested to do so by your teacher. Detailed instructions are not provided. It is hoped that from doing Parts I to IV you have developed a good understanding of the techniques and calculations required in acid-base titrations and can devise your own experiments. Choose a suitable indicator and check your procedure with your teacher before starting. It may be a good idea to get a rough estimate of the volumes required by measuring 10 mL portions with a graduated cylinder until an endpoint is reached, then determining from the results suitable volumes and concentrations to use with the more accurate buret.

Part V   Determination of Acid Concentration in Beverages

Many beverages are acidic. Determine the total concentration of acid in one or more of the following, as instructed: lemon juice, grapefruit juice, apple juice, or a colorless soft drink. Use your standard NaOH solution and phenolphthalein.

Determine the concentration of the approximately $0.1M$ solution of HCl provided by titrating your standard NaOH into 25 mL portions of HCl, using phenolphthalein as an indicator. Then use this standardized HCl in any of the following procedures:

a. Determine the concentration of a household ammonia solution by titrating it with the HCl.

b. Determine the concentration of a saturated solution of limewater (calcium hydroxide, $Ca(OH)_2$) by titrating it with the standard HCl. Use the results to calculate K_{sp} for $Ca(OH)_2$.

c. Determine the number of molecules of water in washing soda or sal soda (hydrated sodium carbonate, $Na_2CO_3 \cdot xH_2O$) by titrating standard HCl against a known mass of the sodium carbonate dissolved in water.

d. Grind up a known mass of antacid tablet, add a measured volume of standardized HCl (enough to dissolve it), and determine how much HCl is left by titrating standard NaOH solution back into the flask. Calculate the amount of acid that is neutralized by the antacid.

Before you leave the laboratory wash your hands thoroughly with soap and water; use a fingernail brush to clean under your fingernails.

CAUTION: Hydrochloric acid is corrosive to skin, eyes, and clothing. When handling NaOH, wear safety goggles, full face shield, gloves, and lab apron. Wash spills and splashes off your skin and clothing immediately using plenty of water. Call your teacher.

CAUTION: Ammonia, limewater, and washing soda solutions are caustic and can harm skin, eyes, and clothing. Wash any spills and splashes off your skin and clothing immediately with plenty of water. Call your teacher.

REAGENT DISPOSAL

Wash solutions that are the end result of titrations down the sink with plenty of water. Your teacher will give you instructions on whether to save for possible reuse the standard solutions of oxalic acid, sodium hydroxide, and hydrochloric acid that are left over, or to neutralize them and rinse them down the sink with copious amounts of water.

POST LAB DISCUSSION

Oxalic acid is a diprotic acid. It can therefore release two hydronium ions when it reacts with a base such as sodium hydroxide. Make certain that you allow for this in your calculations.

In Part III, you may assume that the unknown solid acid is monoprotic unless you are told otherwise.

If you are asked to do Part VI (c), which involves washing soda, you should be aware of the fact that the crystals of hydrated sodium carbonate which make up washing soda tend to lose water on standing in the open air in a process known as *efflorescence*. The molar mass you determine may therefore not correspond to an exact whole number of molecules of water in the formula for the hydrated crystals of sodium carbonate.

DATA AND OBSERVATIONS

It would be a good idea to copy these tables into your notebook before coming to the laboratory.

Part I   Preparation of a Primary Standard Acid

Table 1

Calculated mass of oxalic acid $H_2C_2O_4 \cdot 2H_2O$ (required for 250.0 mL of $0.0500M$ solution (g))	
Mass of beaker (g)	
Mass of beaker + oxalic acid (g)	
Mass of oxalic acid (g)	

Part II   Standardization of an Unknown NaOH Solution

Table 2   Volume of NaOH Needed to Neutralize 25.00 mL of Oxalic Acid

	TRIAL 1	TRIAL 2	TRIAL 3	TRIAL 4	TRIAL 5 (if necessary)
Initial reading of buret					
Final reading of buret					
Volume of NaOH required (mL)					
Average volume of NaOH (mL)					

Part III   Determination of the Molar Mass of an Unknown Solid Acid

Table 3   Volume of NaOH Needed to Neutralize Known Mass of Unknown Solid Acid

UNKNOWN SOLID ACID #____	TRIAL 1	TRIAL 2	TRIAL 3 (if necessary)
Mass of beaker			
Mass of beaker + acid			
Mass of acid			
Initial volume of NaOH			
Final volume of NaOH			
Volume of NaOH used (mL)			

Part IV   Determination of K_a for an Unknown Monoprotic Weak Acid

Table 4

UNKNOWN ACID SOLUTION #____	TRIAL 1	TRIAL 2	TRIAL 3 (if necessary)
pH of unknown acid solution			
Initial volume of NaOH			
Final volume of NaOH			
Volume of NaOH used (mL)			

Part V   Determination of Acid Concentration in Beverages

Part VI   Analysis of Other Solutions

Since these parts are optional procedures in which you design your own experiment, you will also need to prepare tables for the data you will collect.

CALCULATIONS

Always write balanced equations for the reactions studied so that you are aware of the mole relationships to use in your calculations.

Part I   Preparation of a Primary Standard Acid

1. Calculate the mass of one mole of oxalic acid, $H_2C_2O_4 \cdot 2H_2O$.

2. Calculate the number of moles in the measured mass of oxalic acid.

3. Calculate $[H_2C_2O_4 \cdot 2H_2O]$ when the mass in item 1 is dissolved in 250.0 mL of solution.

Part II   Standardization of an Unknown NaOH Solution

1. Calculate the number of moles of oxalic acid in 25.00 mL of standard solution.

2. Calculate the number of moles of NaOH required to neutralize this amount of oxalic acid. (Remember that oxalic acid is diprotic.)

3. Using your average volume of NaOH required and the number of moles present as obtained above, calculate [NaOH] in the standardized solution in mol/L. If your first titration result is somewhat larger than subsequent results, do not include it in calculating the average volume. (In the first titration students often overshoot the endpoint.)

Part III   Determination of the Molar Mass of an Unknown Solid Acid

1. Calculate the number of moles of NaOH used in each titration.

2. Calculate the number of moles of unknown acid neutralized by this amount of NaOH. (Remember that the acid is monoprotic.)

3. Using the relationship

$$\text{molar mass} = \frac{\text{mass of substance (g)}}{\text{number of moles}}$$

calculate the molar mass of the unknown acid.

4. Repeat the calculation in item 3 for each titration performed, and calculate the average molar mass of the acid.

Part IV Determination of K_a for an Unknown Monoprotic Weak Acid

1. Calculate the $[H^+]$ in the unknown acid solution from the relationship $[H^+]$ = inverse log ($-pH$).

2. Calculate the average volume of NaOH required for the titration.

3. Calculate the number of moles of NaOH used to neutralize the acid. (This number is equal to the number of moles of acid, since the acid is monoprotic.)

4. Calculate the concentration of the acid from the relationship

$$\text{molarity} = \frac{\text{number of moles}}{\text{volume (L)}}$$

5. The K_a for a weak acid $HA \rightleftharpoons H^+ + A^-$ is given by the equation

$$K_a = \frac{[H^+][A^-]}{[HA]}$$

Since for every molecule of HA that ionizes, one H^+ ion and one A^- ion are produced, $[H^+] = [A^-]$. Therefore,

$$K_a = \frac{[H^+]^2}{[HA]}$$

The [HA] term here represents the HA molecules left over after ionization has occurred; it should therefore be calculated by subtracting the $[H^+]$ from the total [HA] as obtained from the titration data. In many cases, however, you will find that allowing for this ionization does not make a significant difference to the answer.

Calculate the value of K_a for your acid as outlined in the above discussion.

Part V Determination of Acid Concentration in Beverages

Part VI Analysis of Other Solutions

These calculations are shown in outline only. Set out your own calculation procedure for whichever procedures you followed.

1. Calculate the concentration of acid in each beverage you tested.

2. Calculate the [HCl] from your titration data with NaOH. Then do whichever of the following is appropriate.

    a. Calculate the $[NH_3]$ in household ammonia.
    b. Calculate the $[OH^-]$ in saturated $Ca(OH)_2$ solution, and from the result calculate K_{sp} for $Ca(OH)_2$.
    c. Calculate the number of moles of $Na_2CO_3 \cdot xH_2O$ that must have reacted with the acid, then use the mass and number of moles to calculate the molar mass. From the result, determine the value of x in the formula $Na_2CO_3 \cdot xH_2O$ (that is, the number of molecules of water found in the formula for the hydrated crystal.)
    d. Calculate the number of moles of HCl used up by your mass of antacid, then convert this answer to the volume of $0.100M$ HCl used up by 1 g of antacid. Given that $0.100M$ HCl approximately represents stomach acid, and that it has a density of 1.00 g/mL, calculate the mass of stomach acid neutralized by 1 g of antacid. (Note that this quantity includes the water in the solution as well as the acid itself.)

FOLLOW-UP QUESTIONS

1. A certain soft drink was analyzed and found to contain $0.080M\,H^+$. Other ingredients of the drink include sugar or, in the diet form of the drink, an artificial sweetener. What property of this acid solution is overcome by using sugar or sweetener?

2. Every day, a manufacturing plant produces 5.0×10^3 L of NaOH waste of molarity $0.030M$. In order to comply with environmental regulations, this NaOH must be neutralized before being discharged as effluent. What mass of concentrated HCl will be required to neutralize it? ([HCl] = $12M$; density = 1.2 kg/L)

3. A sample of sodium hydroxide, NaOH, is known to have become contaminated with sodium carbonate, Na_2CO_3, by reaction with CO_2 in the air. A 1.00 g sample is titrated with $0.500M$ HCl, and it is found that 46.5 mL of HCl are required for neutralization. Calculate the percentage by mass of Na_2CO_3 in the sample. (*Hint*: Let mass of Na_2CO_3 = x g.)

4. Why would it be difficult to measure the concentration of acid in red wine or in a cola-type drink using the method in Part V? How could you overcome this difficulty?

5. There are some titrations in which the endpoint is obtained by measuring the electrical conductivity of the solution and watching for the point at which the conductivity is at a minimum. Such a titration is called an *electrometric titration*. An example is the reaction of $Ba(OH)_2$ solution with sulfuric acid, H_2SO_4. Write the net ionic equation for the reaction (remembering the solubility table!), then explain why the conductivity reaches a minimum.

CONCLUSIONS

1. State the molar mass of your unknown solid acid (and its sample number).

2. State the K_a of your unknown weak acid solution (and its sample number).

Titration Curves

You have already performed a number of acid-base titrations in earlier experiments (20C and 20G). You should therefore be well aware of the fact that the pH of a solution changes very rapidly at the equivalence point, the point where the number of moles of H_3O^+ equals the number of moles of OH^-. The rate of change of pH is very clearly seen if a graph is plotted for pH versus the volume of acid or base added as the reaction proceeds. Such a graph is called a *titration curve*. These graphs can also be obtained by interfacing a pH meter with a microcomputer.

In this experiment you will obtain three titration curves by manually plotting your results. The first curve's pH data will be obtained by calculation; it will be for a strong base titrated against a strong acid (Part I). It will be assigned as a pre-lab activity, and will give you useful practice in titration calculations as well as enable you to see the relationship between pH and volume of base added. The second curve will be of the same type, but will be obtained experimentally using a buret to deliver the base solution and a pH meter to measure the pH. The third curve, also obtained experimentally, will be for a strong base titrated against a weak acid, and the shape of the curve will be compared to that for the strong acid.

A pH meter is an instrument with a wide variety of applications, ranging from the testing and monitoring of water quality to manufacturing processes and research. Meters vary in their construction and method of operation, but some general principles apply to all. A glass electrode is connected to the pH meter and inserted into the test solution. A voltage is then produced which is dependent on the pH of the solution. A needle on a scale or a digital readout gives the actual voltage obtained, but a scale showing the pH value directly is generally more useful. The meter must be set for the temperature, then calibrated by placing the electrode in one or more buffers of accurately known pH. Your teacher will give you specific instructions for the pH meter available to you.

OBJECTIVES

1. to calculate the pH at various stages of the titration of a strong base against a strong acid and plot the results on a graph

2. to measure experimentally the pH at various stages of the titration of a strong base against a strong acid and plot the results on a graph

3. to measure experimentally the pH at various stages of the titration of a strong base against a weak acid, plot the results on a graph, and compare the shape to that obtained in Objective 2

MATERIALS

Apparatus		Reagents
pipet (25 mL)	lab apron	0.100M NaOH
buret (50 mL)	safety goggles	0.100M HCl
buret stand and clamp		0.100M acetic acid,
pH meter and electrode		CH_3COOH
beaker (250 mL)		phenolphthalein solution
suction bulb		*or* universal indicator
glass stirring rod		solution

PROCEDURE

Part I   Calculated Titration Curve

In order to become acquainted with titration curves, perform the following calculations as a pre-lab activity:

1. Calculate the pH that results when 25.00 mL of 0.100M HCl is titrated with 0.100M NaOH solution run in from a buret, at each of the following stages of volume of 0.100M NaOH added (in mL): 0.00, 5.00, 10.00, 15.00, 20.00, 22.00, 24.00, 24.50, 24.80, 24.90, 24.95, 24.99, 25.00, 25.01, 25.05, 25.10, 25.20, 25.50, 26.00, 28.00, 30.00, 40.00, 50.00.

    The calculations can be done in either of two ways: (a) Calculate moles of acid or base left over, then divide by the total volume to get [H$^+$] (or [OH$^-$] if the titration has passed the equivalence point). (b) Since the concentrations used are identical, subtraction can give the volume of HCl or NaOH left over. The concentration of 0.100M then has to be reduced by multiplying by the dilution factor (volume unreacted divided by the total volume) to obtain [H$^+$] (or [OH$^-$] if beyond the equivalence point).

    Having now obtained the [H$^+$] or [OH$^-$], you can calculate the pH. Record your calculated results in your copy of Table 1, Part I, in your notebook.

2. Plot a graph of the results, with pH plotted against the volume of NaOH added.

Part II   Experimentally Obtained Titration Curve for NaOH against HCl

1. Put on your lab apron and safety goggles.

2. Set up and calibrate your pH meter according to your teacher's instructions.

3. Using a suction bulb on your pipet, withdraw 25 mL of 0.100M HCl and transfer it to a 250 mL beaker. Remember to rinse your pipet with the HCl first.

4. Add 3 drops of phenolphthalein (or universal indicator solution) to the acid in order to observe the pH changes by means of a color change as well as with the pH meter.

5. Set up the buret in the stand and clamp, and rinse it out with 10 mL of NaOH solution. Discard the rinsings through the tip.

6. Refill the buret with NaOH solution, allow some to drain through the tip to fill it, then adjust the volume to 0.00 mL. (This will make it easier to obtain a large number of volume readings.)

7. Place the electrode of the pH meter in the acid solution in the beaker, and read the pH.

8. Run in as close as possible to 5.00 mL of NaOH solution, stirring the solution in the beaker constantly (with a stirring rod, not the electrode!). Again read the pH.

9. Continue adding NaOH and recording the volume of NaOH added, with its related pH, under Part II of Table 1. Get as close as possible to the volume values for which you calculated the pH in Part I.

CAUTION: The hydrochloric acid and sodium hydroxide solutions are corrosive to skin, eyes, and clothing. Wash any spills and splashes with plenty of water. Call your teacher.

CAUTION: Phenolphthalein solution is harmful when ingested and is flammable. Do not get any in your mouth; do not swallow any. Make sure there are no burners in the vicinity.

The volume increments must become successively smaller as you approach the equivalence point. Be careful in this region, since the equivalence point will only be at 25.00 mL if both solutions were of precisely the same concentration, which may not be the case.

Part III   Experimentally Obtained Titration Curve for NaOH against CH_3COOH

1. Rinse off the electrode for the pH meter before beginning the titration.

2. Repeat the Procedure in Part II, but titrate the NaOH against $0.100\,M$ CH_3COOH instead of HCl. Record all results under Part III of Table 1.

3. Clean up, following the instructions for reagent disposal.

4. Before leaving the laboratory, wash your hands thoroughly with soap and water; use a fingernail brush to clean under your fingernails.

REAGENT DISPOSAL

Wash all solutions formed as a result of the titration down the sink with plenty of water. Return unused portions of original solutions to the container designated by your teacher.

POST LAB DISCUSSION

When an acid and a base react together and neutralize one another, water is formed and a salt is left over in the solution. If the titration is between a strong acid and a strong base, then the salt which is present at the equivalence point will not undergo hydrolysis, and the solution will be neutral. If the titration is between a strong base and a weak acid, then the salt which is present at the equivalence point will undergo anionic hydrolysis, producing OH^- ions. Therefore, the pH at the equivalence point will be on the basic side of neutral; that is, it will be greater than 7. If the titration is between a weak base and a strong acid, then the salt present at the equivalence point will undergo cationic hydrolysis, producing H_3O^+. The pH at the equivalence point will therefore be on the acidic side of neutral, that is, less than 7. By studying the titration curves you can determine which indicator can be used for each type of titration in order to get a color change in the vertical portion of the graph on either side of the equivalence point. The transition point of the indicator should match the equivalence point of the titration as closely as possible.

DATA AND OBSERVATIONS

It would be a good idea to have these tables ready in your notebook before coming to the laboratory. Remember to do the calculations for Part I before coming to the laboratory. Show your calculations in your report, as well as recording the values in the table.

Table 1

PART I (25.00 mL 0.100*M* HCl) CALCULATED VALUES		PART II (25.00 mL 0.100*M* HCl) EXPERIMENTAL VALUES		PART III (25.00 mL 0.100*M* CH₃COOH) EXPERIMENTAL VALUES	
VOLUME OF NaOH (mL)	pH	VOLUME OF NaOH (mL)	pH	VOLUME OF NaOH (mL)	pH
0.00					
5.00					
10.00					
15.00					
20.00					
22.00					
24.00					
24.50					
24.80					
24.90					
24.95					
24.99					
25.00					
25.01					
25.05					
25.10					
25.20					
25.50					
26.00					
28.00					
30.00					
40.00					
50.00					

QUESTIONS AND CALCULATIONS

1. Plot a graph of pH versus the volume of NaOH solution added for each set of results from Parts II and III.

2. State three differences in appearance between the graph in Part II (strong acid) and that in Part III (weak acid).

3. In Part I, for the addition of 0.02 mL (less than half a drop), by how much did the pH change between 24.99 mL and 25.01 mL?

4. In Parts II and III, what was the largest pH change you observed when only one drop was added?

5. The equivalence point in an acid-base titration is found at the middle of the most vertical portion on a titration curve. Find the value of the pH at this point for the graphs in Parts II and III.

6. Explain the reason for the difference between the equivalence points for strong and weak acids, as shown by your answer to question 5.

FOLLOW-UP QUESTIONS

1. Describe the shape of the titration curve if $0.100 M$ HCl were run from a buret into 25.00 mL of $0.100 M$ NaOH.

2. Use the table of indicators in Appendix 4 to select all the indicators which would be acceptable for use in your titration of a strong acid with a strong base.

3. Why is phenolphthalein the best indicator to use for titrating a strong base with a weak acid?

4. From your graph for Part III, read the pH at the point where half the acetic acid has been neutralized. (This corresponds to the point where half the volume of NaOH required for neutralization has been added.) Calculate the $[H_3O^+]$ that corresponds to this pH. How does this concentration compare to the K_a for acetic acid? Explain this result by referring to the K_a expression for acetic acid.

CONCLUSION

Describe the general shapes of the graphs obtained in Parts I, II, and III.

Acid Rain

Acidic precipitation has been identified as a major environmental hazard that has resulted in the destruction of life, natural habitats, and architectural structures. The rise in rainfall acidity can be directly correlated with increasing emissions of sulfur and nitrogen oxides. Released from automobile engines, power plants, steel mills, and other industrial complexes, these atmospheric pollutants combine with water vapor to form sulfurous, sulfuric, and nitric acids.

When fossil fuels that are rich in sulfur impurities are oxidized, great quantities of sulfur dioxide are released into the atmosphere. This noxious by-product may then associate with water vapor, forming sulfurous acid.

$$SO_2 + H_2O \quad \rightleftharpoons \quad H_2SO_3$$

Due to the unstable nature of the product, the reaction is reversible, favoring the spontaneous dissociation of sulfurous acid.

If sufficient oxygen is present, a small percent pf sulfur dioxide may be further oxidized into sulfur trioxide, SO_3. Particulate matter present in coal smoke will catalyze this reaction, increasing the SO_3 yield by over 500%. This gas associates with water to form the stronger and more stable sulfuric acid.

$$SO_2 + 1/2O_2 \quad \rightarrow \quad SO_3$$
$$SO_3 + H_2O \quad \rightarrow \quad H_2SO_4$$

The ecological effects of precipitation containing these and other acids are dependent not only on the acidity of the rainfall, but also on the buffering capability of the soil. Soils rich in lime, CaO, demonstrate a natural protection against acid rain.

The acidity of rain is causing increased environmental problems in Canada. Acid rain leaches minerals from the soil, corrodes metals, dissolves limestone in buildings, and kills fish and other organisms in lakes. Already, thousands of lakes in Canada have been destroyed for aquatic life. The Canadian and United States governments currently have a joint commission studying the problem.

In Part I of this exercise, you will investigate the chemical properties of several acid rainwater solutions. Then in Part II you will observe the neutralizing effect of CaO. Artificial "acid rainwater" will percolate through a funnel containing a soil/CaO mixture. The pH of the filtrate will then be compared to the original value.

OBJECTIVES

1. to observe the effects of artificial acid rainwater solutions on pH paper, calcium carbonate, and magnesium

2. to observe the neutralizing effect of calcium oxide on acid rainwater solutions

MATERIALS

Apparatus

6 small test tubes	funnel
test tube rack	wax pencil
beaker (250 mL)	safety goggles
spatula	lab apron
ring stand and ring	filter paper

Reagents

CaCO₃   Adirondack Mountain
CaO   rainwater
pH indicator paper   (laboratory prepared)
magnesium ribbon   local rainwater sample
Scotland rainwater   distilled water
    (laboratory prepared)   lime-free soil

PROCEDURE

Part I   Effect of Acid Rain Samples on Various Reagents

1. Put on your lab apron and safety goggles.

2. Set up six test tubes labeled *A* to *F*.

3. To test tubes *A* and *B*, add 5 mL of the laboratory-prepared sample of Scotland rainwater.

4. To test tubes *C* and *D*, add 5 mL of the laboratory-prepared sample of Adirondack Mountain rainwater.

5. To test tubes *E* and *F*, add 5 mL of a locally collected rainwater sample.

6. Add a strip of pH paper to test tubes *A*, *C*, and *E*. Record the results in your copy of Table 1 in your notebook.

7. Add a 0.5 g sample of calcium carbonate, CaCO₃, to test tubes *B*, *D*, and *F*. Record your observations in Table 2.

8. Add a 1 cm strip of magnesium ribbon to tubes *A*, *C*, and *E*. Record your observations in Table 3.

Part II   Neutralizing Effect of Calcium Oxide on Acid Rain

1. Fold a piece of filter paper and place it in a funnel. Suspend the funnel in a ring support. Place a clean and dry 250 mL beaker beneath the funnel.

2. Place a 5 g sample of lime-free soil in the funnel.

3. Pour 30 mL of Adirondack Mountain rainwater into the sample and allow it to percolate through the soil.

4. Add a strip of pH paper to the filtrate. Put a 1 cm strip of magnesium ribbon into the beaker. Record your results in your copy of Table 4.

5. To a second 5 g sample of lime-free soil, add 0.1 g of calcium oxide, CaO, and mix thoroughly.

6. Repeat Steps 1 through 4 using this soil sample.

7. Before you leave the laboratory, wash your hands thoroughly with soap and water; use a fingernail brush to clean under your fingernails.

REAGENT DISPOSAL

Wrap any remaining solids in a piece of paper towel and put in a waste-basket. All solutions can be poured down the sink with copious amounts of water.

POST LAB DISCUSSION

In Part I, the properties of several laboratory-prepared rainwater solutions were compared to those of locally obtained samples. The actual Scotland rainwater that your sample simulated fell close to an industrial centre. The Adirondack rainwater fell in unpopulated regions of northern New York State. This precipitation is sufficiently acidic that fish can no longer survive in half of the high-altitude lakes located in this remote mountainous region.

Acid rainfall can rapidly corrode metals such as steel and aluminum. Materials such as limestone and marble are particularly susceptible to acidic environments. Chemically, both limestone and marble are $CaCO_3$. They react as follows:

$$CaCO_3(s) + 2H^+(aq) \rightarrow Ca^{2+}(aq) + CO_2(g) + H_2O\,(l)$$

When lime, CaO, is added to soil or lakes, it reacts with water to form calcium hydroxide, $Ca(OH)_2$. This base is capable of neutalizing the hydrogen ions in acid precipitation as shown in the following reaction:

$$Ca(OH)_2(s) + 2H^+(aq) \rightarrow Ca^{2+}(aq) + 2H_2O\,(l)$$

DATA AND OBSERVATIONS

Part I Effect of Acid Rain Samples on Various Reagents

Table 1

	TEST TUBE CONTENTS	pH
Test tube *A*		
Test tube *C*	COMPLETE IN YOUR NOTEBOOK	
Test tube *E*		

Table 2

	TEST TUBE CONTENTS	REACTION WITH $CaCO_3$
Test tube *B*		
Test tube *D*	COMPLETE IN YOUR NOTEBOOK	
Test tube *F*		

Table 3

	TEST TUBE CONTENTS	REACTION WITH Mg
Test tube *A*		
Test tube *C*	COMPLETE IN YOUR NOTEBOOK	
Test tube *E*		

Part II   Neutralizing Effect of Calcium Oxide on Acid Rain

Table 4

	pH BEFORE PERCOLATION	pH AFTER PERCOLATION	pH DIFFERENCE	Mg STRIP OBSERVATION
Lime-free soil				
Soil with lime				

QUESTIONS

1. How did the addition of lime affect the pH of the soil filtrate in Part II?

2. How might the pH of the filtrate in Part II differ, if twice the amount of CaO is used in Step 5?

3. How does the acidity of your local rainwater compare with the laboratory-prepared samples of acid rainfall?

4. What gas was released when the acid solutions reacted with the magnesium ribbon? Write a balanced equation illustrating this reaction.

FOLLOW-UP QUESTIONS

1. Explain how emissions from taller smokestacks might show contrasting effects on local and distant rainfall.

2. Explain how a spring thaw might present an "acid shock" to the emerging wildlife.

3. Write the equation for the reaction between nitrogen dioxide and water vapor.

4. Why is adding lime to lakes not a very satisfactory way of counteracting the effects of acid rain?

5. A lake 6 km long, 3 km wide, and with an average depth of 10 m is found to have a pH of 4.0 ($[H^+]$ = $1 \times 10^{-4} M$). It is planned to neutralize this acidity by adding calcium carbonate, $CaCO_3$. What mass of $CaCO_3$ is required? (Assume that the acidity is caused by a strong acid.)

CONCLUSION

State the results of Objective 1.

Oxidation-Reduction Reactions of Elements and Their Ions

The process whereby electrons are lost by an atom, molecule, or ion is termed *oxidation*. Conversely, the process whereby electrons are gained by an atom, molecule, or ion is termed *reduction*. Before electrons can be added to a chemical species, they must be removed from another chemical species; therefore, the processes of oxidation and reduction must occur together. The overall reaction is called an *oxidation-reduction reaction*, or, in shorter form, a *redox reaction*.

You have already encountered a number of redox reactions in earlier experiments; for instance, reactions in which a metal reacts with an acid, giving positive ions of the metal and hydrogen gas. The reaction between magnesium and hydrogen ions to give magnesium ions and hydrogen gas is a good example of a redox reaction:

$$Mg(s) + 2H^+(aq) \rightarrow Mg^{2+}(aq) + H_2(g)$$

The reaction consists of two distinct parts which can be writtten as separate reactions, each involving electrons. These are called *half-reactions*.

$$Mg(s) \rightarrow Mg^{2+}(aq) + 2e^- \qquad \text{(oxidation—loss of electrons)}$$
$$2H^+(aq) + 2e^- \rightarrow H_2(g) \qquad \text{(reduction—gain of electrons)}$$

The magnesium brings about reduction of H^+ to H_2, so it is called the *reducing agent*. The H^+ brings about oxidation of Mg to Mg^{2+} and therefore is called the *oxidizing agent*.

The overall equation for the reaction is obtained by adding the equations for the two half-reactions in such a way that the electrons cancel out. (This may mean that one or both of the equations for the half-reactions must be multiplied by some number to make the electrons involved in the oxidation and reduction numerically equal.) Note that the oxidizing agent is the species which itself becomes reduced in the process, and the reducing agent is the species which itself becomes oxidized in the process. Because the reaction proceeds in the direction shown, it can be concluded that magnesium is a stronger reducing agent than H_2, and that H^+ is a stronger oxidizing agent than Mg^{2+}.

In Part I of this experiment you will examine reactions between metals and aqueous solutions of ions of other metals. Then in Part II you will investigate some reactions between free halogen molecules and aqueous solutions of ions of other halogen elements. From your results you will be able to arrange the equations for the reduction half-reactions in sequence from the strongest oxidizing agent down to the weakest. This arrangement will show that any oxidizing agent on the left will be able to react with any reducing agent on the right that is lower on the list. Such a list can be expanded with other experimental results, and is very useful for predicting whether a reaction will proceed. Later in the course you will use it to predict voltages that could be produced in a variety of redox reactions.

OBJECTIVES

1. to investigate various combinations of metals with metal ions and discover which combinations undergo redox reactions

2. to investigate various combinations of the halogen elements chlorine, bromine, and iodine with the related halide salts and discover which combinations undergo redox reactions

3. to list all the reduction half-reactions studied in such a way that the halogen elements and metal ions are arranged in decreasing order of strength as oxidizing agents

MATERIALS

Apparatus

20 test tubes
  (13 mm × 100 mm)
test-tube rack
steel wool or emery paper
water soluble marker
rubber stoppers (size 00)
safety goggles
lab apron

Reagents

$0.1M$ Cu(NO$_3$)$_2$
$0.1M$ Zn(NO$_3$)$_2$
$0.1M$ Mg(NO$_3$)$_2$
$0.1M$ Pb(NO$_3$)$_2$
small strips (approx. 5 mm × 15 mm)
  of copper, zinc, magnesium,
  and lead
$0.1M$ NaCl
$0.1M$ NaBr
$0.1M$ NaI
chlorine water
bromine water
iodine (50% ethanol solution)
n-heptane
$0.1M$ AgNO$_3$ and silver metal strips
  (for teacher demonstration)

PROCEDURE

Part I   Reactions Between Metals and Metal Ions (Cu, Zn, Mg, Ag, and Pb)

CAUTION: The metal nitrate solutions used in this experiment are poisonous. Do not get any in your mouth and do not swallow any.

1. Put on your safety goggles and lab apron.

2. Obtain 3 small strips of each metal (Cu, Zn, Mg, and Pb), and rub each with steel wool or emery paper to remove surface corrosion and reveal the shiny surface underneath. Rinse with water.

3. Place the strips in separate 13 mm × 100 mm test tubes (12 in all), and use your water soluble marker to identify which metal is in each tube.

4. To each of the 3 test tubes containing copper metal, add in turn about 3 mL (one third of a test tube) of a $0.1M$ solution of the nitrate of each other metal. (It is not necessary to try to react copper metal with its own nitrate, Cu(NO$_3$)$_2$.)

5. Repeat with the other three metals, until you have all 12 possible combinations of metals with the nitrates of the others. Label all the combinations. Record your observations in Table 1 in your notebook.

6. Your teacher will display an additional 8 combinations, consisting of silver metal (Ag) with nitrates of Cu^{2+}, Zn^{2+}, Mg^{2+}, and Pb^{2+}, and $0.1 M AgNO_3$ with each of Cu, Zn, Mg, and Pb. Observe which combinations show evidence of reaction, and record your observations in Table 1.

7. In some of the combinations you prepared, a metal will be produced from the positive ion in solution. Note that the metal may be very finely divided and may therefore appear as a black powder. The color and lustre of metals are apparent only when the crystals formed are somewhat larger. Any change in the appearance of a metal or a solution will therefore indicate that a reaction has occurred. Some reactions are slower than others, so leave the test tubes in the rack and take a final look at the results after doing Part II.

Part II Reactions Between Halogens and Halide Ions

The bromine and iodine solutions which are used and which may be produced in this part of the procedure sometimes appear similar in color at certain concentrations. The purpose of Steps 1 and 2 in this part is to demonstrate a way of distinguishing between the two substances Br_2 and I_2. Note that no reaction occurs—the effect seen is simply a selective solubility for the Br_2 and I_2 out of the aqueous phase into the heptane phase.

1. Place 3 mL of bromine water, $Br_2(aq)$, in a test tube, and add 1 mL of n-heptane. Stopper and shake vigorously. Note that the heptane and the water solution do not mix. You will be able to tell which is the heptane layer by observing which layer has the smaller volume. Note the color of the n-heptane, and record it in your notebook.

2. Repeat Step 1 with 3 mL of the I_2 in 50% ethanol solution. Again record the color of the heptane layer.

3. To 3 mL of $0.1 M$ NaBr and 3 mL of $0.1 M$ NaI in separate test tubes add 1 mL of chlorine water. Observe any changes, then to each add 1 mL of heptane, stopper the tube, and shake. Observe the color of the heptane layer, and record what you see in Table 2.

4. Repeat Step 3, but use 1 mL of bromine water with $0.1 M$ NaCl and $0.1 M$ NaI.

5. Repeat Step 3, but use 1 mL of iodine solution in 50% ethanol with $0.1 M$ NaCl and $0.1 M$ NaBr.

6. Now make final observations of results for Part I to check for any further changes.

7. Before leaving the laboratory, wash your hands with soap and water. Use a fingernail brush to clean under your nails.

CAUTION: The n-heptane used in Part II is highly flammable, and its vapors are hazardous if inhaled. Make sure there are no burner flames in the laboratory. Avoid breathing the fumes. Do not get any on your skin. If you do, call your teacher.

CAUTION: The solutions of chlorine water, bromine water, and iodine water are very poisonous and corrosive. Avoid breathing the fumes. Do not get any on your skin. If you do, rinse your skin with the sodium thiosulfate solution which your teacher has available for any such emergencies.

REAGENT DISPOSAL

Return all solutions and metals from Part I to the designated container. DO NOT pour the solutions or the small pieces of metal down the sink.

Pour the solutions from Part II into the designated beaker, which contains a solution of sodium thiosulfate. The sodium thiosulfate can react with unchanged chlorine, bromine, and iodine, which could otherwise be hazardous.

POST LAB DISCUSSION

Note that for every combination of element and ion there is a combination in which the element and ion are reversed. For example, you will have the Cu/Zn^{2+} combination and the Zn/Cu^{2+} combination. Only one of these will react. If a reaction occurred, the conclusion is that the metal ion in the reactants (or in Part II, the halogen molecule) is a stronger oxidizing agent than the other metal ion (or halogen molecule) produced during the course of the reaction.

DATA AND OBSERVATIONS

It would be a good idea to have these tables ready in your notebook before coming to the laboratory.

Part I   Reactions Between Metals and Metal Ions (Cu, Zn, Mg, Ag, and Pb)

Table 1

REACTANTS (METAL + METAL ION)	OBSERVATIONS	REACTION OR NO REACTION	ION THAT IS STRONGER OXIDIZING AGENT
$Cu + Zn^{2+}$			
$Cu + Mg^{2+}$			
$Cu + Pb^{2+}$			
$Zn + Cu^{2+}$			
$Zn + Mg^{2+}$			
$Zn + Pb^{2+}$			
$Mg + Cu^{2+}$			
$Mg + Zn^{2+}$			
$Mg + Pb^{2+}$			
$Pb + Cu^{2+}$			
$Pb + Zn^{2+}$			
$Pb + Mg^{2+}$			
$Ag + Cu^{2+}$			
$Ag + Zn^{2+}$			
$Ag + Mg^{2+}$			
$Ag + Pb^{2+}$			
$Cu + Ag^{+}$			
$Zn + Ag^{+}$			
$Mg + Ag^{+}$			
$Pb + Ag^{+}$			

COMPLETE IN YOUR NOTEBOOK

COMPLETE IN YOUR NOTEBOOK

Part II   Reactions Between Halogens and Halide Ions

Table 2

REACTANTS (HALOGEN + HALIDE ION)	OBSERVATIONS	REACTION OR NO REACTION	HALOGEN THAT IS STRONGER OXIDIZING AGENT
$Cl_2 + Br^-$			
$Cl_2 + I^-$			
$Br_2 + Cl^-$			
$Br_2 + I^-$			
$I_2 + Cl^-$			
$I_2 + Br^-$			

COMPLETE IN YOUR NOTEBOOK

QUESTIONS

1. Write a balanced equation for the half-reaction for reduction of each metal ion. Then arrange the equations in order of decreasing strength of these ions as oxidizing agents. (This is the same as saying "decreasing ease of reduction of the ion".)

2. Write a balanced equation for the half-reaction for reduction of each halogen molecule, then arrange the equations in order of decreasing strength of these molecules as oxidizing agents.

3. With the added information that Ag^+ is a stronger oxidizing agent than I_2, but a weaker oxidizing agent than Br_2, put all the half-reaction equations together in one list, from strongest oxidizing agent to weakest.

4. For every instance in which a reaction did occur, write the balanced overall redox equation by adding together two half-reaction equations, one for the oxidizing agent (from your list), and one for the reducing agent (by reversing one from the list). In some instances you will have to multiply the half-reaction equation by an appropriate number in order to make the number of electrons equal, so that they cancel out.

FOLLOW-UP QUESTIONS

1. On the basis of the results of this experiment, state whether you would expect a reaction in each of the following situations. Give the balanced equation if a reaction does occur.

   a. Br_2 and Pb
   b. I^- and Zn^{2+}
   c. Cl_2 and Cu
   d. I_2 and Mg.

2. What would happen to sterling silver jewelry (an alloy of 92.5% Ag and 7.5% Cu) if it were exposed to fumes of bromine?

3. Some laboratory waste pipes used to be made of lead. What would happen if waste Cu^{2+} solutions were allowed to go down such pipes?

4. To remove Cu^{2+} wastes from a solution before discharging it down the sink, steel wool (an alloy of iron) can be added. This produces copper metal on the steel wool. The solid copper can then be disposed of safely. Is iron a stronger or weaker reducing agent than copper?

CONCLUSIONS

1. State whether halogens are generally oxidizing or reducing agents, and give the periodic trend you observed.

2. State whether metals are generally oxidizing or reducing agents.

Quantitative Redox Reactions Involving Iodine

Redox reactions are involved in a wide variety of techniques for quantitative analysis of chemical substances. The methods for calculating the amounts of substances involved in these reactions (expressed either as mass in grams or as the volume of a solution of known molarity) were introduced in Chapter 6 of the *Heath Chemistry* text. The balanced equations for many of these reactions are complex, and must be obtained either by adding half-reaction equations or by using the oxidation number method, as outlined in Chapter 21 of the *Heath Chemistry* text.

A substance that is often used in quantitative redox reactions is iodine, I_2. It is easily formed by oxidizing I^-, but the reaction can be reversed just as easily, so a wide variety of chemicals can be reacted with iodine. In addition, it gives a characteristic deep blue color with starch solution even when it is in very low concentrations, making it easy to determine when the iodine is all used up, or when it begins to form. Starch is therefore used as the indicator in these reactions.

In Part I of this experiment you will prepare a solution of potassium iodate (KIO_3) of known concentration. This solution makes a good primary standard in redox titrations, since it is stable and can be obtained very pure. In Part II, known volumes of this solution will have excess H^+ and I^- added, and a reaction will occur in which I_2 is produced in a quantity determined by the moles of KIO_3 present initially. A solution of sodium thiosulfate, $Na_2S_2O_3$, of unknown concentration will then be titrated into the solution, which will react with the I_2. Starch will be added when most of the I_2 has reacted with $S_2O_3^{2-}$, and the titration will be continued until the blue color disappears. The concentration of the $Na_2S_2O_3$ solution can now be calculated. This solution can be used to determine the amount of I_2 in other solutions. The further analyses involved in this experiment are to determine the $[Cu^{2+}]$ in a solution (by adding I^-, which reduces Cu^{2+} to copper(I) iodide, CuI, and becomes I_2 in the process) (Part III) and to determine the amount of vitamin C in a sample by analyzing it with a standard I_2 solution (Part IV).

OBJECTIVES

1. to prepare a solution of potassium iodate, KIO_3, of known molarity

2. to standardize a solution of sodium thiosulfate, $Na_2S_2O_3$, by titrating it against standard KIO_3 (with excess I^-, H^+)

3. to determine the molarity of Cu^{2+} in an unknown sample by reacting it with I^- and titrating the liberated I_2 with standard $S_2O_3^{2-}$

4. to use a standard I_2 solution to determine the mass of ascorbic acid (vitamin C) in a juice sample or a vitamin tablet

MATERIALS

Apparatus

centigram balance

3 beakers (100 mL)

funnel

wash bottle

volumetric flask (250 mL)

buret (50 mL) pipet (25 mL)

Erlenmeyer flask (250 mL)

graduated cylinder (10 mL)

beaker (250 mL)

bottle (500 mL) with stopper

graduated cylinder (100 mL)

lab apron

safety goggles

suction bulb

Reagents

solid potassium iodate, KIO_3

$1M$ potassium iodide, KI

$1M$ sulfuric acid, H_2SO_4

sodium thiosulfate solution,

   $Na_2S_2O_3$ (approx. $0.12M$)

starch solution

copper(II) sulfate solution,

   $CuSO_4$ (unknown concentration)

iodine in potassium iodide

   solution

250 mg or 300 mg vitamin C tablets

orange or other citrus juice

PROCEDURE

Part I   Preparation of a Standard Potassium Iodate Solution

1. Before coming to the laboratory, calculate the mass of KIO_3 required to make up 250 mL of a $0.0200M$ solution of KIO_3.

2. Put on your lab apron and safety goggles.

3. Accurately measure the mass of a clean, dry 100 mL beaker and record it in your copy of Table 1 in your notebook.

4. Place solid KIO_3 in the beaker until you have approximately the mass calculated in Step 1. Record the actual mass accurately in Table 1.

5. Dissolve the KIO_3 in water, and pour the solution through a funnel into a 250 mL volumetric flask. Rinse the beaker twice, and add the rinsings to the flask.

6. Add water until the level of the solution is up to the mark. Stopper the flask, and shake it thoroughly to make the solution homogeneous.

CAUTION: Potassium iodate solution is poisonous. Do not get any in your mouth, and do not swallow any. Always use a suction bulb on the pipet.

Part II   Standardization of Sodium Thiosulfate Solution

1. Transfer the standard KIO_3 solution to a clean, dry 250 mL beaker.

2. Obtain in 100 mL beakers approximately 50 mL each of $1M$ KI, $1M$ H_2SO_4, and starch solution. Label each beaker.

3. Using a suction bulb on your pipet, withdraw 25 mL of the KIO_3 solution and transfer it to a 250 mL Erlenmeyer flask, touching the tip to the side of the flask to ensure that the correct volume is delivered.

4. Add to the flask containing the KIO_3 solution approximately 5 mL of $1M$ KI and 5 mL of $1M$ H_2SO_4. These are excess amounts, so precise measurement is not required. Use a 10 mL graduated cylinder for adding the KI and H_2SO_4. (You will notice that a brown precipitate is formed at first, and that it dissolves again to give a clear brown

CAUTION: Sulfuric acid is very corrosive. Wash any spills and splashes on skin or clothing with plenty of water. Call your teacher.

solution. This behavior is characteristic of iodine, I_2. The amount of precipitate formed is determined by the moles of KIO_3 originally present. The iodine will now be made to react with sodium thiosulfate solution, $Na_2S_2O_3$, in order to determine the molarity of the $Na_2S_2O_3$.)

5. Fill a 500 mL bottle with the approximately $0.12M$ $Na_2S_2O_3$ solution provided. Add about 15 mL of the solution to the buret, rinse, and discard.

6. Fill the buret with $Na_2S_2O_3$, then open the valve to allow some to drain through the tip.

7. Close the valve. The tip should be filled with the solution. Read the initial volume of $Na_2S_2O_3$ in the buret and record it in Table 2.

8. Run the $Na_2S_2O_3$ solution into the flask, swirling constantly, until the brown color has faded to a light yellow. Add 5 mL of starch solution, and continue adding the $Na_2S_2O_3$ drop by drop until the blue-black color disappears. Note that the endpoint is a very precise one, and that it is therefore important not to add the starch too soon. Read the final volume in the buret and record it in Table 2.

9. Repeat Steps 3 to 8 until you obtain consistent results. You now have enough data to calculate the molarity of the $Na_2S_2O_3$ solution.

Part III Determination of the Concentration of an Unknown Solution of Copper(II) Sulfate

CAUTION: Copper(II) sulfate solution is poisonous. Do not get any in your mouth. Do not swallow any.

1. Obtain in a beaker approximately 100 mL of the unknown $CuSO_4$ solution provided. Write down its identifying letter or number if more than one unknown is provided.

2. Using a suction bulb, withdraw into a pipet 25 mL of the $CuSO_4$ solution and transfer it to a 250 mL Erlenmeyer flask. Remember— rinse the pipet with the solution first.

3. Add 10 mL of $1.0M$ KI solution to the $CuSO_4$. Use a graduated cylinder; a precise volume is not required.

4. The cloudy brown material produced in the flask consists of brown I_2 solution and a precipitate of white copper(I) iodide, CuI. The iodine can now be titrated with $Na_2S_2O_3$. The CuI does not interfere with this reaction.

5. Read the initial volume of $Na_2S_2O_3$ in the buret and record it in Table 3. Run the solution into the flask until the brown color has faded to light yellow. Add 5 mL of starch solution, and continue adding $Na_2S_2O_3$ drop by drop until the blue-black color disappears. Read and record the volume in the buret. (A light-colored precipitate of CuI will remain.)

6. Repeat Steps 2 to 5 once or twice more until consistent results are obtained. You now have enough data to calculate the molarity of Cu^{2+}, and, therefore, the molarity of the $CuSO_4$ solution.

Part IV Determination of Amount of Vitamin C in a Sample

1. Obtain in a 250 mL beaker about 200 mL of the solution of iodine (in potassium iodide) provided. You will need to standardize it before doing the rest of this part.

2. Using a suction bulb, withdraw 25 mL of the iodine solution into a pipet and transfer it to a 250 mL Erlenmeyer flask.

3. Refill the buret with the standardized $Na_2S_2O_3$ solution, take the initial reading, and record it in Table 4.

4. Run the $Na_2S_2O_3$ solution into the flask until the brown color of the I_2 fades to pale yellow, add 5 mL starch solution, and continue the titration dropwise until the dark blue color just disappears. Again read the final volume in the buret and record it in Table 4.

5. Repeat Steps 2 to 4 until consistent results are obtained. You now have enough data to calculate the molarity of the I_2 solution.

6. Discard the $Na_2S_2O_3$ solution remaining in the buret, wash the buret with water, then rinse it with the I_2 solution. Discard this, then fill the buret again with I_2, and drain some to refill the tip.

7. Obtain a 250 mg (or 300 mg) tablet of vitamin C (ascorbic acid) and place it in an Erlenmeyer flask. Add about 50 mL of water, and shake to dissolve. Add 5 mL of starch solution.

8. Read the initial volume of the I_2 solution in the buret and record it in Table 5. Then allow it to run into the flask. Swirl constantly, watching for the first appearance of the characteristic dark blue color which stays even after swirling. Again read the final volume of the I_2 solution in the buret and record it in Table 5.

9. Repeat Steps 7 and 8 until consistent results are obtained.

10. Obtain a sample of orange or other citrus juice (or other fruit juice to which vitamin C has been added). Using a graduated cylinder, measure out 100 mL of the juice and pour it into a 250 mL Erlenmeyer flask. Add 5 mL of starch solution.

11. Read the initial volume of I_2 solution in the buret and record it in Table 6. Then run it into the flask, swirling until the first permanent blue-black color is produced. Again read the final volume of I_2 solution in the buret and record it in Table 6.

12. Repeat, using another sample or another juice if requested to do so by your teacher.

13. Before leaving the laboratory, wash your hands thoroughly with soap and water; use a fingernail brush to clean under your fingernails.

CAUTION: Iodine causes burns and is a strong irritant to eyes and skin. If any is spilled on your skin, wash first with sodium thiosulfate solution, then with plenty of water.

REAGENT DISPOSAL

Rinse solutions that are left over in the flask after the titrations down the sink with copious amounts of water. Return any leftover KIO_3, KI, $Na_2S_2O_3$, $CuSO_4$, and I_2 in KI solution to the containers designated by your teacher.

POST LAB DISCUSSION

In order to calculate the results for this experiment, you will need to work out the balanced overall redox equation for each reaction that is occurring, then use the mole relationships in the equation to relate reacting quantities.

The half-reactions occurring in this experiment are as follows:

Production of I_2 from KIO_3, KI, H_2SO_4:	$IO_3^- + 6H^+ + 5e^-$	$\rightarrow \frac{1}{2}I_2 + 3H_2O$
	$2I^-$	$\rightarrow I_2 + 2e^-$
Standardization of $Na_2S_2O_3$:	$2S_2O_3^{2-}$	$\rightarrow S_4O_6^{2-} + 2e^-$
	$I_2 + 2e^-$	$\rightarrow 2I^-$
Production of I_2 from Cu^{2+} by I^-:	$Cu^{2+} + I^- + e^-$	$\rightarrow CuI$
	$2I^-$	$\rightarrow I_2 + 2e^-$

You need not show an equation for the reaction of ascorbic acid (vitamin C, $C_6H_8O_6$) with I_2. They react in a 1 to 1 mole ratio.

The deep blue-black color formed by starch and iodine is very useful in a variety of situations. Its formation is not really a chemical reaction—the iodine molecules just happen to fit closely inside the long spiralling starch molecule and interact strongly with it. The combination is unstable above 50°C. You encountered this blue-black color in an earlier experiment on rates of reactions (18B). It is interesting to note that here you are using starch to test for the presence of iodine, but in food chemistry the reverse occurs—iodine solution is used to test for the presence of starch. You may have performed such a test in an earlier science course.

Note that iodine is only slightly soluble in water, but does dissolve well if I^- ions are present. The reaction that occurs is $I_2 + I^- \rightleftharpoons I_3^-$. However, the complex I_3^- breaks down very readily when any chemical is present that can react with I_2 (such as $S_2O_3^{2-}$), and the solution therefore acts as though it were a solution of I_2.

DATA AND OBSERVATIONS

It would be a good idea to have these tables ready in your notebook before coming to the laboratory.

Part I   Preparation of a Standard Potassium Iodate Solution

Table 1   Preparing Standard KIO_3 Solution

Mass of potassium iodate, KIO_3, (g) required for 250.0 mL of $0.0200M$ solution (calculated)	
Mass of beaker (g)	
Mass of beaker + KIO_3 (g)	COMPLETE IN YOUR NOTEBOOK
Mass of KIO_3 (g)	

Part II   Standardization of Sodium Thiosulfate Solution

Table 2   Volume of $Na_2S_2O_3$ Needed to React with Iodine from 25.00 mL of KIO_3

	TRIAL 1	TRIAL 2	TRIAL 3	TRIAL 4 (if necessary)
Initial volume of $Na_2S_2O_3$				
Final volume of $Na_2S_2O_3$		COMPLETE IN YOUR NOTEBOOK		COMPLETE IN YOUR NOTEBOOK
Volume of $Na_2S_2O_3$ required				
Average volume of $Na_2S_2O_3$				

Part III Determination of the Concentration of an Unknown Solution of Copper(II) Sulfate

Table 3 Volume of $Na_2S_2O_3$ Needed to React with Iodine from 25.00 mL of $CuSO_4$

UNKNOWN CuSO₄ SOLUTION #____	TRIAL 1	TRIAL 2	TRIAL 3	TRIAL 4 (if necessary)
Initial volume of $Na_2S_2O_3$				
Final volume of $Na_2S_2O_3$				
Volume of $Na_2S_2O_3$ required				
Average volume of $Na_2S_2O_3$				

Part IV Determination of Amount of Vitamin C in a Sample

Table 4 Volume of $Na_2S_2O_3$ Needed to React with 25.00 mL of I_2 solution

	TRIAL 1	TRIAL 2	TRIAL 3	TRIAL 4 (if necessary)
Initial volume of $Na_2S_2O_3$				
Final volume of $Na_2S_2O_3$				
Volume of $Na_2S_2O_3$ required				
Average volume of $Na_2S_2O_3$				

Table 5 Volume of I_2 Solution Needed to React with Ascorbic Acid (Vitamin C). Mass of Vitamin C in Tablet = ____ mg

	TRIAL 1	TRIAL 2	TRIAL 3 (if necessary)
Initial volume of I_2			
Final volume of I_2			
Volume of I_2 required			
Average volume of I_2			

Table 6 Volume of I_2 Solution Needed to React with Juice

	TRIAL 1	TRIAL 2	TRIAL 3
Type of juice			
Volume of juice			
Initial volume of I_2			
Final volume of I_2			
Volume of I_2 used			

QUESTIONS AND CALCULATIONS

Part I   Preparation of a Standard Potassium Iodate Solution

1. Calculate the concentration of KIO_3 solution formed when you dissolved your calculated mass of KIO_3 in water and made the volume up to 250.0 mL.

2. Calculate the number of moles of KIO_3 (and therefore of IO_3^-) in 25.00 mL of this solution.

Part II   Standardization of Sodium Thiosulfate Solution

1. Work out the overall redox equation for the reaction of IO_3^-, I^-, and H^+ to give I_2.

2. Work out the overall redox equation for the reaction of $S_2O_3^-$ and I_2 to give $S_4O_6^{2-}$ (tetrathionate ion) and I^-.

3. State the relationship between moles of IO_3^- and moles of $S_2O_3^{2-}$, working through moles of I_2.

4. From this relationship and the number of moles of KIO_3 in 25.00 mL of solution, calculate the number of moles of $S_2O_3^{2-}$ with which the KIO_3 reacts..

5. Knowing the average volume and the number of moles of $S_2O_3^{2-}$ used, calculate the $[S_2O_3^{2-}]$.

Part III   Determination of the Concentration of an Unknown Solution of Copper(II) Sulfate

1. Work out the overall redox equation for the reaction $Cu^{2+} + I^- \rightarrow CuI(s) + I_2$

2. Recalling from Part II the relationship between moles of I_2 and moles of $S_2O_3^{2-}$, and using the equation in item 1 above, state the relationship between moles of Cu^{2+} and moles of $S_2O_3^{2-}$.

3. From the average volume (from Part III) and the known concentration (from Part II) of $S_2O_3^{2-}$ used, calculate the number of moles of $S_2O_3^{2-}$ used.

4. Calculate the number of moles of Cu^{2+} originally present.

5. Calculate $[Cu^{2+}]$ in the original sample from the number of moles and the volume used.

Part IV   Determination of Amount of Vitamin C in a Sample

1. Calculate the number of moles of $S_2O_3^{2-}$ used from the average volume used and the molarity from Part II.

2. Calculate the number of moles of I_2 present, using the relationship obtained in Part II.

3. Calculate $[I_2]$ from the number of moles used and the volume in litres.

4. From the average volume of I_2 solution used in the vitamin C titration, calculate the number of moles of I_2 requred to react with the vitamin C.

5. Recalling that it was stated in the Post Lab Discussion that vitamin C and I_2 react in a 1 to 1 mole ratio, and that vitamin C has the formula $C_6H_8O_6$, calculate the mass of vitamin C present, in milligrams.

6. Compare your result with the rated amount of vitamin C for that tablet, and calculate the percentage deviation between your result and the rated amount.

7. In the same manner, calculate the number of milligrams of vitamin C in 100 mL of each juice sample tested.

FOLLOW-UP QUESTIONS

1. Vitamin C was oxidized by iodine in this experiment. By referring to the table of standard reduction potentials in Appendix 5, explain why the vitamin C content of foods is decreased on exposure to air.

2. A chemist who wishes to analyze a sample of hydrated copper(II) nitrate finds that when a sample with a mass of 0.67 g is dissolved in water and excess KI solution is added, 17.7 mL of $0.128 M$ $Na_2S_2O_3$ are required to react with the liberated iodine. What is the number of moles of water in the hydrated crystal?

3. A sample of apple juice states on the label "Contains not less than 35 mg/100 mL of ascorbic acid (vitamin C)." A 25 mL sample was titrated with $0.0080 M$ I_2 solution and found to require 6.55 mL until the starch indicator turned blue. Does this sample meet the stated concentration?

CONCLUSION

State the results of Objectives 3 and 4.

Quantitative Redox Reactions Involving Permanganate Ion

A common laboratory oxidizing agent is the permanganate ion, MnO_4^-, which is usually provided by the compound potassium permanganate, $KMnO_4$. It is especially useful for quantitative redox reactions because the permanganate in solution is an intense purple color, but when reduced all the way to the 2+ state in Mn^{2+} becomes virtually colorless, thereby acting as its own indicator. A sample of a reducing agent can therefore be titrated with $KMnO_4$ solution, and the faint purple color that remains even after the solution is swirled makes the completion of the reaction apparent. You may think that $KMnO_4$ will not be highly accurate in showing the completion of the reaction, since it must be left over to be seen as a purple color. However, its color is very intense; the $0.020 M$ solution you will be using is a very dark purple, and its color can still be detected when 1 mL of the solution is added to 2 L of water, that is, when $[MnO_4^-] = 1.0 \times 10^{-5} M$. This figure represents only 0.05% of the original concentration, which is certainly accurate enough for most situations.

Potassium permanganate is obtainable in analytical reagent quality, so a solution of it can be made up to accurate concentration from a known mass of crystals. However, the solution should be freshly prepared because after a time, any potassium permanganate solution decomposes to a certain extent, and a brown coloration of MnO_2 appears on the side of the container.

The Mn in the permanganate ion has an oxidation number of 7+; in the manganese(II) ion it has an oxidation number of 2+. It has still other common oxidation states; 6+ in the manganate ion (MnO_4^{2-}), which is green, and 4+ in manganese dioxide, which is brown. In order to make sure that all the permanganate ion is reduced completely to Mn^{2+} and not some other state, you must follow the instructions in the experiment carefully. In Part I of the procedure you will look in a qualitative way at the conditions which result in these different compounds, before you go on to use $KMnO_4$ quantitatively in Parts II and III. In Part II you will determine the $[Fe^{2+}]$ in an unknown solution (or the molar mass of an unknown iron compound), then in Part III you will determine the concentration of a solution of hydrogen peroxide, H_2O_2. Your teacher will provide you with a solution of potassium permanganate of known concentration.

OBJECTIVES

1. to determine the conditions under which $KMnO_4$ is reduced completely to Mn^{2+}

2. to determine the $[Fe^{2+}]$ in an unknown solution (or the molar mass of an unknown compound containing Fe^{2+})

3. to determine the $[H_2O_2]$ in a solution of hydrogen peroxide

MATERIALS

Apparatus

buret (50 mL)
stand
buret clamp
Erlenmeyer flask
  (250 mL)
3 test tubes
  (18 mm × 150 mm)
test-tube rack
beaker (250 mL)
beaker (100 mL)

pipet (25 mL)
suction bulb
graduated cylinder
  (10 mL)
centigram balance
medicine dropper
filter funnel
safety goggles
lab apron

Reagents

standard solution of
  $KMnO_4$ (approx. 0.02M)
0.050M Na_2SO_3
3M H_2SO_4
6M NaOH
unknown Fe^{2+} solution
  (or unknown solid
  containing Fe^{2+})
hydrogen peroxide
  solution (approx. 3%)

PROCEDURE

Part I Preliminary Investigation of $KMnO_4$ as an Oxidizing Agent

1. Put on your lab apron and safety goggles.

write Molarity on Bottle

2. Obtain in a 250 mL beaker about ~~150~~ mL of the solution of $KMnO_4$ provided. Note its concentration. *75 mL*

3. Obtain three 18 mm × 150 mm test tubes and place them in the rack. To each add 1 mL of the $KMnO_4$ solution.

4. Next, to one test tube add ~~2 mL~~ *2 drops* of 3M H_2SO_4, to the second add 2 mL of water, and to the third add 2 mL of 6M NaOH.

5. To each test tube add 2 mL of 0.05M Na_2SO_3. Record your observations in your copy of Table 1 in your notebook.

CAUTION: Potassium permanganate ($KMnO_4$) solution is a strong irritant, and will stain skin and clothing. Wash any spills with plenty of water.

CAUTION: Sulfuric acid is very corrosive. Do not get any on your skin, in your eyes, or on your clothing. Wash any spills with plenty of water, and call your teacher.

CAUTION: Sodium hydroxide solution (especially the 6M concentration used here) is very caustic. Do not get any on your skin or in your eyes. Wash any spills immediately with plenty of water. Call your teacher.

CAUTION: Sodium sulfite solution (Na_2SO_3) is a strong irritant to skin and eyes. Wash any spills with plenty of water.

Part II Determining the Concentration of a Solution of Fe^{2+}

1. Using the filter funnel, pour about 15 mL of $KMnO_4$ solution into your buret. Rinse and discard.

2. Fill up the buret with the $KMnO_4$, and allow some to drain in order to fill the tip. Read the volume.

CAUTION: *Ingestion of Fe²⁺ solution can cause intestinal disorders. Always use a suction bulb on your pipet. Do not get any in your mouth. Do not swallow any.*

3. Obtain about 85 mL of unknown Fe^{2+} solution from your teacher. Use a 100 mL beaker. Write down any identifying letter or number if more than one unknown is provided.

4. Using a suction bulb on your pipet, withdraw about 5 mL of the Fe^{2+} solution, and rinse inside the pipet with it. Discard. Refill the pipet to the 25 mL mark with more Fe^{2+} solution, and transfer to a 250 mL Erlenmeyer flask.

clean

volume

10mL 5. Add 10 mL of $3M\ H_2SO_4$ to the flask, then allow the $KMnO_4$ solution to run into the flask, swirling constantly.

4mL

6. When the purple color starts to take a longer time to disperse, slow down the addition of the $KMnO_4$ until you add it a drop at a time. Record the volume in the buret when the faint purple color first stays in the flask.

7. Repeat once or twice if necessary, to obtain consistent results. Record your observations in your copy of Table 2.

8. If instead of using an unknown solution you are instructed to use a particular mass of an unknown solid containing Fe^{2+}, then measure the mass accurately, dissolve the solid in about 30 mL of water, add 10 mL of $3M\ H_2SO_4$, and carry out the titration in the same manner as described above.

Part III   Determining the Concentration of an H_2O_2 Solution

CAUTION: *Hydrogen peroxide is corrosive. It causes burns and is an irritant to skin. Wash any spills with plenty of water.*

1. Obtain in a clean, dry test tube about 5 mL of hydrogen peroxide (H_2O_2) solution, labelled 3% or "10 volume". (This is the type available in drug stores as an antiseptic.)

2. Obtain a clean, dry 250 mL flask and measure its mass.

3. Using a medicine dropper, place 20 to 30 drops of hydrogen peroxide in the flask (about 1 mL to 1.5 mL) and again measure the mass.

10 15

15

4. Add about 30 mL of water and 10 mL of $3M\ H_2SO_4$.

5

5. Read the volume of $KMnO_4$ in the buret (after refilling if necessary), then run the solution in as before to the first appearance of a pale purple color. Record the volume in your copy of Table 3.

weight it

6. Repeat 1 or 2 more times, as necessary, to obtain consistent results. Record all observations in Table 3.

7. Before you leave the laboratory, wash your hands thoroughly with soap and water; use a fingernail brush to clean under your nails.

REAGENT DISPOSAL

Place any unused solutions of $KMnO_4$ and Fe^{2+} in the designated waste containers. Solutions left in the flask after the titrations may safely be rinsed down the sink with copious amounts of water.

POST LAB DISCUSSION

In order to calculate the results for this experiment, you first need to work out the balanced overall redox equation for each reaction. Then you will use the mole relationships in each equation to relate the quantities that are reacting.

The following are the half-reactions occurring in this experiment:

Reduction of MnO_4^-:

In acid:	$MnO_4^- + 8H^+ + 5e^-$	$\rightarrow$ $Mn^{2+} + 4H_2O$
In neutral solution:	$MnO_4^- + 4H^+ + 3e^-$	$\rightarrow$ $MnO_2 + 2H_2O$
In base:	$MnO_4^- + e^-$	$\rightarrow$ MnO_4^{2-}

Oxidation of SO_3^{2-}: $\qquad SO_3^{2-} + H_2O \qquad \rightarrow SO_4^{2-} + 2H^+ + 2e^-$

Oxidation of Fe^{2+}: $\qquad Fe^{2+} \qquad\qquad \rightarrow Fe^{3+} + e^-$

Oxidation of H_2O_2: $\qquad H_2O_2 \qquad\qquad \rightarrow O_2 + 2H^+ + 2e^-$

Remember that the titrations in Parts II and III were done in acidic solution.

DATA AND OBSERVATIONS

It would be a good idea to have these tables ready in your notebook before coming to the laboratory.

Part I   Preliminary Investigation of KMnO₄ as an Oxidizing Agent

Table 1   Preliminary Investigation of $KMnO_4$ as an Oxidizing Agent

TYPE OF SOLUTION	COLOR	ION OR MOLECULE PRESENT
Acidic ($3M$ H_2SO_4)		
Neutral (water)		
Basic ($6M$ NaOH)		

Part II   Determining the Concentration of a Solution of Fe²⁺

Table 2   Volume of $KMnO_4$ to React with 25.00 mL of Fe^{2+} Solution

UNKNOWN # , [KMnO₄] = M	TRIAL 1	TRIAL 2	TRIAL 3 (if necessary)
Initial volume of KMnO₄ (mL)			
Final volume of KMnO₄ (mL)			
Volume of KMnO₄ required (mL)			
Average volume (mL)			

(If you used a solid Fe²⁺ unknown, add a row indicating the mass used.)

Part III   Determining the Concentration of an H₂O₂ Solution

Table 3   Volume of KMnO₄ to React with H₂O₂ Solution

[KMnO₄] = M	TRIAL 1	TRIAL 2	TRIAL 3 (if necessary)
Mass of empty flask (g)	79.70g	79.19	79.21
Mass of flask + H₂O₂ (g)	80.21		79.75
Mass of H₂O₂ (g)	0.51		0.54
Initial volume of KMnO₄ (mL)	5.1	11.3	16.7
Final volume of KMnO₄ (mL)	11.3	16.5	22.6
Volume of KMnO₄ used (mL)	6.2	5.2	5.9

QUESTIONS AND CALCULATIONS

Part I   Preliminary Investigation of KMnO₄ as an Oxidizing Agent

1. Write the overall redox equation for MnO_4^- reacting with SO_3^{2-} to give Mn^{2+} and SO_4^{2-} in acidic solution.

2. Write the overall redox equation for MnO_4^- reacting with SO_3^{2-} to give MnO_2 and SO_4^{2-}. (This occurred in neutral solution, but H^+ ions will appear in the final equation.

3. Write the overall redox equation for MnO_4^- reacting with SO_3^{2-} to give MnO_4^{2-} and SO_4^{2-} (in basic solution).

4. Explain why titrations using permanganate are performed in acid solution.

Part II   Determining the Concentration of a Solution of Fe²⁺

1. Write the balanced overall redox equation for MnO_4^- reacting with Fe^{2+} in acid solution to give Mn^{2+} and Fe^{3+}.

2. From the average volume of MnO_4^- used and the molarity of the solution provided by your teacher, calculate the number of moles of MnO_4^-.

3. Using the mole relationship given by the balanced equation, calculate the number of moles of Fe^{2+} used.

4. Calculate the [Fe²⁺] from the number of moles and the volume of the solution (in litres). (If you used a solid sample, calculate the molar mass or percent of Fe instead, as directed by your teacher.)

Part III Determining the Concentration of an H_2O_2 Solution

1. Write the balanced overall redox equation for MnO_4^- reacting with H_2O_2 in acid solution to give Mn^{2+} and O_2.

2. For the first titration, calculate the number of moles of MnO_4^- from the volume and the molarity.

3. Using the mole relationship given by the balanced equation, calculate the number of moles of H_2O_2 oxidized, and convert to grams using the molar mass of H_2O_2.

4. Using the calculated mass of H_2O_2 above and the mass of the solution from Table 3, calculate the percent of H_2O_2 in the solution.

5. Repeat questions 2 to 4 for each of the other titrations performed, and average your answers for the percent of H_2O_2 in the solution.

FOLLOW-UP QUESTIONS

1. A bottle containing a standard solution of $KMnO_4$ is found to have brown stains on the inside. Why will this $KMnO_4$ be of no further use for quantitative experiments?

2. Hydrogen peroxide is usually labelled 3%, meaning 3 g/100 mL. Assuming that the solution has a density of 1 g/mL, what is the percent deviation between your calculated concentration and the stated 3% figure?

3. Hydrogen peroxide breaks down easily to give water and oxygen as follows:

$$2H_2O_2(aq) \quad \rightarrow \quad 2H_2O(l) + O_2(g)$$

Bottles of hydrogen peroxide are sometimes labelled as 10 volume as well as 3%. This means the volume of oxygen that can be liberated is 10 times the volume of the solution. Remembering that 1 mol of gas occupies 22.4 L at STP, calculate the volume of oxygen at STP that could be produced from 1 L of a 3% solution. Is 10 L a good approximation to your answer?

4. Many different materials can catalyze the breakdown of H_2O_2. (If your dropper is not clean, you may find bubbles of oxygen forming in the dropper!) However, high temperature alone can cause sufficient pressure to build up because of released oxygen to explode a glass container. For this reason, hydrogen peroxide is usually purchased in plastic bottles which often have a venting cap to allow gas to escape. Under what conditions should hydrogen peroxide be stored?

CONCLUSION

State the results of Objectives 2 and 3.

Electrochemical Cells

Electrochemical cells are extensively used in our society. They come in many shapes and sizes and have many applications. For instance, motor vehicles have electrochemical cells in the form of storage batteries that are used to start the engine. Another type of electrochemical cell, the dry cell, is commonly used to provide electrical energy for such things as flashlights, toys, watches, calculators, and smoke alarms. A less common electrochemical cell, the fuel cell, has recently received attention because of its use as a source of electricity and drinking water on the space shuttles.

Although the types of electrochemical cells are varied, the operation of all types is based on the same principle — spontaneous redox reactions. The chemistry involved is the same as that for a redox reaction between species in the same container. However, an electrochemical cell is set up so that the reacting species are not permitted to come in contact with each other. Electrons are transferred from one species to another by means of an external circuit. In this external circuit, the energy of the electrons is "tapped" or put to work, to illuminate a light bulb, for instance.

In this experiment, you will construct laboratory models of three electrochemical cells: a zinc-lead cell in Part I, a lead-copper cell in Part II, and a zinc-copper cell in Part III. In Part IV you will investigate the effect of changing solution concentration on cell voltage. Although your cells will not look like those commonly used, they should enable you to understand the theory of the operation of electrochemical cells better. Before beginning this experiment, you should take the time to review in your textbook the terminology and theory associated with electrochemical cells.

OBJECTIVES

1. to become familiar with the construction and operation of electrochemical cells

2. to predict the reactions and voltages that should result

3. to construct three electrochemical cells and measure their voltages

4. to observe the effect of non-standard conditions on voltage

MATERIALS

Apparatus	Reagents
2 beakers (150 mL)	metal strips (copper, zinc, lead)
U tube	$0.5M$ copper(II) nitrate ($Cu(NO_3)_2$) solution
cotton batting	$0.5M$ zinc nitrate ($Zn(NO_3)_2$) solution
2 wire leads with clips	$0.5M$ lead(II) nitrate ($Pb(NO_3)_2$) solution
voltmeter (0 V–3 V D.C.)	$0.5M$ potassium nitrate (KNO_3) solution
steel wool	$1.0M$ sodium sulfide (Na_2S) solution

PROCEDURE

Part I   Making a Zinc-Lead Cell

1. Put on your lab apron and safety goggles.

2. Obtain 80 mL of each of zinc nitrate and lead(II) nitrate solution in separate 150 mL beakers. Label these beakers so that you do not get them confused.

3. Prepare a salt bridge by filling a glass U tube with potassium nitrate solution and plugging both ends with a small clump of cotton batting. Do not allow air to become trapped in the tube. Carefully invert the U tube and place it in the two beakers, as shown in Figure 21D-1.

CAUTION: Copper(II) nitrate and lead(II) nitrate are extremely poisonous. Do not get any in your mouth; wash any spills or splashes away with plenty of water.

Figure 21D-1 *Construction of an electro-chemical cell.*

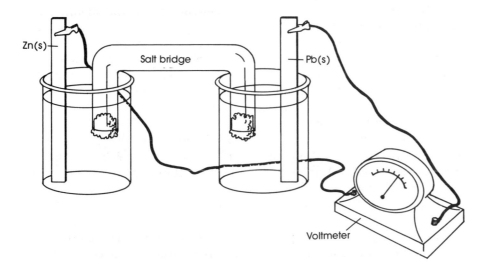

4. Obtain a zinc strip and a lead strip, clean the surfaces with steel wool and a paper towel, and rinse them in water. Place the zinc strip in the zinc nitrate solution and the lead strip in the lead(II) nitrate solution.

5. Connect a voltmeter to the zinc-lead cell as in Figure 21D-1. Connect the leads so that a positive reading results on the voltmeter. Record the measured voltage as soon as the circuit is connected. Make a labelled sketch of your electrochemical cell.

6. While the cell is operating, consult a table of standard reduction potentials and decide at which cell oxidation is occurring. Label this half cell as the anode on your sketch. Before you label the other cell the cathode, first convince yourself that your cell has all the chemical species needed for a redox reaction.

7. Indicate the direction of electron flow (from anode to cathode) on your diagram.

8. Use the table of standard reduction potentials to calculate the theoretical standard state voltage that should result in a zinc-lead cell.

9. Before dismantling the cell, observe the effect of removing the salt bridge or any electrode.

10. Take the cell apart and save the zinc and lead solutions and electrodes for Parts II and III of the experiment.

11. Dismantle the salt bridge, following the instructions for reagent disposal.

Part II   Making a Lead-Copper Cell

1. Obtain 80 mL of copper(II) nitrate solution in a 150 mL beaker. Also obtain a copper strip.

2. Prepare a new salt bridge to avoid contaminating the half-cell solutions.

3. Use the Procedure from Part I to construct and study a lead-copper cell. Here, place the lead strip in the lead(II) nitrate, and the copper strip in the copper(II) nitrate. Remember to record all observations and sketch your lead-copper cell.

Part III   Making a Zinc-Copper Cell

1. In this part you will construct a zinc-copper cell, using the Procedure from Part I. This time you will place the zinc strip in the zinc nitrate and the copper strip in the copper(II) nitrate. You will need to prepare a new salt bridge. Record all observations, and sketch your zinc-copper cell.

2. Disconnect the voltmeter and save the zinc-copper cell for Part IV.

Part IV   The Effect of Solution Concentration on the Cell Voltage of a Zinc-Copper Cell

CAUTION: Sodium sulfide is corrosive; in solution, it reacts with acids to form H_2S gas, which has an offensive odor and is poisonous. Part IV should thus be done only under well-ventilated conditions.

1. Reconnect the zinc-copper cell from Part III and record the initial voltage in a copy of Table 1 in your notebook.

2. Slowly add 40 mL of $1M$ sodium sulfide (Na_2S) solution to the zinc nitrate solution and wait for a few minutes. Record your observations, as well as the new voltage, in Table 1.

3. Repeat Step 2 with the copper half-cell.

4. Clean up and put away all apparatus, following the reagent disposal instructions. Clean the electrodes once again with steel wool before putting them away.

5. Before leaving the laboratory, wash your hands thoroughly with soap and water; use a fingernail brush to clean under your fingernails.

REAGENT DISPOSAL

Use tweezers to remove the cotton plugs from the salt bridge and place them in the designated container. Rinse the KNO_3 solution from the salt bridge down the sink with copious amounts of water. The $Pb(NO_3)_2$ solution should not be contaminated, so it can be poured back into its original container. The remaining $Zn(NO_3)_2$ and $Cu(NO_3)_2$ solutions cannot be re-used; they now contain S^{2-} ions and should be poured into the designated waste container. Return any remaining Na_2S solution to its bottle.

POST LAB DISCUSSION

In any operating electrochemical cell, there will be a net redox reaction, with oxidation taking place at the anode and reduction at the cathode. The specific oxidation and reduction reactions for a cell can be determined by examining a table of standard reduction potentials. (See Appendix 2.) Consider the following example of a magnesium-copper cell using solutions of magnesium nitrate and copper(II) nitrate:

anode (oxidation):	$Mg(s) \rightarrow Mg^{2+} + 2e^-$;	$E° = +2.37$ V
cathode (reduction):	$Cu^{2+} + 2e^- \rightarrow Cu(s)$;	$E° = +0.34$ V
overall:	$Cu^{2+} + Mg(s) \rightarrow Mg^{2+} + Cu(s)$;	$E°_{cell} = +2.71$ V

These half-reactions were chosen as a pair so that the overall cell voltage would be positive. If the reverse reactions had been chosen, then the cell voltage would have been –2.71 V, representing a non-spontaneous reaction uncharacteristic of electrochemical cells.

Once the anode and cathode reactions have been determined, all the other aspects of cell operation, such as direction of electron flow and cation/anion migration, fall into place.

The results in Part IV which involve the addition of Na_2S are another example of Le Chatelier's principle. The voltage changes can be explained by equilibrium shifts of the overall redox reaction. The key to interpreting these shifts is to examine the table of solubilities in Appendix 2 in order to explain the precipitates that formed.

You may have noticed that the measured voltage is usually less than the theoretical voltage. Some internal resistances of the cell can account for this effect. For example, the salt bridge offers a resistance to the flow of ions, thereby decreasing the voltage.

DATA AND OBSERVATIONS

Part I   Making a Zinc-Lead Cell

Part II   Making a Lead-Copper Cell

Part III   Making a Zinc-Copper Cell

For each cell you constructed, you should have a labelled sketch similar to Figure 21D-2. All solutions and electrodes, and the anode, cathode, and direction of electron flow should be labelled in each. Also, the measured voltage should be recorded for each cell, and the theoretical standard state voltage calculated.

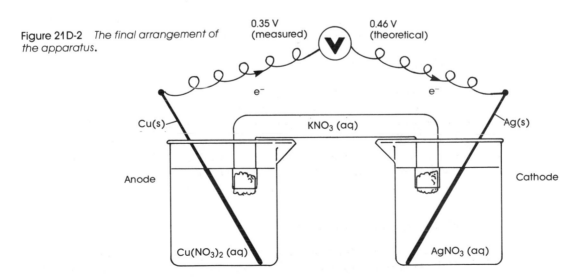

Figure 21D-2   *The final arrangement of the apparatus.*

Part IV The Effect of Solution Concentration on the Cell Voltage of a Zinc-Copper Cell

Table 1

	OBSERVATIONS	VOLTAGE
Initial voltage		
Adding Na₂S to Zn half-cell		
Adding Na₂S to Cu half-cell		

QUESTIONS AND CALCULATIONS

1. For each cell you constructed, write the equations for the following:
   a. the anode half reaction
   b. the cathode half reaction
   c. the overall cell reaction

   Calculate the theoretical standard state cell voltage.

2. a. When Na_2S was added to the Zn half-cell, what precipitate formed?
   b. What change in voltage occurred?
   c. Referring to Le Chatelier's principle, explain why this voltage change occurred.

3. a. When Na_2S was added to the Cu half-cell, what precipitate formed?
   b. What change in voltage occurred?
   c. Referring to Le Chatelier's principle, explain why this voltage change occurred.

4. What effect did removing the salt bridge have on the operation of each electrochemical cell? Explain.

5. In Parts I, II, and III, how did your measured voltages compare to the theoretical voltages? Was there any general pattern?

FOLLOW-UP QUESTIONS

1. Design and draw a diagram of an electrochemical cell that has a magnesium anode and a theoretical standard state voltage of +3.17 V. Label the diagram as you did those in this experiment.

2. Explain why you should not expect an electrochemical cell to operate for an unlimited period of time.

3. Illustrate the migration of all anions and cations in a zinc-copper cell by drawing a labelled diagram of such a cell. What general statement can you make concerning the directions of flow of anions and cations?

4. Predict which ions, Cu^{2+} or Zn^{2+}, should migrate into the salt bridge in question 3. How could you test your prediction?

5. Predict the voltage reading of a zinc-copper cell when the cell reaction reaches equilibrium.

CONCLUSION

State the results of Objective 3.

Electrolytic Cells

In the experiment on electrochemical cells (21D) you assembled apparatus and reagents so that spontaneous redox reactions occurred and produced electrical energy. Here, a chemical change produced electrical energy. Electrolytic cells involve processes opposite to those in electrochemical cells; that is, electrolytic cells require an *external* source of electrical energy (a battery or D.C. power supply) that "forces" a nonspontaneous redox reaction to occur. In electrolytic cells, electrical energy produces a chemical change.

Electrolytic cells are important to the chemical process industries involved in the production of pure metals and gases. Another application of electrolytic cells is in the protection and beautification of metals by silver plating or chrome plating.

Although all electrolytic cells are similar in their assembly, they vary as to how complex it is to interpret the reactions that take place. For example, a cell having more chemical species capable of reacting is more complicated with respect to determining which species react than a cell having fewer chemical species. In order to classify electrolytic cells according to such complexities, it is convenient to describe them as Type 1, Type 2, or Type 3 cells. A Type 1 cell contains unreactive electrodes (usually carbon or platinum) and a molten salt. This type of cell is awkward to operate in a school laboratory since molten salts require extremely high temperatures. A Type 2 cell also contains unreactive electrodes, but the substance to be electrolyzed is part of an aqueous ionic solution. A Type 3 cell is the most complicated cell with regard to interpreting its operation. It contains not only an aqueous ionic solution, but also reactive electrodes.

In this experiment, you will construct and operate both Type 2 and Type 3 electrolytic cells. In Parts I and II, you will carry out an experiment involving the electrolysis of KI and $ZnSO_4$ solutions. Then in Part III you will copper plate a metal object such as a key—remember to bring a suitable object to the laboratory for this part.

For each cell, it will be helpful if you can identify the anode and cathode in advance. In electrolytic cells, the electrodes are determined by the external power supply, which has two terminals, one positive and one negative. Since the negative terminal has a surplus of electrons, it will provide this surplus to any electrode to which it is connected. This electrode consequently becomes the cathode of the electrolytic cell, since reduction can occur only where there is a supply of electrons. By identifying the anode and cathode in advance, you will be able to make appropriate observations at each electrode.

Before beginning this experiment, you should take the time to review the terminology and theory associated with electrolytic cells.

OBJECTIVES

1. to electrolyze a KI solution using carbon electrodes

2. to electrolyze a $ZnSO_4$ solution using carbon electrodes

3. to copper plate a metal object

4. to interpret the products of each electrolytic cell with anode and cathode half-reactions

MATERIALS

Apparatus

U tube
ring stand
buret clamp
250 mL beaker
electrode holder
2 cylindrical carbon
  electrodes
1 copper electrode
  (strip)

copper wire (bare)
6 V battery *or*
  D.C. power supply
2 wire leads with
  alligator clips
steel wool
lab apron
safety goggles

Reagents

1.0*M* KI
1.0*M* ZnSO₄
1.0*M* CuSO₄
phenolphthalein
  solution

PROCEDURE

As a matter of habit, you should clean all electrodes before and after each use. Use a piece of steel wool to remove any surface coatings, then wipe the electrodes clean with paper towel.

Part I Electrolysis of 1.0*M* KI

1. Put on your lab apron and safety goggles.

2. Fill a clean U tube with 1.0*M* KI solution, so that the solution level is about 2.0 cm from the top. Add 5 drops of phenolphthalein to each side of the tube.

3. Place a cylindrical carbon electrode in each side of the U tube and clip a wire end to each electrode. (See Figure 21E-1.) Do not allow the metal ends of the wire leads to contact the solution.

Figure 21E-1 *Electrolysis of KI(aq)*

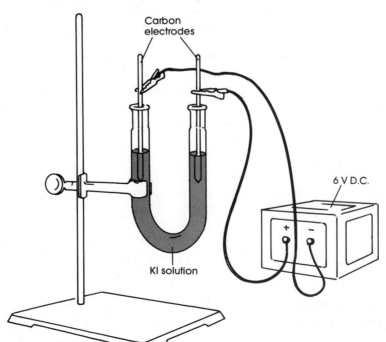

4. Connect the wire leads to a 6 V battery or D.C. power supply. Observe what happens at each electrode during the next several minutes. Record your observations in your copy of Table 1 in your notebook while the cell is operating. Use the table of standard reduction potentials located in Appendix 5 to determine the anode and cathode half-reactions.

5. Disconnect the wire leads, first from the power supply, then from the electrodes.

6. Clean up your apparatus, following the reagent disposal instructions.

Part II Electrolysis of 1.0M ZnSO$_4$

1. Obtain 150 mL of 1.0M ZnSO$_4$ solution in a clean 250 mL beaker.

2. Place an electrode holder on this beaker and insert a cylindrical carbon electrode in each side of the holder. Connect a wire lead to each electrode. (See Figure 21E-2.)

Figure 21E-2 *Electrolysis of ZnSO$_4$(aq)*

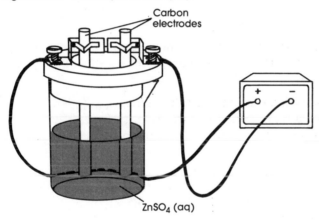

3. Repeat Steps 3, 4, and 5 from Part I, but record all observations in Table 2. Do not operate the cell longer than 5 min to 10 min, as the carbon electrodes will probably start to flake apart due to a physical, rather than chemical, process.

Part III Copper Plating

1. Obtain 200 mL of 1.0M CuSO$_4$ solution in a clean 250 mL beaker.

2. You should have selected a metal object to be plated, such as a coin or a key. Prepare the object for plating by polishing it with steel wool. The idea is to remove any surface film such as oxides or finger grease, so that the copper plating will adhere more effectively. After cleaning the object, avoid touching it with your fingers.

3. Place an electrode holder on a second, empty beaker. Insert a strip of copper metal into one side of the electrode holder.

4. Use a piece of bare copper wire to suspend the metal object from the other terminal of the electrode holder. (See Figure 21E-3.) Ensure that the metal object is completely below the 200 mL mark on the beaker.

Figure 21E-3 *Copper-plating apparatus*

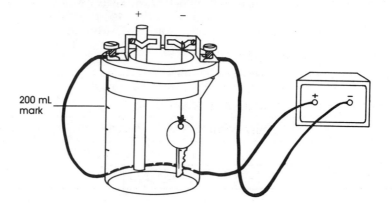

5. Using a wire lead, connect the object to be plated to the NEGATIVE terminal of the power supply. Connect the copper electrode to the POSITIVE terminal and turn on the power supply. Finally, pour the 200 mL of $CuSO_4$ solution into the cell. Observe what happens at each electrode over the next several minutes, and record your observations in Table 3 while the cell is operating.

6. Disconnect the wire leads, first from the power supply, then from the electrodes.

7. Remove both electrodes from the solution. Rinse the object, then pat it dry with a paper towel. You may wish to try polishing the plated surface with a fine abrasive such as chalk dust.

8. Clean up, following the reagent disposal instructions.

REAGENT DISPOSAL

Rinse the KI solution from the U tube down the sink with copious amounts of water. You can return both the $ZnSO_4$ solution and the $CuSO_4$ solution to the containers provided by your instructor.

POST LAB DISCUSSION

The products of electrolysis can be predicted by using a table of standard reduction potentials similar to the one found in Appendix 5. Analysis of the anode and cathode half-reactions listed should provide support for your experimental observations.

The half-reactions in Parts I and III are straightforward and easy to determine. However, to determine the half-reactions for Part II, you may need to review the concept of overpotential.

DATA AND OBSERVATIONS

It would be useful to have these data tables ready in your notebook before you come to the laboratory.

Part I   Electrolysis of 1.0M KI

Table 1   Electrolysis of 1.0M KI (Carbon Electrodes)

ELECTRODE	OBSERVATIONS	HALF-REACTIONS
Anode		
Cathode		

Part II   Electrolysis of 1.0M ZnSO$_4$

Table 2   Electrolysis of 1.0M ZnSO$_4$ (Carbon Electrodes)

ELECTRODE	OBSERVATIONS	HALF-REACTIONS
Anode		
Cathode		

Part III   Copper Plating

Table 3   Copper Plating

ELECTRODE	OBSERVATIONS	HALF-REACTIONS
Anode		
Cathode		

QUESTIONS

1. For Part I, how do the anode and cathode half-reactions explain your observations?

2. For Part II, how do the anode and cathode half-reactions explain your observations?

3. In Part II, what anode and cathode half-reactions would occur if the overpotential effect did not exist?

4. For Part III, how can you explain your observations at (a) the anode, and (b) the cathode?

5. In Part III, predict what might happen if the metal object to be plated were placed in the CuSO$_4$ *before* the power was connected.

FOLLOW-UP QUESTIONS

1. The electrolytic cell in Part I produces reactions similar to those in a chlor-alkali industrial plant, where an NaCl solution is electrolyzed by means of unreactive electrodes.

   a. Predict the anode and cathode half-reactions for a chlor-alkali plant.

b. Suggest a reason why it would be unwise to simulate the chlor-alkali process in Part I of this experiment.

c. What common acid is often manufactured as a byproduct at chlor-alkali plants? (Hint: examine the products of electrolysis.)

2. If the overpotential effect did not exist, which common electroplating process would be impossible? Why?

3. In the electrorefining of copper, highly pure copper metal is produced at the cathode.

a. Consult a reference book, then draw a labelled diagram to illustrate an electrolytic cell capable of refining copper. Identify the materials used for the anode, cathode, and electrolytic solutions.

b. Give two reasons why impurities in the anode do not contaminate the cathode.

4. A $1.0M$ Na_2SO_4 solution is to be electrolyzed in a U tube containing carbon electrodes. Before electrolysis begins, bromthymol blue indicator solution is added to the colorless solution, and the color is adjusted to green (neutral). Predict the colors that will result at each electrode, and support your predictions with anode and cathode half-reactions.

5. When a $ZnSO_4$ cell such as the one in Part II is operated in industry, the $[Zn^{2+}]$ is one critical factor for an efficient recovery of $Zn(s)$. If the $[Zn^{2+}]$ in the cell drops below a certain level, another substance starts to be reduced at the cathode.

a. What undesirable reduction half-reaction occurs?

b. What practical problems could result if this were allowed to happen?

CONCLUSION

State the results of Objective 4.

Corrosion of Iron

Iron is the fourth most abundant element by mass in the earth's crust (after oxygen, silicon, and aluminum) and, therefore, the second most abundant metal. However, it is much easier to obtain from its ores than aluminum. Thus, iron is the most widely used structural metal. Most of it is used in making steel, which is an alloy of iron with carbon, and, in some types of steels, with other elements as well. The wide range of products made from steel includes all types of vehicles, machinery, pipelines, bridges, and reinforcing rods and girders for construction purposes, to name but a few.

Unfortunately, however, iron has one major drawback: under certain conditions it can corrode, or rust. If rusting is allowed to continue unchecked, the iron can eventually corrode completely away. Many millions of dollars are lost annually in replacing items (such as cars!) which have been destroyed by corrosion. It is clearly very important to prevent waste of this magnitude by any available means.

The purpose of this experiment is to acquaint you with the process of corrosion and to demonstrate how it can be slowed or stopped.

OBJECTIVES

1. to expose iron nails to a wide variety of conditions involving access to air, water, acidity, and other materials

2. to deduce from the results the factors which hasten the corrosion process

3. to deduce from the results the factors which retard or prevent the corrosion process from occurring

MATERIALS

Apparatus

12 test tubes
  (18 mm × 150 mm)
test-tube rack
rubber stoppers
steel wool
beaker (250 mL)
water soluble marker
hammer (1 per class)
small piece of scrap wood
lab apron
safety goggles

Reagents

11 iron nails
  (approx. 5 cm long)
acetone or other solvent
galvanized iron nail
$0.05M$ NaCl
$0.05M$ HCl
$0.05M$ NaOH
zinc strip
  (approx. 1 cm × 1 cm)
magnesium ribbon (5 cm long)
copper wire (5 cm long)
lubricating grease
(optional) $0.1M$ $K_3Fe(CN)_6$

PROCEDURE

1. Put on your lab apron and safety goggles.

2. Obtain 11 iron nails. Clean them with steel wool and place them in a 250 mL beaker. Pour acetone or another solvent over them to remove any oil or grease. Agitate, then pour off the solvent and return it to the waste container provided by your teacher. After this, try to handle the nails as little as possible.

CAUTION: Acetone is highly flammable, and its vapors are hazardous if inhaled. Make sure there are no burner flames in the laboratory. Do not breathe the fumes.

3. Place one iron nail in each of 11 test tubes. Place the galvanized iron nail in the final test tube. Label the test tubes 1 to 12 with your water soluble marker.

4. Vary the conditions in each test tube by carrying out the following operations. (Use enough water or solutions to cover each nail, unless otherwise specified.)

   #1 Add water.

   #2 Add water, but only enough to cover half the nail.

   #3 Add 0.05M NaCl solution.

   #4 Add 0.05M HCl solution.

   #5 Add 0.05M NaOH solution.

   #6 Do not add anything—just stopper the test tube.

   #7 Add water that has been boiled for 5 min to remove any dissolved air. Fill the test tube to the top and stopper it.

   #8 Attach the nail to the small piece of zinc by using a hammer to drive the nail through the zinc (place a piece of scrap wood underneath to protect your bench!). This should provide good contact between the zinc and the iron. Place in the test tube and add water.

   #9 Wrap the nail with a piece of magnesium ribbon as tightly as possible to ensure good contact. Place in the test tube and add water.

   #10 Wrap the nail with a piece of copper wire as tightly as possible to ensure good contact. Place in the test tube and add water.

   #11 Smear a small amount of lubricating grease to completely cover the bottom half of the nail. Place in the test tube and add water.

   #12 This test tube contains the galvanized iron nail. Add water.

5. Check whether any changes occur before the end of the period, and record them in your copy of Table 1. Then label the test-tube rack with your name and class and place it in the area designated by your teacher.

6. Before leaving the laboratory, wash your hands thoroughly with soap and water; use a fingernail brush to clean under your fingernails.

7. After two or three laboratory periods, examine your test tubes and record any changes in Table 1.

8. On the day designated by your instructor, make your final observations and record them in your table.

9. On the final day, after making all other observations, remove the nail from test tube 11 and wipe the grease off with a paper towel. Observe the surface of the nail to see whether any corrosion has occurred and if so, where.

10. If no rust has formed in test tube 4, and if you are requested to do so by your teacher, add a small amount of potassium hexacyanoferrate(III) solution ($K_3Fe(CN)_6$) and observe the result.

REAGENT DISPOSAL

Rinse the liquids from the test tubes down the sink with plenty of water. Be careful not to let the nails go down the sink. Place the leftover nails and other metals in the designated container.

POST LAB DISCUSSION

The corrosion of iron is a redox reaction in which iron is initially oxidized to Fe^{2+}:

$$Fe \rightarrow Fe^{2+} + 2e^-$$

The oxidizing agent is oxygen gas, which in the presence of hydrogen ions becomes reduced to water:

$$O_2 + 4H^+ + 4e^- \rightarrow 2H_2O$$

The Fe^{2+} ion itself is unstable, and it can be oxidized to Fe^{3+} by the same half-reaction involving oxygen:

$$Fe^{2+} \rightarrow Fe^{3+} + e^-$$

As you can see, the half-reaction involving oxygen uses up H^+ ions; therefore, the solution becomes basic because OH^- ions are left behind. Both $Fe(OH)_2$ and $Fe(OH)_3$ are virtually insoluble, so a precipitate occurs. What you see as rust in the test tube is mostly $Fe(OH)_3$. Rust that forms on objects exposed to the open air may lose some water from $Fe(OH)_3$ and is often assigned the formula $Fe_2O_3 \cdot xH_2O$, where the amount of water attached can vary with the conditions.

A precipitate may not have occurred in the test tube containing HCl, since, with the larger amount of H^+ present, the amount of H^+ used up by the oxygen was not sufficient to make the solution basic. Evidence for the fact that some iron had actually dissolved was obtainable by adding some $K_3Fe(CN)_6$ solution, if you were asked to do so. A blue color would have indicated the presence of Fe^{2+} ions.

When iron is attached to another metal that can be oxidized more readily (that is, to a metal which is a stronger reducing agent than iron), the electrons given off by this metal travel to the iron and force it to act as a cathode in the process. Since iron is forced to accept electrons, it cannot corrode, as corrosion involves giving off electrons. This method of preventing corrosion is called *cathodic protection*.

DATA AND OBSERVATIONS

It would be a good idea to have this table ready in your notebook before coming to the laboratory.

TEST TUBE NUMBER	CONTENTS	FIRST OBSERVATION	SECOND OBSERVATION	FINAL OBSERVATION	AMOUNT OF CORROSION COMPARED TO TEST TUBE #1 (MORE, LESS, SAME)
1	Water				
2	Half water, half air				
3	0.05M NaCl				
4	0.05M HCl				
5	0.05M NaOH				
6	Air				
7	Boiled water (no air)				
8	Fe nail + Zn, water				
9	Fe nail + Mg, water				
10	Fe nail + Cu, water				
11	Grease on nail, water				
12	Galvanized nail, water				

QUESTIONS AND CALCULATIONS

1. Compare the results observed in test tubes 1, 2, and 7. In which test tube did the greatest amount of corrosion occur? In which did the least corrosion occur? What chemical is therefore necessary for corrosion?

2. Compare the results observed in test tubes 1 and 6. What substance in addition to the one from question 1 is necessary for corrosion?

3. Compare the results observed in test tubes 3, 4, and 5. In which test tube was the amount of corrosion greatest? In which was the amount of corrosion least? What ion is therefore responsible for hastening the corrosion process?

4. Using the table of reduction potentials in Appendix 5, write down the half-reactions for O_2 reacting with $1M$ H^+ to give H_2O, and for O_2 reacting with $10^{-7}M$ H^+ to give H_2O, along with their $E°$ values. Which of these half-reactions will occur to the greater extent?

5. Write the balanced overall equation for iron reacting to give Fe^{2+}. Give the overall $E°$ value for both $1M$ H^+ and $10^{-7}M$ H^+.

6. Write the balanced overall equation for Fe^{2+} reacting with O_2 and H^+ to give Fe^{3+} and water. Again, work out both overall $E°$ values, one for $1M$ H^+ and one for $10^{-7}M$ H^+.

7. Write the net ionic equation for the reaction between Fe^{3+} and the OH^- ions left in solution which gives $Fe(OH)_3$.

8. Compare the results observed in test tubes 8, 9, and 10. Which metal(s) seemed to slow the corrosion process? Which metal(s) hastened corrosion? Do the results agree with the relative position of these four metals in the reduction potential table?

9. On the basis of your understanding of the factors involved in corrosion, explain the result in test tube 11.

10. Galvanized iron nails such as the one in test tube 12 are made by dipping the iron nail into molten zinc to coat them with a layer of zinc. Explain the result observed in this test tube.

FOLLOW-UP QUESTIONS

1. Blocks of magnesium are connected at intervals to underground pipelines or to hulls of ships, to prevent corrosion of the iron. However, they have to be replaced periodically because they dissolve. (They are called "sacrificial anodes" since they sacrifice themselves to prevent the iron from corroding.) Why does it make sense economically to keep replacing the blocks of magnesium?

2. Using a reference book, find out why objects that are galvanized (coated with zinc) do not need to have the zinc replaced, even though it is more active than the iron.

3. Name some objects made of galvanized iron, other than nails, which you have in or around your home.

4. Explain why the salts put on roads in winter to melt ice can hasten the corrosion of a car if they are not thoroughly washed off.

5. Corrosion can be prevented by keeping air and water away from iron. Some ways of doing this are plating the iron with another metal that does not corrode (as in the chrome plated bumpers, etc., on a car) or painting the iron. However, these methods cannot always be used. For instance, gardeners should protect their gardening tools from rusting when stored in an outside tool shed over the winter, but cannot plate or paint them. What method of protecting gardening tools would you suggest?

6. What is stainless steel? From a reference book, discover its composition.

7. Copper does not react with $1M$ H^+ to give Cu^{2+} and H_2, since the $E°$ for the reaction is negative. However, if a strip of copper is half submerged in $1M$ HCl in a test tube, after a few days a blue color (indicating Cu^{2+}) is seen in the solution, showing that a reaction has occurred. Explain this result. Write an overall redox equation for the reaction, and calculate its $E°$. (Your teacher may demonstrate this reaction to you, or you may want to try it yourself. Ask permission first.)

CONCLUSION

State the results of Objectives 2 and 3.

Observing Reactions of Ions

All the solutions in this experiment are *electrolytes*. Electrolytes contain ions. When solutions containing ions are mixed, a reaction may or may not take place. If no macroscopic changes occur, you can assume that all the ions are present as a mixture and you write N. R., which means no reaction.

Macroscopic observations that indicate a reaction are: bubbles of a gas, a color change, an energy change, an odor, or the formation of an insoluble substance called a precipitate.

To write an equation for the reaction that occurs when ionic solutions are mixed, the formulas for the reagents are written to show that ions are initially present. For example, if mercury(II) bromide, $HgBr_2(aq)$, reacts with sodium iodide, $NaI(aq)$, the reactants are written as follows in ionic form:

$$Hg^{2+}(aq) + 2Br^-(aq) + Na^+ + I^-(aq)$$

This notation shows that for every $Hg^{2+}(aq)$ ion in solution, there are two $Br^-(aq)$ ions, while there is one $I^-(aq)$ ion for every $Na^+(aq)$ ion.

When these solutions are mixed, an orange precipitate forms. This precipitate is an insoluble solid that forms when two oppositely charged ions are attracted to each other. The precipitate cannot be $Hg^{2+}(aq)$ combined with $Na^+(aq)$ because both those ions are positively charged. Similarly, the precipitate cannot be Br^- combined with I^-. This means the precipitate is either $HgI_2(s)$ or NaBr (s). If you refer to the Solubility Table in your text, you will note that HgI_2 is insoluble and NaBr is soluble. Therefore, the precipitate is HgI_2.

The balanced ionic equation for the reaction is:

$$Hg^{2+}(aq) + 2Br^-(aq) + 2Na^+(aq) + 2I^-(aq) \rightarrow$$
$$HgI_2(s) + 2Na^+(aq) + 2Br^-(aq)$$

The $Na^+(aq)$ and $Br^-(aq)$ ions are called spectator ions. The equation written without the spectator ions is called the net ionic equation:

$$Hg^{2+}(aq) + 2I^-(aq) \quad \rightarrow \quad HgI_2(s)$$

In making your observations, note any macroscopic changes and include the color of the precipitate and any recognizable odor. A number of inorganic salts exhibit some brilliant colors which, along with their solubilities, make them valuable commercial pigments for paints or glazes. For example, the pigment known as "cobalt yellow" is prepared by precipitation, after which it is washed with water to remove the soluble impurities.

OBJECTIVES

1. to make the macroscopic observations necessary to determine when a chemical reaction takes place

2. to write ionic formulas for the reactants

3. to write net ionic equations for the reactions that occur

4. to use the process of elimination to determine the identity of a precipitate

MATERIALS

Apparatus

8 test tubes
  (13 mm × 100 mm)
test tube rack
test tube brush
thermometer
safety goggles
lab apron
plastic gloves
full face shield

Reagents

dropper bottles
  containing:
$MnCl_2(aq)$
$NH_4I(aq)$
$BaCl_2(aq)$
$CoSO_4(aq)$

$K_2CO_3(aq)$
$NaOH(aq)$
$HCl(aq)$
$Pb(NO_3)_2(aq)$
$CuSO_4(aq)$

CAUTION: Most of these solutions are corrosive, poisonous, or irritants. Therefore, protect your skin, eyes, and clothing. Wear safety goggles, lab apron, full face shield, and use plastic gloves. Do not get these solutions in your mouth, do not swallow any. Wash spills and splashes off your skin and clothing immediately, using plenty of water. Call your teacher.

CAUTION: You should always detect odors with caution. Hold the test tube 30 cm away and 15 cm below your nose. Waft the odor toward your nose sniffing cautiously.

PROCEDURE

1. Put on your safety goggles, lab apron, full face shield, and plastic gloves.

2. Add 10 drops of each solution listed in the vertical column of Table 1 to each of eight test tubes.

3. Add 10 drops of solution 1 in the horizontal row of Table 1 to the first test tube, one drop at a time. Use a thermometer to determine if energy is absorbed or evolved. Record your observations of heat evolved, bubbles of a gas, an odor, or the formation of a precipitate (note the color) in your copy of Table 1 in your notebook.

4. Repeat Step 3 until solution 1 on the horizontal row has been added to each of the eight test tubes. Empty and clean the test tubes according to the reagent disposal instructions.

5. Repeat Steps 2, 3, and 4 for solution 2 from the vertical column of Table 1.

6. Continue until all eight of the solutions in the vertical column have been reacted with each solution from the horizontal row and all spaces in your copy of Table 1 contain observations.

7. Before leaving the laboratory, wash your hands thoroughly with soap and water; use a fingernail brush to clean under your fingernails.

REAGENT DISPOSAL

Pour the solutions from the test tubes into the appropriate waste chemical containers provided by your teacher. Rinse the test tubes with copious amounts of water.

POST LAB DISCUSSION

Compare your observations to those made by other students. If you are in doubt about a reaction, repeat it. If there is no observable macroscopic change, assume that no reaction occurred.

In a reaction that produces a gas, it may be helpful to first write a double replacement reaction to identify the product. For example, if sodium carbonate is reacted with sulfuric acid, bubbles of an odorless gas that turns limewater milky are produced. The equation is:

$$Na_2CO_3(aq) + H_2SO_4(aq) \rightarrow Na_2SO_4(aq) + H_2CO_3(aq)$$

Sodium sulfate, Na_2SO_4, is an ionic compound and has a high melting point so it is not the gas. Carbonic acid, H_2CO_3, is an unstable acid that decomposes readily to form carbon dioxide, CO_2, a gas, and H_2O, water.

$$H_2CO_3 \rightarrow H_2O(l) + CO_2(g)$$

Sodium carbonate and sulfuric acid are not present in solution as molecules but are dissociated as ions. This can be shown by testing both solutions with the light bulb conductivity apparatus shown in the text. An ionic equation is a better representation of what is occurring in solution:

$$2Na^+(aq) + CO_3^{2-}(aq) + 2H^+(aq) + SO_4^{2-}(aq) \rightarrow$$
$$2Na^+(aq) + SO_4^{2-}(aq) + H_2O(l) + CO_2(g)$$

DATA AND OBSERVATIONS

Table 1

	1. $MnCl_2$	2. NH_4I	3. $BaCl_2$	4. $CoSO_4$	5. K_2CO_3	6. $NaOH$	7. HCl	8. $Pb(NO_3)_2$
A. $MnCl_2$								
B. NH_4I								
C. $BaCl_2$								
D. $CoSO_4$								
E. K_2CO_3								
F. $NaOH$								
G. HCl								
H. $CuSO_4$								

COMPLETE IN YOUR NOTEBOOK

QUESTIONS AND CALCULATIONS

1. Compare your observations with those of your classmates. If your results are different and you are not sure which results are correct, how should you decide which are correct?

2. Reaction H-8 produced a precipitate. Write the reactants in ionic form and draw an arrow.

3. Explain why the precipitate for the reaction in item 2 is not CuPb(s).

4. Explain why the precipitate for the reaction in item 2 is not SO_4NO_3(s).

5. Write the formulas for the two remaining possibilities for the precipitate in reaction H-8.

6. Refer to Table 16-3 in the text and identify the precipitate in reaction H-8.

7. List the spectator ions in reaction H-8.

FOLLOW-UP QUESTIONS

1. Write the complete balanced ionic equation for reaction H-8.

2. Write the net ionic equation for reaction H-8.

3. The reaction C-4 produces a precipitate. Write a balanced ionic equation for the reaction.

4. What are the spectator ions in reaction C-4?

5. Write a net ionic equation for reaction C-4.

6. Write a balanced ionic equation for reactions:
   a. A-5
   b. A-6
   c. A-7
   d. C-2
   e. C-5
   f. C-8

7. Write a balanced ionic equation for the reactions that were exothermic. Include the energy term.
   a. F-7
   b. G-6

8. Write a balanced ionic equation for the reactions that gave off a gas having the odor of ammonia.
   a. B-6
   b. F-2

9. Write balanced ionic equations for the reactions that gave off an odorless gas.
   a. E-7
   b. G-5

CONCLUSION

State the results of Objective 3.

Predicting the Results of Reactions, Including Precipitation, Acid-Base, and Redox Reactions

The scientific method involves three major phases. The first consists of making observations (doing experiments). Second, as a result of these experiments, relationships may become apparent, and theories are put forward to explain these relationships. The third phase involves testing the theory. This is usually done by making predictions as to the outcome of an experiment and then performing the experiment to test the prediction.

At this point in your study of chemistry, you have been exposed to a large body of chemical knowledge, but you have not often been asked to predict a result. In this experiment you will have a chance to do so. In Part I of the experiment you will look at a large number of chemical combinations as a pre-lab activity, and you will draw on your knowledge of precipitation reactions (Chapter 16), acid-base reactions (Chapter 20), and redox reactions (Chapter 21) in order to come up with a predicted result for the reaction. In the few situations where no reaction is possible, your prediction will be "no reaction".

After making your predictions and justifying them on the basis of the solubility tables, acid-base theory, or $E°$ values, you will perform the investigations and see whether your predictions were correct (Part II). If you do not predict a given result correctly, you will have to reassess your prediction and try to explain what happened.

In Part III of the experiment, the reactions are somewhat more complex, so you will simply perform the investigations and attempt to explain the results.

OBJECTIVES

1. to predict the results of a large number of chemical reactions of different types

2. to perform investigations in order to test the predictions

3. to carry out a number of other reactions and interpret their results

MATERIALS

Apparatus

20 test tubes
  (13 mm × 100 mm)
test-tube rack
lab apron
safety goggles

Reagents

$0.1M$ $Ca(NO_3)_2$	$0.1M$ KBr
$0.1M$ Na_2CO_3	$0.2M$ Na_2SO_3
phenolphthalein	$0.1M$ $K_2Cr_2O_7$
saturated $Ba(OH)_2$	$0.5M$ Na_2CO_3
(about $0.1M$)	$1M$ HNO_3
$0.2M$ H_2SO_4	$0.1M$ K_2SO_4
$0.1M$ KI	$0.1M$ $BaCl_2$
$1M$ H_2SO_4	$0.1M$ $MgSO_4$
3% H_2O_2	$0.1M$ $(NH_4)_2SO_4$
$0.1M$ $Zn(NO_3)_2$	$0.1M$ $FeSO_4$
$0.1M$ NH_3	household bleach
$6M$ HCl	(NaClO)
$0.02M$ $KMnO_4$	starch solution
$0.1M$ $FeCl_3$	$0.1M$ $Cr(NO_3)_3$
$0.1M$ $Fe_2(SO_4)_3$	$1M$ NaOH

PROCEDURE

Part I Predicting Experimental Results

1. As a pre-lab activity, predict whether or not a reaction will occur in each of the following situations. Justify your predictions on the basis of $E°$ values, solubility tables, etc. The relative amounts are not important for your prediction; they are put in as a guide for the investigations in which you will test your predictions.

   a. To 2 mL $0.1M$ $Ca(NO_3)_2$ add 2 mL $0.1M$ Na_2CO_3.

   b. To 2 mL of saturated $Ba(OH)_2$ add 1 drop of phenolphthalein, then 2 mL of $0.2M$ H_2SO_4.

   c. To 2 mL of $0.1M$ KI add 1 mL of $1M$ H_2SO_4, then 2 mL of 3% H_2O_2.

   d. To 2 mL of $0.1M$ $Zn(NO_3)_2$ add 2 mL of $0.1M$ NH_3.

   e. To 2 mL of $6M$ HCl add 2 drops of $0.02M$ $KMnO_4$.

   f. To 2 mL of $0.1M$ KI add 2 mL of $0.1M$ $FeCl_3$.

   g. To 2 mL of $0.1M$ KBr add 2 mL of $0.1M$ $FeCl_3$.

   h. To 2 mL of $0.2M$ Na_2SO_3 add 1 mL of $1M$ H_2SO_4, then 10 drops of $0.1M$ $K_2Cr_2O_7$.

   i. To 2 mL of $0.5M$ Na_2CO_3 add 2 mL of $1M$ HNO_3.

   j. To 2 mL of $0.1M$ $AgNO_3$ add 2 mL of $0.1M$ KBr.

   k. To 2 mL of $0.1M$ K_2SO_4 add 2 mL of $0.1M$ $FeCl_3$.

   l. To 2 mL of $0.1M$ Na_2CO_3 add 2 mL of $0.1M$ $BaCl_2$, then 1 mL of $1M$ HNO_3.

   m. To 2 mL of $0.1M$ $MgSO_4$ add 2 mL of $0.1M$ KI.

   n. To 2 mL of $0.1M$ $(NH_4)_2SO_4$ add 2 mL of saturated $Ba(OH)_2$.

   o. To 2 mL of $0.1M$ $FeSO_4$ add 1 mL $1M$ H_2SO_4, then 10 drops of $0.1M$ $K_2Cr_2O_7$.

   p. To 2 mL of $0.1M$ Na_2SO_3 add 1 mL $1M$ H_2SO_4, then 10 drops of $0.02M$ $KMnO_4$.

   q. To 2 mL of $0.1M$ $Fe_2(SO_4)_3$ add 2 mL of saturated $Ba(OH)_2$, then 1 mL of $1M$ HNO_3.

Part II Confirming Predictions Experimentally

1. Put on your lab apron and safety goggles.

2. Using 13 mm × 100 mm test tubes, and estimating volumes rather than actually measuring quantities, carry out all the investigations listed in Part I, (a) to (q). (2 mL is about one-fifth of the depth of a 13 mm × 100 mm test tube, or a 2 cm depth; 1 mL is one-tenth the depth of a 13 mm × 100 mm test tube, or a 1 cm depth.) Watch for color changes, cloudiness (indicating precipitates), the productions of gases, and the production of odors. Do not be biased by your predictions; record what you actually see.

HAZARD

CAUTION: Most of these chemicals are poisonous, corrosive, or irritants. Treat each one with the utmost care. Do not get any on your skin, in your eyes, or on your clothing. Do not get any in your mouth, and do not swallow any. Wash any spills and splashes with plenty of water. Call your teacher in order to obtain specific instructions as to how to handle any spills of a particular chemical.

Part III Further Examples of Redox Reactions

1. To 2 mL of $0.1M$ KI add 5 drops of starch solution; then add bleach (sodium hypochlorite, NaClO) until a color change is observed. Continue adding the bleach until a second color change is observed.

2. To 2 mL of $0.1M$ $Cr(NO_3)_3$ add $1M$ NaOH drop by drop, until the precipitate dissolves again. Finally, add 3 mL 3% hydrogen peroxide, H_2O_2.

3. To 2 mL of $0.1M$ $K_2Cr_2O_7$ add 1 mL of $1M$ H_2SO_4. Then add 3 mL of 3% H_2O_2.

4. Wash your hands thoroughly with soap and water before leaving the laboratory; use a fingernail brush to clean under your fingernails.

REAGENT DISPOSAL

Place the contents of test tubes containing chromium compounds, barium compounds, and silver compounds in separate designated waste containers. The contents of all other test tubes may be rinsed down the sink with plenty of water.

POST LAB DISCUSSION

The reactions predicted in Part I and subsequently carried out in Part II are relatively straightforward, so you should have had good success in predicting your results. For Part III, however, some explanations are required. In Step 1, the blue color characteristic of I_2 with starch should have been seen to form and then dissolve again. The ClO^- is an oxidizing agent and is able to oxidize I^- to I_2, but it can also oxidize the I_2 to a higher oxidation state of 5+ in IO_3^-. This reaction occurs in basic solution, since NaClO solution will be basic by hydrolysis.

The color changes you observed in the remainder of Part III would indicate that in Step 2 Cr, with an oxidation number of 3+ (in $Cr(OH)_4^-$), was oxidized to 6+ (CrO_4^{2-}), but in Step 3 Cr, with an oxidation number of 6+ (in $Cr_2O_7^{2-}$), was reduced to the green Cr^{3+}. In both cases the reagent added was hydrogen peroxide. This shows that H_2O_2 (which has an oxidation number of 1–) can either act as an oxidizing agent (becoming H_2O, in which the oxygen has an oxidation number of 2–), or act as a reducing agent (becoming O_2 gas, with an oxidation number of 0). Note that for the oxidation of Cr^{3+} a basic solution was required, but the reduction of Cr from the 6+ state had to occur in an acidic solution.

DATA AND OBSERVATIONS

Your observations in this experiment are best not put in table form, as some experiments have more observations to be made than others, and a table restricts the amount of information you record. For each experiment, just describe everything you saw and state whether your observations agree with your predictions. If you did not predict correctly, try to explain what happened and why.

QUESTIONS AND CALCULATIONS

1. For each situation in Part II in which a reaction occurred, write the net ionic equation and state what type of reaction it is (precipitation, acid-base, or redox). If the reaction was a redox reaction, also calculate its E°.

2. On the basis of the additional information given in the Post Lab Discussion, write equations for the half-reactions occurring in each step of the Procedure in Part III, then combine them to give the overall equation for each reaction. Remember that Steps 1 and 2 occurred in basic solution, but Step 3 occurred in acidic solution.

3. Calculate the E° for the reaction in Step 3 of Part III. (The other two steps do not have the appropriate E° values in the standard reduction potentials table in Appendix 5.)

FOLLOW-UP QUESTIONS

1. Why is it more difficult to predict whether a redox reaction will proceed than it is to predict whether either an acid-base or a precipitation reaction will proceed?

2. Some redox reactions having positive predicted $E°$ values do not actually occur. What factor(s) could be responsible?

CONCLUSION

Make a statement as to the amount of success you had in predicting the correct results of the chemical reactions listed in Part I.

Flame Tests

In your attempts to identify unknown solutions, you have noted that sodium, potassium, and lithium ions do not react with any other ions that you have used. Carbonate, CO_3^{2-}, forms a precipitate with all the other positive ions except Na^+, K^+, Li^+, H^+, and NH_4^+. When CO_3^{2-} is added to an unknown and no reaction occurs, the unknown contains Li^+, Na^+, K^+, H^+, or NH_4^+. The addition of OH^- can be used to detect H^+ and NH_4^+, but how can Na^+, K^+, and Li^+ be identified?

In Chapter 10, you learned that when energy is added to an atom the electrons can absorb the energy and be raised to a higher energy level. When these "excited" electrons return to the ground state, they emit energy in the form of electromagnetic radiation. The frequency of the radiation is as unique as a fingerprint. All elements can be identified by the electromagnetic radiation they emit. However, only a few elements give off their characteristic frequency in the visible region of the spectrum. For most elements, the electromagnetic radiation emitted is in the ultraviolet or infrared part of the spectrum. For these elements, photographic film or an electronic device called a spectroscope is required. Copper, barium, strontium, sodium, potassium, lithium, and calcium show a spectrum in the visible range, and these ions can be identified chemically by doing a flame test.

The brilliant illuminations of entertainment fireworks, as well as safety flares and a variety of military applications (such as signal flares and tracer bullets) are largely based on the combustion of magnesium powder. The brilliant colors are obtained by including salts such as the ones used in this investigation.

OBJECTIVES

1. to identify lithium, sodium, and potassium using a flame test

2. to learn to recognize the characteristic flame test for copper, barium, strontium, and calcium

3. to confirm the presence of these elements in an unknown solution

MATERIALS

Apparatus	Reagents
8 test tubes	Solutions of
(75 mm × 100 mm)	LiCl(aq)
test tube rack	KCl(aq)
platinum wire or	NaCl(aq)
wood splints	CuCl₂(aq)
laboratory burner	BaCl₂(aq)
safety goggles	SrCl₂(aq)
lab apron	CaCl₂(aq)
full face shield	1M HCl

PROCEDURE

1. Put on your lab apron, safety goggles, and full face shield.

2. Add 10 drops of LiCl(aq) to a clean test tube.

3. Heat the platinum wire in the hottest part of the burner flame until it glows but shows no color above the wire. If necessary, clean the wire by dipping it in a test tube that contains 10 drops of $1M$ HCl(aq) and then heating the wire in the burner flame.

4. When the platinum wire is clean, dip the wire in the test tube containing LiCl(aq) solution and hold it in the hottest part of the burner flame. See Figure 22C-1. Record your observations in your copy of Table 1 in your notebook. Sometimes the color appears for a very short time so it may be necessary to dip the wire in the LiCl(aq) solution and put it in the flame several times.

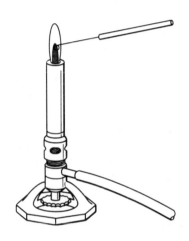

Fig. 22C-1

CAUTION: LiCl and CuCl$_2$ are poisonous, and BaCl$_2$ is very poisonous. Do not get them in your mouth; do not swallow any.

CAUTION: SrCl$_2$ and CaCl$_2$ are irritating to skin and eyes. Wash any spills or splashes with plenty of water. Call your teacher.

CAUTION: Hydrochloric acid is corrosive to skin, eyes, and clothing. When handling hydrochloric acid, wear safety goggles, full face shield, gloves, and lab apron. Wash spills and splashes off your skin and clothing immediately using plenty of water. Call your teacher.

5. Repeat Steps 2-4 for KCl(aq) and NaCl(aq), CuCl$_2$(aq), CaCl$_2$(aq), SrCl$_2$(aq), and BaCl$_2$(aq).

6. If a platinum wire is not available, a wood splint can be placed in each test tube of solution overnight and then heated the following day.

7. Obtain the unknown test solutions labeled A-E from your teacher. Test the unknown solutions as in Step 4 and record your observations in your copy of Table 2.

8. Before leaving the laboratory, wash your hands thoroughly with soap and water; use a fingernail brush to clean under your fingernails.

REAGENT DISPOSAL

Pour the solutions from the test tubes into the appropriate waste chemical containers provided by your teacher. Rinse the test tubes with copious amounts of water.

DATA AND OBSERVATIONS

Table 1

SOLUTION	OBSERVATIONS
LiCl(aq)	
KCl(aq)	
NaCl(aq)	
CuCl₂(aq)	COMPLETE IN YOUR NOTEBOOK
BaCl₂(aq)	
SrCl₂(aq)	
CaCl₂(aq)	

Table 2

unknown A	
unknown B	
unknown C	COMPLETE IN YOUR NOTEBOOK
unknown D	
unknown E	

QUESTIONS

1. What is the characteristic color of the lithium ion flame?

2. What is the characteristic color of the potassium ion flame?

3. What is the characteristic color of the sodium ion flame?

FOLLOW-UP QUESTIONS

1. All the solutions you tested were $0.5M$. How would the experimental results differ if the solutions were $0.10M$ or $1.00M$?

2. What would you observe if you tested a solution that contained both LiCl(aq) and KCl(aq)?

3. If solutions of $LiNO_3$(aq), KNO_3(aq), Na_2SO_4(aq), and Na_2CO_3(aq) are separately tested, what results would you expect?

4. A common type of bright street light on major highways and bridges gives off an orange light. This lamp utilizes the vapor of a metallic element. Which element is used?

5. A student who had handled the platinum wire and then not cleaned it before dipping it in an unknown solution was fooled into thinking that the result of the flame test indicated that the unknown was sodium. Why did the student obtain this result?

CONCLUSION

State the results of Objective 3.

Molecular Model Building (Isomerism)

The chemical and physical properties of substances can often be inferred from their molecular structures. Electron dot and structural (line) diagrams can show molecular geometry in simplified, two-dimensional notation. Although many molecules can be adequately illustrated by drawings, certain structures are more easily understood if they can be seen in three dimensions. To aid in three-dimensional visualization, ball and stick molecular models can be assembled.

Substances having the same molecular formula, but different structural configurations are known as *isomers*. There are two categories of isomers to be considered here: structural and geometric.

Structural isomers can arise in several ways. The arrangement of the carbon atoms in the carbon skeleton or backbone of the molecule may differ. For example, butane, C_4H_{10}, may exist with its four carbon atoms linked in a straight chain or as a branched chain hydrocarbon:

Other types of structural isomers occur when, even though the carbon skeleton is identical, the position of the functional group attached to the carbon skeleton in the molecule may vary. Note the placement of the OH group in each of the following isomers of propanol:

Sometimes, the two structural isomers may belong to two totally different classes of compound, even though they have the same molecular formula. In this case they may have very different chemical and physical properties. For example, the following two isomers with molecular formula C_3H_8O belong to two different classes of compounds:

Geometric isomerism occurs in some molecules that have at least one double bond. The sequence for the atoms and bonds in the molecule is the same for each, but they differ in having a different orientation for the atoms or groups attached to the carbon atoms in the double bond. Since rotation about a double bond is restricted, the parts of the molecule on either side of the double bond remain in fixed positions. Note that in order to have this type of isomerism, each carbon atom in the double bond has to have two different groups attached to it. The compound dichloroethene exhibits this kind of isomerism:

$$\begin{array}{ccc} Cl & & Cl \\ \backslash & & / \\ & C = C & \\ / & & \backslash \\ H & & H \end{array} \qquad \begin{array}{ccc} H & & Cl \\ \backslash & & / \\ & C = C & \\ / & & \backslash \\ Cl & & H \end{array}$$

cis-dichloroethene (both chlorines are on the same side of the double bond)   trans-dichloroethene (the two chlorines are on opposite sides of the double bond)

Before doing this experiment, if necessary, refresh your memory as to the number of bonding sites for each atom by referring back to Experiment 12B.

OBJECTIVES

1. to represent molecular structures with electron dot and structural (line) diagrams

2. to construct molecular models of simple substances

3. to construct molecular models illustrating the different types of isomers

MATERIALS

molecular model kit

PROCEDURE

1. Construct ball and stick models for each of the following alkanes. In your notebook, draw the structural (line) and electron dot diagrams for each of these molecules.

    a. methane, CH_4
    b. ethane, C_2H_6
    c. propane, C_3H_8

2. Construct the ball and stick models for all structural isomers for each of the following compounds. Draw the structural diagram for each isomer, and then name each one.

    a. butane, C_4H_{10}
    b. pentane, C_5H_{12}
    c. hexane, C_6H_{14}
    d. cyclohexane, C_6H_{12}
    e. methylhexane, C_7H_{16}

3. Construct the ball and stick models for all structural isomers of butene, C_4H_8. Draw the structural diagram for each, and then name them. (Note that one of the structures has geometric isomers.)

4. Construct ball and stick models for all structural isomers of propyne, C_3H_4, and butyne, C_4H_6. Draw the structural diagram for each, and then name them.

5. Construct a ball and stick model for each of the isomers of the following molecule. Identify the position of the OH group and draw the structural diagram for each isomer, and name them: n-hexanol, $C_6H_{13}OH$ (the n- designates a straight-chained molecule).

6. Construct a ball and stick model for the following structural isomers. Compare their structures and the placement of the oxygen atom. Draw the structural diagram for each isomer in your notebook.

   a. ethanol, C_2H_5OH
   b. dimethyl ether, CH_3OCH_3

POST LAB DISCUSSION

It can be seen that even with the above relatively simple molecules, there are often many structures possible. The IUPAC system for naming organic compounds was introduced so that there would be no confusion as to the name of a compound of a particular structure. Once you know the rules, the structural formula can be written from the name, and vice versa. Many common names for chemicals are in fact shortened versions of their IUPAC names. For instance, the insecticide DDT takes its name from shortening the name *DichloroDiphenylTrichloroethane*. Likewise, the common name for the herbicide 2,4-dichlorophenoxyacetic acid is 2,4-D.

QUESTIONS

1. How many isomers are possible for the following alkanes?

   a. methane   d. butane
   b. ethane   e. pentane
   c. propane   f. hexane

2. Can cyclopentane (C_5H_{10}) be considered an isomer of pentane? Explain.

3. Can the model set you used illustrate the proper geometry of benzene, C_6H_6? Explain.

4. In procedure 2d you made a model for cyclohexane, C_6H_{12}, and were probably able to find only one isomer. In fact, there are two—one in which the carbon skeleton looks like a chair, and another that looks like a boat. Try to show in structural diagram form the difference between the two.

CONCLUSION

Explain why there is such a huge number of organic compounds.

Preparation of Esters

Organic chemistry is the study of carbon compounds. There are a great number of types of carbon compounds, ranging from the simple alkanes, alkenes, and alkynes to the very complicated long chains of proteins or nucleic acids. Many organic compounds are too hazardous to be used in a high school chemistry laboratory.

The *esters* are a group of organic compounds best known for their interesting odors. Many perfumes and artificial flavorings are esters. Esters are formed when a carboxylic acid reacts with an alcohol in the presence of a strong acid. A general equation for the formation of esters is:

$$R\!-\!OH + R'\!-\!\overset{\displaystyle O}{\overset{\|}{C}}\!-\!OH \;\;\rightarrow\;\; HOH + R'\!-\!\overset{\displaystyle O}{\overset{\|}{C}}\!-\!O\!-\!R$$

The R and R' represent alkyl groups such as methyl, ethyl, or propyl. The esters are named after the compounds from which they are formed. The first part of the name comes from the alcohol, and the second part of the name comes from the carboxylic acid. Thus when ethyl alcohol (ethanol) combines with acetic acid, the resulting ester is named ethyl acetate.

The synthesis of an ester must be done in the presence of an acid in order to push the reaction closer to completion. The reaction can be reversed by adding a strong base, such as NaOH. The acid that you will be using as a catalyst in this experiment is sulfuric acid.

Many of the aromas of natural fruits and flowers are due to simple esters. Octyl ethanoate has the odor of oranges, while apricots owe their characteristic aroma to pentyl butanoate.

OBJECTIVES

1. to observe the synthesis of several esters and to identify the odor of each

2. to write the chemical equations for the formation of each ester

MATERIALS

Apparatus

5 test tubes	beaker (250 mL)
(18 mm × 150 mm)	thermometer
test tube rack	lab apron
dropper pipet	safety goggles
centigram balance	full face shield
glazed paper	plastic gloves
hot plate	graduated cylinder
	(10 mL)

Reagents

methanol
ethanol
2-methylpropanol
1-pentanol
1-octanol
glacial acetic acid
formic acid solution
salicylic acid
concentrated sulfuric
acid, H_2SO_4

PROCEDURE

1. Put on your lab apron, face shield, gloves, and safety goggles.

2. Label the five test tubes *A* to *E*. Place the test tubes in the test tube rack.

3. Into the appropriate test tube, pour the correct amount of an alcohol and add a carboxylic acid as indicated in the table below. (Use the centigram balance to measure the solid salicylic acid.) Add four drops of concentrated sulfuric acid to each test tube.

TEST TUBE	CARBOXYLIC ACID	ALCOHOL
A	1 mL acetic acid	1 mL ethanol
B	1 mL formic acid	1 mL 2-methylpropanol
C	1 mL acetic acid	1 mL 1-octanol
D	1 g salicylic acid	1 mL methanol
E	1 mL acetic acid	1 mL 1-pentanol

4. Put about 150 mL of water in a 250 mL beaker. Place the test tubes into the water and heat the water on a hot plate to a temperature of 60°C. Leave the test tubes in the hot water bath for 15 min.

5. Cool the test tubes by immersing them in a cold water bath.

6. Add 5 mL of distilled water to each of the test tubes.

7. Carefully note the odor of the contents of each of the test tubes in your copy of Table 1 in your notebook. Your teacher will demonstrate how to safely smell chemicals in the laboratory. Each of the odors should be somewhat familiar to you (plants, fruits, vegetables, or animals).

8. Dispose of all materials following the reagent disposal instructions.

9. Before leaving the laboratory, wash your hands thoroughly with soap and water; use a fingernail brush to clean under your fingernails.

REAGENT DISPOSAL

Any remaining concentrated H_2SO_4 must first be diluted before disposal. To dilute, slowly add the acid to at least ten times its volume of water in a beaker. All liquids can be rinsed down the sink with copious amounts of water.

POST LAB DISCUSSION

The balanced equations for these reactions require the knowledge of the structures of the molecules involved. The structures of the alcohols and carboxylic acids used in this experiment are shown on the next page.

CAUTION: Concentrated sulfuric acid is a strong oxidizing agent. It will start a fire if mixed incorrectly with any of the alcohols or other acids used in this experiment. Use it exactly as directed.

CAUTION: All of the liquid acids used in this experiment are corrosive to skin, eyes, and clothing. While working on this experiment, wear safety goggles, full face shield, gloves, and lab apron. Wash spills and splashes off your skin and clothing immediately, using plenty of water. Call your teacher.

CAUTION: The alcohols and the organic acids used in this experiment are all flammable. Be sure all burners and other flames in the laboratory are extinguished before you start this experiment.

CAUTION: You should always detect odors with caution. Breathing the vapors of some of these esters can cause sore throat, dizziness, headache, and drowsiness. Hold the test tube 30 cm away and 15 cm below your nose. Waft the odor toward your nose, sniffing cautiously, once or twice. Do not breathe deeply while sniffing.

acetic acid
(ethanoic acid)
CH₃COOH

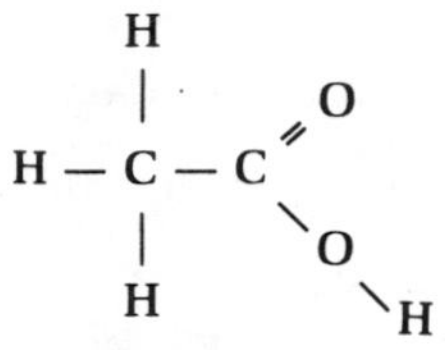

salicylic acid
(2-hydroxybenzoic acid)
HOC₆H₄COOH

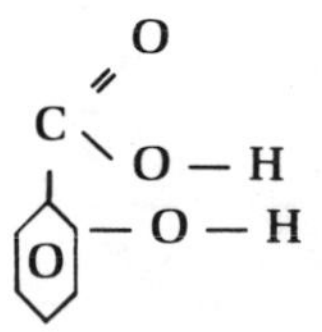

methanol

CH₃OH

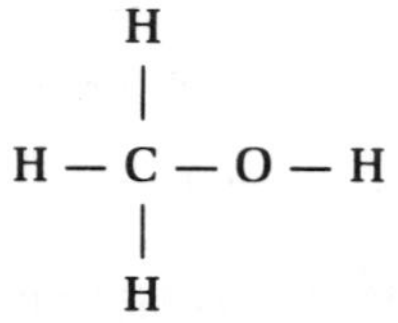

formic acid
(methanoic acid)
HCOOH

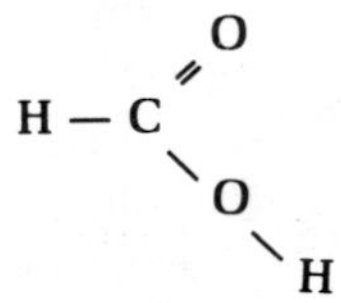

ethanol
C₂H₂OH

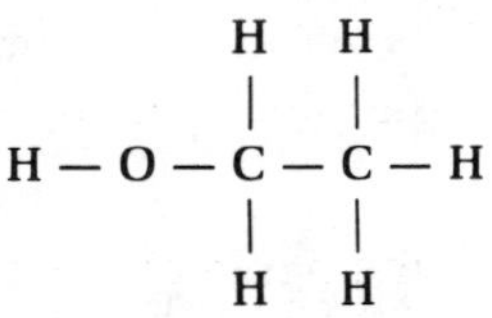

1-pentanol

C₅H₁₁OH

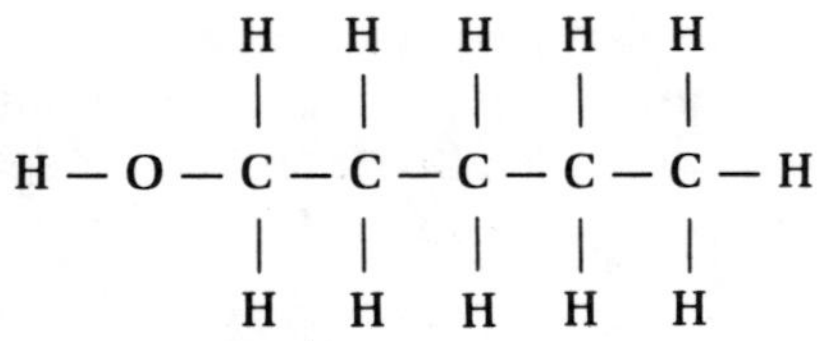

1-octanol
C₈H₁₇OH

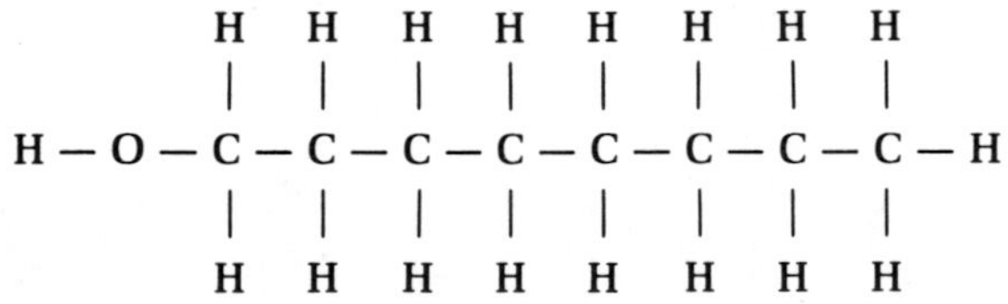

2-methyl propanol
C₄H₉OH

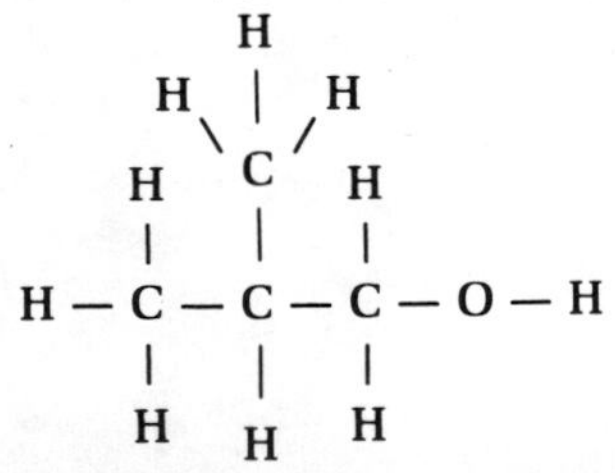

DATA AND OBSERVATIONS

Table 1

TEST TUBE	ODOR
A	
B	
C	
D	
E	

COMPLETE IN YOUR NOTEBOOK

QUESTIONS

1. Write the equations that represent the reactions in each of the test tubes.

2. What is the name of the compound formed in each of the test tubes?

FOLLOW-UP QUESTIONS

1. Formic acid is the common name for methanoic acid. This acid is commonly found in ants. How might the formic acid be used by these organisms?

2. What is another name for acetic acid? What common household chemical is a solution of acetic acid?

3. What is the name of the ester formed from each of the following combinations?
   a. ethanol and benzoic acid
   b. propanol and toluic acid

4. What combination of alcohol and acid will form the following esters?
   a. octyl benzoate
   b. ethyl acetate

5. The ester methyl salicylate is also known as "oil of wintergreen". Name some commercial products that you know that contain this substance.

CONCLUSION

For any odors that you recognize, state the name of the ester responsible.

Preparation of a Soap

The term "detergent" refers to any substance with strong cleansing power. Detergents are commonly classified as either soaps or synthetic detergents. Synthetic detergents are prepared from synthetically produced chemicals, whereas soaps are prepared from natural fats and oils. (The word "soap" has its roots in a Latin word meaning "animal fat".)

The history of soap making can be traced back 5000 years to the Middle East, where it was discovered that treating fat with alkali resulted in a substance with cleansing and healing powers. In fact, for many centuries soap was used medicinally only, in the treatment of skin wounds. Soap making remained relatively primitive until the 16th century, when techniques that produced a purer soap were developed. The reaction which produces soap is called *saponification*.

In more precise terms, soaps are salts of mixed fatty acids. Today they are prepared by reacting fats (which are esters) with alkali solutions such as sodium hydroxide or potassium hydroxide. For example, stearin, an ester, is a principal component of animal fat. It is the glycerol (1, 2, 3-propanetriol) ester of stearic acid, glycerol stearate or stearin.

Stearin, when heated with sodium hydroxide, is broken down into glycerol and sodium stearate, a soap:

In a typical commercial process, a sodium hydroxide solution is added slowly and intermittently to a molten mixture of fats and oils. High temperatures and good mixing are maintained by passing steam through the mixture. After a time, the fat is broken down to form an emulsified mixture of soap, glycerol, and unreacted NaOH. At this point, an NaCl solution is added which causes the soap to separate as a curd and float to the top of the mixture. In the final stages, perfumes, colorings, antiseptics, and other ingredients are added as necessary.

In Part I of this experiment you will prepare a soap by reacting a fat with a fairly concentrated NaOH solution. Unlike the commercial process, ethanol will be added to help speed up the reaction. The ethanol serves as a solvent to bring the reacting materials into closer contact so that the procedure can be conducted in one laboratory period. Then in Part II you will test your soap, a commercial soap, and lard for solubility, sudsing, and acidity.

OBJECTIVES

1. to prepare soap by saponification

2. to compare the results of tests on the soap prepared in the experiment and a soap prepared commercially

MATERIALS

Apparatus

1 beaker (250 mL)	beaker tongs (or
2 beakers (150 mL)	crucible tongs)
pan (such as a dissect-	plastic spoon
ing tray)	test-tube rack
3 wooden splints	3 test tubes
glass stirring rod	(16 mm × 150 mm)
ring stand with	neutral litmus paper or
ring support	universal indicator solution
wire gauze	metric ruler
hotplate	lab apron
heat resistant mat	safety goggles

Reagents

lard, fat, or oil
commercially prepared bar of soap
saturated NaCl solution
6M NaOH
ethanol (denatured)
distilled water

PROCEDURE

Part I   Saponification

1. Put on your lab apron and safety goggles.

2. Obtain a 150 mL beaker and, using a water soluble marker, label it "NaCl(aq)".

3. Place about 60 mL of saturated NaCl solution in this beaker and heat it on a hotplate until the solution just begins to boil. Set the solution aside on a heat resistant mat and save it for Step 9. Label a second 150 mL beaker "H₂O", place 100 mL of distilled H₂O in it, and set it aside as well.

4. Place about 15 g of fat (lard) in a 250 mL beaker. Heat the lard over a hotplate until it melts. Stir the fat carefully with a glass stirring rod while it is melting. Be prepared to remove the beaker from the heat should overheating occur. Record the time of melting, as well as your observations, in your copy of Table 1 in your notebook.

5. Remove the beaker from the heat, then carefully and *slowly* pour 25 mL of ethanol into the molten lard. Stir the mixture and resume heating.

6. *Slowly* pour 25 mL of 6M NaOH solution into the mixture in a thin steady stream, stirring constantly and slowly. (Rapid addition or fast stirring may cause the fat to separate from the mixture.)

7. Continue to heat the mixture slowly and stir it regularly for the next 10 min or 15 min, until no evidence of fat globules remains. Occasionally, you will need to add distilled water (from the 150 mL beaker) to maintain a constant volume of mixture. Record the time at which no fat remains, as well as your observations, in Table 1. Turn off the hotplate.

8. Place some cold tap water in a tray for a cold water bath. Set the 250 mL beaker containing the mixture in the cold water bath, then add 40 mL of distilled water to the mixture while stirring it.

9. Allow the mixture to cool for several minutes in the cold water bath, then slowly add the 60 mL of warm NaCl solution from Step 2. Stir the mixture while adding the NaCl solution. In Table 1, record the time at which soap begins to form, as well as your observations.

10. The soap should now be visible as curds on the top of the mixture. Use a plastic spoon to scoop off a sample of soap and place it on a piece of paper towel that has been folded several times.

11. Save your soap sample for Part II. Clean up the rest of your apparatus according to the reagent disposal instructions.

Part II   Laboratory Tests

1. Label 3 test tubes A, B, and C with a water soluble marker, and place them in a test-tube rack.

2. Use separate wooden splints to add a small sample of each of the following substances to the test tubes: a sample of lard to test tube A, a sample of your lab soap to test tube B, and a sample of commercially prepared soap to test tube C.

3. Half-fill each test tube with distilled water and perform the following tests.
   Solubility and Sudsing: Place your thumb over the end of each test tube and shake vigorously for 15 s. Record your results in your copy of Table 2.
   Acidity: Test the resulting water mixtures with neutral litmus paper or universal indicator solution and record your results in Table 2.

4. Clean up according to the reagent disposal instructions.

5. Before leaving the laboratory, wash your hands thoroughly with soap and water; use a fingernail brush to clean under your fingernails.

~GENT DISPOSAL

~art I, the solution that remains after the soap has been removed ~ glycerol, NaCl, and NaOH. It can be washed down the drain with ~arm water.

~ pour both the contents of test tube A and the solid soap into ~d waste container. The contents of the other test tubes can be ~ the drain with plenty of water.

~ISSION

~its and oils combined with different basic solutions ~'s of soaps. Soaps containing shorter carbon chains ~erally more soluble than those containing longer ~arbons). Also, soaps prepared from potassium ~re soluble than those prepared from sodium

~ydroxide was commercially available, soap ~otash (K_2CO_3) as the source of their basic ~f wood ash prepared in an iron pot. When ~r, a strong basic solution of KOH is

~noticed that the curds of soap were ~us liquid. This liquid was glycerol. ~ the glycerol, formed into shapes, ~(those sold in pump dispensers),

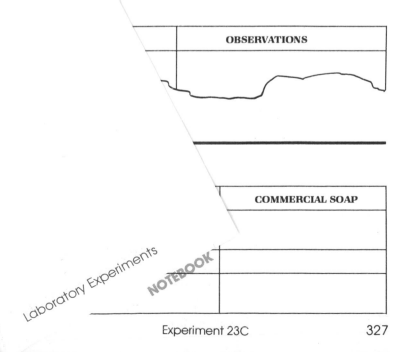

	OBSERVATIONS

	COMMERCIAL SOAP

Laboratory Experiments   NOTEBOOK

QUESTIONS

1. Describe the soap you prepared.

2. The soap you prepared is likely to be harsh on the skin. Why?

3. In Part II, what properties of your soap were similar to those of a commercially prepared soap?

FOLLOW-UP QUESTIONS

1. a. What practical problem might you encounter if you were to filter your final mixture to recover your soap?
   b. Suggest some solutions to this problem.

2. One popular brand of hand soap is made from a mixture of palm oil and olive oil. What do you think is the name of that brand of soap?

3. Soft soaps in pump dispensers are common in homes. State three criteria necessary to making a soft soap. (Refer to the Post Lab Discussion.)

4. During World War II, the Army was very interested in the by-product of soap, glycerol (glycerol). Find out what it was used for.

CONCLUSION

State the results of Objective 2.

Oxidation of Alcohols

One of the amazing features of organic chemistry is the tremendous number of organic compounds which can react in a variety of ways to form new organic compounds. As a result, the number of organic compounds which can be synthesized in the laboratory is limitless. Many of the materials people take for granted today are a result of organic synthesis reactions. Some of the most familiar synthetic compounds include nylon, Teflon®, rayon, polyester, and a variety of plastics. Since the molecules of these synthetics are quite complex in structure, it is preferable to study synthesis reactions involving simpler molecules first.

One typical method of synthesis involves the process of oxidation. Oxidation, as it applies to organic molecules, usually involves the addition of an oxygen atom or the removal of a hydrogen atom, or both. Oxidation reactions can be carried out by reacting organic compounds either with oxygen or with oxidizing agents such as potassium dichromate ($K_2Cr_2O_7$).

In the three parts of this experiment, three alcohols, methanol, ethanol, and 2-propanol, will undergo separate oxidation reactions to form new organic compounds. Alcohols can be classified as *primary* or *secondary*, depending on where the hydroxyl (OH) group is attached to the carbon chain. Primary alcohols have their hydroxyl groups attached to the end carbon, whereas secondary alcohols have their hydroxyl groups attached to an intermediate carbon on the chain.

When each of the above alcohols is oxidized, the products of oxidation can be identified by characteristic odors.

OBJECTIVES

1. to investigate different methods of carrying out oxidation reactions

2. to oxidize primary and secondary alcohols

3. to identify the synthesized organic compounds by comparing their odors with those of known samples

MATERIALS

Apparatus

3 test tubes
  (16 mm × 150 mm)
test-tube rack
graduated cylinder
medicine dropper
bare copper wire
  (22 gauge)

lab burner
crucible tongs
metric ruler
beaker (250 mL)
lab apron
safety goggles

Reagents

methanol
ethanol
2-propanol
methanal sample
propanone sample
3M sulfuric acid
0.1M potassium dichromate
  solution

PROCEDURE

Part I   Simple Oxidation of Methanol

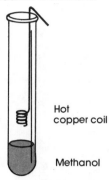

Figure 23D-1
Oxidation of methanol

Hot
copper coil

Methanol

CAUTION: You should always detect odors with caution. Hold the test tube 30 cm away from and 15 cm below your nose. Waft the odor toward your nose with your hand, sniffing cautiously.

1. Put on your lab apron and safety goggles.

2. Place about 3 mL of methanol in a clean test tube. Observe and record its odor in your notebook.

3. Obtain a 30 cm length of bare copper wire. Make a coil at one end by wrapping the wire around a pencil 6 times; use the rest of the wire as a handle. Lower the coil into the test tube to just above the surface of the methanol, and bend the handle over the edge of the test tube so that the coil is suspended above the methanol. See Figure 23D-1.

4. Hold the bent handle of the wire in a pair of crucible tongs and heat the coil in a burner flame for a few minutes.

5. Remove the hot coil from the flame, then immediately reinsert it in the test tube. Observe both the appearance of the copper coil and — cautiously — any odors produced during the process.

6. Compare the odor produced with the odor of methanal and propanone and record your observations in your notebook.

7. Clean up, following the instructions for reagent disposal. Save your copper coil for Part III.

Part II   Oxidation of Ethanol

CAUTION: Sulfuric acid is corrosive to the skin, eyes, and clothing. When handling it, wear safety goggles, full face shield, apron, and gloves. Wash spills and splashes off your skin and clothing immediately, using plenty of water. Call your teacher.

1. Place 3 mL of 0.1M K₂Cr₂O₇ solution in a test tube, then add 3 mL of 3M sulfuric acid.

2. Obtain a 2 mL sample of ethanol and note its odor. Add the sample of ethanol to the contents of the test tube.

3. Set the test tube upright in a beaker containing hot tap water. Record any color changes that occur during the next 5 min. (Cr³⁺(aq) ions have a characteristic green color.)

4. Compare the odor produced with the odors of methanal and propanone and record your observations in your notebook.

5. Clean up, following the reagent disposal instructions.

Part III   Oxidation of 2-Propanol

1. Repeat Part I, using 2-propanol instead of methanol.

2. Clean up all materials following the reagent disposal instructions.

3. Before leaving the laboratory, wash your hands thoroughly with soap and water; use a fingernail brush to clean under your nails.

CAUTION: Most of the organic liquids used in this experiment are poisonous and flammable. Therefore, do not get any in your mouth and keep them away from open flame.

REAGENT DISPOSAL

Collect all liquids in the designated waste container(s).

POST LAB DISCUSSION

The reaction is Part I involved the oxidation of a primary alcohol, methanol, by the removal of hydrogen atoms from the methanol molecule.

The reaction in Part II also involved the oxidation of a primary alcohol, ethanol, during which process hydrogen atoms were removed from the ethanol molecule. Ethanal, whose odor is similar to that of methanal, was produced. The color change was merely an indication of a change in the oxidizing agent as $Cr_2O_7^{2-}$ ions (orange) changed to Cr^{3+} ions (green).

The alcohol in alcoholic beverages is ethanol. Upon being consumed, it is absorbed into the bloodstream and slowly metabolized by the body. However, a small amount of it is vaporized from the blood into the lungs. The subsequent ethanol concentration in the exhaled air can be related to that in the blood. The "breathalyzer" used by police to detect drinking drivers utilizes a reaction similar to the one carried out in Part II of this experiment. The breathalyzer contains an acid solution of potassium dichromate solution. When a deep breath is exhaled through it, the ethanol in the exhaled air is oxidized to ethanal by the dichromate ion.

$$3CH_3CH_2OH + Cr_2O_7^{2-} + 8H^+ \longrightarrow 3CH_3C\!\!\begin{smallmatrix}\nearrow O \\ \searrow H\end{smallmatrix} + 2Cr^{3+} + 7H_2O$$

| ethanol | orange color | | ethanal | green color |

An instrument measures the degree to which the intensity of the orange color is reduced, and the results are registered on a dial which is calibrated to read blood-alcohol concentration.

The reaction in Part III was similar to that in Part I; however, since a secondary rather than primary alcohol was oxidized, an entirely different class of organic compound was produced.

DATA AND OBSERVATIONS

Part I   Simple Oxidation of Methanol

Odor of methanol

Appearance of copper coil during the reaction

Odor after the reaction

Part II   Oxidation of Ethanol

Odor of ethanol

Color changes during the reaction

Odor after the reaction

Part III   Oxidation of 2-Propanol

Odor of 2-propanol

Odor after the reaction

QUESTIONS

1. a. On the basis of comparing odors, what was the product of the oxidation of methanol?
    b. What was the product of the oxidation of ethanol?
    c. Therefore, which type of organic compound forms as a result of the oxidation of a primary alcohol?

2. a. On the basis of comparing odors, what was the product of the oxidation of 2-propanol?
    b. Therefore, which type of organic compound forms as a result of the oxidation of a secondary alcohol?

3. a. Compare the structural formulas of methanol and methanal, and comment on the differences between them.
    b. Compare the structural formulas of ethanol and ethanal, and comment on the differences between them.
    c. Compare the structural formulas of 2-propanol and propanone, and comment on the differences between them.

FOLLOW-UP QUESTIONS

1. Consult a reference book to find a common name and use for methanal.

2. Consult a reference book to find a common name and use for propanone.

3. Wine contains the alcohol ethanol. Sometimes a wine will spoil and develop a vinegary taste. Explain how this can happen.

CONCLUSION

Summarize the results of all three Objectives.

Hydrolysis of Starch

Carbohydrates are organic compounds having the empirical formula CH_2O. Monosaccharides such as glucose and fructose are the simplest carbohydrates. These basic units may be polymerized by dehydration synthesis into more complex sugars, starch, or cellulose molecules.

Starch is a polysaccharide containing over 1000 monosaccharides joined in an end-to-end fashion. Bonds linking the units can be broken or *hydrolyzed* by the addition of water molecules. When hydrolyzed, the starch molecule separates into its component monosaccharides. Most often, the final product of starch hydrolysis is the simple sugar, glucose.

Much of the carbohydrate in the plants we eat is present as starch. However, starch molecules are much too large to pass through the walls of the intestines into the blood. To get the benefit of these foods, our bodies have to break down the starch into smaller sugar molecules. You can test this by chewing a piece of dry bread. After a period of time it begins to taste sweet.

Chemical reactions that take place in living organisms are dependent upon the action of enzymes. These organic catalysts increase reaction rates by lowering the amount of energy needed to start the reaction. Without the assistance of enzymes, most biological reactions would proceed too slowly to sustain life. Since they are protein in composition, enzymes are easily denatured and inactivated. To function efficiently, they require a specific range of temperature and pH.

Amylase, a digestive enzyme found in saliva, catalyzes the hydrolysis of starch. Later, in the small intestine, ingested starch is broken down into its component monosaccharides. These simple sugars are then readily absorbed and processed by the circulatory system.

In this laboratory, you will investigate the hydrolysis of starch by both an acid and an enzyme.

OBJECTIVES

1. to be able to differentiate between the presence of simple sugars and starch using a qualitative test

2. to perform the hydrolysis of starch using a $4M$ HCl solution

3. to determine an effective temperature for the amylase-catalyzed hydrolysis of starch

MATERIALS

Apparatus

4 test tubes
(18 mm × 150 mm)
test tube rack
graduated cylinder
(10 mL)
test tube holder
laboratory burner
ring stand and ring
wire gauze

beaker (600 mL)
3 beakers (250 mL)
safety goggles
lab apron
plastic gloves
full face shield
marking pen

Reagents

glucose solution
starch solution
Benedict's solution
iodine solution
4M HCl
4M NaOH
amylase solution
distilled water
ice water

PROCEDURE

Part I   Qualitative Tests for Glucose and Starch

CAUTION: Benedict's
solution is irritating to skin
and eyes. Wash off spills
and splashes with plenty
of water. Call your
teacher.

CAUTION: Iodine and its
solutions are corrosive to
skin and eyes; wash spills
and splashes off your skin
with plenty of water. Ask
your teacher how to
remove the brown stain.

1. Put on your lab apron and safety goggles.

2. Set up four test tubes labeled A, B, C, and D.

3. To test tubes A and B, add 10 drops of glucose solution. To test tubes C and D, add 10 drops of starch solution.

4. Add 3 mL of Benedict's solution to test tubes A and C.

5. Place a 600 mL beaker filled with 400 mL of hot water on a ring stand with ring and wire gauze. Heat the water to boiling. Place test tube A in the boiling water bath. Record any color change in your copy of Table 1 in your notebook.

6. Repeat Step 5 using test tube C.

7. Add two drops of iodine solution to test tubes B and D. Record your observations in Table 1.

Part II   Effects of Acidic and Basic Solutions on Starch

CAUTION: Hydrochloric
acid is corrosive to skin,
eyes, and clothing. When
handling HCl, wear safety
goggles, full face shield,
gloves, and lab apron.
Wash spills and splashes
off your skin and clothing
immediately using plenty
of water. Call your
teacher.

1. Set up four test tubes labeled A, B, C, and D.

2. Place 2 mL of a starch solution into each of the four tubes.

3. Put on the plastic gloves and full face shield. Add 1 mL of a 4M HCl solution to test tubes A and B. Add 1 mL of distilled water to tubes C and D. (Test tubes C and D will serve as controls.)

4. Place a 600 mL beaker filled with 400 mL of hot water on a ring stand with ring and wire gauze. Heat the water to boiling.

5. Place all four test tubes into the boiling water bath.

6. After five minutes, remove the tubes. Add 1 mL of a 4 M NaOH solution to test tubes A and B. (Benedict's test does not work in an acidic environment.) Add 1 mL of distilled water to the control test tubes C and D.

7. Add 3 mL of Benedict's solution to test tubes A and C. Return the test tubes to the boiling water bath for a few minutes. Record your observations in your copy of Table 2.

8. Add 2 drops of iodine to test tubes B and D. Record your observations in Table 2.

CAUTION: Sodium hydroxide solution is corrosive to skin, eyes, and clothing. When handling NaOH, wear safety goggles, full face shield, gloves, and lab apron. Wash spills and splashes off your skin and clothing immediately using plenty of water. Call your teacher.

Part III Effect of the Enzyme Amylase on Starch at Various Temperatures

1. Add 200 mL of ice water to a 250 mL beaker. Place a second 250 mL beaker filled with hot water on a ring stand with ring and wire gauze. Heat the hot water to boiling. Fill a third 250 mL beaker with 200 mL of water at approximately body temperature, 38°C (mix hot and cold tap water to achieve this temperature).

2. Set up three test tubes labeled A, B, and C.

3. Add 1 mL of starch solution to each of the tubes.

4. Place test tube A in the ice water bath, test tube B in the boiling water bath, and test tube C in the 38°C water bath.

5. Wait five minutes for the contents of each tube to reach the temperature of the water bath. Add five drops of a prepared amylase solution to each of the three test tubes. Wait two minutes.

6. Add 3 mL of Benedict's solution to each of the test tubes.

7. Place a 600 mL beaker filled with 400 mL of hot water on a ring stand with ring and wire gauze. Heat the water to boiling.

8. Put test tubes A, B, and C in the boiling water bath for a few minutes. Examine the contents and record your observations in your copy of Table 3.

9. Before leaving the laboratory, wash your hands thoroughly; use a fingernail brush to clean under your fingernails.

REAGENT DISPOSAL

Any remaining solids should be wrapped in a piece of paper towel and put in a wastebasket. All solutions can be rinsed down the sink with copious amounts of water.

POST LAB DISCUSSION

Monosaccharides and certain disaccharides are easily oxidized. The presence of these carbohydrates can be identified by their reaction with the reagent, Benedict's solution. Copper(II) ions found in this buffered reagent give Benedict's solution its characteristic blue color. When reacted with some simple carbohydrates, the blue Cu^{2+} ions are reduced to the brick red Cu_2O complex.

When iodine is added to a starch solution, a dark blue color appears. This test can be useful in the identification of more complex carbohydrates. Starch polymer chains do not readily decompose in water. However, in an acidic environment or when catalyzed by amylase, the bonds linking the monosaccharides are hydrolized. Free monosaccharides result from the hydrolysis and their presence may be confirmed by a positive Benedict's test.

Protein molecules can be permanently inactivated or denatured by high temperatures. Low temperatures reduce the number of substrate molecules that possess sufficient energy to react with the enzyme.

DATA AND OBSERVATIONS

Part I   Qualitative Tests for Glucose and Starch

Table 1

TEST TUBE	CONTENTS	BENEDICT'S TEST	IODINE TEST
A			
B			
C			
D			

Part II   Effects of Acidic and Basic Solutions on Starch

Table 2

TEST TUBE	REAGENTS ADDED	BENEDICT'S TEST	IODINE TEST
A			
B			
C			
D			

Part III   Effect of the Enzyme Amylase on Starch at Various Temperatures

Table 3

TEST TUBE	TEMPERATURE	BENEDICT'S TEST RESULTS
A		
B		
C		

QUESTIONS

1. Does a negative Benedict's test indicate the complete absence of carbohydrates?

2. If the concentration of HCl used in Part II was decreased to $2M$, how would this affect the volume of $4M$ NaOH needed in Step 6?

3. Explain the results obtained in Part II.

4. Which of the three temperatures presented the most favorable condition for the amylase-catalyzed hydrolysis? Give a reason for this observation.

5. Would you expect the amylase placed at 0°C to regain its activity? Why?

6. How might you explain a positive Benedict's test for test tube A in Part III?

FOLLOW-UP QUESTIONS

1. Suggest a way in which to quantitatively determine the percent of glucose in a solution.

2. What is the eventual fate of glucose molecules in the body?

3. Why will starch be better digested if it is thoroughly chewed in the mouth for some time before being swallowed?

4. The majority of enzyme reactions increase in rate as the temperature is raised, but a maximum rate is reached in the neighborhood of 38°C, after which their catalyzing ability is lessened and eventually destroyed. Explain the reason for this phenomenon.

CONCLUSION

State the results of Objective 1.

APPENDIX 1

MEASURING LIQUID VOLUMES

Chemists use several types of apparatus for measuring liquid volumes. All of these devices are graduated but it is important to note that there are two methods of graduation. Some devices are graduated to contain (TC) a certain volume of liquid and some are graduated to deliver (TD) a certain volume. In fact, the letters TC or TD are often labelled on the apparatus so that you will know how the scales were calibrated. Any scale must be carefully examined so that all of the calibrations are understood. When reading a scale you must ensure that you look on a level line at the scale as in Figure A1-1. Also, you will notice that the top surface of a liquid usually forms a depression called a *meniscus*. Always read the bottom of the meniscus. Three specialized volumetric devices will now be described:

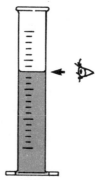

Figure A1-1 *When reading a scale such as this, take care to have a level line of sight*

1. A *volumetric flask* is used whenever a specific liquid volume must be measured and is calibrated TC. The flask is graduated with a line etched around the neck of the flask. If a 1.0 L volumetric flask is being used to prepare 1.0 L of a solution, the volume can be quickly measured simply by filling the flask to the graduation. See Figure A1-2.

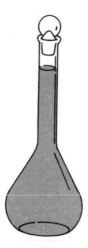

Figure A1-2 *A volumetric flask*

2. A *pipet* is designed to measure and deliver volumes of liquids that are usually 25.0 mL or less. Pipets, then, are calibrated TD. Like a volumetric flask, some pipets have only one calibration and are used for only one specific volume. Other pipets may be graduated.

   Do not try to fill a pipet by holding it in your mouth, especially when handling corrosive or poisonous liquids. As a matter of habit, you should always use a rubber suction bulb to draw the liquid into the pipet. (See Figure A1-3.) When draining the pipet into a flask, do not blow the liquid out; instead, allow the pipet to drain at its own rate. Touch the tip of the pipet against the side of the flask to get the last few drops of liquid out. Practise your pipetting technique with water before using a pipet in an experiment.

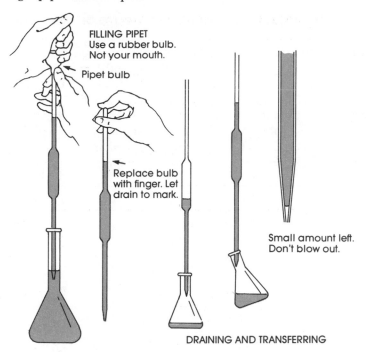

Figure A1-3   *Using a pipet*

3. A *buret* is used for dispensing variable volumes of liquids, therefore, it is calibrated TD. (See Figure A1-4.) There are a variety of valves available on burets so you should familiarize yourself with the type in your lab. Always rinse your buret first with the solution to be used so that your solution does not become diluted by any water inside the buret. (Be sure to run a small amount of solution through the tip as a part of the rinsing process.) When filling your buret, simply pour the solution into the top using a small beaker and adjust the initial TD reading to zero. Each time a volume is dispensed, it is not necessary to refill the buret to zero, since the volume dispensed can be determined by difference. However, it is important that you do not allow the liquid to drain below the last graduation of the buret, because you will be unable to take readings in this region. As with the pipet, the last drops of liquid can be retrieved by touching the flask to the tip of the buret. Finally, the buret should be cleaned with a warm soap solution and rinsed out with water.

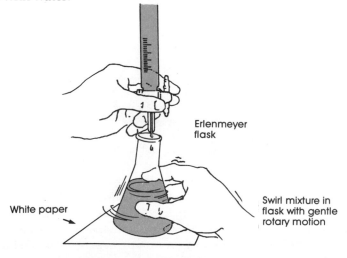

Figure A1-4   *Using a buret*

APPENDIX 2

SOLUBILITY OF COMMON COMPOUNDS IN WATER

NEGATIVE IONS (Anions)	POSITIVE IONS (Cations)	SOLUBILITY OF COMPOUNDS
All	Alkali ions Li^+, Na^+, K^+, Rb^+, Cs^+, Fr^+	Soluble
All	Hydrogen ion, H^+	Soluble
All	Ammonium ion, NH_4^+	Soluble
Nitrate, NO_3^-	All	Soluble
Acetate, CH_3COO^-	All	Soluble
Chloride, Cl^- Bromide, Br^- Iodide, I^-	Ag^+, Pb^{2+}, Hg_2^{2+}, Cu^+ All others	Low Solubility Soluble
Sulfate, SO_4^{2-}	Ba^{2+}, Sr^{2+}, Pb^{2+} All others	Low Solubility Soluble
Sulfide, S^{2-}	Alkali ions, H^+, NH_4^+, Be^{2+}, Mg^{2+}, Ca^{2+}, Sr^{2+}, Ba^{2+} All others	Soluble Soluble Low solubility
Hydroxide, OH^-	Alkali ions, NH_4^+, Sr^{2+}, Ba^{2+} All others	Soluble Low Solubility
Phosphate, PO_4^{3-} Carbonate, CO_3^{2-} Sulfite, SO_3^{2-}	Alkali ions, H^+, NH_4^+ All others	Soluble Low Solubility

RELATIVE STRENGTHS OF BRÖNSTED-LOWRY ACIDS AND BASES

in aqueous solution at room temperature

Reaction: $HB_{(aq)} \rightleftharpoons H^+_{(aq)} + B^-_{(aq)}$ $K_a = \dfrac{[H^+][B^-]}{[HB]}$

STRENGTH OF ACID	NAME OF ACID	ACID	BASE	K_a	STRENGTH OF BASE
Strong	Perchloric acid	$HClO_4 \rightarrow H^+ + ClO_4^-$		........very large	Weak
	Hydriodic acid	$HI \rightarrow H^+ + I^-$		........very large	
	Hydrobromic acid	$HBr \rightarrow H^+ + Br^-$		........very large	
	Hydrochloric acid	$HCl \rightarrow H^+ + Cl^-$		........very large	
	Nitric acid	$HNO_3 \rightarrow H^+ + NO_3^-$		........very large	
	Sulphuric acid	$H_2SO_4 \rightarrow H^+ + HSO_4^-$		........very large	
	Hydronium ion	$H_3O^+ \rightleftharpoons H^+ + H_2O$		........1.0	
	Iodic acid	$HIO_3 \rightleftharpoons H^+ + IO_3^-$		........1.7×10^{-1}	
	Oxalic acid	$HOOCCOOH \rightleftharpoons H^+ + HOOCCOO^-$		...5.4×10^{-2}	
	Sulphurous acid ($SO_2 + H_2O$)	$H_2SO_3 \rightleftharpoons H^+ + HSO_3^-$		........1.7×10^{-2}	
	Hydrogen sulphate ion	$HSO_4^- \rightleftharpoons H^+ + SO_4^{2-}$		........1.3×10^{-2}	
	Phosphoric acid	$H_3PO_4 \rightleftharpoons H^+ + H_2PO_4^-$		........7.1×10^{-3}	
	Ferric ion	$Fe(H_2O)_6^{3+} \rightleftharpoons H^+ + Fe(H_2O)_5(OH)^{2+}$		6.0×10^{-3}	
	Citric acid	$H_3C_6H_5O_7 \rightleftharpoons H^+ + H_2C_6H_5O_7^-$		.....8.7×10^{-4}	
	Hydrofluoric acid	$HF \rightleftharpoons H^+ + F^-$		........6.7×10^{-4}	
	Nitrous acid	$HNO_2 \rightleftharpoons H^+ + NO_2^-$		........5.1×10^{-4}	
	Formic (methanoic) acid	$HCOOH \rightleftharpoons H^+ + HCOO^-$		......1.8×10^{-4}	
	Chromic ion	$Cr(H_2O)_6^{3+} \rightleftharpoons H^+ + Cr(H_2O)_5(OH)^{2+}$		1.5×10^{-4}	
	Benzoic acid	$C_6H_5COOH \rightleftharpoons H^+ + C_6H_5COO^-$		....6.6×10^{-5}	
	Hydrogen oxalate ion	$HOOCCOO^- \rightleftharpoons H^+ + OOCCOO^{2-}$		....5.4×10^{-5}	
	Acetic (ethanoic) acid	$CH_3COOH \rightleftharpoons H^+ + CH_3COO^-$		.....1.8×10^{-5}	
	Dihydrogen citrate ion	$H_2C_6H_5O_7^- \rightleftharpoons H^+ + HC_6H_5O_7^{2-}$		.....1.8×10^{-5}	
	Aluminum ion	$Al(H_2O)_6^{3+} \rightleftharpoons H^+ + Al(H_2O)_5(OH)^{2+}$		1.4×10^{-5}	
	Monohydrogen citrate ion	$HC_6H_5O_7^{2-} \rightleftharpoons H^+ + C_6H_5O_7^{3-}$		.......4.0×10^{-6}	
	Carbonic acid ($CO_2 + H_2O$)	$H_2CO_3 \rightleftharpoons H^+ + HCO_3^-$		........4.4×10^{-7}	
	Hydrogen sulphide	$H_2S \rightleftharpoons H^+ + HS^-$		........1.0×10^{-7}	
	Dihydrogen phosphate ion	$H_2PO_4^- \rightleftharpoons H^+ + HPO_4^{2-}$		.......6.3×10^{-8}	
	Hydrogen sulphite ion	$HSO_3^- \rightleftharpoons H^+ + SO_3^{2-}$		........6.2×10^{-8}	
	Boric acid	$H_3BO_3 \rightleftharpoons H^+ + H_2BO_3^-$		........6.5×10^{-10}	
	Ammonium ion	$NH_4^+ \rightleftharpoons H^+ + NH_3$		........5.7×10^{-10}	
	Hydrogen Cyanide	$HCN \rightleftharpoons H^+ + CN^-$		........4.8×10^{-10}	
	Phenol	$C_6H_5OH \rightleftharpoons H^+ + C_6H_5O^-$		.......1.3×10^{-10}	
	Hydrogen carbonate ion	$HCO_3^- \rightleftharpoons H^+ + CO_3^{2-}$		........4.7×10^{-11}	
	Hydrogen peroxide	$H_2O_2 \rightleftharpoons H^+ + HO_2^-$		........2.4×10^{-12}	
	Monohydrogen phosphate ion	$HPO_4^{2-} \rightleftharpoons H^+ + PO_4^{3-}$		........4.4×10^{-13}	
	Hydrogen sulphide ion	$HS^- \rightleftharpoons H^+ + S^{2-}$		........1.3×10^{-13}	
	Water	$H_2O \rightleftharpoons H^+ + OH^-$		........1.0×10^{-14}	
	Hydroxide ion	$OH^- \leftarrow H^+ + O^{2-}$		........very small	
Weak	Ammonia	$NH_3 \leftarrow H^+ + NH_2^-$		........very small	Strong

Tendency to lose protons increases (left side, arrow upward from Weak to Strong)

Tendency to gain protons increases (right side, arrow downward from Weak to Strong)

COMMON INDICATORS

INDICATOR	pH RANGE IN WHICH COLOR CHANGE OCCURS	COLOR CHANGE AS pH INCREASES
Methyl violet	0.5 — 1.6	yellow to blue
Thymol blue	1.2 — 2.8	red to yellow
Orange IV	1.4 — 2.8	red to yellow
Methyl orange	3.2 — 4.4	red to yellow
Bromcresol green	3.8 — 5.4	yellow to blue
Methyl red	4.8 — 6.0	red to yellow
Chlorophenol red	5.2 — 6.8	yellow to red
Bromthymol blue	6.0 — 7.6	yellow to blue
Phenol red	6.6 — 8.0	yellow to red
Neutral red	6.8 — 8.0	red to yellow-orange
Thymol blue	8.0 — 9.6	yellow to blue
Phenolphthalein	8.2 — 10.0	colorless to magenta
Thymolphthalein	9.4 — 10.6	colorless to blue
Alizarin yellow	10.1 — 12.0	yellow to red
Indigo carmine	11.4 — 13.0	blue to yellow

STANDARD REDUCTION POTENTIALS OF HALF-CELLS

Ionic Concentrations, 1 M in water at 25°C

STRENGTH	OXIDIZING AGENTS	REDUCING AGENTS	E° (VOLTS)	STRENGTH
Very strong oxidizing agents	$F_2(g) + 2e^- \rightleftharpoons 2F^-$		+2.87	Very weak reducing agents
	$S_2O_8^{2-} + 2e^- \rightleftharpoons 2SO_4^{2-}$		+2.05	
	$H_2O_2 + 2H^+ + 2e^- \rightleftharpoons 2H_2O$		+1.78	
	$BrO_3^- + 6H^+ + 5e^- \rightleftharpoons \frac{1}{2}Br_2(l) + 3H_2O$		+1.52	
	$MnO_4^- + 8H^+ + 5e^- \rightleftharpoons Mn^{2+} + 4H_2O$		+1.49	
	$Au^{3+} + 3e^- \rightleftharpoons Au(s)$		+1.42	
	$ClO_4^- + 8H^+ + 8e^- \rightleftharpoons Cl^- + 4H_2O$		+1.37	
	$Cl_2(g) + 2e^- \rightleftharpoons 2Cl^-$		+1.36	
	$Cr_2O_7^{2-} + 14H^+ + 6e^- \rightleftharpoons 2Cr^{3+} + 7H_2O$		+1.33	
	$\frac{1}{2}O_2(g) + 2H^+ + 2e^- \rightleftharpoons H_2O$		+1.23	
	$MnO_2(s) + 4H^+ + 2e^- \rightleftharpoons Mn^{2+} + 2H_2O$		+1.21	
	$IO_3^- + 6H^+ + 5e^- \rightleftharpoons \frac{1}{2}I_2(s) + 3H_2O$		+1.20	
	$Br_2(l) + 2e^- \rightleftharpoons 2Br^-$		+1.06	
	$AuCl_4^- + 3e^- \rightleftharpoons Au(s) + 4Cl^-$		+0.99	
	$NO_3^- + 4H^+ + 3e^- \rightleftharpoons NO(g) + 2H_2O$		+0.96	
	$Hg^{2+} + 2e^- \rightleftharpoons Hg(l)$		+0.85	
	$\frac{1}{2}O_2(g) + 2H^+(10^{-7}\,M) + 2e^- \rightleftharpoons H_2O$		+0.82	
	$Ag^+ + e^- \rightleftharpoons Ag(s)$		+0.80	
	$\frac{1}{2}Hg_2^{2+} + e^- \rightleftharpoons Hg(l)$		+0.80	
	$NO_3^- + 2H^+ + e^- \rightleftharpoons NO_2(g) + H_2O$		+0.78	
	$Fe^{3+} + e^- \rightleftharpoons Fe^{2+}$		+0.77	
	$O_2(g) + 2H^+ + 2e^- \rightleftharpoons H_2O_2$		+0.68	
	$MnO_4^- + 2H_2O + 3e^- \rightleftharpoons MnO_2(s) + 4OH^-$		+0.59	
Increasing strength of oxidizing agents	$I_2(s) + 2e^- \rightleftharpoons 2I^-$		+0.53	Increasing strength of reducing agents
	$Cu^+ + e^- \rightleftharpoons Cu(s)$		+0.52	
	$H_2SO_3 + 4H^+ + 4e^- \rightleftharpoons S(s) + 3H_2O$		+0.45	
	$Cu^{2+} + 2e^- \rightleftharpoons Cu(s)$		+0.34	
	$SO_4^{2-} + 4H^+ + 2e^- \rightleftharpoons H_2SO_3 + H_2O$		+0.20	
	$Cu^{2+} + e^- \rightleftharpoons Cu^+$		+0.16	
	$Sn^{4+} + 2e^- \rightleftharpoons Sn^{2+}$		+0.15	
	$S(s) + 2H^+ + 2e^- \rightleftharpoons H_2S(g)$		+0.14	
	$2H^+ + 2e^- \rightleftharpoons H_2(g)$		0.00	
	$Pb^{2+} + 2e^- \rightleftharpoons Pb(s)$		−0.13	
	$Sn^{2+} + 2e^- \rightleftharpoons Sn(s)$		−0.14	
	$Ni^{2+} + 2e^- \rightleftharpoons Ni(s)$		−0.23	
	$H_3PO_4 + 2H^+ + 2e^- \rightleftharpoons H_3PO_3 + H_2O$		−0.28	
	$Co^{2+} + 2e^- \rightleftharpoons Co(s)$		−0.28	
	$Se(s) + 2H^+ + 2e^- \rightleftharpoons H_2Se$		−0.36	
	$Fe^{2+} + 2e^- \rightleftharpoons Fe(s)$		−0.41	
	$Cr^{3+} + e^- \rightleftharpoons Cr^{2+}$		−0.41	
	$2H_2O + 2e^- \rightleftharpoons H_2 + 2OH^-(10^{-7}\,M)$		−0.41	
	$Te(s) + 2H^+ + 2e^- \rightleftharpoons H_2Te$		−0.69	
	$Ag_2S(s) + 2e^- \rightleftharpoons 2Ag(s) + S^{2-}$		−0.71	
	$Cr^{3+} + 3e^- \rightleftharpoons Cr(s)$		−0.74	
	$Zn^{2+} + 2e^- \rightleftharpoons Zn(s)$		−0.76	
	$2H_2O + 2e^- \rightleftharpoons H_2(g) + 2OH^-$		−0.83	
	$Mn^{2+} + 2e^- \rightleftharpoons Mn(s)$		−1.03	
	$Al^{3+} + 3e^- \rightleftharpoons Al(s)$		−1.66	
	$Mg^+ + 2e^- \rightleftharpoons Mg(s)$		−2.37	
	$Na^+ + e^- \rightleftharpoons Na(s)$		−2.71	
	$Ca^{2+} + 2e^- \rightleftharpoons Ca(s)$		−2.76	
	$Sr^{2+} + 2e^- \rightleftharpoons Sr(s)$		−2.89	
	$Ba^{2+} + 2e^- \rightleftharpoons Ba(s)$		−2.90	
	$Cs^+ + e^- \rightleftharpoons Cs(s)$		−2.92	
Very weak oxidizing agents	$K^+ + e^- \rightleftharpoons K(s)$		−2.92	Very strong reducing agents
	$Rb^+ + e^- \rightleftharpoons Rb(s)$		−2.92	
	$Li^+ + e^- \rightleftharpoons Li(s)$		−3.00	

Overpotential Effect

APPENDIX 6

VAPOR PRESSURES OF WATER

TEMPERATURE (°C)	VAPOR PRESSURE (kPa)
– 10 (ice)	0.260
– 5 (ice)	0.402
0	0.610
5	0.872
10	1.228
15	1.705
16	1.818
17	1.937
18	2.063
19	2.197
20	2.338
21	2.486
22	2.643
23	2.809
24	2.983
25	3.167
26	3.361
27	3.565
28	3.780
29	4.005
30	4.243
35	5.623
40	7.376
45	9.583
50	12.33
55	15.74
60	19.92
65	25.00
70	31.16
75	38.54
80	47.34
85	57.41
90	70.10
95	84.51
100	101.32

Source: *Handbook of Chemistry and Physics*, CRC Press, 1980–81.

CHARGES OF SOME COMMON IONS

POSITIVE IONS (CATIONS)		NEGATIVE IONS (ANIONS)	
aluminum	Al^{3+}	acetate	CH_3COO^-
ammonium	NH_4^+	bromide	Br^-
barium	Ba^{2+}	carbonate	CO_3^{2-}
cadmium	Cd^{2+}	hydrogen carbonate, bicarbonate	HCO_3^-
calcium	Ca^{2+}	chlorate	ClO_3^-
chromium (II),* chromous	Cr^{2+}	chloride	Cl^-
chromium (III), chromic	Cr^{3+}	chlorite	ClO_2^-
cobalt	Co^{2+}	chromate	CrO_4^{2-}
copper (I),* cuprous	Cu^+	dichromate	$Cr_2O_7^{2-}$
copper (II), cupric	Cu^{2+}	fluoride	F^-
hydrogen, hydronium	H^+, H_3O^+	hydroxide	OH^-
iron (II),* ferrous	Fe^{2+}	hypochlorite	ClO^-
iron (III), ferric	Fe^{3+}	iodide	I^-
lead	Pb^{2+}	nitrate	NO_3^-
lithium	Li^+	nitrite	NO_2^-
magnesium	Mg^{2+}	oxalate	$C_2O_4^{2-}$
manganese (II), manganous	Mn^{2+}	hydrogen oxalate	$HC_2O_4^-$
mercury (I),* mercurous	Hg_2^{2+}	perchlorate	ClO_4^-
mercury (II), mercuric	Hg^{2+}	permanganate	MnO_4^-
nickel	Ni^{2+}	phosphate	PO_4^{3-}
potassium	K^+	monohydrogen phosphate	HPO_4^{2-}
scandium	Sc^{3+}	dihydrogen phosphate	$H_2PO_4^-$
silver	Ag^+	sulfate	SO_4^{2-}
sodium	Na^+	hydrogen sulfate, bisulfate	HSO_4^-
strontium	Sr^{2+}	sulfide	S^{2-}
tin (II),* stannous	Sn^{2+}	hydrogen sulfide, bisulfide	HS^-
tin (IV), stannic	Sn^{4+}	sulfite	SO_3^{2-}
zinc	Zn^{2+}	hydrogen sulfite, bisulfite	HSO_3^-

* Aqueous solutions are readily oxidized by air.
Note: In ionic compounds the relative number of positive and negative ions is such that the sum of their electric charges is zero.

APPENDIX 8

Alphabetic Listing of the Elements

Atomic mass values have been rounded to the first decimal place for ease of calculation. If more accurate values are required, use the periodic table in Appendix 9 or on pages 308-309 of the Heath Chemistry Textbook.

ELEMENT	SYMBOL	ATOMIC NO.	ATOMIC MASS	ELEMENT	SYMBOL	ATOMIC NO.	ATOMIC MASS
Actinium	Ac	89	(227)	Mercury	Hg	80	200.6
Aluminum	Al	13	27.0	Molybdenum	Mo	42	95.9
Americium	Am	95	(243)	Neodymium	Nd	60	144.2
Antimony	Sb	51	121.8	Neon	Ne	10	20.2
Argon	Ar	18	39.9	Neptunium	Np	93	(237)
Arsenic	As	33	74.9	Nickel	Ni	28	58.7
Astatine	At	85	(210)	Niobium	Nb	41	92.9
Barium	Ba	56	137.3	Nitrogen	N	7	14.0
Berkelium	Bk	97	(249)	Nobelium	No	102	(254)
Beryllium	Be	4	9.0	Osmium	Os	76	190.2
Bismuth	Bi	83	209.0	Oxygen	O	8	16.0
Boron	B	5	10.8	Palladium	Pd	46	106.4
Bromine	Br	35	79.9	Phosphorus	P	15	31.0
Cadmium	Cd	48	112.4	Platinum	Pt	78	195.1
Calcium	Ca	20	40.1	Plutonium	Pu	94	(242)
Californium	Cf	98	(251)	Polonium	Po	84	(210)
Carbon	C	6	12.0	Potassium	K	19	39.1
Cerium	Ce	58	140.1	Praseodymium	Pr	59	140.9
Cesium	Cs	55	132.9	Promethium	Pm	61	(147)
Chlorine	Cl	17	35.5	Proctactinium	Pa	91	(231)
Chromium	Cr	24	52.0	Radium	Ra	88	(226)
Cobalt	Co	27	58.9	Radon	Rn	86	(222)
Copper	Cu	29	63.5	Rhenium	Re	75	186.2
Curium	Cm	96	(247)	Rhodium	Rh	45	102.9
Dysprosium	Dy	66	162.5	Rubidium	Rb	37	85.8
Einsteinium	Es	99	(254)	Ruthenium	Ru	44	101.1
Erbium	Er	68	167.3	Samarium	Sm	62	150.4
Europium	Eu	63	152.0	Scandium	Sc	21	45.0
Fermium	Fm	100	(253)	Selenium	Se	34	79.0
Fluorine	F	9	19.0	Silicon	Si	14	28.1
Francium	Fr	87	(223)	Silver	Ag	47	107.9
Gadolinium	Gd	64	157.2	Sodium	Na	11	23.0
Gallium	Ga	31	69.7	Strontium	Sr	38	87.6
Germanium	Ge	32	72.6	Sulphur	S	16	32.1
Gold	Au	79	197.0	Tantalum	Ta	73	180.9
Hafnium	Hf	72	178.5	Technetium	Tc	43	(99)
Helium	He	2	4.0	Tellurium	Te	52	127.6
Holmium	Ho	67	164.9	Terbium	Tb	65	158.9
Hydrogen	H	1	1.0	Thallium	Tl	81	204.4
Indium	In	49	114.8	Thorium	Th	90	232.0
Iodine	I	53	126.9	Thulium	Tm	69	168.9
Iridium	Ir	77	192.2	Tin	Sn	50	118.7
Iron	Fe	26	55.8	Titanium	Ti	22	47.9
Krypton	Kr	36	83.8	Tungsten	W	74	183.8
Lanthanum	La	57	138.9	Uranium	U	92	238.0
Lawrencium	Lr	103	(257)	Vanadium	V	23	50.9
Lead	Pb	82	207.2	Xenon	Xe	54	131.3
Lithium	Li	3	6.9	Ytterbium	Yb	70	173.0
Lutetium	Lu	71	175.0	Yttrium	Y	39	88.9
Magnesium	Mg	12	24.3	Zinc	Zn	30	65.4
Manganese	Mn	25	54.9	Zirconium	Zr	40	91.2
Mendelevium	Md	101	(256)				

Based on $^{12}_{6}C$ = 12.0000. For elements not found in nature, the atomic mass value is shown in parenthesis, and this represents the mass number of the most stable isotope.

PERIODIC TABLE OF THE ELEMENTS
(based on $^{12}_{6}C = 12.0000$)

TRANSITION METALS

Key:
14
Si
Silicon
28.0855

— Atomic number
— Symbol
— Name
— Atomic mass

1*	2	3	4	5	6	7	8	9	10	11	12	13	14	15	16	17	18
1 H Hydrogen 1.007																	2 He Helium 4.0026
3 Li Lithium 6.941	4 Be Beryllium 9.012											5 B Boron 10.81	6 C Carbon 12.0111	7 N Nitrogen 14.0067	8 O Oxygen 15.9994	9 F Fluorine 18.998	10 Ne Neon 20.179
11 Na Sodium 22.98977	12 Mg Magnesium 24.305											13 Al Aluminum 26.9815	14 Si Silicon 28.0855	15 P Phosphorus 30.973	16 S Sulfur 32.06	17 Cl Chlorine 35.453	18 Ar Argon 39.948
19 K Potassium 39.098	20 Ca Calcium 40.08	21 Sc Scandium 44.955	22 Ti Titanium 47.88	23 V Vanadium 50.9415	24 Cr Chromium 51.996	25 Mn Manganese 54.938	26 Fe Iron 55.847	27 Co Cobalt 58.933	28 Ni Nickel 58.69	29 Cu Copper 63.546	30 Zn Zinc 65.39	31 Ga Gallium 69.72	32 Ge Germanium 72.59	33 As Arsenic 74.92	34 Se Selenium 78.96	35 Br Bromine 79.904	36 Kr Krypton 83.80
37 Rb Rubidium 85.467	38 Sr Strontium 87.62	39 Y Yttrium 88.905	40 Zr Zirconium 91.224	41 Nb Niobium 92.906	42 Mo Molybdenum 95.94	43 Tc Technetium (98)	44 Ru Ruthenium 101.07	45 Rh Rhodium 102.906	46 Pd Palladium 106.42	47 Ag Silver 107.868	48 Cd Cadmium 112.41	49 In Indium 114.82	50 Sn Tin 118.71	51 Sb Antimony 121.75	52 Te Tellurium 127.60	53 I Iodine 126.905	54 Xe Xenon 131.29
55 Cs Cesium 132.905	56 Ba Barium 137.3	57 La Lanthanum 138.906	72 Hf Hafnium 178.49	73 Ta Tantalum 180.948	74 W Tungsten 183.85	75 Re Rhenium 186.207	76 Os Osmium 190.2	77 Ir Iridium 192.22	78 Pt Platinum 195.08	79 Au Gold 196.967	80 Hg Mercury 200.59	81 Tl Thallium 204.383	82 Pb Lead 207.2	83 Bi Bismuth 208.980	84 Po Polonium (209)	85 At Astatine (210)	86 Rn Radon (222)
87 Fr Francium (223)†	88 Ra Radium (226.0)	89 Ac Actinium 227.028	104 (261)	105 (262)	106 (263)	107 (262)	108	109 (266)									

INNER TRANSITION METALS

Lanthanide series

58 Ce Cerium 140.12	59 Pr Praseodymium 140.908	60 Nd Neodymium 144.24	61 Pm Promethium (145)	62 Sm Samarium 150.36	63 Eu Europium 151.96	64 Gd Gadolinium 157.25	65 Tb Terbium 158.925	66 Dy Dysprosium 162.50	67 Ho Holmium 164.930	68 Er Erbium 167.26	69 Tm Thulium 168.934	70 Yb Ytterbium 173.04	71 Lu Lutetium 174.96

Actinide series

90 Th Thorium 232.038	91 Pa Protactinium 231.036	92 U Uranium 238.029	93 Np Neptunium (244)	94 Pu Plutonium (244)	95 Am Americium (243)	96 Cm Curium (247)	97 Bk Berkelium (247)	98 Cf Californium (251)	99 Es Einsteinium (252)	100 Fm Fermium (257)	101 Md Mendelevium (258)	102 No Nobelium (259)	103 Lr Lawrencium (260)

*The numbers heading each column represent group numbers recommended by the American Chemical Society Committee on nomenclature.

†Masses in parentheses are the mass numbers of the most stable isotope.

981